A Bird's-eye View of Robert Browning's

'The Ring and the Book'

By
Nicholas M
Romano

A Bird's-eye View of Robert Browning's 'The Ring and the Book'

Author: Nicholas M Romano

Copyright © Nicholas M Romano (2025)

The right of Nicholas M Romano to be identified as author of this work has been asserted by the author in accordance with section 77 and 78 of the Copyright, Designs and Patents Act 1988.

First Published in 2025

ISBN 978-1-83538-654-5 (Paperback)
978-1-83538-655-2 (Hardback)
978-1-83538-656-9 (E-Book)

Cover Design and Book Layout by:
Maple Publishers
www.maplepublishers.com

Published by:
Maple Publishers
Fairbourne Drive, Atterbury,
Milton Keynes,
MK10 9RG, UK
www.maplepublishers.com

A CIP catalogue record for this title is available from the British Library.

All rights reserved. No part of this book may be reproduced or translated by any form or by any means, electronic or mechanical, including photocopying, recording or by any information storage and retrieval system without written permission from the author.

The views expressed in this work are solely those of the author and do not necessarily reflect the views of the publisher, and the publisher hereby disclaims any responsibility for them.

Whydunit

A Bird's-Eye view of Robert Browning's *The Ring and the Book*

By

Nicholas M. Romano

White shall not neutralize the black, nor good compensate bad in man, absolve him so: Life's business being just the terrible choice.

Pope Innocent XII

ABOUT ROBERT BROWNING (1812-1889)

A native of London, Robert Browning shared with his father a fondness for detective fiction. He had already gained a reputation as the author of 'Dramatic Romances and Lyrics' when, following elopement with Elizabeth Barnett, he moved to his beloved Italy in 1846.

During a second visit to Florence he chanced on an 'old yellow Book' revolving around a Tuscan Count's triple murder and court case in the 17th century papal Rome. It turned out to be the source of 'The Ring and the Book'(1868-69). In the following years his ongoing interest in deviant minds led to poems such as 'Red Cotton Night-Cap Country' and 'The 'Inn-Album'.

Some time after the loss of his darling wife - a lyricist in her own right and a fervent supporter of the Risorgimento, i.e. the movement for the birth of Italy as a nation, the poet composed 'Dramatic Idyls, First Series' in a lighter mood. They were followed by 'Ixion' in a rebellious frame of mind.

In 1889 the ageing poet visited dear old Asolo in the Veneto Region before retiring to the Venetian abode of his son 'Pen'. It was to be his last place as a living man. Before the end of the year he took leave of the world, but not before telling his fellow human beings that 'held we fall to rise, are baffled to fight better, sleep to wake'. He is buried in Westminster.

Major Characters

Robert Browning Author & Harbinger
Guido Franceschini Aretine Count
Pompilia Franceschini Guido's wife
Paolo Franceschini Guido's brother. Abbot.
Pietro Comparini Bourgeois Roman citizen
Violante Comparini Pietro's wife
Giuseppe Caponsacchi Aretine Priest
Four Guido's henchmen
Tertium Quid Upper-class gentleman
Giacinto Arcangeli Guido's defender
Giovanni Battista Bottini Public Prosecutor
Innocent XII Incumbent Pontiff

Place: Rome and Arezzo, Italy
Time: Late 10907th century

Prologue

Warwick Crescent in Paddington, Central London.
Autumn, 1864 A.D.

"Do you see this ring? 'T is Rome-work, made to match Etrurian circlets found some happy morn, spark-like 'mid unearthed slope-side fig tree roots that roof old tombs at Chiusi – soft, you see, yet crisp as jewel cutting. There's one trick, craftsmen instruct me, one approved device ere the stuff grow a ring-thing right to wear; that trick is: the artificer melts up wax with honey, so to speak; he mingles gold with gold's alloy and, duly tempering both, effects a manageable mass, then works. But his work ended, once the thing a ring, oh, there's repristination! Just a spirt o' the proper fiery acid o'er its face, and forth the alloy unfastened flies in fume while, self-sufficient now, the shape remains, the rondure brave, the lilied loveliness, gold as it was, is, shall be evermore: prime nature with an added artistry – no carat lost, and you have gained a ring!"

Ensconced in his dwelling at the core of London Paddington, the Victorian poet Robert Browning was addressing imaginary visitors. He wore a long dark jacket above bright baggy pants; his neatly combed hair was sprinkled with off-white patches, his luxuriant white beard cascaded down a fleshy neck, his high forehead spread above deep-set black eyes, and his noble nose sat in the middle of a romantically tinged face.

"What of it?" the would-be host continued, "'T is a figure, a symbol, say; a thing's a sign: now for the thing signified", Slipping the ring onto his forefinger, he moved to a silvery table and picked up a printed sheaf. "Do you see this *square old yellow book* I toss i' the air, and catch again, and twirl about? Examine it yourselves! I found this book, – mark the predestination, – when a Hand, always above my shoulder, pushed me once across a Square in Florence, crammed with booths, and 'Stall!', cried I: a *lira* made it mine." The narrator's bookworm's eyes sparkled with excitement. "Here it is, this I toss and take again: a book in shape but, really, pure crude fact secreted from man's life when hearts beat hard and brains, high-blooded, ticked two centuries since. Give it me back! The thing's restorative i' the touch and sight."

A smile prompted by the recollection of a momentous event crisscrossed the poet's lineaments. "That memorable day I leaned a little and overlooked my prize through fire irons, tribes of tongs, shovels in sheaves, skeleton bedsteads, wardrobe drawers agape, and worse, cast clothes a-sweetening in the sun; none of them took my eye from my prize, – still read I on, from written title page to written index; on, through street and street, till, by the time I stood at home again, I had mastered the contents, knew the whole truth gathered together, bound up in this book. '*Romana Homicidiorum*' – nay, better translate – 'A Roman murder case; position of the entire criminal cause of Guido Franceschini, nobleman, with certain Four, the cutthroats in his pay: that was this *old square yellow book* about."

A touch of gravitas enhanced the story. "Now, as the ingot, ere the ring was forged, lay gold, – beseech you, hold that figure fast! – so, in this book lay absolutely truth, fanciless fact, the documents indeed, – put forth and printed, as the practice was at Rome, in the Apostolic Chamber's type, and so submitted to the eye o' the Court. There was a Hall of Justice: that came last, for justice had a chamber by the hall where she took evidence first, summed up the same, then sent accuser and accused alike, in person of the advocate of each, to weigh that evidence's worth, arrange, array the battle.

'T was the so-styled Fisc began, pleaded, and since he only spoke in print, the printed voice of him lives now as then. Thus was the paper put before the court in the next stage, – no noisy work at all, – to study the case. In due time like reply came from the so-styled Patron of the Poor, official mouthpiece of the five accused. Pages of proof this way, and that way proof; and always, once again the case postponed! Lastly, what made all safe, the Pope was kind: much more unlikely then, in extreme age, to take a life the general sense bade spare. 'It was plain that Guido would go scatheless yet. But human promise, oh, how short of shine! How topple down the piles of hope we rear! Suddenly starting from a nap, as it were, cried the Pope's great self, – Innocent by name and nature too, and eighty-six years old, Antonio Pignatelli of Naples, Pope who had trod many lands, known many deeds, probed many hearts, beginning with his own. He cried of a sudden, this great good old Pope, when they appealed in last resort to him: 'I have mastered the whole matter; I nothing doubt. Though Guido stood forth priest from head to heel, instead of, as alleged, a piece of one, I and Christ would renounce all right in him. Am I not Pope and presently to die, and shall I wait a day ere I decide on doing or not doing justice here?'"

The speaker stood in silence for a moment, breathed in and out, recommenced. "This is the bookful; thus far take the truth, the untampered gold, the fact untampered with, the mere ring-metal ere the ring be made! You know the tale already: I may ask, ask you not merely who were he and she, husband and wife, what manner of mankind, but how you hold concerning this and that other yet-unnamed actor in the piece, the priest declared the lover of the wife, Giuseppe Caponsaccchi; – his strange course i' the matter, was it right or wrong or both? Then the old couple slaughtered with the wife by the husband as accomplices in crime, those Comparini, Pietro and his spouse, – what say you to the right and wrong of that when, at a known name whispered through the door of a lone dwelling on a Christmas night, it opened that the joyous hearts inside might welcome as it were an angel-guest, and so did welcome devils and their death?" Further inhaling and exhaling intervened and then "Well, British Public, ye who like me not, truth must prevail, the proverb vows; and truth, here is it all i' the book at last, as first there it was all i' the heads and hearts of Rome. I took my book to Rome first, tried truth's power on likely people: "Have you met such names? Is a tradition extant of such facts? Your law-courts stand, your records frown a-row; what if I rove and rummage?" And the response was: 'Why, you'll waste your pains and end as wise as you began!' Everyone snickered:' names and facts thus old are newer much than Europe news we find down in today's *Diario*. Records, quotha? Why, the French burned them; what else do the French? Content you with your treasure of a book, a pretty piece of narrative enough. Do you tell the story, now, in off-hand style, straight from the book? Or simply here and there?'

"From the book, yes", said the speaker in response; "thence bit by bit I dug the lingot truth, that memorable day, assayed and knew my piecemeal gain was gold, – yes; but from something else surpassing that, something of mine which, mixed with the mass, made it bear hammer and be firm to file. Fancy with fact is just one fact the more; to-wit, that fancy has informed, transpierced, thridded and so thrown fast the facts else free. I fused my live soul and that inert stuff, before attempting smithcraft, on the night after the day when, – truth thus grasped and gained, – the book was shut and done with and laid by. The life in me abolished the death of things, deep calling unto deep: as then and there acted itself over again once more the tragic piece. I saw with my own eyes in Florence as I trod the terrace, breathed the beauty and the fearfulness of night, how it had run, this round from Rome to Rome. Because, you are to know, they lived at Rome, Pompilia's parents, as they thought themselves, two poor ignoble hearts who did their best to somehow make a shift and scramble through the world's mud, careless if it splashed and spoiled, provided they might so hold high, keep clean their child's soul, one soul white enough for three, and lift it to whatever star should stoop. I saw the star stoop, that they strained to touch, and did touch and depose their treasure on, as Guido Franceschini took away Pompilia to be his for evermore. I saw the star supposed, but fog o' the fen, gilded star-fashion by a glint from hell; having been heaved up, haled on its gross way, by hands unguessed before, invisible help from a dark brotherhood, and specially two obscure goblin creatures, – fox-faced this, cat-clawed the other, called his next of kin by Guido the main monster, – cloaked and caped, making as they were priests, to mock God more , – Abate Paul,

Canon Girolamo. These two had rolled the starlike pest to Rome and stationed it to suck up and absorb the sweetness of Pompilia, rolled again that bloated bubble, with her soul inside, back to Arezzo and a palace there. It touched home, broke, and blasted far and wide. I saw the cheated couple find the cheat and guess what foul rite they were captured for. I saw them, in the potency of fear, in recrudescency of baffled hate, prepare to wring the uttermost revenge from body and soul thus left them; all was sure, fire laid and cauldron set, the obscene ring traced, the victim stripped and prostrate. What of God? The cleaving of a cloud, a cry, a crash, as, in a glory of armour like Saint George, out again sprang the young good beauteous priest, bearing away the lady in his arms, saved for a splendid minute and no more."

At Yuletide the hard-luck story had taken a turn for the worse. "The second of the year, and oh so cold! All was silent, sinister, – when, ha! glimmeringly did a pack of werewolves pad the snow: those flames were Guido's eyes in front, and all five found and footed it, the track, to where a threshold-streak of warmth and light betrayed the dwelling-door with life inside, while an inch outside were those blood-bright eyes and black lips wrinkling o'er the flash of teeth. They parleyed in their language. Then one whined; deep in his throat whispered what seemed a name.

'Open to Caponsacchi! Guido cried.

'Gabriel!' cried Lucifer at Eden-gate.

Wide as a heart, opened the door at once, showing the joyous couple and their child the two-weeks' mother, to the wolves, the wolves to them. Close eyes! And when the corpses lay stark-stretched, and those the wolves, their wolf-work done, were safe-embosomed by the night again, I knew a necessary change in things. Lo, the first ray protruded on those five! It reached them, and each felon writhed transfixed. Awhile they palpitated on the spear motionless over Tophet: stand or fall? 'I say, the spear should fall – should stand, I say!' cried the world come to judgment, granting grace or dealing doom according to world's wont, those world's bystanders grouped on Rome's crossroad at prick and summons of the primal curse which bids man love as well as make a lie. There prattled they, discoursed the right and wrong, turned wrong to right, proved wolves sheep and sheep wolves, so that you scarce distinguished fell from fleece; till out spoke a great guardian of the fold, stood up, put forth his hand that held the crook, and motioned that the arrested point decline: horribly off, the wriggling dead-weight reeled, rushed to the bottom and lay ruined there. Though still at the pit's mouth, despite the smoke o' the burning, tarriers turned again to talk and trim the balance, and detect at least a touch of wolf in what showed whitest sheep, a cross of sheep redeeming the whole wolf, – vex truth a little longer: – less and less, because years came and went, and more and more brought new lies with them to be loved in turn. Till at once the memory of the thing, why, this proved sandstone, friable, fast to fly and give its grain away at wish o' the wind. Ever and ever more diminutive, base gone, shaft lost, only entablature, dwindled into no bigger than a book, lay of the column; and that little, left by the roadside 'mid the ordure, shards and weeds.

Until I haply, wandering that way, kicked it up, turned it over and recognized, for all the crumblement, this abacus, this *square old yellow book*, – could calculate by this the lost proportions of the style."

A tinge of self-gratification coloured the random discoverer's voice. "Well, now; there's nothing in nor out o' the world good except truth: yet this, the something else, what's this then, which proves good yet seems untrue? This that I mixed with truth, motions of mine that quickened, made the inertness malleolable o' the gold was not mine, – what's your name for this? Is fiction which makes fact alive, fact too? *The somehow may be thishow.*"

The poet ambled to the fashionable bay window overlooking Warrington Crescent. "I find first 'In the beginning God made heaven and earth'. Man, – as befits the made, the inferior thing,

– repeats God's process in man's due degree, creates, no, but resuscitates, perhaps. For such man's feat is, in due degree, – mimic creation, galvanism for life, but still a glory portioned in the scale." He gave himself a slap on the brow. "The book! I turn its medicinable leaves in London now till, as in Florence erst, a spirit laughs and leaps through every limb, and lights my eye, and lifts me by the hair, letting me have my will again with these – how title I the dead alive once more? Let this old woe step on the stage again! Act itself o'er anew for man to judge, not by the very sense and sight indeed – since, how heart moves brain, and how both move hand, what mortal ever in entirety saw? No dose of purer truth than man digests, but truth with falsehood, milk that feeds him now – to-wit, by voices we call evidence, for how else know we save by worth of word? Here are the voices presently shall sound in due succession. First, the world's outcry around the rush and ripple of any fact fallen stonewise, plumb on the smooth face of things, – say, Half-Rome's feel after the vanished truth: honest enough, as the way is, – all the same, harbouring in the centre of its sense a hidden germ of failure, shy but sure, should neutralize that honesty and leave that feel for truth at fault, as the way is too. Who shall say how, who shall say why? 'T is there – the instinctive theorizing where a fact looks to the eye as the eye likes the look. Gossip in a public place, a sample speech, all for truth's sake, mere truth, nothing else! How Half-Rome found for Guido much excuse.

Next, from Rome's Other Half, the opposite feel for truth with a like swerve, like unsuccess, – or if success, by no more skill but luck: this time, through rather siding with the wife. A piece of public talk to correspond at the next stage of the story; just a day let pass and a new day bring the proper change. Another sample speech i' the marketplace o' the Barberini by the Capucins; where the old Triton, at his fountain-sport, Bernini's creature plated to the paps, puffs up steel sleet which breaks to diamond dust, a spray of sparkles snorted from his conch. A-smoke i' the sunshine, Rome lies gold and glad: so, listen how, to the other half of Rome, Pompilia seemed a saint and martyr both!

Then, yet another day let come and go, hear a fresh speaker! – neither this nor that half-Rome aforesaid; something bred of both: the elaborate product, *tertium quid*. Rome's first commotion in subsidence gives the curd o' the cream, flower o' the wheat, as it were, and finer sense o' the city. Is this plain? Here, after ignorance, instruction speaks in person of some man of quality who, – breathing musk from lace-work and brocade, his solitaire amid the flow of frill, powered peruke on nose and bag at back, and cane dependent from the ruffled wrist, – harangues in silvery and selectest phrase 'neath waxlight in a glorified saloon, courting the approbation of no mob, but Eminence This and All-Illustrious That. Still, spite its weight and worth, a sample-speech. How quality dissertated on the case.

So much for Rome and rumour; smoke comes first. The actors, no mere rumours of the act, intervene. First you hear Count Guido' voice, in a small chamber that adjoins the court, where Governor and Judges, summoned thence, find the accused ripe for declaring truth. He proffers his defence, in tones subdued near to mock-mildness now, so mournful seems the obtuser sense truth fails to satisfy; now, moved, from pathos at the wrong endured, to passion; for the natural man is roused at fools who first do wrong, then pour the blame of their wrong-doing, Satan-like, on Job. Also his tongue at times is hard to curb; incisive, nigh satiric bites the phrase, rough-raw, yet somehow claiming privilege, modified forthwith by a fall o' the fire. He feels he has a fist, then folds his arms crosswise and makes his mind up to be meek despite, – what twitches brow and makes lip wince, – his limbs' late taste of what was called the Cord, or Vigil-torture more facetiously. Even so, they were wont to tease the truth out of loath witness toying, trifling time, by torture: 't was a trick, a vice of the age. That is all history: and what is not now, was then, defendants found it to their cost. How Guido, after being tortured, spoke." The racounter gave a measured sniff and introduced another voice.

"Also hear Caponsacchi who comes next, man and priest – could you comprehend the coil! – in days when that was rife which now is rare. How, mingling each its multifarious wires, now heaven, now earth, now heaven and earth at once, had plucked at and perplexed their puppet here, played off the young frank personable priest, a courtly spiritual Cupid, – squire of dames by law of love and mandate of the mode. All is changed now, as he tells the court how he had played the part excepted at; since, for his cause of scandal, his own share i' the flight from home and husband of the wife, he has been censured, punished in a sort by relegation, – exile, we should say. Here sit the old Judges then, but with no grace of reverend carriage, magisterial port, as he speaks rapidly, angrily, speech that smites and they keep silence, bear blow after blow, because the seeming solitary man, speaking for God, may have an audience too, invisible, no discreet Judge provokes. How the priest Caponsacchi said his say."

A third character stole the limelight and made herself heard. "Then a soul sighs its lowest and its last. How, while the hireling and the alien stoop, and folk, allowably inquisitive, encircle the low pallet where she lies in the good house that helps the poor to die, Pompilia tells the story of her life, as if the bystanders gave each his straw, which, plaited all together, made a Cross fit to die looking on and praying with. So, to the common kindliness she speaks. How she endeavoured to explain her life."

Browning's attention turned to the courts of law. "One orator, of two on either side, shall teach us the puissance of the tongue, that is, o' the pen which simulated tongue; that point of vantage, law let nobly pass. How Don Giacinto of the Arcangeli, called Procurator of the Poor at Rome, – now advocate for Guido and his mates, the jolly learned man of middle age, cheek and jowl all in laps with fat and law, constant to that devotion of the earth, still captive in those dear domestic ties! – how he, having a cause to triumph with, wheezes out law and whiffles Latin forth, makes logic levigate the big crime small, sprinkling each flower appropriate to the time; how he turns, twists, and tries the oily thing shall be – first speech for Guido against the Fisc.

On the other side, some finished butterfly, some breathing diamond-flake with leaf-gold fans: Giovambattista o' the Bottini, Fisc, Pompilia's patron by the chance of the hour, odds of age joined in him with ends of youth. A man of ready smile and facile tear, improvised hopes, despairs at nod and beck, and language – ah, the gift of eloquence! – language that goes as easy as glove o'er good and evil, smoothens both to one. Rashness helps caution with him, fires the straw, while calm sits Caution, rapt with heavenward eye, as, in his modest studio, all alone, the tall wight stands a-tiptoe, strives and strains, – both eyes shut, like the cockerel that would crow, – speaks out the poesy which, penned, turns prose.

Then comes the all but end, the ultimate judgment save yours, Pope Innocent the Twelfth. Simple, sagacious, mild yet resolute, having attained to fourscore years and six; when the court found Guido and the rest guilty, but law supplied a subterfuge and passed the final sentence to the Pope, how he is wont to do God's work on earth. In the plain closet where he does such work with, from all Peter's treasury, one stool, one table and one lathen crucifix, *there* sits the Pope, his thoughts for company, grave but not sad; nay, something like a cheer leaves the lips to be benevolent. He reads, notes, lays the papers down at last, unclasps a huge tome in an antique guise, finds place where falls the passage to be conned according to an order long in use, starts somewhat, solemnizes straight his smile, and at the end lets flow his own thoughts forth, till by the dreary relics of the west wan through the half-moon window, – all his light, – he bows the head while the lips move in prayer, writes some three brief lines, signs and seals the same, tinkles a hand-bell, bids the obsequious Sir who puts foot presently o' the closet-sill he watched outside of, bear as superscribed that mandate to the Governor forthwith; then heaves abroad his cares in one good sigh, and so to sup as a clear conscience should. The manner of the judgment of the Pope.

Then must speak Guido yet a second time; all a man hath, *that* will he give for life. On a stone bench in a close fetid cell, where the hot vapour of an agony, struck into drops on the cold wall, runs down horrible worms made out of sweat and tears – *there* crouch, well-nigh to the knees in dungeon-straw, two awestruck figures: this a Cardinal, that an Abate, both of old styled friends of the part-man part-monster in the midst, – so changed is Franceschini's gentle blood. The tiger-cat screams now, that whined before; then you know how the bristling fury foams. They listen, this wrapped in his folds of red; the other, as beseems a stouter heart, working his best with beads and cross to ban the enemy that comes in like a flood spite of the standard set up, verily and in no trope at all, against him there, – when inside, from the true profound, a sign shall bear intelligence that the foe is foiled, that Guido Franceschini has confessed, and is absolved and reconciled with God. How Guido made defence a second time."

'Here are the voices presently shall sound in due succession', Browning had let his imagined visitor know, and now that the voices had sounded, he drew a conclusion. "Action now shrouds, now shows the informing thought. Man, like a glass ball with a spark atop, out of the magic fire that lurks inside, shows one tint at a time to take the eye, suffuses bright with dark and baffles so your sentence absolute for shine or shade." He tapped on his *old yellow book*. "Such, British Public, ye who like me not, – God love you! – whom I yet have laboured for, such labour had such issue". The poet pattered on the ring he was wearing on his fingers. "So I wrought this arc, by furtherance of such alloy, and so, by one spirt, take away its trace till, justifiably golden, rounds my ring."

He cast a questioning look. "A ring without a posy, and that ring mine?"

He gave a far-reaching smile while his eyes focussed on a distant place and a near past. "O lyric Love, – half-angel and half-bird, and all a wonder and a wild desire, yet human at the red-ripe of the heart – hail then and hearken from the realms of help! Never may I commence my song, my due to God who best taught song by gift of thee, except with bent head and beseeching hand; never conclude, but raising hand and head thither where eyes, that cannot reach, yet yearn for all hope, all sustainment, all reward, their utmost up and on, – so blessing back in those thy realms of help, that heaven thy home, some whiteness which, I judge, thy face makes proud, some wanness where, I think, thy foot may fall!"

It would not go amiss to highlight Browning's statement at the outset, "A thing's a sign: now for the thing signified", for the author appears to have pinpointed a linguistic centre in his work and in so doing foreshadowed the modern linguistic concern with the signifier/signified dichotomy, not to mention the notion that 'signs allow and even require the interposing and incorporation of a certain amount of human culture into reality.'[1] It ought to be added that it has been pointed out, early in linguistic days, that 'a linguistic sign is not a link between a thing and a name, but between a concept and a sound pattern.'[2] However, the Victorian poet has stopped short of maintaining that the linguistic sign is arbitrary and made no mention of the 'perpetual sliding of the signified under the signifier' subsequently descried from a post-structuralist angle.[3]

As the story goes, Robert Browning had purchased an *old yellow book* at a Florentine flea market: "'Stall!' cried I: a *lira* made it mine", he has recalled, and it is easy to imagine that, while voraciously reading the peculiar contents en route to the house he shared with his wife Elisabeth *Casa Guidi*, the impulsive buyer let out the phenomenological *cri de coeur*, 'Back to the things themselves!'[4] In addition, he may well have come up with one of those 'empirical or object-sentences' later theorized by logical positivists, albeit it remains to be seen whether he ever came up with one of those 'pseudo-object sentences' the positivists have deemed to be as seemingly relating to things but in reality making statements about words.[5] Back home from Italy, the fortunate owner of the *yellow book* has boasted that "the thing's restorative i' the touch and sight", and the feeling has, to all appearances, made him behave, say, in the manner of a *bricoleur*, i.e., like a handyman who 'addresses himself to a collection of oddments left over from human endeavours' and 'speaks through things'.[6]

One of the 'things' under scrutiny has been the lengthy legal procedure in the Franceschini trial: "Pages of proof this way, and that way proof, and always – once again the case postponed!" In other words, the law's delay has been part and parcel of the scene – one is put in mind of *Jarndyce and Jarndyce* as another instance of the vicissitudes depicted in *The Ring and the Book*[7] – yet the Court has had its say, and the Pope has been in a position to utter the last word. "Fancy with fact is just one fact the more," Browning has stated qua a commentator on the characters' interaction, – notably on how Guido, standing at the Comparini's front door, had adopted somebody else's identity, just as Lucifer had done at Eden-gate. By and large, the poet has brooded over the *square old yellow book* and on the ethical features of truth: "Well, now, there's nothing in nor out o' the world good except truth", he has affirmed. "Yet this, the something else, what's this then, which proves good yet seems untrue?" he has asked. Then, "is fiction which makes fact alive, fact too?" he has wondered. "The somehow may be *thishow*", he has declared hopefully." 'Truth must prevail', it had been asserted in days of yore, and, centuries later, his belief that the Florentine script was based on truth has made him utter in accordance with the latter-day phenomenological tenet that 'truth is an ongoing project rather than a fixed possession, a task of living experience rather than a *fait after accompli*.[8] It is on record that the poet paid a visit to York Street Chapel and was mesmerized by "the harvestings of truth's stray ears singly gleaned, and in one sheaf bound together for belief."[9]

To crown it all, Browning has told his imaginary guest about his skilfully moulding an ingot into a ring: "So I wrought this arc by furtherance of such alloy and so, by one spirt, take away its trace till, justifiably golden, rounds my ring:" It had been a momentous feat on all counts and he had linked the *old yellow book* with the *ring* in the hope that a gentle rub of the latter would summon a genie willing to rid the craftsman of his bedazzlement.

Awesomely contiguous, his plea to the "lyric Love" soaring as a "half-angel and half bird and all a wonder a wild desire' has resonated with St. Bernard of Clairvaux's extolment of the Virgin Mary: 'Lady, thou art so great and so powerful, that who seeks grace without recourse to thee would have his wish fly upwards without wings'[10]. Along similar lines, the pleader has expressed the hope that his song of praise would allow him to rise to a heavenly sphere where his eyes yearning for comfort and sustenance would be blessed with the eternal light.

The all-out mystic utterance has been preceded by the presentation of characters making utterances on a speaking rota and metamorphosing the verse novel into a kind of 'play for voices' able to conjure up a 'fairy-tale milk wood'[11] despite being enacted in a concrete jungle.

To start with, Browning has disclosed, *Half-Rome* will support Guido – "all for truth's sake, mere truth, nothing else", he has commented not without a hint of irony.

Conversely, leaving aside the irony of it, the *Other Half-Rome* will side with Pompilia and see her as "a saint and martyr both".

Well apart from the two halves of Rome, a personage described as a *Tertium Quid* and "the curd o' the cream, flower o' the wheat", will take a sort of unbiased stand.

Then Guido Franceschini will engage in self-defence by dint of a language "rough-raw, yet somehow claiming privilege"; in effect, he will be oscillating between Religion and Humanity.

Following the Aretine aristocrat, Giuseppe Caponsacchi will act as a "young frank personable priest ... a courtly spiritual Cupid."

Guido's wife, Pompilia Comparini, will appear to be caught in the crossfire and appeal to "the common kindliness ... there being scarce more privacy at last for mind than body, but she is used to bear."

The next two voices will be raised by lawyers, one being the "advocate for Guido and his mates ... mirthful as mighty, yet, as great hearts use ... still captive in those domestic ties!", and the other acting as "Pompilia's patron by the chance of the hour ... a man of ready smile and facile tear, and language."

Finally, Pope Innocent the Twelfth, called in to give his inappellable verdict on the Franceschini case, will sound "grave but not sad, – nay, something like a cheer leaves the lips free to be benevolent, which, all day long, did duty firm and fast."

In a kind of aftergame, Guido will speak again while being visited in his cell by "two awe-struck figures, this a Cardinal, that an Abate, both of old styled friends of the part-man part-monster in the midst", – a sort of bivalved creature in the depths of despair.

Browning's introduction of characters and events has been enhanced by a riot of colour inherent in the impressive array. By way of sample, Pietro and Violante Comparini were "two poor ignoble hearts who did their best to ... scramble through the world's mud" and did not hesitate to lay their treasured offspring on a "stooping star" twinkling in the Roman sky. As it happened, Guido Franceschini, the hoped-for recipient of the treasure, had the contours of a "star supposed, but fog o' the fen, gilded star-fashion by a glint from hell" and "heaved up, haled on its gross way" by two dark brothers known as Abbot Paolo and Canon Girolamo.

As for Canon Giuseppe Caponsacchi, he could be seen as a redivivus Saint George by virtue of "bearing away the lady in his arms, saved for a splendid minute and no more."

Common-or-garden people have come on the scene in the aftermath of the crime in Via Paulina and been excitedly confabulating about "a pack of werewolves", turned wrong to right, and proved wolves sheep and sheep wolves.

At the end of the line, a great guardian of the folk has stood up and searched for the truth about the *Romana Homicidiorum*, i.e., the Rome-based homicide.

As a corollary, Truth has been panegyrised by Browning as the one and only good "in or out o' the world." By the same token the poet has acknowledged that something good may seem untrue: a blend of fiction and truth, means and end, may be of great help in many respects, yet can fiction make fact alive? Well, he might have asked from a linguistic perspective whether truth could 'reside in the processes of language and not simply in in an external word which language is called to represent.'[12] "The somehow may be *thishow*", he has concluded with linguistic overtones and in quick succession added a touch of metaphysics to the speculation by asserting that "Man, as befits an inferior thing purposed to grow but not make in turn, does not create; he resuscitates, perhaps. For such man's feat is, in the due degree, – mimic creation, galvanism for life, but still a glory portioned in the scale. "

Soon afterwards, the fluky-possessor of the Yellow Book has welcomed the uplifting impact of its "medicinable leaves" on his spirit; in so doing, he has deemed the Florentine textbook to be not only as a link between storytelling and reality but also as a precondition for knowledge: "For how else know we save by worth of word?" he has put forth.

In this respect, it is worthwhile to mention that the 'cognitive' function has been featured by linguists as a vital constituent of a verbal communication. On the other hand, it has been argued that any transmission of information, far from being confined to cognition, is part and parcel of an 'emotive' function: the final stage of the process is, of course, the production of a 'poetic' spark, which is in effect the primary purpose of verbal art.[13] Bearing this in mind, there is every reason to assume that Browning's emotional response to the Florentine text connotes the approach of a literary critic as well as a linguist.

At this critical juncture, it seems apposite to elaborate on the thought-provoking behaviour of characters peculiarly dealing with *Veritas*, i.e. the Goddess of Truth.

Pietro and Violante Comparini were moderately well-off. Pietro was a homeowner well past his prime, reputedly a gourmet and layabout. His wife, equally mature, was known to be dutiful yet liable to miscarriage – hence no children had enriched their wedded life up to the day when, out of the blue, *Signora* Comparini made her husband privy to her unexpected pregnancy. In due course a baby daughter was delivered in Pietro's absence and christened as Pompilia in *San Lorenzo*, the couple's parish church. Thirteen years later, the miracle baby had grown into a tall slender girl with raven-black hair, large dark eyes and an eaglet-like nose. Traditional mores had been the staple diet of her rearing, and indeed modesty appeared to be an endearing quality of hers. Moreover, the fact that her parents were financially at ease made her an attractive choice as a bride.

By sheer coincidence, the Aretine Count Franceschini had travelled to Rome in search of a female companion hopefully blessed with an adequate dowry; as it happened, the pulling of a few strings put the thin and pale, beaky-nosed, grey-bearded nobleman in touch with the pretty and ethereal Pompilia. The prospect of her becoming a *Contessina* enticed Violante despite her misgivings about a conjugal bond between an aristocratic fellow and a lower middle-class girl. In effect, she welcomed the noble pursuer. For his part, Pietro, suspicious of the Count's so far uncorroborated financial position, kept his options open until he gave in to pressure, – from his brother Paolo most of all.

In a short space of time the Comparini household had moved, lock, stock, and barrel, into the Palazzo Franceschini up at Arezzo and soon enough got entangled in a complex web of social intercourse. Indeed, class divide coupled with inadequate family funds proved to be thorny issues, and things went from bad to worse in spite of Pompilia's best efforts to cope with the demands of a middle-aged husband exceedingly keen on having a son and consequently a heir. Soon they were at the end of their tether and moved to back to their less palatial abode. The domestic drama reached its epiphanic moment the moment when Violante disclosed that Pompilia was not her natural daughter: the child had been bought from a destitute widow, she confessed and, lo and behold, Pietro cottoned on to the cause of his wife's leaving home while the alleged childbearing was in progress; nevertheless, he plumped for forgiveness: at long last he was a father!

In the meantime, miles away from her parents, Pompilia was finding it increasingly difficult, even painful, to come to terms with a consort endowed with the qualities of a bullyboy, and the outcome of the predicament was that she found solace in the proximity of a youthful subdeacon named Giuseppe Caponsacchi and made sure of availing herself of the golden opportunity. His frequent appearances at close quarters were welcome to a certain extent, but in the long run they aroused suspicions. Pangs of jealousy caused marital problems and, to rub salt into Pompilia's wound, her dealings with Beatrice, Guido's elderly mother, became ever so troublesome.

To cut a long story short, the girl found herself unable to grin and bear it any longer and looked for a way out of the impasse with a little help from her new-found friend. The agreeable subdeacon pondered briefly and then held out a hand: written messages were exchanged for some time and finally, in the small hours of an April day, Pompilia and Giuseppe hopped on a carriage and embarked on a perilous journey along the *Via Consolare* leading to Rome. Fatigue obliged the couple to take a rest at an inn and the next morning they came face to face with the uncalled-for Guido. After an abortive skirmish, the runaways were taken into custody: Caponsacchi was banished to the coastal town of Civita Vecchia while Pompilia was confined to an institution for fallen women known to one and all as *Le Scalette*.

As for Guido, he took the sentence to be an insult to his acute sense of honour, but worse was to come: in a short space of time Pompilia was in the family way and permitted to rejoin her parents. Soon a son was born and christened Gaetano after Violante's cherished saint. It was the last straw for the alleged father: he saw his honour in tatters and for good measure it irked him to think that Pietro had so far failed to give him the due dowry in full. The notion of a revenge justified by an unconditional moral principle flashed on his mind, and on Christmas Eve he galloped to the Eternal City in the company of four young rustics. On the strength of a letter allegedly sent by Caponsacchi the new arrivals gained access to Comparini's villa; a murderous attack was over and done with in a flash. The perpetrators vanished into the Roman night but, alas, the law was in hot pursuit. The ensuing capture represented a watershed in the life of Count Franceschini as well as in that of his kith and kin.

Such had been the chain of events prior to the murder. "Let this old woe step on the stage again!" the reader of the Yellow Book has exclaimed. "Here are the voices presently shall sound in due succession," he has added, and the 'play for voices' has commenced in Guido Franceschini's *Milk Wood*. Indeed, Browning's preview may be taken to be the presentation of 'different voices and multiple codes which are at once interwoven and unfinished.'[14]

1. Levi-Strauss, as quoted in *Modern Criticism and Theory*, Ed. David Lodge, Longman 1992 p. 65
2. Ferdinand de Saussure, in *Op. Cit.*, p. 10.
3. *Jacques Lacan, in Op. Cit.* pp. *79 & 87*
4. Edmund Husserl's slogan, *as quoted in*
   Western Philosophy and Philosophers, Unwin Hyman, 1991, p. 233
5. *Logical Positivism*, in *Op. Cit.* p. 186
6. Levi-Strauss, as quoted in *Modern Criticism and Theory. Ed. David Lodge. Longman, 1992* pp. 64-66
7. Charles Dickens, *Bleak House*, Penguin Books, p. 52
8. Maurice Merleau-Ponty, in *Western Philosophy and Philosophers*, p. 200
9. Robert Browning, *Christmas-Eve*, ll. 606-09
10. Dante Alighieri, *La Divina Commedia, Paradiso*, Canto XXXIII, ll. 3-15
11. Dylan Thomas, *Under Milk Wood*
12. Colin Mac Cabe, in *Language,*
13. *Linguistics and the study of Literature'*, in *Modern Criticism and Theory*, p. 438
14. Roman Jakobson, *Linguistics and Poetics*, in *Op. Cit*, p. 32ff
15. Roland Barthes, *Textual Analysis: Poe's 'Valdemar'*, in *Modern Criticism and Theory*, p. 193

HALF-ROME

A vast crowd had gathered inside the austere walls of *San Lorenzo in Lucina* in order to pay its last respects to the late Pietro and Violante Comparini.

In the wake of the funeral two mourners ran into each other on the steps leading to the temple. "What, you, Sir, come too?" said one of the two in surprise. "What a roaring day we've had!" he exclaimed. "Whose fault? Why, today's lucky pearl is cast to swine! They laid both bodies in the church, this morn the first thing, on the chancel two steps up; disposed them, – Pietro, the old, murdered fool, to the right of the altar, and his wretched wife on the other side. In trying to count stabs, people supposed Violante showed the most, till somebody explained us that mistake: his wounds had been dealt out indifferent where, but she took all her stabbings on the face, since punished thus solely for honour's sake; it was Violante gave the first offence, while Pietro, who helped merely, his mere death answered the purpose, so his face went free. Why did not he roll down altar-step, roll on through nave, roll fairly out of church, deprive *Lorenzo* of the spectacle? For see, at that same altar where he lies, to that same inch of step, was brought the babe for blessing after baptism, and there styled Pompilia and a string of names beside, by his bad wife, seventeen years ago, who purchased her simply to palm on him, flatter his dotage and defraud the heirs. Wait awhile! Also to this very step did this Violante, twelve years afterward, bring, the mock-mother, that child-cheat full-grown, yes, made her daughter, as the girl was held, marry a man, and honest man beside, and man of birth to boot, – clandestinely. Ay, 'tis four years since man and wife they grew, this Guido Franceschini and this same Pompilia, foolishly thought, falsely declared a Comparini and the couple's child: just at this altar where, beneath the piece of Master Guido Reni, Christ on cross, that couple lie now, murdered yestereve.

Even the blind can see a providence here: enough that here the bodies had their due."

The other guy, a fellow proletarian by the look of him, gave a nod and a wink. The speaker took his cue and carried on.

"These wretched Comparini were once gay and galiard, – of the modest middle class, – and married young. They lived the accustomed life, citizens as they were of good repute and, childless, naturally took their ease since Pietro was possessed of house and land. He owned some usufruct, had moneys' use lifelong, but to determine with his life in heirs' default: so, Pietro craved an heir. Hence, seventeen years ago, conceive his glee when first Violante, 'twixt a smile and a blush, announced that, spite of her unpromising age, an heir's birth was to happen." Half-Rome broke into a knowing smile. "And it did: a child was born, Pompilia, for his joy, a saints' grace or, say, grant of the good God ... a fiddle pin's end. What imbeciles are we! She, whose trick brought the babe into the world, she it was, – when the babe was grown a girl, – judged a new trick should reinforce the old: she who had caught one fish could make that catch a bigger still, in angler's policy. Her minnow was set wriggling on its barb and tossed to the midstream; that is, this grown girl with the great eyes and bounty of black hair and first crisp youth that tempts a jaded taste was whisked i' the way of a certain man, who snapped."

The narrator gave a loud sniff. "Count Guido Franceschini *l'Aretino* was head of an old noble house enough, – not over-rich, you can't have everything, but such a man as riches rub against. As such folks do, he had come up to Rome to better his fortune and since many years was friend and follower of a cardinal. He waited, and learned waiting, thirty years. The end was: Guido, when the warning showed, the first white hair i' the glass, gave up the game, determined on returning to his town, making the best of bad incurable, patching the old palace up and lingering there where honour helps to spice the scanty bread. Just as he trimmed his lamp and girt his loins, who but Violante sudden spied her prey and threw her bait, Pompilia, where he sulked. A gleam i' the gloom! What if he gained thus much, wrung out this sweet drop from the bitter past and, after all, brought something back from Rome? Would not a wife serve at Arezzo well to light the dark house, lend a look of youth to the mother's face grown meagre, left alone and famished with the emptiness of hope? Such were the pinks and greys about the bait persuaded Guido gulp down hook and all."

The lower-class chap gave a dry cough and looked his mate in the eye. "What constituted him so choice a catch? Why, first, here was a nobleman with friends, a palace one might run to and be safe: is birth a privilege and power or no? The Count was made woo, win, and wed at once with sanction of some priest-confederate properly paid to make short work and sure. So, did old Pietro's daughter change her style for Guido Franceschini's lady-wife ere Guido knew it well. And why this haste and scramble and indecent secrecy? 'Lest Pietro, all the while in ignorance, should get to learn, gainsay and break the match.' She remedied the wilful man's mistake.'

All parties made perforce the best o' the fact; Pietro could play vast indignation off, be ignorant and astounded, dupe alike at need of wife, daughter, and son in law. Guido's broad back was saddled to bear all: Pietro, Violante, and Pompilia too, – three lots cast confidently in one lap, three dead-weights with one arm to lift the three out of their limbo up to life again. They, for their part, turned over, first of all, their fortune in its rags and rottenness to Guido, – he who guaranteed, for better or for worse, to Pietro and Violante, house and home, kith and kin, with the pick of company and life o' the fat o' the land while life should last."

Half-Rome flashed an interrogative look. "How say you to the bargain at first blush? Why did a middle-aged not-silly man show himself thus besotted at once?" There was no reply, and he gave one: "Quoth Salomon, 'One black eye does it all.'" He looked thrilled by the wise king's asseveration.

"They went to Arezzo", he continued, "Pietro and his spouse, with just the dusk o' the day of life to spend, eager to use the twilight, taste a treat, enjoy for once with neither stay nor stint the luxury of lord-and-lady-ship, while Guido, – who should minister the sight, stay all this qualmish greediness of soul with apples and with flagons – for his part, was set on life diverse as pole from pole: suppose He hoped now to walk softly all his days in soberness of spirit, if haply so, till times, that could not well grow worse, should mend." A wry smile enhanced the rosy picture. "Thus minded then, two parties mean to meet and make each other happy. The first week, and fancy strikes fact and explodes in full: 'This,' shrieked the Comparini, 'this the Count, the palace, the signorial privilege, the pomp and pageantry were promised us? For this have we exchanged our liberty, our competence, our darling of a child? To house as spectres in a sepulchre, under this black stone heap, the street's disgrace? Where's the foregone housekeeping good and gay, the neighbourliness, the companionship called common by the uncommon fools we were? Even the sun that used to shine at Rome, where is it? Robbed and starved and frozen too? We will have justice, justice if there be!' Did not they shout, did not the town resound!" The narrator's mouth tightened into a compact line. "Four months' probation of this purgatory, dog-snap and cat-claw, curse and counterblast, – then, their worst done that way, they struck tent, marched, renounced their share o' the bargain, flung what dues Guido was bound to pay in Guido's face, left their hearts' darling, treasure of the twain and so forth, the poor inexperienced bride, to her own devices, bade Arezzo rot and the life signorial, and sought Rome once more."

Loquacious Half-Rome went through a flicker of doubt about the whole caboodle and sharpened his stare. "I see the comment on your lip: 'The better fortune, Guido's – free at least by this defection of the foolish pair, he could begin make profit in some sort of the young bride and the new quietness, lead his own life now, henceforth breathe unplagued.' Could he? You know the sex like Guido's self. Learn the Violante-nature!" He dried up for an instant and recommenced composedly. "Once in Rome, her first act to inaugurate return was, she got pricked in conscience: Jubilee gave her the hint. Our Pope, as kind as just, attained his eighty years, announced a boon should make us bless the fact, held Jubilee: short shrift, prompt pardon for the light offence, and no rough dealing with the regular crime. Our sage Violante had a sin of a sort she must compound for now or not at all: now be the ready riddance! She confessed Pompilia was a fable not a fact: she never bore a child in her whole life. The babe had been a find i' the filth-heap, Sir, catch from the kennel! There was found at Rome a woman who professed the wanton's trade under the requisite thin coverture: ordinary harlot and washer-wife; she sold this babe eight months before its birth to our Violante, Pietro's honest spouse: she it was, bought and paid for, passed the thing off as the flesh and blood and child of her despite the flagrant fifty years, – and why? Partly to please Pietro, fill his cup with wine at the late hour when lees are left, partly to cheat the rightful heirs, agape, for that same principal of the usufruct it vexed him he must die and leave behind.

Such was the sin had come to be confessed. Which of the tales, the first or the last, was true? Did she so sin once, or, confessing now, sin for the first time? Either way you will. One sees a reason for the cheat; one sees a reason for a cheat in owning cheat where no cheat had been. What of the revenge? What prompted the contrition all at once, made the avowal easy, the shame slight? Why, prove they but Pompilia not their child, no child, no dowry; this, supposed their child, had claimed what this, shown alien to their blood, claimed nowise: Guido's claim was through his wife, null then and void with hers. The biter bit!"

The commoner's eyes grew wider while he asked, "Is this your view?" before adding in a modulated tone, "'T was Guido's anyhow and colourable: he came forward then, protested in his very bride's behalf. This makes the first act of the farce; anon the stealing sombre element comes in till all is black or blood-red in the piece. Guido, thus made a laughingstock abroad, a proverb for the marketplace at home, what did the Count? Revenge him on his wife? Plainly, did Guido open both doors wide, spurn thence the spurn-cast creature, and clear scores? No, birth and breeding, and compassion, too, saved her such scandal: she was young, he thought, not privy to the treason, punished most i' the proclamation of it; why make her a party to the crime she suffered by? Then the black eyes were now her very own, not any more Violante's: let her live, lose in a new air, under a new sun, the taint of the imputed parentage truly or falsely, take no more the touch of Pietro and his partner anyhow! All might go well yet."

The lower-class representative pursed his lips with distaste. "So she thought, herself, it seems, since what was her first act and deed when news came how these kindly ones at Rome had stripped her naked to amuse the world with spots here, spots there, and spots everywhere? For I should tell you that they noised abroad of how the promised glory was a dream, the power a bubble, and the wealth, – why, dust. What side did our Pompilia first espouse? Her first deliberate measure was she wrote, pricked by some loyal impulse, straight to Rome and her husband's brother the Abate there, who, having managed to effect the match, might take men's censure for its ill success. She made a clean breast also in her turn: she qualified the couple handsomely since whose departure hell, she said, was heaven, and the house, late distracted by their peals, quiet as Carmel where lilies live. Their game had been to thwart her husband's love and cross his will, malign his words and ways, – whose last injunction to her simple self had been – what parents'-precept, do you think? that she should follow after with all speed, join them at Rome again, but first of all pick up a fresh companion in her flight: some gay, daredevil, cloak-and-rapier spark capable of adventure; helped by whom she, some fine eve when lutes were in the air, having put poison in the posset cup, laid hands on money, jewels and the like, and, to conceal the thing with more effect, by way of parting benediction too, fired the house, – one would finish famously i' the tumult, slip out, scurry off and away, and turn up merrily at home once more. Fact this, and not a dream o' the devil, Sir!"

The skilful presentation of a slice of life was received with a dismissive wave of the hand, which was dismissed by a sly smile. "The cause thus carried to the courts at Rome, Guido away, the Abate had no choice but stand forth, take his absent brother's part, defend the honour of himself beside. He made what head he might against the pair, maintained Pompilia's birth legitimate and all her rights intact – hers, Guido's now – and so far by his tactics turned their flank that, though the courts allowed the cheat for fact, suffered Violante to parade her shame and let the tale o' the feigned birth pass for proved, yet they stopped there, refused to intervene: they would not take away the dowry now wrongfully given at first, nor bar at all succession to the aforesaid usufruct, established on a fraud, nor play the game of Pietro's child and now not Pietro's child as it might suit the gamester's purpose. Thus was justice ever ridiculed in Rome: whence, on the Comparini's part, appeal; counter-appeal on Guido's. That's the game, and so the matter stands, even to his hour, bandied as balls are in a tennis court, and so might stand, unless some heart broke first, till doomsday."

A stream of nods enhanced the utterance. "Leave it thus, and now revert to the old Arezzo whence we moved to Rome. Pompilia, left alone now, found herself; found herself young too, sprightly, fair enough, matched with a husband old beyond his age; found too the house dull and its inmates dead; so, looked outside for light and life. And lo, there in a trice did turn up life and light: the man with the aureole, sympathy made flesh, the all-consoling Caponsacchi, Sir! A priest – what else should the consoler be? – with goodly shoulder blade and proper leg, a portly make and a symmetric shape, and curls that clustered to the tonsure quite; a canon full-blown so far; priest, and priest nowise exorbitantly overworked, the courtly Christian, not so much Saint Paul as a saint of Caesar's household: there posed he sending his god-glance after his shot shaft. He, not a visitor at Guido's house, scarce an acquaintance, but in prime request with the magnates of Arezzo, was seen here, heard there, felt everywhere in Guido's path if Guido's wife's path be her husband's too. Now he threw comfits at the theatre into her lap, – what harm in Carnival? – now he pressed close till his foot touched her gown, his hand touched hers, – how help on promenade? While – how do accidents sometimes combine! – Pompilia chose to cloister up her charms just in a chamber that o'erlooked the street, sat there to pray, or peep there at mankind." A couple of extra-lusty nods sliced the air. "This passage of arms and wits amused the town: 'Somebody courts your wife, Count? Where and when? How and why? Mere horn madness; have a care! Your lady loves her own room, sticks to it, locks herself in for hours, you say yourself. And … what, it's Caponsacchi means you harm? The Canon? We caress him, he's the world's, a man of such acceptance! Never dream he'd risk his brush for your particular chick when the wide town's his hen-roost. Fie o' the fool!' So they dispensed their comfort of a kind. Guido at last cried, 'Something is in the air; the trouble of eclipse hangs overhead. Let Caponsacchi take his hand away from the wire, disport himself in other paths than lead precisely to my palace gate, look where he likes except one window's way where, cheek on hand and elbow set on sill, happens to lean and say her litanies every day and all day long, just my wife! Or wife and Caponsacchi may fare the worse!'"

Half-Rome put a finger behind his ear. "Admire the man's simplicity: 'I'll do this, I'll not have that, I'll punish and prevent!' 'Tis easy saying, but to a fray, you see, two parties go. The badger shows his teeth; the fox nor lies down sheeplike nor dares fight. Oh, the wife knew the appropriate warfare well, the way to put suspicion to the blush! She bade the Governor do governance, cried out on the Archbishop, – why, there now, take him for sample! Three successive times had he to reconduct her by main force back to the husband and the house she fled. Judge if that husband warmed him in the face of friends or frowned on foes as heretofore! Judge if he missed the natural grin of folk, or lacked the customary compliment of cap and bells, the luckless husband's fit!" The speaker gave a little chuckle. "One merry April morning, Guido woke with an inordinate yawning of the jaws, ears plugged, eyes gummed together, palate, tongue and teeth one mud-paste made of poppy milk; and found his wife flown, his scrutoire the worse for a rummage; jewelry that was, was not, some money there had made itself wings too; the door lay wide and yet the servants slept sound as the dead, or dosed which does as well. This lamb-like innocent of fifteen years had simply put an opiate in the drink of the whole household overnight and then spoiled the Philistine and marched out of doors. All neighbours knew; no mystery in the world: the lovers left at nightfall; overnight had Caponsacchi come to carry off Pompilia, not alone: a friend of his, Lord and a Canon also, – what would you have? such are the red-clothed milk-swollen poppy heads that stand and stiffen 'mid the wheat o' the Church, – this worthy came to aid, abet his best. And so the house was ransacked, booty bagged, the lady led downstairs and out of doors. A carriage lay conveniently at the gate. Goodbye to the friendly Canon; the loving one could peradventure do the rest himself. In jumps Pompilia; after her, the priest: 'Whip, driver! Money makes the mare to go, and we've a bagful. Take the Roman road!'

The hearer's eyes sparkled with growing interest. "Guido heard all, swore the befitting oaths, got horse, was fairly started in pursuit, trod soon upon their very heels, too late by a minute only at Camoscia, at Chiusi, Foligno, – ever the fugitives just ahead, just out as he galloped in, till, lo, at the last stage of all, last post before Rome; as we say, in sight of Rome and safety, – there's impunity at Rome for priests, you know – at … what's the little place? some call it *Castelnuovo*, some just call it *L'*

Osteria, because o' the post-house inn, – triumph deceived them and undid them both: there they did halt at early evening; *there* did Guido overtake them; 't was daybreak, – one couch in one room, and one room for both." The narrator let out a belly laugh. "Sir, what's the sequel? Lover and beloved fall on their knees? No impudence serves here? They beat their breasts and beg for early death? This you expect? Indeed, then, much you err. The die was cast: over shoes over boots, and just as she – I presently shall show – Pompilia, soon looked Helen to the life, recumbent upstairs in her pink and white, so, in the inn-yard, bold as 't were Troy town, there strutted Paris in correct costume: cloak, cap and feather, no appointment missed, even to a wicked-looking sword at side, he seemed to find and feel familiar at. Nor wanted words as ready and as big as the part he played, the bold abashless one: 'I interposed to save your wife from death, yourself from shame, the true and only shame. What I have done I answer, anywhere, here, if you will; you see I have a sword: or, since I have a tonsure as you taunt, at Rome, by all means, – priests to try a priest.' And then he fingered at the sword again."

A knowing smile added colour to the impromptu speech. "So, Guido called, in aid and witness both, the Public Force; the Commissary came, Officers also. They secured the priest; then, for his more confusion, mounted up to the bedroom where still slept or feigned a sleep his paramour and Guido's wife. *In* burst the company and bade her wake and rise. Her defence? This. She woke, saw, sprang upright i' the midst and stood as terrible as truth, sprang to her husband's side, caught at the sword and, in a moment, out flew the bright thing full in the face of Guido; but for help o' the guards who held her back and pinioned her with pains enough, she had finished you my tale with a flourish of red all round it, pinked her man prettily; but she fought them one to six. They stopped that, but her tongue continued free: she spat forth such invective at her spouse, o'erfrothed him with such foam of murderer, thief, pandar – that the popular tide soon turned, the favour of the very *sbirri*, straight ebbed from the husband, set toward the wife, people cried, 'Hands off, pay a priest respect!' and 'persecuting fiend' and 'martyred saint' began to lead a measure from lip to lip while the Count, mortified in mien enough, and, nose to face, an added palm in length, was writ 'husband' every piece of him. Capture once made, release could hardly be. Beside, the prisoners both made appeal, 'Take us to Rome!'

Half-Rome pulled out a handkerchief embroidered with a Capitoline Wolf and blew his aquiline nose.

"Taken to Rome they were, – the husband trooping after piteously, tail between legs, no talk of triumph now, no dubious salve to honour's broken pate; for Guido's first search, – ferreting, poor soul, here, there and everywhere in the vile place abandoned to him when their backs were turned, found, – furnishing a last and best regale, – all the love-letters bandied betwixt the pair: mad prose, mad verse, fears, hopes, triumph, despair, avowal, disclaimer, plans, dates, names, – was nought wanting to prove, if proof consoles at all, that this had been but the fifth act o' the piece whereof the due *proemium*, months ago these playwrights had put forth, and ever since matured the middle, added 'neath his nose. He might go cross himself: the case was clear."

The proletarian observer of Caponsacchi's and Pompilia's bourgeois theatrics clapped while wallowing in the quag of a sly smile. "Therefore to Rome with the clear case; there plead each party its best and leave the law do right, let her shine forth and show, as God in heaven, vice prostrate, virtue pedestalled at last, the triumph of truth! What else shall glad our gaze when once authority has knit the brow and set the brain behind it to decide between the wolf and sheep turned litigants?

'This is indeed a business', Law shook head; "a husband charges hard things on a wife, the wife as hard o' the husband; whose fault here? A wife that flies her husband's house does wrong, the male friend's interference looks amiss, lends a suspicion; but suppose the wife, on the other hand, be jeopardized at home – nay, that she simply hold, ill-groundedly, an apprehension she is jeopardized, and further, if the friend partake the fear, and, in a commendable charity which trusteth all, trust her that she mistrusts, – what do they but obey the natural law? Pretence may this be and a cloak for sin, and circumstances that concur i' the close hint as much, loudly – yet scarce loud enough to drown the answer "strange my yet be true:" innocence often looks like guiltiness. The accused declare that in thought, word, and deed, innocent were they both from first to last. Difficult to believe, yet possible, as witness Joseph, the friend's patron-saint. The night at the inn – there charity nigh chokes ere swallow what they both asseverate; so long a flight necessitates a fall on the first bed, though in a lion's den. Last come the letters' bundled beastliness; the accused, both in a tale, protest, disclaim, abominate the horror: 'Not my hand' asserts the friend; 'nor mine' chimes in the wife. 'Twas pearls to swine: she read no more than wrote, while for his part the friend vows ignorance alike of what bears his name and bears hers: 'tis forgery, a felon's masterpiece, home manufacture and the husband's work; though he confesses, the ingenuous friend, that certain missives, letters of a sort, flighty and feeble, which assigned themselves to the wife, no less have fallen, far too oft, in his path; wherefrom he understands just this, that they were verily the lady's own. But, now he sees her face and hears her speech, much he repents him if, in fancy-freak for a moment the minutest measurable, he coupled her with the first flimsy word o' the self-spun fabric some mean spider-soul furnished forth: stop his films and stamp on him!" The ad hoc orator gesticulated wildly. "Never was such a tangled knottiness, but thus authority cuts the Gordian through, and mark how her decision suits the need! Here's troublesomeness, scandal on both sides, plenty of fault to find, no absolute crime: let each side own its fault and make amends!" The speaker clapped again. "The

Canon Caponsacchi, then, was sent to change his garb, re-trim his tonsure, tie the clerkly silk round, – every plait correct, – make the impressive entry on his place of relegation, thrill his Civita: what were a couple of years to while away? Pompilia, as enjoined, betook herself to the aforesaid Convertites, the sisterhood in Via Lungara, where the light ones live, spin, pray, then sing like linnets o'er the flax. 'Anywhere, anyhow, out of my husband's house, is heaven', cried she, – was therefore suited so. But for Count Guido Franceschini, he – the injured man thus righted – found no heaven i' the house when he returned there, I engage, was welcomed by the city turned upside down in a chorus of inquiry. 'What, back – you? And no wife? Left with the penitents? Ah, being young and pretty, 't were a shame to have her whipped in public: leave the job to the priests who understand! Such priests as yours – our mad Caponsacchi: think of him! So, he fired up, showed fight and skill of fence? Ay, you drew also, but you did not fight!' Ask yourself, had you borne a baiting thus? Was it enough to make a wise man mad?" Half-Rome gave a wry smile. "Ever in due succession, drop by drop, came slow distilment from the alembic here, corrosive keeping the man's misery raw: inadequate her punishment, no less punished in some slight sort his wife had been; then, punished for adultery, what else? He claimed in due form a divorce at least. This claim was met now by a counterclaim: Pompilia sought divorce from bed and board; so was the engine loaded, wound up, sprung on Guido, who received the bolt in breast, but no less bore up, giddily perhaps. He had the Abate Paolo still in Rome, brother and friend and brother on his side as if to shame supine law from her sloth and, waiting her award, let beat the while Arezzo's banter, Rome's buffoonery. Guido had thought in his simplicity – that lying declaration of remorse, that story of the child which was no child and motherhood no motherhood at all, – that even this sin might have its sort of good: the parents had abjured all right, at least, i' the woman still his wife; to plead right now were to declare the abjuration false; he was relieved from any fear henceforth their hands might touch, their breath defile again Pompilia with his name upon her yet."

The lowly bloke thrust his hand into his coat-pocket and, hey presto, the mythically patterned handkerchief resurfaced. "Well, no," he said while energetically wiping his forehead. "The next news was: Pompilia's health demanded change after full three long weeks spent in devotion with the Sisterhood. She had demanded, had obtained indeed, not freedom, scarce remitted penalty, solely the transfer to some private place where better air, more light, new food might be, – *domus pro carcere*, in Roman style: you keep the house i' the main, as most men do and all good women, but free otherwise, should friends arrive, to lodge and entertain." The storiated hankie disappeared under his collar. "What house obtained Pompilia's preference? Why, just the Comparini's – just, do you mark, theirs who renounced all part and lot in her so long as Guido could be robbed thereby: they took Pompilia to their hiding-place at *Via Paolina*, not so hard to miss by the honest eye, easy enough to find in twilight by marauders: where perchance some muffled Caponsacchi might repair, employ odd moments when he too tried change. Here's Guido poisoned to the bone, you say, your boasted still's full strain and strength: not so! One master-squeeze from screw shall bring to birth the hoard i' the heart o' the toad, hell's quintessence. Pompilia – what? sang, danced, saw company? – gave birth, Sir, to a child, his son and heir, or Guido's heir and Caponsacchi's son. In fury of the moment – the first news fell on the Count among his vines, it seems, doing his farm work, – why, he summoned steward, called in the first four hard hands and stout hearts from field and furrow, poured forth his appeal and, whereas law and gospel held their peace, what wonder if the sticks and stones cried out?" Half-Rome rolled his eyes, as though he was being confronted with an uncalled-for presence. "All five soon somehow found themselves at Rome, at the villa door: there was the warmth and light – the sense of life so just an inch inside – some angel must have whispered 'One more chance!'

He gave it: bade the others stand aside, knocked at the door.

'Who is it knocks?' cried one.

'I will make,' surely Guido's angel said, 'one final essay, last experiment: speak the word, name the name from out all names. If I should bring my lips to breathe that name and they be innocent, – nay, by one touch of innocence redeemed from utter guilt, – that name will bar the door and bid Fate pass.'

Why, Sir, the stumbling-block is cursed and kicked, block though it be; the name that brought offence will bring offence: the burnt child dreads the fire although that fire feed on a taper-wick which never left the altar nor singed fly, – and had a harmless man tripped you by chance, how would you wait him, stand or step aside, when next you heard he rolled your way? Enough.

'Giuseppe Caponsacchi!' Guido cried, and open flew the door: enough again. Vengeance, you know, burst, like a mountain-wave that holds a monster in it, over the house, and wiped its filthy four walls free again with a wash of hell-fire, – father, mother, wife, killed them all, bathed his name clean in their blood o' the day all this was. Now the whole is known, and how the old couple come to lie in state though hacked to pieces, – never, the expert say, so thoroughly a study of stabbing – while the wife viper-like, very difficult to slay, writhes through every ring of her, poor wretch, at the Hospital hard by – survives, we'll hope, to somewhat purify her putrid soul by full confession, make so much amends.

For Caponsacchi, – why, they'll have him here, the hero of the adventure, who so fit to tell it in the coming Carnival? 'Twill make the fortune of whate'er saloon hears him recount, with helpful cheek, and eye, hotly indignant now, now dewy-dimmed, the incidents of flight, pursuit, surprise, capture – while Guido, the most unromantic spouse, no longer fit to laugh at since the blood gave the broad farce an all too brutal air, why, he and those four luckless friends of his may tumble in the straw this bitter day – laid by the heels i' the New Prison, I hear. If the law thinks to find them guilty, Sir, there's an end to all hope of justice more: Astrea's gone indeed, let hope go too!"

The outburst was followed by the grotesque depiction of an event that, for being in harmony with the natural law and God's word 'The faithless wife shall die', would have provoked general commendation. Had Guido, in the twinkling of an eye, summed up the reckoning, promptly paid himself, cloven each head, by some Rolando-stroke, in one clean cut from crown to clavicle, – slain the priest-gallant, the wife-paramour, sticking, for all defence, in each skull's cleft the rhyme and reason of the stroke thus dealt, to-wit, those letters and last evidence of shame, each package in its proper place, – I say, the world had praised the man. But no! That were too plain, too straight, too simply just! He hesitates, calls law forsooth to help. When honour is beforehand and would serve, what wonder if law hesitate in turn, plead her disuse to calls o' the kind, reply: 'What you touched with so light a fingertip, – you whose concern it was to grasp the thing, – why must law gird herself and grapple with? What you dealt lightly with, shall law make out heinous forsooth?' Sir, what's the good of law in a case o' the kind?" There was no response from the one-man audience and the questioner hastened to give his own reply. "None, as she all but says."

A measure of graphic elaboration ensued like a dose of salts: Guido preferred the new path, – for his pains, stuck in a quagmire, floundered worse and worse until he managed somehow scramble back into the safe sure rutted road once more, revenged his own wrong like a gentleman. Once back 'mid the familiar prints, no doubt he made too rush amends for his first fault, vaulted too loftily over what barred him late, and lit i' the mire again, – the common chance, the natural over-energy: the deed maladroitly yields three deaths instead of one. All which is worse for Guido, but, be frank – the better for you and me and all the world, husbands of wives, especially in Rome. The thing is put right, in the old place, – ay, the rod hangs on its nail behind the door, fresh from the brine: a matter I commend to the notice, during Carnival that's near, of a certain what's-his-name and jackanapes somewhat too civil of eves with lute and song about a house here, where I keep a wife."

The innuendo made up a sort of marital coda in Half-Rome's deepfelt response to the sight of the Comparini lying lifeless inside *San Lorenzo in Lucina*.

A bisection of the Roman populace has made its voice heard *uno ore* and in the process betrayed a "feel after the vanished truth" which has conjured up the finger of a prejudiced feeler aiming "to find and fix truth at the bottom, that deceptive speck" inside a pool, and falling wide of the mark. Interestingly, the poet's metaphor appears to go hand in hand with the subjectivistic contention that the veracity of a statement hinges on the mental state of the speaker and, by virtue of that, mankind's achievement of relative truths invites comparison with God's absolute *veritas*. In this respect, Jesus didn't mince his words when he said to Pontius Pilate that he had come into the world 'to bear witness to the truth'[1], and it is hardly surprising that the aforementioned procurator, provoked into thinking seriously about the issue, asked him, 'What is truth?'[2] It is equally interesting to know that he felt bound to tell the accusing crowd that he found no crime in Jesus[3]; by the same token he was implying that the truth is a matter of living experience rather than a pre-given.

Half-Rome's depiction of the slain couple on view in the church has linked Browning's appreciation of the quest for truth with the subject of honour: Violante's disfigured face *honoris causa*, i.e. for the sake of the Count's honour, has provided the proletarian observer with a significant clue as to the whys and wherefores of the murder. In this connection, one is put in mind of young Mildred saying to her brother Thorold after he has murdered Earl Mortoun, 'Your code of honour bids you hear before you strike; but at the end, as he looked up for life into your eyes, you struck him down!'[4] Mildred's ethical standards suggest high seriousness and conjure up by contrast Sir John Falstaff's paradoxical air of *gravitas* when he sees honour as 'air. A trim reckoning ... a mere scutcheon'[5].

Half-Rome may well have been in earnest when commenting, "Even the blind can see a providence here", yet a common-sense approach to linguistic analysis may equally well lead to the detection of a touch of gothic awkwardness in the mention of a divine force controlling life and death, – the latter being seen as 'the aim of all life', as Freud would have it.

Within the space of a few words, the speech act has been spiced up by the portrayal of Pompilia as a "plaything at once and prop, a fairy gift, a saint's grace or, say, grant of the good God" and, as a finishing touch, "a fiddle-pin's end! What imbeciles are we!" Yes, quite. The dichotomy between the speaker's transcendental approach and his mock-serious comment points to a highly suspicious, possibly sceptical, mind.

Half-Rome's perception of Violante's qualities has brought to the fore an inclination to weigh a serious attitude against its comic equivalent. Interestingly, the banter has persisted and an octave leap been performed through the comment on the bargain struck by Guido and the Comparini: "Quoth Solomon, one black eye does it all."

Keeping the mood, Half-Rome has expatiated on how Violante had seized the golden opportunity provided by the Jubilee and confessed her sin; subsequently, the mouthpiece has added fuel to the fire by stressing that Pompilia had – how sweet of her! – blackened her parents' character by letting the Abate Paolo know that they had distorted Guido's 'words and ways', affectionately (sic) urged her to decamp without forgetting to put some toxic stuff in her husband's posset cup and 'by way of parting benediction' set fire to the house. Last but not least, the young woman had been urged to do a bunk, hopefully escorted by a 'fresh companion', and happily rejoin her dear parents at their Roman abode. The 'fresh companion' had materialised in the priestly figure of Giuseppe Caponsacchi and, the coast being now blissfully clear, the flight had been a fait accompli. In the wake of it, lawsuits had been filed and the courts had pronounced mock-Solomonic sentences. Hence an "appeal on the Comparini's part and counter-appeal on Guido's ... bandied as balls are in a tennis court'. The whole enchilada had left a nasty taste in the mouth of Joe Public and made justice an object of ridicule. In that regard, it is worth bringing up the cynical view aired by the bank employee Joseph K. while conversing with a warder: 'I don't know this Law ... and it probably exists nowhere but in your head.'[6]

The subsequent goings-on at Arezzo have prompted Half-Rome to take a dig at the chivalrous Caponsacchi, now portrayed as a 'courtly Christian' and 'a saint of Caesar's household'. As to Guido Franceschini, he had sniffed out the presence of a fox and, as a result, wordmongers had seen fit to offer an ambiguous kind of comfort by talking of mere horn madness and maintaining that the foxy Caponsacchi would hardly risk his brush for a chick like Pompilia 'when the wide town's his hen-roost!' Regrettably, the solacing thought had been of little avail: Guido had speedily retorted, 'Let Caponsacchi take his hand away from the wire!'

At this juncture, Half-Rome has invited his listener to admire the noble man's simplicity and made a comment imbued with a carnivalesque flavour when he has requested the fellow to judge whether Guido had "missed the natural grin of folk, or lacked the customary compliment of cap and bells, the luckless husband's fit!" Soon after, sounding in an equally jocular mood, the Roman observer has commented on the Count's recovery from the incredible feat of Pompilia, 'candid soul', and his capture of the run-away couple. In the same vein, he has likened Caponsacchi strutting "in correct costume, cloak, cap and feather" to the Homeric Paris and Pompilia to a slumbering Helen abruptly up and about again. To cap it all, Half-Rome has recounted how the epithet 'martyred saint' was on the lips of folk compelled to bear the sorry sight of an ashamed husband. Soon afterwards, the garrulous monologist has related how, back in Rome, the parties concerned had pleaded in deadly earnest and left "the law do right, let her shine forth and show, as God in heaven, vice prostrate, virtue pedestalled at last". For its part, the law had scrutinised every facet of the strange 'business' and judged it to be compliant with nature's diktats while admitting that specific circumstances pointed up the fact that 'strange may yet be true'. Along similar lines, the working-class chap has emphasized the accused's protestation of innocence "in thought, word and deed" and repeatedly stated, perhaps not without a touch of *double entendre*, that the 'business' was, notably in the light of the overnight stay at a wayside inn, "difficult to believe, yet possible". To crown it all, the batch of love letters discovered by Guido, "poor soul", had provided – on the strength of plans, dates and names – vital clues about the goings-on; in the final reckoning, the judicial authority had given a Solomonic judgement.

Half-Rome subsequent description of events and characters has focused on Arezzan citizens making utterances evocative of a chorus in a Greek tragedy; it has also brought to light gut feelings engendered by the belief that Guido had been affected by "corrosives keeping the man's misery raw" while endeavouring "to wring from out the sentence passed – poor, pitiful, absurd although it were". By all appearances a *black* comedy has been in full swing.

At the end of his strikingly enacted speech act, the performer has struck another mock-serious note by comparing the conflict between Caponsacchi as a participant in a pre-carnival amorous adventure with Guido as an unromantic spouse heading for the *mannaia*: the people of Rome, he has argued, would have eulogised the latter if he had "by some Rolando-stroke" slain "the priest-gallant, the wife-paramour" on the spot; unfortunately, the nobleman had dithered over the quid pro quo and appealed to an equally shillyshallying judicial system in order to vindicate his deep sense of honour. At a later time, however, he had "revenged his own wrong like a gentleman."

Half-Rome, a Rolando hailing from the slopes of the plebeian Aventine and yet displaying a tongue barely tinged with class colouration, has wound up his dramatic performance with a little help from his Roman horn: "The better for you and me and all the world. The thing is put right, in the old place, – ay, the rod hangs on its nail behind the door, fresh from the brine", he has told his fellow citizen before bringing the reassuring detail to the notice of "a certain what's-his-name and jackanapes somewhat too civil of eves with lute and song" only a stone's throw from the house where the speaker kept his wife.

By way of conclusion, the critical mind may find it of use to take a look at Half-Rome's version of events from a semiotic angle and on the strength of this perspective ascertain whether the commoner's humour and verbal wit have merged into the play of a world replete with signs pointing up the lack of a signifier/signified bond. Indeed, the guy's claim to fully understand often laughable characters and events needs careful scrutiny, and it makes sense to wonder whether, qua a stand-in for the author of the poem, the fellow has in effect paid tribute to the cathartic power of laughter by means of a double-talk redolent of a satyr play set against a carnivalesque background. In effect, Half-Rome has more than once conjured up pictures of ribald theatrics and in so doing brought out parody/travesty as a key component of his performance.[7] Take, for instance, the throwing of comfits to Pompilia: was a sign of familiar and free interaction between people as well as of the eccentric behaviour that make up two categories of the carnivalesque? Similarly, has Caponsacchi been making a parodic-travestying speech which might prove to be a catalyst for cultural change?

At the end of the day, it is tempting to see the theatrics at Arezzo and Rome in the shape of a drama centred on Guido Franceschini as a family-conscious character pervaded by what has been anthropologically identified with 'a sort of nostalgia for origins, of archaic and natural innocence'.[8] When all's said and done, the debased Count's attitude can be deemed to be the expression of a world of signs free of unforgivable weaknesses; confronted with the latter, the plebeian onlooker has ended his presumably class-conscious analysis on a personal note which has evinced his vested interest in the crime story as well as in Guido Franceschini's plight. The Count's hinting at a concept of truth founded on utility has highlighted again the timeless significance of Pontius Pilate's disturbing question about the essence of truth: has Guido's pragmatic mind touched on a partial, ego-driven, view of truth? In this respect, it has been cogently argued that 'no man can see reality any reality steadily and see it whole; each approach is partial and incommensurate with other approaches.'[9] On the other hand, 'each approach may be partial and confined, but each does disclose its own particular element of truth.[10] It is safe to concur with the philosophical notion that it is essentially a matter of degree: a partially adequate yet self-consistent human experience may help truth-seekers to achieve a degree of reality and in virtue of it enter the realm of *Veritas*.[11] At this final point, it is worthwhile to recall Browning's perception of Half-Rome's "feel after the vanished truth; honest enough, as the way is: all the same, harbouring in the centre of its sense a hidden germ of failure, shy but sure". The Victorian poet, one may conclusively assert, has cut the Gordian knot.

1. *The Gospel According to John*, 18.37
2. *Op. Cit.*, 38
3. *Ibid*
4. Robert Browning, *A Blot in the 'Scutcheon*, Act 3, Sc. 2
5. William Shakespeare, *Henry IV*, 1, 5.
6. Franz Kafka, *The Trial*, Penguin Books, 1953, p.13
7. A reference to the parodic/travestying element in a discourse, as highlighted by Michael Bakhtin in *From the Prehistory of Novelistic Discourse*. Vide *Modern Criticism and Theory*, pp. 145ff.
8. As quoted by Jacques Derrida in *Structure, Sign and Play* in *The Discourse of the Human Sciences*. See *Op. Cit.* p. 121
9. W. Dilthey, as quoted by E. D. Hirsh Jr. in *Modern Criticism and Theory*, p. 258
10. *Ibid.*
11. F. H. Bradley, in *Western Philosophy and Philosophers*, p. 53

THE OTHER HALF-ROME

Another section of the populace had congregated within sight of Father Tiber in the wake of the persistent rumours about the heinous event in Via Paolina. A chubby middle-aged fellow took his place in front of Bernini's statue of the sea god Triton and, on hearing somebody in the throng commiserate an ill-starred young woman called Pompilia Comparini, stepped on a tree stump and launched into utterance.

"Another day that finds her living yet, little Pompilia, with the patient brow and lamentable smile on those poor lips, and, under the white hospital array, a flower-like body, to frighten at a bruise you'd think, yet now, stabbed through and through again, alive i' the ruins. 'T is a miracle: the angels love to do their work betimes. Old Monna Baldi chatters like a jay, swears – but that, prematurely trundled out, the miracle was snapped up by somebody, – her palsied limb 'gan prick and promise life! Cavalier Carlo – well, there' some excuse for him – Maratta who paints Virgins so – ' a lovelier face is not in Rome', cried he. Then, oh that pair of eyes, that pendent hair, black this, and black the other! Mighty fine, but nobody cared ask to paint the same nor grew a poet over hair and eyes four little years ago when, ask and have, the woman who wakes all this rapture leaned flower-like from out her window long enough. Truth lies between: there's anyhow a child ruined. Who did it shall account to Christ.

Somebody, at the bedside, said much more, took on him to explain the secret cause o' the crime: quoth he, 'Such crimes are very rife, explode nor make us wonder now-a-days, seeing that Antichrist disseminates that doctrine of the Philosophic Sin'.

'Nay,' groaned Don Celestine, 'what's there new? Crime will not fail to flare up from men's hearts while hearts are men's and so born criminal.'"

The self-appointed soapbox speaker scratched his head. "Pompilia, living so and dying thus, has had undue experience how much crime a heart can hatch. Why was she made to learn what Guido Franceschini's heart could hold? Thus saintship is effected probably." He gave a few nods. "For see now: Pietro's and Violante's life till seventeen years ago, all Rome might note. What could they be but happy? – balanced so, nothing above, below the just degree. But, as 't is said a body, rightly mixed, each element in equipoise, would last too long and live for ever, – accordingly, not otherwise a fatal germ lurked here: out of the very ripeness of life's core a worm was bred: 'Our life shall leave no fruit. 'T is in a child man and wife grow complete, one flesh. God says so; let him do his work!'

Eve saw the apple was fair and good to taste; so, plucked it, having asked the snake advice: she told her husband God was merciful, and his and her prayer granted at the last: their house continued to them by an heir, their vacant heart replenished with a child."

The Other Half-Rome put on a long face. "We have her own confession at full length made in the first remorse. 'T was Jubilee pealed in the ear o' the conscience and it woke: she found she had offended God no doubt, misfortune on misfortune; but she harmed no one i' the world, so far as she could see: the act had gladdened Pietro to the height, while at least one good work had she wrought, – good, clearly, and incontestably: her cheat, – what was it to its subject, the child's self, but charity and religion? See the girl! Well then, she had caught up this castaway, – this fragile egg some careless wild bird dropped, – and put in her own breast till forth broke finch able to sing God praise on mornings now." The speaker's mouth twisted. "Well, having gained Pompilia, the girl grew i' the midst of Pietro here, Violante there – each, like a semicircle with stretched arms, joining the other round her preciousness – two walls that go about a garden plot where a chance sliver, branchlet slipt from bole of some tongue-leaved eye-figured Eden tree, filched by two exiles and borne far away, patiently glorifies their solitude. But on the twelfth sun that brought April there what meant that laugh? The coping-stone was reached: Pompilia's root, stem and a branch or two home enclosed still, the rest would be the world's. All which was taught our couple though obtuse, since walls have ears, when one day brought a priest, the notable Abate Paolo, known as younger brother of a Tuscan house whereof the actual representative, Count Guido, had employed his youth and age in culture of Rome's most productive plant – a cardinal. But years pass and change comes, in token of which, here was our Paolo brought to broach a weighty business. Might he speak? Yes, to Violante somehow caught alone.

He dissertated on that Tuscan house, those Franceschini: very old they were, not rich however – say rather, well enough, i' the way, indeed, ha, ha, to better fortune than the best. Their house might wear the red cloth that keeps warm, would but the Count have patience – there's the point! In short, call him fantastic as you choose, Guido was homesick, yearned for the old sights and usual faces, – fain would settle himself and have the patron's bounty, when it fell, go fertilize Arezzo, not flood Rome. Sooth to say, 't was the wiser wish: the Count proved wanting in ambition, – let us avouch, humble but self-sustaining, calm and cold, having, as one who puts his hand to the plough, renounced the over-vivid family feel, – but that, to light his mother's visage up with second youth, hope, gaiety again, he must find straightway, woo, and haply win and bear triumphantly back some wife. Well now, the man was rational in his way; indeed, the Abate's little interest was somewhat nearly touched i' the case, they saw: no lack of mothers here in Rome, – no dread of daughters lured as larks by looking glass! No, that at least the Abate could forestall. He read the thought within his brother's word, knew what he purposed better than himself. Come, cards on table; was it true or false that here – here in this very tenement – yea, Via Vittoria did a marvel hide, a daughter with the mother's hands still clasped over her head for fillet virginal, a wife worth Guido's house and hand and heart? Then with the great air did he kiss, devout, Violante's hand, and rise up his whole height and go forth grandly, – as if the Pope came next. And so Violante rubbed her eyes awhile, got up too, walked to wake her Pietro soon and pour into his ear the mighty news how somebody had somehow somewhere seen their tree-top-tuft bloom above the wall; whereon did Pietro wipe his eyes in turn, then, periwig on head and cane in hand, sally forth dignifiedly into the Square of Spain across *Babbuino*, walk the six steps to *La Barcaccia* where our idlers lounge.

Heartily laughed the world in his fool's face: Guido and Franceschini; a Count, – ay, but a cross i' the poke to bless the Countship? No! All gone except sloth, pride, rapacity; he had hung long, and now – let go, said some – tired of the trade and something worse for wear, was wanting to change town for country quick.

Home again, shaking oft the puzzled pate, went Pietro to announce a change indeed, yet point Violante where some solace lay of a rueful sort: the taper, quenched so soon, had ended merely in a snuff, not stink. Violante wiped away the transient tear, praised much her Pietro's prompt sagaciousness, found neighbours' envy natural, lightly laughed at gossips' malice, fairly wrapped herself in her integrity three folds about and, by the hand holding a girl veiled too, stood, one dim end of a December day, in *San Lorenzo* on the altar step, just where she lies now and that girl will lie – only with fifty candles' company now in the place of the poor winking one which saw, – doors shut and sacristan made sure, – a priest, perhaps Abate Paolo, wed Guido clandestinely, irrevocably, to his Pompilia aged thirteen years.

Transfer complete, why, Pietro was apprised: Violante sobbed the sobs and prayed the prayers and said the serpent tempted so she fell, till Pietro had to clear his brow apace and make the best of matters: wrath at first, how else? pacification presently. Trust's politic, suspicion does the harm, there is but one way to browbeat this world: to go on trusting, namely, till faith move mountains."

The Other Half-Rome's eyes shifted skyward. "And faith here made the mountains move. Why, friends whose zeal cried 'Caution ere too late!' – bade 'Pause ere jump, with both feet joined, on slough!' – heard for their pains that Pietro had closed eyes, jumped and was in the middle of the mire. Words to the wind! The parents cast their lot into the lap o' the daughter, and the son, now with a right to lie there, took what fell. Into this quag, 'jump!' bade the Cardinal, and neck-deep in a minute *there* flounced they." The eyes fell and lit up mischievously. "But they touched bottom at Arezzo: there – four months' experience of how craft and greed, quickened by penury and pretentious hate of plain truth, brutify and bestialize, – four months' taste of apportioned insolence, and lo, the work was done, success clapped hands. The starved, stripped, beaten brace of stupid dupes broke at last in their desperation loose and, careless what came after, carried their wrongs to Rome, – I nothing doubt, with such remorse as folly feels, since pain can make it wise, but crime, past wisdom, which is innocence, needs not be plagued with till a later day."

The ocular glitter dimmed. "Pietro went back to beg from door to door, in hope that memory not quite extinct of cheery days and festive nights would move friends and acquaintance – after the natural laugh and tributary 'Just as we foretold'. Not so Violante: ever a-head i' the march, she went first to the best adviser, God. Here was the prize of sin, luck of a lie! But here too was the Holy Year would help to lift the leadenest of lies, let soar the soul unhampered by a feather-weight. So, with the crowd she mixed, made for the dome, through the great door new-broken for the nonce marched, muffled more than ever matron-wise, up the left nave to the formidable throne, and then knelt down and whispered in his ear how she had bought Pompilia, palmed the babe on Pietro, passed the girl off as their child to Guido, and defrauded of his due this one and that one, more than she could name. Replied the throne: 'Ere God forgive the guilt, make man some restitution. Do your part! Then, penance so performed, may pardon be.'

Home went Violante and disbosomed all; and Pietro who, six months before, had borne word after word of such a piece of news like so much cold steel inched through his breast-blade, now at its entry gave a leap for joy: 'What? All that used to be, may be again? What, the girl's dowry never was the girl's? And, unpaid yet, is never now to pay? Then the girl's self, my pale Pompilia child that used to be my own with her great eyes – he who drove us forth, why should he keep her when proved as very a pauper as himself? Ay, let him taste the teeth o' the trap, this fox, give us our lamb back, golden fleece and all; let her creep in and warm our breasts again!' And so, he carried case before the courts; and there Violante, blushing to the bone, made public declaration of her fault, renounced her motherhood, and prayed the law to interpose, frustrate of its effect her folly and redress the injury done. Guido pronounced the story one long lie lied to do robbery and take revenge; or say it were no lie at all but truth, then, it both robbed the right heirs and shamed him without revenge to humanize the deed: what had he done when first they shamed him thus? they lied to blot him though it brand themselves.

Wherefore the court, its customary way, inclined to the middle course the sage affect: they held the child to be a changeling. Good, but, lest the husband got no good thereby, they willed the dowry, though not hers at all, should yet be his, if not by right then by grace – part-payment for the plain injustice done. But then, that other contract, Pietro's work, renunciation of his own estate, that must be cancelled: 'Give him back his goods, he was no party to the cheat at least!' So ran the judgement; whence a prompt appeal on both sides, seeing right is absolute; till law said, 'Reinvestigate the case!' And so the matter pends, unto this day."

The working-class, i.e. on a par with Half-Rome, commentator shrugged his shoulders and spread his hands. "Hence new disaster.

That no outlet seemed, no path whereby the fatal man might march victorious, – wreath on head and spoils in hand, – nor cranny whence, desperate and disgraced, stripped to the skin, he might be fain to crawl. No, he was pinned to the place there, left alone with his immense hate and, the solitary subject to satisfy that hate, his wife. What if the girl-wife, tortured with due care, should take, as though spontaneously, the road it were impolitic to thrust her on; if, goaded, she broke out in full revolt, followed her parents i' the face o' the world, branded as runaway not castaway, self-sentenced and self-punished in the act? So should the loathed form and detested face launch themselves into hell and there be lost while he looked o'er the brink with folded arms; so should the heaped-up shames go shuddering back o' the head o' the heapers, Pietro and his wife, and bury in the breakage three at once: while Guido, left free, no one right renounced, should ask law what it was law paused about – if law were dubious still whose words to take, the husband's – dignified and derelict, or the wife – the … what I tell you it should be.

Guido's first step was to take pen, indite a letter to the Abate, – not his own, his wife's, – she should re-write, sign, seal and send. She liberally told the household-news, rejoiced her vile progenitors were fled, revealed their malice – how they even laid a last injunction on her, when they fled, that she should forthwith find a paramour, complot with him to gather spoil enough, then burn the house down, – taking previous care to poison all its inmates overnight, – and so companioned, so provisioned too, follow to Rome and all join fortunes gay. This letter, traced in pencil-characters, Guido as easily got re-traced in ink by his wife's pen, guided from end to end. She had as readily re-traced the words of her own death-warrant, – in some sort 't was so. Accordingly did Guido set himself to worry up and down, across, around, the woman hemmed in by her household bars, – chased her about the coop of daily life, having first stopped each outlet thence save one which, like bird with a ferret in her haunt, she needs must seize as sole way of escape from tooth and claw of something in the dark: Giuseppe Caponsacchi."

The all-for-one and one-for-all orator moved his head downwards and upwards more than once. "Now begins the tenebrific passage of the tale: how hold a light, display the cavern's gorge? How, in this phase of the affair, show truth? Here is the dying wife who smiles and says, 'So it was, so it was not, – how it was, I never knew nor ever care to know.' Confessor Celestino groans ''T is truth, all truth and only truth: there's something else, some presence in the room beside us all, something that every lie expires before: no question she was pure from first to last.'

So far is well and helps us to believe: but beyond, she the helpless, simple-sweet or silly-sooth, unskilled to break one blow at her good fame by putting finger forth, – how can she render service to the truth? Here be facts, charactery; what they spell determine, and thence pick what sense you may! There was a certain young bold handsome priest popular in the city, far and wide famed, – for Arezzo's but a little place, – as the best of good companions, gay and grave at the decent minute, settled in his stall, or sideling, lute on lap, by lady's couch. Men are men; why then need I say one word more than this, that our man the Canon here saw, pitied, loved Pompilia? This is why: 'tis strange then that this else abashless mouth should yet maintain that, for truth's sake which is God's, that, even ere word had passed between the two, Pompilia penned him letters, passionate prayers: there *must* be falsehood somewhere. For her part, Pompilia quietly constantly avers she never penned a letter in her life nor to the Canon nor any other man, – being incompetent to write and read. Is that credible? Well, yes: as she avers with calm mouth dying. I do think 'Credible!' you'd cry–did not the priest's voice come to break the spell, which damns the story credible otherwise. Or what do you say to a touch of the devil's worst? Can it be that the husband, – he who wrote the letter to his brother I told you of, i' the name of her it meant to criminate, – what if *he* wrote those letters to the priest? Further the priest says, – when it first befell, this folly o' the letters, – that he checked the flow, put them back lightly, each with its reply.

Here again vexes new discrepancy: there never reached her eye a word from him; he did write, but she could not read – she could burn what offended wifehood, womanhood, so did burn; never bade him come to her, yet when it proved he must come, let him come, and when he did come though uncalled, she spoke prompt by an inspiration. *Thus* it was."

The Other Half-Rome nodded again with vim, in harmony with a plebeian's modus operandi.

"When first, pursuant to his plan, there sprung, like an uncaged beast, Guido's cruelty on the weak shoulders of his wife, she cried to those whom the law appoints resource for such: the secular guardian, that's the Governor, and the Archbishop, that's the spiritual guide, – and prayed them take the claws from out her flesh. The Archbishop, not to be outdone by the Governor, break custom more than he, coached her and carried her to the Count again: his old friend should be master in his house, rule his wife and correct her faults at need!

Well, driven from post to pillar in this wise, she, as a last resource, betook herself to one, should be no family-friend at least, a simple friar o' the city; confessed to him, then told how fierce temptation of release by self-dealt death was busy with her soul. So, the course being plain, – with a general sigh at matrimony the profound mistake, – he threw reluctantly the business up, having his other penitents to mind. At last she took to the open, stood and stared with her wan face to see where God might wait, and *there* found Caponsacchi wait as well for the precious something at perdition's edge he only was predestined to save. How do you say? It were improbable? So is the legend of my patron saint." The hard-boiled protégé let his hand glide across his furrowed brow.

"Whatever way in this strange world it was, Pompilia and Caponsacchi met, in fine, – she at her window, he i' the street beneath, – and on a certain April evening, late i' the month, this girl of sixteen, bride and wife, stole from the side o' the sleeping spouse – who knows? Sleeping perhaps, silent for certain, – slid ghost-like from great dark room to great dark room, descended staircase, gained last door of all and there stood, first time, last and only time, at the city gate by Caponsacchi's side: hope there, joy there, life and all good again; the carriage there, the convoy there, light there. Up she sprang, in he followed, they were safe.

The husband quotes this for incredible, sees the priest's hand throughout upholding hers, traces his foot to the alcove, that night, whither and whence blindfold he knew the way.

She says, 'God put it in my head to fly. I took the favour, had the help, how else? And so we did fly rapidly all night, all day, all night – a longer night – again, and then another day, longest of days. I talked with my companion, told him much, knowing that he knew more, knew me, knew God and God's disposal of me, – but the sense o' the blessed flight absorbed me in the main till, at the end of that last longest night in a red daybreak, when we reached an inn, sudden the weak flesh fell like piled-up cards. Then something like a white wave o' the sea broke o'er my brain and buried me in sleep blessedly, till it ebbed and left me loose, and where was I found but on a strange bed in a strange room like hell, roaring with noise, ruddy with flame, and filled with men, in front who but the man you call my husband, ay, Count Guido once more between heaven and me, – for *there* my heaven stood, my salvation, yes, that Caponsacchi all my heaven of help! I sprang up, reached him with one bound, and seized the sword o' the felon trembling at his side, and would have pinned him through the poison-bag to the wall and left him there to palpitate, as you serve scorpions, but men interposed, disarmed me, gave his life to him again that he might take mine and the other lives. And he has done so. I submit myself!'

The priest says – oh, and in the main result the facts asseverate, he truly says – 'The flight was for flight's sake, no pretext for aught except to set Pompilia free.' He says, 'I cite the husband's self's in proof of my best world for both of us. Be it conceded that so many times we took our pleasure in his palace; then, what need to fly at all? – or flying no less, what need to outrage the lips sick and white of a woman, and bring ruin down beside, by halting when Rome lay one stage beyond?' So does he vindicate Pompilia's fame, confirm her story in all points but one: she makes confusion of the reddening white which was the sunset when her strength gave way, and the next sunrise and its whitening red which she revived in when her husband came. She mixes both times, morn and eve, in one, having lived through a blank of night 'twixt each though dead-asleep, unaware as a corpse, – when up came Guido.

Guido's tale begins – how he and his whole household, drunk to death by some enchanted potion, poppied drugs plied by the wife, lay powerless in gross sleep till noontide, then made shift to get on horse and did pursue: which means, he took his time, pressed on no more than lingered after, step by step, just making sure o' the fugitives, till at the nick of time he saw his chance, seized it, came up with and surprised the pair. The guardian angel gave reluctant place, Satan stepped forward with alacrity, Pompilia's flesh and blood succumbed, perforce a halt was, and her husband had his will. Do you see the plan deliciously complete? Success did seem not so improbable: body and soul one holocaust to hell. Anyhow, of this natural consequence did just the last link of the long chain snap: for his eruption was o' the priest, alive and alert, calm, resolute and formidable. Yes, *there* stood he in secular costume complete from head to heel, with sword at side; there was no prompt suppression of the man as he said calmly, 'I have saved your wife from death; there was no other way but this; of what do I defraud you except death? Charge any wrong beyond, I answer it.'"

The Other-Half-Rome flashed a tight smile. "Guido, the valorous, had met his match, was forced to demand help instead of fight, bid the authorities o' the place lend aid and make the best of a broken matter so. He knew his wife so well and the way of her: this was the froward child, 'the restive lamb used to be cherished in his breast', he groaned – 'eat from his hand and drink from out his cup, the while his fingers pushed their loving way through curl on curl of that soft coat – alas, and she all silverly baaed gratitude while meditating mischief!' – and so forth. He must invent another story now!

The ins and outs o' the rooms were searched: he found or showed for found the abominable prize: love-letters from his wife who cannot write; love letters, in reply, o' the priest – thank God! – who can write and confront his character with this, and prove the false thing forged throughout: spitting whereat, he needs must spatter who but Guido's self that forged and falsified one letter called Pompilia's, past dispute?

So was the case concluded then and there: Guido preferred his charges in due form, called on the law to adjudicate, consigned the accused ones to the Prefect of the place. The captured parties were conveyed to Rome; investigation followed here i' the court. That was the prelude; this, the play's first act."

The Other-Half-Rome stood with his arms akimbo and gave a loud sniff. "Well, the result was something of a shade on the parties thus accused – how otherwise? Shade, but with shine as unmistakable. Each had a prompt defence.

Pompilia first – 'Earth was made hell to me who did no harm: I only could emerge one way from hell by catching at the one hand held me, so I caught at it and thereby stepped to heaven; if that be wrong, do with me what you will!'

Then Caponsacchi with a grave grand sweep o' the arm as though his soul warned baseness off – 'If as a man, then much more as a priest I hold me bound to help weak innocence: if so my worldly reputation burst, being the bubble it is, why, burst it may. But use your sense first, see if the miscreant here has not both laid the trap and fixed the lure over the pit should bury both body and soul! His facts are lies: his letters are the fact. As for the fancies: whether ... what is it you say? the lady loves me, whether I love her in the forbidden sense of your surmise ... I never touched her lip nor she my hand nor either of us thought a thought, much less spoke a word which the Virgin might not hear. Be that your question, thus I answer it.'

Then the court had to make its mind up, spoke.

'It is a thorny question, and a tale hard to believe, but not impossible. Here has a blot surprised the social blank, and we're unclean and must be purified; here is a wife makes holiday from home, a priest caught playing truant to his church; here is a husband, ay and man of mark, who comes complaining here, demands redress as if he were the pattern of desert. Husband, wife, priest, scot-free not one shall 'scape: first, let the husband stomach as he may, his wife shall neither be returned him, no – nor branded, whipped and caged, but just consigned to a convent and the quietude she craves; so is he rid of his domestic plague. Next, let the priest retire unshent, unshamed, unpunished as for perpetrating crime, but relegated – not imprisoned, Sirs! – sent for three years to clarify his youth at Civita, a rest by the way to Rome. All parties may retire, content, we hope.'"

The Roman citizen smiled fleetingly while remarking, "That's Rome's way, the traditional road of law; whither it leads is what remains to tell. Guido had gained not one of the good things he grasped at by his creditable plan o' the flight and following and the rest: the suit that smouldered late was fanned to fury new. Oh it was rare, and naughty all the same! Brief, the wife's courage and cunning; the priest's show of chivalry and adroitness; last but not least, the husband – how he ne'er showed teeth at all, whose bark had promised biting, but just sneaked back to his kennel, tail 'twixt legs, as 't were; all this was hard to gulp down and digest,

– so pays the devil his liegeman, brass for gold. Brave Paolo bore up against it all – he knew his Rome, what wheels we set to work. As for the Comparini's counterplea, he met that by a counterplea again, made Guido claim divorce – with help so far by the trial's issue: for, why punishment however slight unless for guiltiness however slender? – and a molehill serves much as a mountain of offence this way. So was he gathering strength on every side and growing more and more to menace – when all of a terrible moment came the blow that beat down Paolo's fence, ended the play o' the foil and brought *Mannaia* on the stage."

The speaker jerked a hand at his neck as if to make sure that no hideous blade was touching it. "Five months had passed now since Pompilia's flight, months spent in peace among in peace among the convert nuns. The Convent's self makes application bland that, since Pompilia's health is fast o' the wane, she may have leave to go combine her cure of soul with cure of body, mend her mind together with her thin arms and sunk eyes that want fresh air outside the convent wall, say in a friendly house, – and which so fit as a certain villa in Via Paolina, that happens to hold Pietro and his wife? What would *you* answer? All so smooth and fair, even Paul's astuteness sniffed no harm i' the world. He authorised the transfer, saw it made and, two months after, reaped the fruit of the same, having to sit down, rack his brain and find what phrase should serve him best to notify our Guido that by happy providence a son and heir, a babe was born to him; yes, such had been Pompilia's privilege: she, when she fled, was one month gone with child, known to herself or unknown, either way availing to explain – say men of art – the strange and passionate precipitance of maiden startled into motherhood which changes body and soul by nature's law.

'I shall have quitted Rome ere you arrive to take the one step left,' wrote Paolo. Then did the winch o' the winepress of all hate, vanity, disappointment, grudge and greed, take the last turn that screws out pure revenge with a bright bubble at the brim beside

– by an heir's birth he was assured at once o' the main prize, all the money in dispute: Pompilia's dowry might revert to her or stay with him as law's caprice should point, – but now – *now* – what was Pietro's shall be hers, what was hers shall remain her own, – if hers, why then, – oh, not her husband's but – her heir's! That heir being his too, all grew his at last by this road or by that road, since they join. Before, why, push he Pietro out o' the world – the current of the money stopped, you see, Pompilia being proved no Pietro's child; or let it be Pompilia's life he quenched, again the current of the money stopped, – Guido debarred his rights as husband soon, so the new process threatened; – now, the chance, now, the resplendent minute! Clear the earth, cleanse the house, let the three but disappear, a child remains, depositary of all, that Guido may enjoy his own again! Repair all losses by a masterstroke, wipe out the past, all done and left undone, swell the good present to best evermore, die into new life, which let blood baptize!"

An ominous silence intervened, but it was speedily broken by a vocal crescendo. "So, i' the blue of a sudden sulphur-blaze, he saw the ins and outs to the heart of hell and took the straight line thither swift and sure. He rushed to Vittiano, found four sons o' the soil, harangued, equipped, instructed, pressed each clod with his will's imprint; then took horse, plied spur, and so arrived, all five of them, at Rome on Christmas Eve, and forthwith found themselves installed i' the vacancy and solitude left them by Paolo, the considerate man who, good as his word, disappeared at once as if to leave the stage free.

A whole week did Guido spend in study of his part, then played it fearless of a failure. *One*, struck the year's clock whereof the hours are days, and off was rung o' the little wheels the chime 'Good will on earth and peace to man': but *Two*, proceeded the same bell and, evening come, the dreadful five felt finger-wise their way across the town by blind cuts and black turns to the little lone suburban villa; knocked.

'Who may be outside?' called a well-known voice.

'A friend of Caponsacchi's bringing friends a letter.'

What bait had been i' the name to ope the door? The promise of a letter? Stealthy guests have secret watchwords, private entrances; the man's own self might have been found inside and all the scheme made frustrate by a word. No: but since Guido knew, none knew so well, the man had never since returned to Rome.

'Come in', bade poor Violante cheerfully, drawing the door-bolt: that death was the first, stabbed through and through. Pietro, close on her heels, set up a cry – 'Let me confess myself! Grant but confession!' Cold steel was the grant. Then came Pompilia's turn.

Then they escaped. They had forgotten just the one thing more which saves i' the circumstance, the ticket to-wit which puts post-horses at a traveller's use: so, all on foot, desperate through the dark reeled they like drunkards along open road, stumbled at last, deaf, dumb, blind through the feat, into a grange and, one dead heap, slept there till the pursuers hard upon their trace reached them and took them, red from head to heel, and brought them to the prison where they lie. The couple were laid i' the church two days ago, and the wife lives yet by miracle."

The Other-Half-Rome stood glued to the spot, visibly affected by the murder and its sequel. "All is told. You hardly need ask what Count Guido says, since something he must say: 'I own the deed, just and inevitable, since no way else was left me, but by this of taking life to save my honour, which is more than life. I exercised a husband's right.'

To which the answer is as prompt. 'There was no fault in any one o' the three to punish thus: neither i' the wife, who kept all faith to you, nor in the parents, whom yourself first duped, robbed and maltreated, then turned out of doors. You wronged and they endured wrong; yours the fault. Next, had endurance overpassed the mark and turned resentment needing remedy,

– nay, put the absurd impossible case, for once – you were all blameless of the blame alleged and they blameworthy where you fix all blame, still, why this violation of the law? Yourself elected law should take its course, avenge wrong, or show vengeance not your right; why, only when the balance in law's hand trembles against you and inclines the way o' the other party, do you make protest, renounce arbitrament, flying out of court, and crying 'Honour's hurt the sword must cure'? What? You may chop and change and right your wrongs leaving the law to lag as she thinks fit? That were too temptingly commodious, Count! One's honour forsooth? Does that take hurt alone from the extreme outrage? I who have no wife, being yet sensitive in my degree as Guido, – must discover hurt elsewhere which, half compounded-for in days gone by, may profitably break out now afresh, need cure from my own expeditious hands. The lie that was, as it were, imputed me when you objected to my contract's clause; the theft as good as, one may say, alleged, when you, co-heir in a will, excepted, Sir, to my administration of effects, – aha, do you think law disposed of these? Count, that were too commodious, I repeat! If any law be imperative on us all, of all are you the enemy: out with you from the common light and air and life of man!"

The vibrant apostrophe wound up the proletarian bachelor's harangue. As he stepped down from his make-shift platform, a light rain began to fall. Hands stretched out to feel the increasing intensity of the cloudburst, heads shook in protest at Jove's intrusion, collars straightened up and shadowy human beings faded away in the all-engulfing darkness.

The Other Half-Rome, rooted likewise in a plebeian ground, has gathered in the time-honoured *Piazza Barberini* and made itself heard. A self-elected mouthpiece has highlighted by way of overture the "lamentable smile" on the "poor lips" of Pompilia still "alive in the ruins" and focused on the "flower-like body" of a "lamb-pure, lion-brave" lass. Intriguingly, the metaphor evokes

Dante Alighieri's *'Tanto Gentile e tanto Onesta* Pare'[1], – albeit not without a caveat: Dante's Tuscan maiden was imbued with a spirit full of love urging the enthralled wooer to 'suspire' whereas the Roman girl eulogised by The Other Half-Rome has barely embodied a *donna angelicata*.

For his part, Robert Browning has depicted Pompilia as "a saint and a martyr both" and in so doing conjured up the image of a *Blessed Damozel* gazing at the world from her celestial abode with eyes *'deeper than the depth of waters stilled at even'*,[2] holding three lilies in her hand and displaying seven stars in her hair.

Half-Rome's counterpart has metaphysically as well as ethically maintained that the feminine specimen at issue was neither a child nor an adult. Furthermore, he has pointed out that she had had "undue experience how much crime a heart can hatch"; by the same token, he appears to have unwittingly supported Browning's appreciation by positing that 'thus saintship is effected probably.'

At this critical juncture, the issue of truth has re-emerged in the shape of an enigma, and it is worth recalling Aristotle's contention that divergent views are partially true and a clarification of how conclusions have been reached is a sine qua non for obviating any inconsistency between the solutions that have been offered.[3]

As to Pompilia's alleged mother, her frame of mind, leading her to a disclosure of the truth about her motherhood, has been portrayed in a similar vein: "'T was Jubilee pealed i' the ear of the conscience and it woke'; moreover, 'her cheat – what was it to its subject, the subject's self, but charity and religion?' By all appearances, the mixture of ethics and metaphysics likewise occurring in Violante's psyche has stirred the conscience of the common-or-garden observer.

Guido has been next in line for analysis, and prominence has been given to matters of the hearth: in the eyes of his younger brother, the "notable" Abate Paolo, the Count was a son devoutly conscious of the fact that 'to light his mother's visage up with second youth, hope, gaiety again, he must find straightway, woo and haply win and bear away triumphant back, some wife.' To be sure, 'poor brother Guido … was rational in his way', the compassionate Abate has acknowledged, somehow in accord with the empiricist John Locke's view that human beings possess enough power of reason to deserve trust while they deal with the norms of civilized society. In addition, to Paolo's mind the Count's undertaking for the sake of honour upheld a tradition, and it is important to recall that conventional morals have often been philosophically justified on grounds outside the boundaries of reason.

As regards Pompilia, the Other Half-Rome has rekindled the ethical dichotomy between truth and falsity when he has rhetorically asked, "Come, cards on the table: was it true or false that here – here in this very tenement – yea, Via Vittoria did a marvel hide, lily of a maiden, white with intact leaf, a wife worth Guido's house and hand and heart?"

Then Pietro has come under scrutiny. A note imbued with a parodying/travestying nuance has been struck by quidnuncs laughing in his "fool's face" and hinting at a major crisis hanging over his would-be-wealthy son-in-law's realm; in reality, it was 'all gone except sloth, pride, rapacity.' Here language has been used as a weapon in a battle for power between speakers, and it could be argued that some of the voices ushered in by Browning in his prologue have unwittingly pointed up to what has in latter days been linguistically seen as an existential 'conflict between freedoms, each one trying to "nihilate" the other in order to preserve its own sovereign autonomy.'[4]

Elaborating further on the features of the characters in the drama, the Other Half-Rome has depicted the surreptitiously wedded Pompilia as a "lamb brought forth from basket and set out for sale", and it seems fair to posit that the portrayal has furnished the figure of a *donna angelicata* with the traits of a marketable commodity.

At such pivotal stage in the narrative, metaphysics has reinstated itself and struck a mock-serious overtone: trust has been the name of the game, and a faith based on trust has made the mountains move. 'Why, friends whose zeal cried, 'Caution ere too late! Pause ere jump, with both feet joined, on slough!' had 'heard for their pains that Pietro had closed eyes, jumped and was in the middle of the mire'. His wife, too, had been dragged into the mess and both had leapt into the quagmire, mainly in compliance with the order issued by the Cardinal who happened to be their distinguished patron. Sometime later and back in Arezzo, Violante had returned to the church and been urged at the confessional to do her part by giving something back: it would make her more eligible for pardon.

As for Guido, he had felt that he had been duped by the Comparini, who had "lied to blot him though it brand themselves." Consequently, he had been "left alone with his immense hate and, the solitary subject to satisfy that hate, his wife": a strong dislike had induced him to oblige her to trace his letters over again. Paradoxically, it may be argued, his feelings have helped him give a meaning and a purpose to the activities of Giuseppe Caponsacchi; by the same token he may be seen as the provider of an instance of interrelation between love and hate, anger and pity.

At this "tenebrific passage of the tale" the badly hurt Pompilia had raised an enlightening issue: "How, in this phase of the affair, show truth?" she had asked before ambivalently declaring that 'so it was, so it was not', thus unwittingly echoing the Majorca storyteller's statement, "*Aixo era y no era*"[6] before telling the small audience at her bedside, 'How it was, I never knew nor ever care to know'. In saying so, she appeared to have preferred truth of fiction to truth of fact, – in contrast to, one may remark, the chief alchemist Paracelsus' belief that 'truth is within ourselves … and there is an inmost centre in us all, where truth abides in fulness'[7]; interestingly, the reappearance of Brother Celestino in the next sequence has redressed the balance by dint of asserting that it was 'truth, all truth and only truth … no question she was pure from first to last.'

In this connection, the Other Half-Rome has wondered whether Pompilia had been able to "render service to the truth", and it is only fitting to link his doubts with Browning's early question: "Since, how heart moves brain, and how both move hand, what mortal ever in entirety saw?' Indeed, the overall effect of the heart on the brain and of both on the body has not yet been fully ascertained, yet it would be barely reasonable to dispute the Other-Half-Rome's belief that Caponsacchi had compassionately loved Pompilia and consequently to discard the idea that such a belief has engendered the question of the young woman's ethical stance. Here Aristotle springs to mind again on the strength of his opinion that a virtuous human being takes pity on wretched fellow humans at a suitable time, for a good reason, and in a proper manner.[8]

What next? Considering Aristotle's outlook in association with that of Pompilia's character and situation, it appears that the Other Half-Rome's juxtaposition of pity and love connotes his presumption that virtue was indeed an asset of the compassionate priest/lover. But then, had he been telling the truth, the whole truth, nothing but the truth? What about the decisive missives supposedly penned by Pompilia, an obdurate denier in that respect? "There must be falsehood somewhere", the commoner has remarked; he, for one, was inclined to believe that Caponsacchi had taken the utilitarian view that if the outcome of a lie is more favourable than that of a truthful statement, mendacity is a healthy option. Arguably, that the canon was subconsciously paying tribute to Aristotle's ethics through letting his desire determine his ends and using means conducive to the fulfilment of his aims.

At this critical stage it is fair to remark that, on a par with Half-Rome, the Other Half has failed to grasp the truth in its entirety; in effect, the two Halves of the City on the Tiber have made a half-baked effort to achieve veracity and in so doing adumbrated the corollary that human beings had better be content with a perception of the particular and take comfort from the hope that truth can still be intuited with the help of the imagination.

At the end of the day, a dichotomy between truthfulness and falsehood has established itself as a major theme, which has remained preponderant in the course of the gothically-tinged depiction of Pompilia sliding 'ghost-like from great dark room to great dark room' – was she on her own or was Caponsacchi already with her? – and finally doing a bunk with the priest inside a pitch-black carriage vis-à-vis the surrounding light. When all is said and done, the detailed account of the couple sitting side by side inside the vehicle has invigorated a string of conventional and often contradictory contentions reminiscent of Francis Bacon's disapproval of the *Idols of the Tribe* for being an expression of the limitations of the human mind as well as of an empirical perception; in this connection, it is pertinent to consider the Renaissance thinker's quotation of Pontius Pilate's question, 'What is truth?' without so much as a wait for an answer. Ages before Bacon, the sceptic Carneades of Cyrene had asserted that the detection of a clear difference between trustworthy and unreliable impressions was beyond the power of the human mind and the perceptual apparatus. Following in Bacon's footsteps, the Royal Society has held that language possesses truth only in representational terms, and it seems reasonable to assume that the notion does not conflict with Augustine of Hippo's tenet that some figurative uses of language do allow access to the realm of divine truth. In subsequent times, the empiricist

David Hume has called for a destruction of anything false and adulterate with the help of an earnest probe into the nature of human understanding. What's more, latter-day literary theory has significantly contributed to a proper appreciation of the burning question by asserting that 'the dimension of truth emerges only with the appearance of language' and is in fact determined by it[9]. In this context, a search for the transcendental presence of *alētheia*, i.e. truth, is liable to be a flop, notably because 'the original or transcendental 'signified' is never absolutely present outside a system of differences'.[10] In other words, *differance* is the name of the game, and a natural consequence of the absence of a conclusive *signified* is that the quest for truth is destined to continue *ad infinitum*.[11]

With regard to the latest developments, it would not come amiss to underscore the Other Half-Rome's borderline tribute to Count Franceschini's mental agility: "He must invent another story now!" he has exclaimed, but then again, there was no need for another figment of Guido's imagination because the court had decided to follow a medium course, thus sanctioning 'Rome's way, the traditional road of law'. "Wither it leads is what remains to tell", the Roman fellow has commented with mixed feelings, thus hinting that conflicting emotions had been the likely *fons et origo* of the Aretine nobleman's mendacity, murderous assault and inglorious retreat, – all of which being, at an educated guess, the embodiment of Vice in a morality play as well as of a split personality redolent of an Augustan poet's inconsistent feelings and desperate plight: 'I hate and I love. Why I do this, you may ask, I know not, but I feel it happening and am on the rocks.'[12]

The speaker's monologue has climaxed with an indignant rejection of the Count's self-professed sense of honour. His marriage-related assertion, "I who have no wife, being sensitive in my degree as Guido, must discover hurt elsewhere", has associated him, an ethically self-conscious plebeian, with an ethically questionable aristocrat; nonetheless the former has sounded less biased than his counterpart, the latter being a married guy suspicious of his vulnerable wife's behaviour. In this context, it ought to be noted that he has ended his speech with a contemptuous statement and a valedictory curse: "Count, that were too commodious, I repeat! If any law be imperative on us all, of all are you the enemy; out with you from the common light and air and life of man!" The outburst, it can finally be remarked, has once again subverted linguistic representation by treating language in terms of a constant battle between utterers'[13]; furthermore, it has reignited the perennial conflict between language and truth. The Other Half-Rome's domain of truth has been the manipulation of the word with the help of the 'letter', i.e. thanks to the support given by speech; admittedly, 'the letter killeth while the spirit giveth life', yet the letter has proved that 'it can produce all the effect of truth in man without involving the spirit at all.'[14]

In the final analysis it does appear that the Other Half-Rome has tested – well ahead of a latter-day speech-act theory[15] – a 'performative language', and the linguistic event has taken place on an inter-class plane. If that is the case, the entire 'discourse' of the second half of the city may well be taken, in consort with that of the first half, to be the articulation of a 'signifier' conducive to the 'signified' Robert Browning has been in quest of from the outset.

1. *'So Kind and so Honest She Looks'*
2. Dante Gabriele Rossetti, *The Blessed Damozel.*
3. Aristotle, in *Western Philosophy and Philosophers*, p. 24
4. Jean-Paul Sartre, as quoted in *Western Philosophy and Philosophers*, p. 288
5. Martin Heidegger, as referred to in *Op. Cit.* p. 129
6. See Roman Jakobson's citation in *Linguistics and Poetics, Modern Criticism and Theory*, p. 50
7. Robert Browning, *Paracelsus*, ll.726-729

8. Aristotle's *Ethics*, in *Western Philosophy and Philosophers*, pp. 29-30
9. Jacques Lacan, *The Insistence of the Letter in the Unconscious*, in *Modern Criticism and Theory*, p. 102
10. Jacques Derrida, *Structure, Sign and Play in the Discourse of the Human Sciences*, in *Modern Criticism and Theory*, p.110
11. *Ibid*
12. Gaius Valerius Catullus, *Odi et Amo*
13. See Colin MacCabe apropos of Falstaff's speech, in *Language, Linguistics and the study of Literature*, in *Modern Criticism and Theory*, pp. 434-435
14. Jacques Lacan, *The Insistence of the Letter in the Unconcscious*, in *Op. Cit.* p. 91
15. Terry Eagleton, *Literary Theory – An Introduction*, Blackwell Publishers, 1993, p. 118

TERTIUM QUID

Conspicuously aloof from the vociferous plebs, a lawyer and 'man of quality' sedately mingled with a select few inside a posh drawing room. Prompted by the assertions of a couple of dignitaries, *Tertium Quid* set about expatiating on the Franceschini criminal trial. "True, Excellency – as his Highness says, though she's not dead, she's as good as stretched symmetrical beside the other two; though he's not judged yet, he's the same as judged, so do the facts abound and superabound: and nothing hinders, now, we lift the case out of the shade into the shine, allow qualified persons to pronounce at last, nay, edge in an authoritative word between this rabble's brabble of dolts and fools who make up reasonless unreasoning Rome. Law's a machine from which, to please the mob, Truth the divinity must needs descend and clear things at the play's fifth act – aha! To hear the rabble and brabble, you'd call the case fused and confused past human finding out: one calls the square round, t'other the round square; it makes a man despair of history! Why, Excellency, we and His Highness here would settle the matter as sufficiently as ever will Advocate This and Fiscal that and Judge the Other, with even – a word and a wink – we well know who for ultimate arbiter. Bethink you that you have to deal with *plebs*, the commonalty? This is an episode in burgess-life, – why seek to aggrandize, idealize, denaturalize the class?" The upper-class gentleman's forehead furrowed. "This Pietro, this Violante, live their life at Rome in the easy way that's far from worst even for their betters, – themselves love themselves, spend their own oil in feeding their own lamp that their own faces may grow bright thereby.

Well, having got through fifty years of flare, they burn out so, indulge so their dear selves, that Pietro finds himself in debt at last. Creditors grow uneasy, talk aside, take counsel, then importune all at once. For if the good fat rosy careless man, who has not laid a ducat by, decease – let the lamp fall, no heir at hand to catch –

why, being childless, there's a spilth i' the street o' the remnant, there's a scramble for the dregs by the stranger: so, they grant him no long day but come in a body, clamour to be paid. What's his resource? He asks and straight obtains the customary largesse, dole dealt out to, what we call our 'poor dear shame-faced ones', in secret once a month to spare the shame o' the slothful and the spendthrift, – pauper-saints the Pope puts meat i' the mouth of, ravens they, and providence he – just what the mob admires! That is, instead of putting a prompt foot on selfish worthless human slugs whose slime has failed to lubricate their path in life, why, the Pope picks the first ripe fruit that falls and gracious puts it in the vermin's way. Pietro could never save a dollar? Straight he must be subsidized at our expense; and for his wife – the harmless household sheep one ought not to see harassed in her age – judge, by the way she bore adversity, o' the patient nature you ask pity for! Violante, the old innocent burgess-wife, in her first difficulty showed great teeth fit to crunch up and swallow a good round crime. She meditates the tenure of the Trust, – these funds that only want an heir to take, – then makes her mind up, sees the thing to do, posts off to vespers, missal beneath arm, passes the proper San Lorenzo by, dives down a little lane to the left, is lost in a labyrinth of dwellings best unnamed, selects a certain blind one, black at base, blinking at top, – the sign of we know what, – gropes for the door i' the dark, ajar of course, raps, opens, enters in.

Up starts a thing: 'Mercy on me, poor sinner that I am! What may your pleasure be, my bonny dame?' One of those women that abound in Rome, whose needs oblige them eke out one poor trade by another vile one: her ostensible work was washing clothes, out in the open air at the cistern by Citorio, but true trade at home, that eve, i' the house where candles blinked decorously above, and all was done i' the holy fear of God and cheap beside. Violante, now, had seen this woman wash, and now was come to tempt her and propose a bargain far more shameful than the first which trafficked her virginity away for a melon and three pauls at twelve years old. Struck was the bargain, business at an end: 'Then, six months hence, that person whom you trust, comes, fetches whatsoever babe it be; I keep the price and secret, you the babe, paying beside for Mass to make all straight: meantime, I pouch the earnest money-piece.'"

Tertium Quid, a man of the world *coram populi*, landed a gloved hand on his peruke à la mode and stroked it. The speech act resumed. "Violante, triumphing in a flourish of fire from her own brain, self-lit by such success, – gains church in time for the *Magnificat*; then home to Pietro, the enraptured-much but puzzled-more when told the wondrous news. Accordingly, when time was come about, he found himself the sire indeed of this Francesca Vittoria Pompilia and the rest o' the names whereby he sealed her his next day. A crime complete in its way is here, I hope?" The suggestion was for the ears of the nearest distinguished fellow. The speaker added by way of comment, "Your Highness, – healthy minds let bygones be, leave old crimes to grow young and virtuous-like i' the sun and air; so time treats ugly deeds: they take the natural blessing of all change. There was the joy o' husband silly-sooth, the softening of the wife's old wicked heart, virtues to right and left, profusely paid if so they might compensate the saved sin. Why, moralist, the sin has saved a soul! Moreover, say that certain sin there seem, the proper process of unsinning sin is to begin well-doing somehow else. Pietro, – remember, with no sin at all i' the substitution, – why, this gift of God steadied him in a moment, set him straight on the good path he had been straying from: all sort of self-denial was easy now for the child's sake, the chatelaine to be. As for the wife, – I said, hers the whole sin: so, hers the exemplary penance. 'T was a text whereon folk preached and praised, the district through!"

His Highness raised his eyebrows in surprise. Tertium Quid countered the facial expression pronto. "Here you put by my guard, pass to my heart by the home-thrust" – 'There's a lie at base of all.'

Why, thou exact Prince, is it a pearl or no, yon globe upon the Principessa's neck? Do you call it worthless for the worthless core? You see so far i' the story, who was right, who wrong, who neither, do n't you? What, you do n't? Leap over a dozen years: you find, these passed, an old good easy creditable sire, a careful housewife's beaming bustling face, both wrapped up in the love of their one child, the strange tall pale beautiful creature grown lily-like out o' the cleft i' the sun-smit rock to bow its white miraculous birth of buds. Indeed, the prize was simply full to a fault; exorbitant for the suitor they should seek, and social class to choose among, these cits. For, Guido Franceschini was the head of an old family in Arezzo, old to that degree they could afford be poor better than most: the case is common too. The family instinct felt out for its fire to the Church. The Church traditionally helps a second son, and such was Paolo, who played the regular game, – priest and Abate. Even our Guido, eldest brother, went as far i' the way o' the Church as safety seemed, but main promotion must fall otherwise, though still from the side o' the Church: and here was he, at Rome since first youth, worn threadbare of soul, getting fast tired o' the game whose word is 'Wait!' when one day, – he too having his Cardinal to serve in some ambiguous sort, as serve to draw the coach the plumes o' the horses' heads, – the Cardinal saw fit to dispense with him, ride with one plume the less; and off it dropped. Guido thus left, – with a youth spent in vain and not a penny in purse to show for it, advised with Paolo, bent no doubt in chafe the black brows somewhat formidable the while.

'Patience', pats Paolo the recalcitrant – 'you have not had, so far, the proper luck; you are the Count however, yours the style, heirdom and state, – you can't expect all good. Come, clear your looks, and choose your freshest suit, and, after function's done with, down we go to the woman-dealer in perukes, a wench I and some others settled in the shop at Place Colonna: she's an oracle. Hmm!' And so plumped out Pompilia's name the first: the wench "told them of the household and its ways in Via Vittoria; how the tall young girl, with hair black as yon patch and eyes as big as yon pomander to make freckles fly, would have so much for certain, and so much more in likelihood. Why, it suited, slipt as smooth as the Pope's pantoufle does on the Pope's foot!

I'll to the husband!' Guido ups and cries.

'Ay, so you'd play your last court-card, no doubt!' puts Paolo in with a groan – Only, you see, 'tis I, this time, that supervise your lead. Priests play with women, maids, wives, mothers; why, these play with men and take them off our hands. Go, brother, stand you rapt in the anteroom of Her Efficacity my Cardinal while I betake myself to the grey mare, the better horse, – how wise the people's word! – and wait on Madam Violante.'

Tertium Quid gave a chuckle. "Said and done. He was at Via Vittoria in three skips: proposed at once to fill up the one want o' the burgess family which, wealthy enough, and comfortable to heart's desire, yet crouched outside a gate to heaven, – locked, bolted, barred, whereof Count Guido had a key he kept under his pillow, but Pompilia's hand might slide behind his neck and pilfer thence. The key was fairy; mention of it, made Violante feel the thing shoot one sharp ray that reached the heart o' the woman. 'I assent: yours be Pompilia, hers and ours that key to all the glories of the greater life!'

Then was the matter broached to Pietro; then did Pietro make demand and get response that in the Countship was a truth, but in the counting up of the Count's cash, a lie: he thereupon stroked grave his chin, looked great, declined the honour. Then the wife wiped one – winked with the other eye turned Paolo-ward, whispered 'Pompilia', stole to church at eve, found Guido there and got the marriage done.

Quoth Pietro, 'Let us make the best of things.'

'I knew your love would licence us,' quoth she.

Quoth Paolo once more, 'Mothers, wives and maids, these be the tools wherewith priests manage men.'"

Tertium Quid produced a knowing smile. "Now, here take breath and ask, – which bird o' the brace decoyed the other into clapnet? Who was fool, who knave? Neither and both, perchance. On each side, straight and plain and fair enough; there was the blunder incident to words, and in the clumsy process, fair turned foul. Hence was the need, on either side, of a lie to serve as decent wrappage: so, Guido gives money for money and they bride for groom, – having, he, not a doit, they not a child honestly theirs, but this poor waif and stray. Why, you know where the gist is of the exchange: each sees a profit, throws the fine words in. No party blamed the other, – so, starting fair, all subsequent fence of wrong, returned by wrong i' the matrimonial thrust and parry, at least had followed on equal terms! But, as it chanced, one party had the advantage, saw the cheat of the other first and kept its own concealed, – and the luck o' the first discovery fell, beside, to the least adroit and self-possessed o' the pair: 'twas foolish Pietro and his wife saw first the nobleman was penniless and screamed 'We are cheated!'"

The speaker's impish smile metamorphosed into a snigger. "Such unprofitable noise angers at all times, but when those who plague do it from inside your own house and home, noise goes too near the brain and makes you mad.

On the other hand, 'Not so!' Guido retorts – 'I am the wronged, solely, from first to last, who gave the dignity I engaged to give. You thought nobility gained at any price would suit and satisfy, – find the mistake, and now retaliate, not on yourselves, but me. There's not one truth in this odious tale o' the buying, selling, substituting; prove your daughter was and is your daughter, – well, and her dowry hers and therefore mine, – what then? Why, where's the appropriate punishment for this enormous lie hatched for mere malice's sake to ruin me? Is that a wrong or no? And if I try revenge for remedy, can I well make it strong and bitter enough?'" The questioner's frilly foot hit the floor. "Which brownness is least black, – decide who can, wager-by-battle-of cheating! What do you say, Highness? Suppose, your Excellency, we leave the question at this stage, proceed to the next, both parties step out, fight their prize upon, in the eye o' the world? They brandish law 'gainst law; the grinding of such blades, each parry of each, throws terrible sparks off, over and above the thrusts, and makes more sinister the fight to the eye. Guido, – whose cue is to dispute the truth o' the tale, reject the shame it throws on him, – he may retaliate, fight his foe in turn; law may meet law, – but all the gibes and jeers, those libels on his House, – how reach at them? Two hateful faces, grinning all a-glow, not only make parade of spoil they filched, but foul him from the height of a tower, you see. These fools forgot their pet lamb, fed with flowers, then 'ticed as usual by the bit of cake out of the bower into the butchery. Plague her, he plagues them threefold: but how plague? The word may have its word to say to that: you can't do some things with impunity. What remains … well, it is an ugly thought … but that he drive herself to plague herself, herself disgrace herself and so disgrace who seek to disgrace Guido?"

The speaker darted forward a look pregnant with gravitas. "*There*'s the clue to what else seems gratuitously vile: the aim o' the cruelty being so crueller still, that cruelty almost grows compassion's self could one attribute it to mere return o' the parents' outrage, wrong avenging wrong. The pair had nobody but themselves to blame, – being selfish beasts throughout, no less, no more. They baited their own hook to catch a fish with this poor worm, failed o' the prize and then sought how to unbait tackle, let worm float or sink, amuse the monster while they 'scaped. Given, a fair wife aged thirteen years, a husband poor, care-beaten, sorrow-sunk, little, long-nosed, bush-bearded, lantern-jawed, forty-six-years full, – place the two grown one, how evolve happiness from such a match? 'T were hard to serve up a congenial dish out of these ill-agreeing morsels, Duke, but let two ghastly scullions concoct mess with brimstone, pitch, vitriol and devil's dung, throw in abuse o' the man, – his body and soul,

– then end by publishing , for fiend's arch-prank, that, over and above sauce to the meat's self, why, even the meat, bedevilled thus in dish, was never a pheasant but a carrion-crow, what wonder if this, the compound plague o' the pair, pricked Guido not to take the course they hoped, that is, submit him to their statement's truth, accept its obvious promise of relief, and thrust them out of doors the girl again? Rather did rage and hate so work in him that he should plot ad plan and bring to pass his wife might, of her own free will and deed, relieve him of her presence, get her gone, while blotting out, as by a belch of hell, their triumph in her misery and death."

Tertium Quid's countenance was unyieldingly dignified as he went on to say, "You see, the man was Aretine, had touch o' the subtle air that breeds the subtle wit; was noble too, of old blood thrice-refined that shrinks from clownish coarseness in disgust. Substitute for the clown a nobleman, and you have Guido, practising, 't is said, the finer vengeance: this, they say, the fact o' the famous letter shows, the writing traced at Guido's instance by the timid wife over the pencilled words himself writ first. They also say: to keep her straight therein, all sort of torture was piled, pain on pain, on either side Pompilia's path of life, built round about and over again by fear, close, closer and yet closer with pain, – no outlet from the encroaching pain save just where stood one saviour like a piece of heaven; Hell's arms would strain round but for this blue gap whereat stood Caponsacchi, who cried, 'This way, out by me! Hesitate one moment more and the fire shuts *out* me and shuts *in* you. Here my hand holds your life out!' Whereupon she clasped the hand, which closed on hers and drew Pompilia out o' the circle now complete."

The distinguished fellow narrowed his eyes in the manner of a narrator focusing on a visual image. "But then this is the wife's – Pompilia's tale – Eve's ... no, not Eve's, since Eve, to speak the truth, was hardly fallen – our candour might pronounce – when simply saying in her own defence, 'The serpent tempted me, and I did eat.' Her daughters ever since prefer to urge 'Adam so starved me I was fain accept the apple any serpent pushed my way.' What an elaborate theory have we here! Ingeniously nursed up, pretentiously brough forth, pushed forward amid trumpet-blast, to account for the thawing of an icicle, to solve the problem why young fancy-and-flesh slips from the dull side of a spouse in years, betakes it to the breast of brisk-and-bold whose love-scrapes furnish talk for all the town." Tertium Quid wagged his head.

"Accordingly, one word on the other side tips over the piled-up fabric of a tale. Guido says – that is, always, his friends say – it is unlikely from the wickedness, that any man treat any woman so. The letter in question was her very own, unprompted and unaided: she could write – as able to write as ready to sin, or free, when there was danger, to deny both facts. He bids you mark, herself from first to last attributes all the so-styled torture just to jealousy, – jealousy of whom but just this very Caponsacchi! How suits here this with the other alleged motive, Prince? Would Guido make a terror of the man he meant should tempt the woman, as they charge? Do you fright your hare that you may catch your hare? He further asks – Duke, note the knotty point! – how he, – concede him skill to play such part and drive his wife into a gallant's arms, – could bring the gallant to play his part too, to undertake this strange and perilous feat? Take the wife's tale as true, say she was wronged, – pray, in what rubric of the breviary do you find it registered the part of a priest that to right wrongs he skip from the church door, go journeying with a woman that's a wife, and be pursued, o'ertaken and captured … how? in a lay dress, playing the sentinel where the wife sleeps – says he who best should know – and sleeping, sleepless, both have spent the night! Could no one else be found to serve at need – no woman – or if man, no safer sort than this not well-reputed turbulence?"

There was a momentary pause as the speaker wiped his brow with a cutely embroidered silk handkerchief.

He recommenced. "Then, look into his own account o' the case! He, being the stranger and astonished one, yet received protestations of her love from lady neither known nor cared about: love, so protested, bred in him disgust after the wonder, – or incredulity, such impudence seeming impossible. But, soon assured such impudence might be, when he had seen with his own eyes at last letters thrown down to him i' the very street from behind lattice where the lady lurked, and read their passionate summons to her side, why then, a thousand thoughts swarmed up and in: *there* flashed the propriety, expediency of treating, trying they might come to terms, – at all events, granting the interview prayed for, and so adapted to assist decision as to whether he advance, stand or retire, in his benevolent mood. Therefore the interview befell at length; he saw the sole and single course to take, bade her dispose of him, – head, heart and hand, – not for the natural end, the love of man for woman whether love be virtue or vice, but, please you, altogether for pity's sake – pity of innocence and helplessness!"

Tertium Quid raised his eyes to otherwordly decorations on the ceiling as if seeking inspiration.

"'And now, do hear my version', Guido cries. 'I accept argument and inference both. Cheating and lies: they used the hackney chair Satan jaunts forth with, shabby and serviceable. That same officious go-between, the wench that gave and took the letters of the two, bears testimony to visits night by night when all was safe, the husband far and away, – too many a timely slipping out at large by light o' the morning star, ere he should wake. And when the fugitives were found at last, why, with them were found also, to belie what protest they might make of innocence, all documents yet wanting, if need were, to establish guilt in them, disgrace in me: letters from wife to priest, from priest to wife, – here they are, read and say where they chime in with the other tale, superlative purity o' the pair of saints! I stand or fall by these." The haranguer frowned, and deep lines materialised between his eyebrows. "But then on the other side again, – how say the pair of saints? That not one word is theirs – no syllable o' the batch or writ or sent or yet received by either of the two.

Guido rejoins, 'Did the other end o' the tale match this beginning! 'Tis alleged I prove a murderer at the end, a man of force prompt, indiscriminate, effectual: good! Then what need all this trifling woman's-work, letters and embassies and weak intrigue, when will and power were mine to end at once safely and surely? Murder had come first not last with such a man, assure yourselves! Moreover, what o' the future son and heir, the unborn babe about to be called mine, – what end in heaping all this shame on him, were I indifferent to my own black share? Would I have tried these crookednesses, say, willing and able to effect the straight?'

'Ay, would you!' – one may hear the priest retort, 'you, a born coward, try a coward's arms, trick and chicane, – and only when these fail, does violence follow, and like fox you bite caught out in stealing. Also, the disgrace, you hardly shrunk at, wholly shrivelled her: you plunged her thin white delicate hand i' the flame along with your coarse horny brutish fist. Your hurt would heal forthwith at ointment's touch – namely, succession to the inheritance which bolder crime had lost you: let things change, the birth o' the boy warrant the bolder crime, why, murder was determined, dared and done.'"

The sound pattern expanded. "Highness, decide! Pronounce, Her Excellency! Or … even leave this argument in doubt, account it a fit matter, taken up with all its faces, manifold enough, to put upon – what fronts us, the next stage, next legal process! – Guido, in pursuit, coming up with the fugitives at the inn, caused both to be arrested then and there and sent to Rome for judgment on the case – thither, with his armoury of proof betook himself, and there we'll meet him now, waiting the further issue.

Here some smile 'Passion and madness irrepressible? Why, Count and cavalier, the husband comes and catches foe i' the very act of shame. There's man to man, – nature must have her way, – we look he should have cleared things on the spot. But when he stands, the stockfish, – sticks to law – can stand, can stare, can tell his beads perhaps, oh, let us hear no syllable o' the rage! Whereas the grey innocuous grub, of yore, had hatched a hornet, tickle to the touch, the priest was metamorphosed into a knight, and even the timid wife, whose cue was – shriek, bury her brow beneath his trampling foot, – she too sprang at him like a pythoness: so, gulp down rage, passion must be postponed, calm be the word! Well, our word is – we brand this part o' the business, howsoever the rest befall.'

'Nay,' interpose as prompt his friends – 'this is the world's way! So you adjudge reward to the forbearance and legality yourselves begin by inculcating – ay, you publish all, with the kind comment here, "Its victim was too cowardly for revenge." '

Tertium Quid took a deep breath, then exhaled slowly. "Make it your own case, – you who stand apart! The husband wakes one morn from heavy sleep, with a taste of poppy in his mouth, – rubs eyes, finds his wife flown, his strong box ransacked too, follows as he best can, overtakes i' the end. You bid him use his privilege: well, it seems he's scarce cool-blooded enough for the right move; he'll know in a minute, but till then, he doubts. Admit the worst: his courage failed the Count; he's cowardly like the best o' the burgesses he's grown incorporate with, – a very cur. Still, the Church-door lies wide to take him in, and the Court-porch also; *in* he sneaks to each. Religion and Law lean forward from their chairs: 'Well done, thou good and faithful servant!' Ay, not only applaud him that he scorned the world, but punish should he dare do otherwise.

The courts would nor condemn nor yet acquit this, that or the other, in so distinct a sense as end the strife to either's absolute loss; pronounced, in place of something definite, 'For the wife, – let her betake herself, for rest, after her run, to a House of Convertites – keep there, as good as real imprisonment. For the priest, spritely strayer out of bounds, let him relegate to Civita, circumscribed by its bounds till matters mend. And finally for the husband, whose rash rule has but itself to blame for this ado, let him be comforted with the thought, no less, that, turn each sentence howsoever he may, there's satisfaction to extract therefrom. Oh, ay, you, all of you, want the other thing, the extreme of law, some verdict neat, complete, but we've no mind, we children of the light, to miss the advantage of the golden mean, and push things to the steel point.'

Thus the courts. Is it settled so far? Settled or disturbed, console yourselves: 't is like ... an instance, now! You've seen the puppets, of Place Navona, play, – Punch and his mate: how threats pass, blows are dealt, and a crisis comes; the crowd or clap or hiss accordingly as disposed for man or wife – when down the actors duck awhile perdue, donning what novel rag-and-feather trim best suits the next adventure, new effect. There's a whistle, up again the actors pop in t' other tatter with fresh tinseled staves, to re-engage in one last worst fight more shall show, what you thought tragedy was farce. Note, that the climax and the crown of things invariably is, the devil appears himself, armed and accoutred, horns and hoofs and tail! Just so, nor otherwise it proved – you' ll see! Move to the murder, never mind the rest!"

The speech-act progressed with a diminuendo.

"Well, at such crisis and extreme of straits, happened the strangest accident of all: the wife's withdrawal from the Convertites, visit to the house wherein her parents lived, and birth there of his babe. Divergence here! I simply take the facts, ask what they show. First comes this thunderclap of a surprise; then follow all the signs and silences premonitory of earthquake. Paolo first vanished, was swept off somewhere, lost to Rome; then Guido girds himself for enterprise, comes to terms with four peasants young and bold, and starts for Rome the Holy, reaches her at very holiest – for 't is Christmas Eve – and then, rest taken, observation made and plan completed, all in a grim week, the five proceed in a body, reach the place, Pietro's, by the Paolina, silent, lone, at one in the morning, knock.

A voice: 'Who's there?'

'Friends with a letter from the priest your friend.'

At the door, straight smiles old Violante's self. She falls; her son-in-law stabs through and through, reaches thro' her at Pietro.

With your son this is the way to settle suits, good sire!'

He bellows 'Mercy for heaven, not for earth! Leave to confess and save my sinful soul; then do your pleasure on the body of me!'

'Nay, father, soul with body must take its chance!'

He presently got his portion and lay still.

And last, Pompilia rushes here and there like a dove among lightnings in her brake, falls also: Guido's, this last husband's-act. He lifts her by the long, dishevelled hair, looks out his whole heart's hate on the shut eyes, draws a deep satisfied breath, 'So – dead at last!', throws down the burthen on dead Pietro's knees.

And, as they left by one door, in at the other tumbled the neighbours – for the shrieks had pierced to the mill and the grange, this cottage and that shed. Soon followed the Public Force; pursuit began. So, that same night was he, with the other four, overtaken near Baccano, – where they sank by the wayside, in some shelter meant for beasts, and now lay heaped together, nuzzling swine, each wrapped in bloody cloak, each grasping still his unwiped weapon, sleeping all the same the sleep o' the just, – a journey of twenty miles bringing just and unjust to a level, you see.

The only one i' the world that suffered aught by the whole night's toil and trouble, flight and chase, was just the officer who took them, Head o' the Public Force, – Patrizi, zealous soul, who, having duty to sustain the flesh, got heated, caught a fever and so died: a warning to the over-vigilant, – virtue in a chafe should change her linen quick, lest pleurisy get start of providence."

The narrator paused for an instant, arguably with the aim of giving His Excellency and His Highness time to appreciate the therapeutic caveat.

"Well, they bring back the company to Rome. Says Guido, 'By your leave, I fain would ask how you found out 't was I who did the deed, what put you on my trace, a foreigner, supposed in Arezzo, – and assuredly safe except for an oversight: who told you, pray?'

'Why, naturally your wife!'

Down Guido drops, so strange it seemed his wife should live and speak! She had prayed – at least so people tell you now – for but one thing to the Virgin for herself, not simply, as Pietro did 'mid the stabs, – time to confess and get her own soul saved – but time to make the truth apparent, truth for God's sake, lest me should believe a lie. The self-command and even the final prayer, our candour must acknowledge explainable as easily by the consciousness of guilt.

'But we left this man many another way, and *there's* his fault', 't is answered – 'he himself preferred our arm o' the law to fight his battle with. No doubt we did not open him an armoury to pick and choose from, use, and then reject. He tries one weapon and fails, – he tries the next and next: he flourishes wit and common sense, they fail him, – he plies logic doughtily, it fails him, too, – thereon discovers last he has been blind to the combustibles – that all the while he is aglow with ire, boiling with irrepressible rage, and so may try explosives and discard cold steel, – so hire assassins, plot, plan, execute! Is this the honest self-forgetting rage we are called to pardon? Does the furious bull pick out four helpmates from the grazing herd and journey with them over hill and dale till he find his enemy?'" Tertium Quid wagged his forefinger to left and right. "What rejoinder? save that friends accept our bull-similitude." His Highness and His Excellency displayed a perplexed countenance. "In truth you look as puzzled as ere I preached", he remarked promptly. "How is that? There are difficulties perhaps on any supposition, and either side. Each party wants too much, claims sympathy for its object of compassion, more than just. Cry the wife's friends, 'O the enormous crime caused by no provocation in the world!' Why, here you have the awfulest of crimes for nothing! Hell broke loose on a butterfly, a dragon born of rose-dew and the moon!" A soft sniff accompanied the utterance. "Yet here is the monster! Why, he's a mere man – born, bred and brought up in the usual way. The Governor of his town knows and approves, the Archbishop of the place knows and assists: here he has Cardinal This to vouch for the past, Cardinal That to trust for the future, – match and marriage were a Cardinal's making. In short, what if a tragedy be acted here impossible for malice to improve, and innocent Guido with his innocent four be added, all five, to the guilty three, that we of these last days be edified with one full taste o' the justice of the world?"

Propelled by the ethical conjecture, the speaker reached the pinnacle of his verbal flight: "The long and the short is, truth is what I show: – undoubtedly no pains ought to be spared to give the mob an inkling of our lights. It seems unduly harsh to put the man to the torture, as I hear the court intends, though readiest way of twisting out the truth: he is noble, and he may be innocent; on the other hand, if they exempt the man, what crime that ever was, ever will be, deserves the torture? Then abolish it! You see the *reductio ad absurdum*, Sirs?" He made eye contact with His Excellency and His Highness only to perceive that the former was about to join the nearby game players while the latter was keen to retire. "I am of their mind", he said to himself; "only, all this talk, talked, both know as much about it, now, at least, as all Rome. No particular thanks, I beg!" It was the final spark in Tertium Quid's pyrotechnic display, – a performance centred, to echo Browning's words in the Prologue, on the 'silvery and selectest phrase'. Visibly gratified, the fireworks craftsman sauntered out of the salon that was out of bounds to Half-Rome and the Other Half-Rome.

"So do the facts abound and superabound: and nothing hinders, now, we lift the case out of the shade into the shine, allow qualified persons to pronounce at last, nay, edge in an authoritative word between this rabble's brabble of dolts and fools who make up reasonless unreasoning Rome." Such has been the initial statement of a posh Roman citizen, a '*tertium quid*' in Robert Browning's eyes.

Ages before him, Plato had come up with the idea of a *Triton Ti*, namely a Third Thing that could be grasped solely on the strength of some spurious logic; not much later, Aristotle had, by contrast, gone as far as to put forth the theory of a logical-minded *Triton Ti*. Taking a leaf out of the Hellenic philosophers' books, the Roman Horace and the Carthaginian Tertullian had examined the wider implications of the concept.

The Victorian Browning has walked up the well-trodden path and made Tertium Quid sound like one of those agents of Reason whom the hedonist Epicurus had deemed capable of an autonomous attitude and consequently deserving either praise or blame.

Interestingly, the 17th-century free-thinking 'man of quality' has stolen the show by seeing law as "a machine from which, to please the mob, Truth the divinity must needs descend and clear things at the play's fifth act". The metaphor has echoed Browning's assertion in the Prologue that 'here, after ignorance, instruction speaks; here, clarity of candour, history's soul; the critical mind, in short, no gossip guess'.

As a matter of fact, the obverse of the coin has displayed a socialite striving to understand the complex nature of the human mind, whereas the reverse has conveyed the impression of an upper-class fellow baulking at the prospect of being bracketed with the *plebs*. In this connection, the gentleman has objected to a juxtaposition of the bourgeois Comparini with the nobility: "Why seek to aggrandize, idealize, denaturalize the class?" he has put to *Sua Eccellenza* and *Sua Altezza* in the course of a party not designed for the hoi polloi. Soon afterwards, he has revealed a knack for detecting humorous streaks in human nature, – witness his mention of the Pope's decision to subsidize an impecunious Pietro. Moreover, he has given a detailed account of how a local washerwoman would reassure nocturnal male visitors to her small abode "blinking at top – the sign of we know what" – that "all was done i' the fear of God and cheap beside. Lo and behold, "the old innocent" Violante had, after due consideration, called on the wench and obtained her pledge to quietly deliver a baby before too long. Her own donation to the parish priest in order to have a mass that would 'make all straight' had been an integral part of the compact. Mission accomplished, she had rushed to her cherished San Lorenzo in time for the *Magnificat*, and dashed home where, hey presto, her mesmerized husband had been apprised of 'orisons and works of charity' that had borne fruit in the autumn of his life – they, or the *Orvieto* in a double dose.'

Tertium Quid's expanding discourse has borne the hallmark of a speaker anxious to talk about "lies to God, lies to man, every way lies to nature and civility and the mode. In respect of that, he has subsequently asserted that, moral imperatives notwithstanding, "healthy minds let bygones be, leave old crimes to grow young and virtuous-like i' the sun and air; so time treats ugly deeds: they take the natural blessing of all change." "Why, moralist, the sin has saved a soul!' he has exclaimed, thereby calling to mind the Aristotelian dictum that an action is virtuous only if it strikes a mean between two extremes; he has likewise rekindled memories of Kant's hypothetical imperative – videlicet, of the moral rule primarily relating to the use of suitable means motivated by a yearning for a good result rather than by a compelling sense of duty. In addition, it is worth comparing the Roman observer's standpoint to the latter-day poststructuralist tenet concerning a play of potentially endless substitutions of means for ends and of ends for means, i.e. a play that takes place by means of a supplementarity which turns out to be a precondition for the existence of an equally necessary complementarity.[1]

Tertium Quid has gone on to take a prescriptive tone when he has held that "the proper process of unsinning sin is to begin well-doing somehow else": unintentionally in harmony with Aristotelian ethics[2], he has eulogised Pietro's return to a good life and contrasted it with Violante's "whole sin" and consequent "exemplary penance."

'There's a lie at base of all.' This much the 'Prince' present at the gathering has asserted, and the statement has prompted Tertium Quid to ask the "exact royal" if he would call the pearly globe adorning a *Principessa*'s neck 'worthless for the worthless core'.

In a short space of time, the discourse has undergone a psychological twist: while dealing with Guido's search for a Roman wife, the speaker has quoted the hard-boiled Abate Paolo as saying that 'priests play with women, maids, wives, mothers' because 'these play with men and take them off our hands'. What's more, Guido's brother had sarcastically added that 'mothers, wives and maids; these be the tools wherewith priests manage men.'

Expanding on his analysis, Tertium Quid has focused his attention on the Comparini's and Guido Franceschini's approach to the burning issue: "Who was fool, who knave?" he has discerningly asked, and his own reply has been: "neither and both, perchance. There was a bargain mentally proposed on each side, straight and plain and fair enough" but then again, there was a "need, on either side, of a lie to serve a decent wrappage" and "according to the words, each cheated each"; in effect, both parties had scented a profit and chosen their words to the best of their ability.

Heavens above, what finesse! The disenchanted observer has, by the sound of it, emphasised the need to regard the upshot of the awkward agreement between the Count and the bourgeois couple as a specimen of the human stain. Guido's question, "And if I try revenge for remedy, can I well make it strong and bitter enough?" has highlighted a link between morality and religion. By the same token, his request for *Sua Altezza*'s and *Sua Eccellenza*'s views on the ethical issue has betrayed an acute sense of dependence on the attitude of the two personages.

However, there's more to it than meets the eye: Tertium Quid's altruistic state of mind has been made conspicuous by his contention that Guido's household lacked the living wherewithal prior to asserting by way of postscript, "That's one more wrong than needs." It does make sense to suppose that the gentleman's emotive perception of the difference between right and wrong has entailed a code common to him and his audience. In the wake of the shared set of values, a rationalistic approach has taken centre stage and captured the essence of a descriptive meaning which, while being somewhat in line with Aristotelian precepts, has exuded a rhetorical flavour consonant with the sophisticated character's analysis of ethical questions.

At the end of the day, Tertium Quid's standpoint appears to have been on a par with that of a society inclined to believe that 'you can't do some things with impunity'; hence his claim to impartiality when censuring the Comparini's negativity concerning Pompilia, Guido's "rage and hate" conducive to vengeance, and his wife's recourse to unresponsive authorities before clasping the hand of the chivalric-minded Caponsacchi. Interestingly, the picture of Pompilia's last-ditch contact with a cleric has been adjusted through biblical lenses: in contrast to Eve who had confessed, 'The serpent tempted me and I did eat', Pompilia had aligned herself with the daughters of Eve who would rather say, 'Adam so starved me I was fain to accept the apple any serpent pushed my way'.

Be that as it may, the ambiguity inherent in the evaluation of Pompilia's tale has not altered the unequivocal tone of the narrative. As a matter of fact, the narrator has sounded anxious to keep his distance – witness his statement: "Guido says – that is, always, his friends say – it is unlikely from the wickedness, that any man treat any woman so." On the other hand, he has provided an instance of the 'ambiguity' which linguists have identified with any verbal nuance capable of resolving alternative meanings into one[3]; in this connection, it has been propounded that in point of fact 'ambiguity is an intrinsic, inalienable character of any self-focused message.'[4] By the sound of it, there has been not an iota of ambiguity in Tertium Quid's assertion that, regarding Caponsacchi, "pity of innocence and helplessness" had been the big issue on the carpet. Accordingly, he has urged the 'Prince' to take note of the heart-rending topics and then asked, in the light of the Canon's ability to feel the truth by instinct, "What do you say to it, trying its truth by your own instinct too, since that's to be the expeditious mode?"

As for Guido, the Count has mockingly labelled Pompilia and the Canon a 'pair of saints' and contextually spurned the young woman's allegations of criminal activity on his part as well as the priest's assertion that he had tried "a coward's arms, trick and chicane" and resorted to violence when 'murder was determined, dared and done.'

In connection with the above, Tertium Quid has boomed out, "Highness, decide! Pronounce, Her Excellency!" Nonetheless he has not ruled out the possibility of an ambiguous alternative: "or ... even leave this argument in doubt", he has hesitatingly conceded. Then, pursuing the question about Guido' motives, the considerate observer has consistently reported how commoners had scrutinized the Count's attitude and exclaimed with a chilly smile, 'And never let him henceforth dare to plead his irrepressible wrath at honour's wound! Passion and madness irrepressible? Oh, let us hear no syllable o' the rage!' Conversely, the nobleman's supporters had emphasised how the Church and the Court had been in no doubt about the validity of the pleader's claims: confronted with Guido's contention that his behaviour had been motivated by the loss of his honour and his wife – not to mention the risk to his safety – Religion and Justice had exclaimed in unison, 'Well done, thou good and faithful servant!'

On finding himself faced with polarities, Tertium Quid has reiterated his inclination to steer a middle course by letting the nobility and the clergy have the final say on the Franceschini case. As for the law courts, they had been blessed, in contrast to Guido's groping around in a pall of "smother and smoke", with the blue sky of hindsight; moreover, driven by their dogged determination not 'to miss the advantage of the golden mean', they had come up with a Solomonic sentence. In this regard, the theatrical-minded fellow has been overcome by an irresistible urge to associate the characters in the calamitous Roman play with *Piazza Navona* puppets popping up 'with fresh-tinseled staves to re-engage in one last worst fight more shall show what you thought tragedy was farce'; in this connection, the birth of Gaetano, Pompilia's baby, could be seen as "the strangest accident of all."

At this point, the speaker has pinpointed his modus operandi: "I simply take the facts, ask what they show," he has declared. Suddenly, the mind takes wing and alights on E.A. Poe's 'Valdemar', 'It is now rendered necessary that I give the facts – as far as I comprehend them myself.'[5] It is a short step from the above attitude to the concept that a 'fact has as its structural function that of authenticating the story, not that of making the reader believe that it really happened'[6].

In spite of the high seriousness inherent in the interaction between the cognitive and the real, the Roman murder mystery has intimated the subtext of a *double entendre* and done so when the upper-class narrator, after mentioning the death from pleurisy of the upright officer who had caught up with the fugitive murderers, has commented that "virtue in a chafe should change her linen quick". Arguably, as a parodic/travestying gloss on a hideous event, laughter has come up as a signifier in the narrative.

Tertium Quid has gone on to disclose that another fact analysed by him had been Pompilia's prayer to the Madonna that she would be allowed time to make the truth apparent, truth for God's sake, lest men should believe a lie. Her friends had highlighted the vicissitudes of her married life and seen her survival as 'attestation of her probity'. "Does it strike your Excellency?" the 'man of quality' has wanted to know and without delay confessed to having been struck by Pompilia's perceptibly guilty feelings about her inability to save her partner. People had cried, 'confession of the moribund is true!', and he has raised a question about the nature of the confession: "This public one, or the private one we shall never know? You criticize the drunken reel, fool's speech, maniacal gesture of the man. We grant, but who poured poison in his cup?" The bottom line was that Pompilia had been permitted to safely rejoin her parents' household whereas her husband had been wounded in the soul: there was no denying that "men, plagued this fashion, get to explode this way. It left no other."

At this critical juncture, the would-be impartial observer has tangibly veered in the direction of Guido, in his eyes a guy who, after having vainly availed himself of weapons, wit, common sense and logic, had become "aglow with ire, boiling with irrepressible rage" leading him to deal with his victims in the manner of a furious bull. "Do you blame a bull?" the salon sophist has rhetorically queried. Some sympathisers had roared, 'Here you have the awfulest of crimes for nothing, hell broke loose on a butterfly'. But then again, the villain of the piece was "a mere man – born, bred and brought up in the usual way" – greatly esteemed by the civil as well as by the ecclesiastical authorities; taking the whole lot into account, "what if a tragedy be acted here and innocent Guido with his innocent four be added, all five, to the guilty three?"

The last stage of the monologic performance has corroborated Tertium Quid's sympathetic switch from the Comparini household to Guido Franceschini. Witness the former's statement: "The long and the short is, truth is what I show: undoubtedly no pains ought to be spared to give the mob an inkling of our lights." The aristocratic fellow, it would appear, has dredged up a code of descriptive ethics and associated it with a subtle hint at a class engaged in a quest for truth consonant with a correspondence theory of it: the top-ranking members of society, including himself, deemed truth to be something bound up with fact and consequently providing a clue about the criterion or criteria used by the authorities in order to make room for manoeuvre on the thorny issue of the veracity or falsehood of a statement. The Court might well be prone to inflict torture on the Count as the "readiest way of twisting out the truth", but it would be inhuman to gainsay that a criminal offence, heinous though it might be, did not *per se* justify the resort to torment; furthermore, the accused was a man of high standing and, more importantly, an official declaration of his guilt was not etched in stone. Indeed, what was the sweeping corollary of the twofold premise? It unquestionably was that the cruel practice sanctioned by law ought to be abolished once and for all; surely no fair-minded law courts would conceive of the rack as a means of avoiding the illusion of a mental balance and the enticements of insanity; on that score, *Sua Eccellenza* and *Sua Altezza* were doubtless capable of providing a convincing argument. For all that, should *Sua Eccellenza* be more inclined to join players having a game somewhere else and *Sua Altezza* be anxious to beat a retreat, he would be only too happy to let both go their own way, for he was sure that his speech had helped them see the light about the Franceschini pitch-dark case: "Both know as much about it, now, at least, as all Rome. No particular thanks, I beg", he has stated, and it is tempting to see a carnivalesque hue pervade his closing request, for it has evinced an awkward alliance of young and old as well as a penchant for scot-free murderous deeds. As such, it has left the nature of the speaker open to the question: has he has proved to be a reliable user of discourse? In other words, has Tertium Quid's manipulation of language conferred on him an identity of his own as against that of Half-Rome and the Other Half-Rome? If the premises are that "we know what it is we are talking about, though there is probably no word to be found in the language that is so overdetermined, self-evasive, disfigured and disfiguring as 'language'[7], the conclusion will be that the utterer has been creating his own truth with the help of a metaphorically distorted tongue purportedly grounded in ethics. It can be argued that, as a member of the local community, the high-up gentleman has perceived, unwittingly in tune with Virginia Woolf's 'Orlando', that 'society is the most powerful concoction in the word and society has no existence whatsoever'[8]; in consequence, he has kept his distance by suggesting a different albeit not indifferent truth, and it is worth bearing in mind that, on a similar plane, relativist thinkers have held that what is true in one situation may not be true in another.

An additional conclusion will be that it is essentially a matter of ethics to be associated with the logico-positivist tenet that moral judgments may well fail to bring ethical facts to notice because they are conditioned by the state of mind of a speaker eager to win the hearts and minds of a responsive audience. Keeping this end in view, Tertium Quid has baulked at tackling difficulties arising from ethical issues and consequently steered clear of a clear-cut pertinent judgement. At the end of the day, the only remaining question is whether he has succeeded in his effort "to give the mob an inkling of his lights", and a straight answer may well be that a clear dividing line between the gentleman and the two lower halves of Rome has been provided by the fact that the working-class observers have pursued the truth by consciously using the resources of the spirit, whereas he, an upper-class onlooker, has aimed at objectivity and truth by subconsciously availing himself of the 'letter' which, it has been cogently held, 'can produce all the effects of truth without involving the spirit at all.'[9] Regrettably, the aristocrat's lights have been dimmed by his class prejudice as well as by his yearning for recognition qua a refined Roman citizen ready to make allowance for the grievous wounds in the soul of an Aretine Count, – and here one is reminded of the platonic notion of a *Third Thing* perceivable solely by dint of a contradictory use of reason. A flash of light has nevertheless been provided by Tertium Quid's syllogistic *reductio ad absurdum* in support of the abolition of torture as well as by his parodic/travestying admission that he had failed to make headway. Paradoxically, by virtue of a latent leaning towards the equally failure-prone Franceschini as well as of an obvious hankering for a bond with close-at-hand dignitaries, the high-class sophist appears to have pointed in the direction of a kind of Aristotelian substantial Form capable of giving a measure of consistency to an ambivalent attitude and therefore suggesting the possibility of a way out of a problematic *tertia quidditas*.

1. Jacques Derrida, *Structure, Sign and Play in the Discourse of the Human Sciences*, in *Modern Crticism and Theory*, pp. 118-119

2. *Western Philosophy and Philosophers*, p. 29

3. In *Dictionary of Literary Terms and Literary Theory*, Penguin, 1991, pp. 32-33

4. Roman Jakobson, *Linguistics and Poetics*, in *Modern Criticism and Theory*, p. 49
5. As quoted by Roland Barthes in *Textual Analysis: Poe's 'Valdemar'*, in *Op. Cit.* p. 175
6. Roland Barthes, *Ibid.* p. 179
7. Paul de Man, *The Resistance to Theory*, in *Modern Criticism and Theory*, p. 364
8. Virginia Woolf, *Orlando*, Granada Publishing, 1977, p. 121
9. Jacques Lacan, *The Insistence of the Letter in the Unconscious*, in *Modern Criticism and Theory*, p. 91

COUNT GUIDO FRANCESCHINI

Il Palazzo di Giustizia oozed authority and charm on the strength of symmetrical Baroque and Renaissance motifs enhanced by a massive central balcony surrounded by composite columns and stylish rectangular windows. Inside the spacious main courtroom, mahogany furniture was shot through with colour at variance with sombre streaks running the length of age-old walls. Up in the ceiling, the dignified ensemble was crowned by the goddess Themis holding the pans of a balance in one hand and a dagger in the other above an *amoretto* flanked by cherubs.

Count Guido Franceschini was taken to the palace for being the author of the criminal offence he had committed in Via Paolina. Compelled to face the jury sitting in an austere chamber, he stood aslant, visibly low-spirited, and, on being asked by a member of the panel to take a seat, countered in a mock-sostenuto manner "Thanks, Sir, but, should it please the reverend Court, I feel I can stand somehow, half sit down without help, make shift to even speak, you see, fortified by the sip of ... why, 't is wine, Velletri, – and not vinegar and gall, so changed and good the times grow! Thanks, kind Sir! How cautious and considerate ... aie, aie, aie, not your fault, sweet Sir! Come, you take to heart an ordinary matter. Law is law. Noblemen were exempt, the vulgar thought, from racking, but, since law thinks otherwise, I have been put to the rack. All's over now; much could not happen, I was quick to faint, being past my prime of life and out of health. This getting tortured merely in the flesh amounts to almost an agreeable change. Four years have I been operated on i' the soul, do you see – its tense or tremulous part – my self-respect, my care for a good name: *that*, and not this you now oblige me with, *that* was the Vigil-torment, if you please! What? 'T is my wrist you merely dislocate for the future when you mean me martyrdom?

A trifle of torture to the flesh, like yours, while soul is spared such foretaste of hell-fire, is naught. May it content my lords, the gracious Court, to listen only half so patient-long as I will in that sense profusely speak, and – fie, they shall not call-in screws to help! I killed Pompilia Franceschini, Sirs; killed too the Comparini: husband, wife, who called themselves, by a notorious lie, her father and her mother to ruin me. There's the irregular deed: you want no more than right interpretation of the same, and truth so far – am I to understand?"

A thought-provoking silence pervaded the chamber whilst the presiding judge's eyes focussed on *Justitia* enthroned in the panelled ceiling: was not Truth lying in the goddess's set of scales? Guido followed the rising gaze, gave a nervous cough and recommenced.

"I' the name of the indivisible Trinity! Noble, I recognized my nobler still, the Church, my suzerain – no mock-mistress, she – and now am whealed, one wide wound all of me; my own fault, I am stiffened by my work; my own reward, I help the Court to smile!" The speaker broke into a tight smile himself. "I am representative of a great line, one of the first of the old families in Arezzo, ancientest of Tuscan towns. This struck me: I was poor who should be rich; therefore I must make move forthwith, transfer my stranded self, born fish with gill and fin fit for the deep sea, now left flap bare-backed in slush and sand, – a show to crawlers vile reared of the low tide and aright therein. I asked my fellows, "How came this about?"

'Why, Jack, the suttler's child, perhaps the camp's, went to the wars, fought sturdily, took a town and got rewarded as was natural.'

'Well, let me go, do likewise. War's the word; I'll take my turn, try soldiership.'

'What? You, the eldest son and heir and prop o' the house, so do you see your duty? *Here*'s your post, stand fast, stick tight;

conserve your gods at home!' 'Well then, the quiet course, the contrary trade: the tonsure, and, since heresy's but half-slain, have at Molinos!'

'Have at a fool's head! You a priest? How were marriage possible? There must be Franceschini till time ends – that's your vocation. Make your brothers priests but save one Franceschini for the age! Be not a priest but gird up priesthood's loins, with one foot in Arezzo stride to Rome, spend yourself there and bring the purchase back!'

Abruptly louder, the speaker's voice floated down the spacious room. "Bidden qualify for Rome, I, having a field, went, sold it, laid the sum at Peter's foot, started for Rome, and led the life prescribed. Close to the Church, though clean of it, I assumed three or four orders of no consequence while, for the world's sake, I rode, danced and gamed, quitted me like a courtier, measured mine with whatsoever blade had fame in fence. Prepared for any event, Sirs, I said 'Here wait, do service, – serving and to serve!' A string of nods unfolded in quick succession. "I waited thirty years, may it please the Court, saw meanwhile many a denizen o' the dung hop, skip, jump o'er my shoulder, make him wings and fly aloft, – succeed, in the usual phrase, – while I kept fasts and feasts innumerable, matins and vespers, functions to no end i' the train of Monsignor and Eminence, as gentleman-squire, and for my zeal's reward have rarely missed a place at the table foot except when some Ambassador, or such like, brought his own people. Brief, one day I felt the tick of time inside me, turning-point and slight sense that there was now enough of this: better not press it further, – be content with living and dying only a nobleman. 'The mother must be getting old,' I said; 'the sisters are well wedded away; our name can manage to pass a sister off, at need, and do for dowry: both my brothers thrive – regular priests they are, nor, bat like, 'bide 'twixt flesh and fowl with neither privilege; my spare revenue must keep me and mine. I am tired: Arezzo's air is good to breathe; let me bid hope goodbye, content at home!' "

The reminiscing Count took a deep breath, then exhaled slowly. "Thus, one day, I disbosomed me and bowed. Whereat began the little buzz and thrill o' the gazers round me; each face brightened up: 'How, Sir? So scant of heart and hope indeed? Retire with neither cross nor pile from play just when luck turns and the fine throw sweeps all?' "Whereon protested Paolo, 'Go hang yourselves! Leave him to me. Count Guido and brother of mine, a word in your ear! Take courage since faint heart ne'er won … a fair lady, do n't men say? Count you are counted: still you've coat to back, not cloth of gold and tissue as we hoped, but cloth with sparks and spangles on its frieze from Camp, Court, Church, enough to make a shine, entitle you to carry home a wife with the proper dowry, let the worst betide. Why, it was just a wife you meant to take!'

Now, Paul's advice was weighty; priests should know, and Paul apprised me ere the week was out that Pietro and Violante, the easy pair, had just the daughter and exact the sum to truck for the quality of myself: 'She's young, pretty and rich; you are noble, classic, choice. Is it to be a match?'

"A match," said I.

Done! He proposed all, I accepted all. Will the Court of its charity teach poor me anxious to learn of any way i' the world, allowed by custom and convenience, save this same which, taught from my youth up, I trod? Take me along with you; where was the wrong step? If what I gave in barter, style, and state were worthless, – why, society goes to ground, its rules are idiot's-rambling. Honour of birth, – if that thing has no value, cannot buy something with value of another sort, your social fabric, pinnacle to base, comes down a-clatter like a house of cards. Get honour and keep honour free from flaw, aim at still higher honour, – gabble o' the goose! All my privation and endurance, all love, loyalty and labour dared and did, fiddle-de-dee! – why, doer and darer both, – Count Guido Franceschini had hit the mark far better, spent his life with more effect, as a dancer or a prizer, trades that pay! On the other hand, bid this buffoonery cease, admit that honour is a privilege, the question follows, privilege worth what? Why, worth the market price, – now up, now down, just so with this as with all other ware: therefore essay the market, sell your name, style and condition to who buys them best! This time 'twas my scale quietly kissed the ground, mere rank against mere wealth – some youth beside, some beauty too, thrown into the bargain, just as the buyer likes or lets alone. I thought to deal o' the square; others find fault, it seems: the thing is, those my offer most concerned, Pietro, Violante, cried they fair or foul? What did they make o' the terms?"

Guido crossed his arms and stood akimbo.

"Preposterous terms? Why then accede so promptly, close with such nor take a minute to chaffer? Bargain struck, they straight grew bilious, wished their money back, repented them, no doubt. Why, so did I: I falsified and fabricated, wrote myself down roughly richer than I prove; mere grace, mere coquetry such fraud, I say, a flourish round the figures of a sum for fashion's sake, that deceives nobody. They knew and I knew where the back-bone lurked i' the writhings of the bargain, lords, believe! I paid down all engaged for, to a doit, delivered them just that which, their life long, they hungered in the hearts of them to gain – incorporation with nobility thus in word and deed: for that they gave me wealth. But when they came to try their gain, my gift, quit Rome and head for Arezzo, take the tone o' the new sphere that absorbed the old, why, then, they found that all was vanity, vexation, and what Solomon describes! Poverty and privation for pride's sake proved unendurable to the sobered sots, – one dish at supper and weak wine to boot! And this you admire, you men o' the world, my lords? *This* moves compassion, makes you doubt my faith, if this be other than the daily hap of purblind greed that dog-like still drops bone, grasps shadow, and then howls the case is hard?"

A handkerchief exquisitely embroidered with a tree and a dog jutting out of it for an improbable flight made an appearance and reached the Count's nostrils for a gentle blow. "So much for them so far; now for myself, my profit or loss i' the matter: married am I – there is the law; what sets this law aside in my particular case? My friends submit, 'Guide, guardian, benefactor, – fee, faw, fum, the fact is you are forty-five years old; girls must have boys.' Why, let girls say so then. Come, cards on table! When you chaunt us next a conjugal song full to overflow with praise and glory of white womanhood, – the chaste and pure – troll no such lies o'er lip. No! I shall still think nobler of the sex, believe a woman still may take a man for the short period his soul wears flesh; with a wife I look to find all wifeliness, as when I buy, – timber and twig, – a tree, I buy the song o' the nightingale inside."

A telling smile spread across the musical-minded fellow's lineaments. "Such was the pact: Pompilia from the first broke it, refused from the beginning day either in body or soul to cleave to mine. She found I was a devil and no man, – made common cause with those who found as much, her parents, Pietro and Violante, – moved heaven and earth to the rescue of all three. Say my resentment grew apace: what then? Do you cry out on the marvel? When I find that pure smooth egg which, laid within my nest, could not but hatch a comfort to us all, issues a cockatrice for me and mine, do you stare to see me stamp on it? Swans are soft: is it not clear that she you call my wife, that any wife of any husband, caught whetting a sting like this against his breast, proves a plague prodigy to God and man? I would have rummaged, ransacked at the word those old odd corners of an empty heart for remnants of dim love the long disused, and dusty crumblings of romance! But here we talk of just a marriage, if you please – the everyday conditions and no more. Pompilia was no pigeon, Venus' pet, that shuffled from between her pressing paps to sit on my rough shoulder, – but a hawk I bought at a hawk's price and carried home. I have paid my pound, await my penny's worth, so, hoodwink, starve and properly train my bird, and, should she prove a haggard, – twist her neck! Did I not pay my name and style, my hope and trust, my all? Through spending these amiss I am here! 'T is scarce the gravity of the Court will blame me that I never piped a tune, treated my falcon-gentle like my finch. The obligation I incurred was just to practise mastery, prove my mastership; Pompilia's duty was – submit herself, afford me pleasure, perhaps cure my bile. Am I to teach my lords what marriage means, what God ordains thereby and man fulfils who, docile to the dictate, treads the house? If I was overharsh, – the worse i' the wife who did not win from harshness as she ought, wanted the patience and persuasion, lore of love, should cure me and console herself. Put case that I mishandle, flurry and fright my hawk through clumsiness in sportsmanship, – what, shall she bite and claw to mend the case? And, if you find I pluck five more for that, shall you weep 'How he roughs the turtle there?' "

Another pause ensued, arguably in hopes for a response, but no response came. The disquisition resumed. "Such was the starting. Now of the further step: the couple, father and mother of my wife, returned to Rome, published before my lords, put into print, made circulate far and wide that they had cheated me, who cheated them Pompilia, I supposed their daughter, drew breath first 'mid Rome's worst rankness, through the deed of a drab and a rogue, was bye-blow bastard-babe of a nameless strumpet, passed off, palmed on me as the daughter with the dowry. Daughter? Dirt o' the kennel! Dowry? Dust o' the street! Nought more, nought less, nought else but – oh – ha – assuredly a Franceschini and my very wife!" The alleged victim of deceit gazed piercingly at the jury. "Now, take this charge as you will, for false or true, – this charge, preferred before your very selves who judge me now, – I pray you, adjudge again, classing it with the cheats or with the lies, by which category I suffer most! Whichever point o' the charge might poison most, Pompilia's duty was no doubtful one. You put the protestation in her mouth: 'I should have been remembered and withdrawn from the first o' the natural fury, not flung loose a proverb and a byeword men will mouth at the crossway, in the corner, up and down Rome and Arezzo, – there, full in my face, if my lord, missing them and finding me, content himself with casting his reproach to drop i' the street where such impostors die. Ah, did he do thus, what a friend were he! What grace were his, what gratitude were mine!'

Such protestation should have been my wife's. Looking for this, do I exact too much? Why, here's the, – word for word so much, no more, – avowal she made, her pure spontaneous speech to my brother the Abate at first blush, ere the good impulse had begun to fade.

'Ay, the false letter,' interpose my lords – 'the simulated writing, – 't was a trick: you traced the signs, she merely marked the same, the product was not hers but yours.' "

The alleged letter-writer sniffed at the assertion. "Alack, I want no more impulsion to tell truth from the other trick, the torture inside there! Mine and not hers the letter, – conceded, lords! Impute to me that practice! – take as proved I taught my wife her duty, made her see what it behoved her see and say and do, forced her to take the right step, – I myself marching in mere marital rectitude! And who finds fault here, say the tale be true? It was in the house from the window, at the church from the hassock, – where the theatre lent its lodge, or staging for the public show left space, – that still Pompilia needs must find herself launching her looks forth, letting looks reply, till one day, what is it knocks at my clenched teeth but the cup full, curse-collected all for me? And I must needs drink, drink this gallant's praise, that minion's prayer, the other fop's reproach, and come at the dregs to ... Caponsacchi! Sirs, I, – chin deep in a marsh of misery, struggling to extricate my name and fame and fortune from the marsh would drown them all, – must free me from the attacking lover too! Men say I battled ungracefully enough – was harsh, uncouth and ludicrous beyond the proper part o' the husband: have it so!"

The reputedly Draconian husband ran his smudgy fingers across his shabby shirt. "Tell me: if on that day when I found first that Caponsacchi thought the nearest way to his church was some half-mile round by my door, and that he so admired, shall I suppose, the manner of the swallows' come-and-go between the props o' the window over-head, – that window happening to be my wife's – if I, instead of threatening, talking big, showing hair-powder, a prodigious pinch, for poison in a bottle, – making believe at desperate doings with a bauble-sword, had, with the vulgarest household implement calmly and quietly cut off, clean thro' bone, but one joint of one finger of my wife, saying 'For listening to the serenade here's your ring-finger shorter a full third', why, there had followed a quick sharp scream, some pain, much calling for plaister, damage to the dress, a somewhat sulky countenance next day, perhaps reproaches, – but reflections, too! I don't hear much of harm that Malchus did after the incident of the ear, my lords! Saint Peter took the efficacious way; Malchus was sore but silenced for his life. So, by this time, my true and obedient wife might have been telling beads with a gloved hand; awkward a little at pricking hearts and darts on sampler possibly, but well otherwise: not where Rome shudders now to see her lie. I give that for the course a wise man takes; I took the other however, tried the fool's, the lighter remedy, brandished rapier dread with cork-ball at the tip, boxed Malchus' ear instead of severing the cartilage, called her a terrible nickname and the like and there an end: and what was the end of that? What was the good effect o' the gentle course? Why, one night I went drowsily to bed, dropped asleep suddenly, not suddenly woke, but did wake with rough rousing and loud cry, to find noon in my face, a crowd in my room, fumes in my brain, fire in my throat, my wife gone God knows whither, – rifled vesture-chest, and ransacked money-coffer.

'What does it mean?'

"The servants had been drugged too, stared and yawned, 'It must be that our lady has eloped!'

'Whither and with whom?'

'With whom but the Canon's self? One recognizes Caponsacchi there! 'T is months since their intelligence began, – a comedy the town was privy to, – he wrote and she wrote, she spoke, he replied, and going in and out your house last night was easy work for one … to be plain with you … accustomed to both, at dusk and dawn when you were absent, – at the villa, you know. And presently, bit by bit, the full and true particulars of the tale were volunteered; bit by bit thus made-up mosaic-wise, flat lay my fortune, – tessellated floor, imperishable tracery devils should foot and frolic it on, around my broken gods, over my desecrated hearth. So much for the terrible effect of threatening, Sirs!"

The beleaguered husband released a twisted smile. "Well, this way I was shaken wide awake, doctored and drenched, somewhat unpoisoned so; then, set on horseback and bid seek the lost, floundered thro' day and night, another day and yet another night, and so at last tumbled into the court-yard of an inn and fell on whom I thought to find, even Caponsacchi, – what part was once priest cast to the winds now with the cassocks-rags: in cape and sword, a cavalier confessed, and though the lady, tired, – the tenderer sex, – still lingered in her chamber, – to adjust the limp hair, look for any blush astray, – she would descend in a twinkling, – 'Have you out the horses therefore!' "

The handkerchief reappeared and a barely audible nasal sound followed. "So did I find my wife. Is the case complete? Do your eyes see with mine?"

'Why, that then was the time,' you interpose, 'to take the natural revenge: there and thus 't was requisite to slay the couple, Count!'

"Just so my friends say – 'Kill!' they cry in a breath. Then, when I claim and take revenge, 'So rash?' they cry – 'so little reverence for the law?' "

The posh piece of cloth sank inside the aristocrat's hair-goat cloak. "At first, I called in Law to act and help. Seeing I did so, 'Why, 't is clear,' they cry, 'you shrank from gallant readiness and risk, were coward: the thing's inexplicable else.' Sweet my lords, let the thing be! I fall flat, play the reed, not the oak, to breath of man. Only, inform my ignorance! Say I stand convicted of the having been afraid, proved a poltroon, no lion but a lamb, – does that deprive me of my right of lamb and give my fleece and flesh to the first wolf? Cowardice were misfortune and no crime! I still could recognise no time mature unsanctioned by a move o' the judgment-seat: this is just why I slew nor her nor him, but called in law, law's delegate in the place, and bade arrest the guilty couple, Sirs! Ah, the Court! yes, I come to the Court's self. Law renovates even Lazarus, – cures me! Caesar thou seekest? To Caesar thou shalt go! Caesar's at Rome; to Rome accordingly!" The self-confident assertion synchronised with a click of his fingers. "The case was soon decided: both weights, cast i' the balance, vibrate, neither kicks the beam, here away, there away, this now and now that. To every one o' my grievances law gave redress, could purblind eye but see the point. The wife stood a convicted runagate from house and husband, – driven to such a course by what she somehow took for cruelty, oppression and imperilment of life – not that such things were, but that so they seemed: therefore, the end conceived lawful, – since to save life there's no risk should stay or leap – it follows that all means to the lawful end are lawful likewise, – poison, theft and flight. As for the priest's part, did he meddle or make, enough that he too thought life jeopardized; what did he else but act the precept out, leave, like a provident shepherd, his safe flock to follow the single lamb and strayaway? Best hope so and think so, – that the ticklish time i' the carriage, the tempting privacy, the last somewhat ambiguous accident at the inn, – all may bear explanation: may? then must! The letters, – do they so incriminate? But what if the whole prove a prank o' the pen, flight of the fancy, none of theirs at all, bred of the vapours of my brain belike, or at worst mere exercise of scholar's wit in the courtly Caponsacchi: verse, convict? Did not Catullus write less seemly once? Yet *doctus* and unblemished he abides."

Guido's face grew solemn. "Still, I did righteously in bringing doubts for the law to solve, – take the solution now! Word for word, there's your judgment! Read it, lords, re-utter your deliberate penalty: you mete out punishment such and such, yet so punish the adultery of wife and priest! While I stood rapt away with wonderment, voices broke in upon my mood and muse: 'Do you sleep?' began the friends at either ear, 'the case is settled, – you willed it should be so – none of our counsel, always recollect; with law's award, budge! Back into your place! Leave us to bury the blunder, sweep things smooth!' " The facial solemnity abated. "I was in humble frame of mind, be sure! I bowed, betook me to my place again; station by station I retraced the road, traversed the length of sarcasm in the street, found myself in my horrible house once more, and after a colloquy – no word assists – with the mother and the brothers, stiffened me strait out from head to foot as dead man does, and, thus prepared for life as he for hell, marched to the public Square and met the world. I played the man as I best might, bade friends put non-essentials by and face the fact: Law has pronounced there's punishment, less or more, and I take note o' the fact and use it thus – for the first flaw in the original bond, I claim release. My contract was to wed the daughter of Pietro and Violante. Both protest they never had a child at all. Then I never made a contract: good! Cancel me quick the thing pretended one. You shall not laugh me out of faith in law! I listen, through all your noise, to Rome!'"

The Aretine citizen, avowedly respectful of the Roman law, took a deep breath and carried on his speech act.

"Rome spoke. In three months, letters admonished me: 'Your plan for the divorce is all mistake. It would hold, now, had you, taking thought to wed Rachel of the blue eye and golden hair, found swarth-skinned Leah cumber couch next day: but Rachael, blue-eyed golden-haired aright, proving to be only Laban's child, not Lot's, remains yours all the same for ever more; you did the wrong and have to answer it. As for the circumstance of imprisonment, never fear, that point is considered too! The convent-quiet preyed upon her health, she is transferred now to her parents' house; do not afflict your brains with trifles now. You have still three suits to manage, all and each ruinous truly should the event play false. It is indeed the likelier so to do, that Brother Paul, your single prop and stay, after a vain attempt to bring the Pope to set aside procedures, sit himself and summarily use prerogative, afford us the infallible finger's tact to disentwine your state of affairs. Paul, – finding it moreover past his strength to stem the irruption, bear Rome's ridicule of ... since friends must speak ... to be round with you ... of the old outwitted husband, wronged and wroth, pitted against a brace of juveniles: a brisk priest who is versed in Ovid's art more than his Summa, and a gamesome wife able to act Corinna without book, beside the waggish parents who played dupes, – Paul, finally, in such a state of things, after a brief temptation to go jump and join the fishes in the Tiber, drowns sorrow another and a wiser way: house and goods, he has sold all off, is gone, leaves Rome, whether for France or Spain – who knows? – or Britain almost divided from our orb. You have lost him anyhow.'

The deserted brother's voice and features filled with dusky shadows. "Now, – I see my lords shift in their seat, – would I could do the same!" He engaged in a make-believe attempt to shake his legs. "When I sought home with such news, mounted stair and sat a last in the sombre gallery, as I supped, ate the coarse bread, drank the wine weak once, now acrid with the toad's-head-squeeze, my wife's bestowment, – I broke silence thus: 'Let me, a man, manfully meet the fact, confront the worst o' the truth, end, and have peace! I am irremediably beaten here, the gross illiterate vulgar couple, – bah! Why, they have measured forces, mastered mine, made me their spoil and prey from first to last. They have got my name, – 't is nailed now fast to theirs, the child or changeling is anyway my wife. They gain all, and I lose all – even to the lure that led to loss, – they have the wealth again they hazarded awhile to hook me with, have caught the fish and find the bait entire: they even have their child or changeling back to trade with, turn to account a second time. Well, are we demigods or merely clay? Is this, we live on, heaven and the final state, or earth which means probation to the end? Why claim escape from man's predestined lot of being beaten and baffled? – God's decree, in which I, bowing bruised head, acquiesce.' " He stood motionless, his head bowed in submission. "And I believe t' was in no unmeet match for the stoic mood, with something like a smile, that, when morose December roused me next, I took into my hand, broke seal to read the new epistle from Rome. 'All to no use! Whate'er the turn next injury take,' smiled I, 'here's one has chosen his part and knows his cue. Is the parentage of my wife demonstrated infamous to her wish? Parades she now loosed of the cincture that so irked the loin? Has the priest, with nobody to court beside, courted the Muse in exile, hitched my hap into a rattling ballad-rhyme which, bawled at tavern- doors, wakes rapture everywhere? My brothers are priests, and childless so; that's well – and, thank God most for this, no child leave I – none after me to bear till his heart break the being a Franceschini and my son!'

'Nay,' said the letter, 'but you have just that! A babe, your veritable son and heir, and he's already hidden away and safe from any claim on him you mean to make.' "

The avowedly childless aristocrat stared defiantly at the Lords "Then I rose up like fire, and fire-like I roared. There's to be my representative, another of the name shall keep displayed the flag with the ordure on it, brandish still the broken sword has served to stir a jakes? Who will he be, how will you call the man but a Caponsacchi? Oh, be very sure! Or say, by some mad miracle of chance, is he indeed my flesh and blood, this babe? Was it because fate forged a link at last betwixt my wife and me, and both alike found we had henceforth some one thing to love, the child I had died to see though in a dream, the child I was bid strike out for, beat the wave and baffle the tide of troubles where I swam? Rather be the town-talk true, Square's jest, street's jeer true, my own inmost heart's confession true, and he's the priest's bastard and none of mine! This bastard then, a nest for him is made, as the manner is of vermin, in my flesh – shall I let the filthy pest buzz, flap and sting, busy at my vitals, and nor hand nor foot lift, but let be, lie still and rot resigned? No, I appeal to God, – what says Himself, how lessons Nature when I look to learn? Why, that I am alive, am still a man with brain and heart and tongue and right- hand too. No more of law; a voice beyond the law enters my heart: 'Who is on the Lord's side?'"

The self-proclaimed heavenly-and-earthly inspired nobleman hastened to labour the point by providing details about the *fons et origo* of the judicial summons and his presence in court. "Myself, in my own Vittiano, told the tale to my own serving-people summoned there. I fixed on the first whose eyes caught mine, some four, resolute youngsters with the heart still fresh, took whatsoever weapon came to hand, and out we flung and on we ran or reeled Romeward. I have no memory of our way; only that, when at intervals the cloud of horror about me opened to let in life, I listened to some song in the ear, some snatch of a legend, relic of religion, stray fragment of record very strong and old of the first conscience, the anterior right, the God's-gift to mankind, impulse to quench the antagonistic spark of hell and tread Satan and all his malice into dust, declare to the world the one law: right is right. Then the cloud re-encompassed me, and so

I found myself, as on the wings of winds, arrived: I was at Rome on Christmas Eve."

The narrator narrowed his eyes: was he attempting to recapture the peculiar atmosphere of the place and the time? "Festive bells – everywhere the Feast o' the Babe, joy upon earth, peace and goodwill to man! I am baptized. I started and let drop the dagger. 'Where is it, His promised peace?' Nine days o' the Birth-Feast did I pause and pray to enter into no temptation more; I stopped my ears even to the inner call of the dread duty, heard only the song *Peace upon Earth*, saw nothing but the face o' the Holy Infant and the halo there. But, day by day, joy waned and withered off: the Babe's face, premature with peak and pine, sank into wrinkled ruinous old age, suffering and death, then mist-like disappeared and showed only the Cross at end of all." The avenger's pupils dilated. "On the ninth day, this grew too much for man. I started up – 'Some end must be!' At once, silence; then, scratching like a death-watch tick, slowly within my brain was syllabled, 'One more concession, one decisive way and but one, to determine thee the truth. Now doubt, anon decide, thereupon act!' And so, all yet uncertain save the will to do and the daring aught save leave right undone, I did find myself at last i' the dark before the villa with my friends, and made the experiment, the final test, ultimate chance that ever was to be for the wretchedness inside. I knocked – pronounced the name, the predetermined touch for truth, 'What welcome for the wanderer? Open straight …' to the friend, physician, friar upon his rounds, traveller belated, beggar lame and blind? – no, but … 'to Caponsacchi!' And the door opened."

The blow-by-blow account reached a crescendo. "And then, – why, even then, I think, i' the minute that confirmed my worst of fears, had but Pompilia's self, – the tender thing who once was good and pure, was once my lamb, – fronted me in the door-way, stood there faint with the recent pang, perhaps, of giving birth to what might, though by miracle, seem my child, – nay more, I will say, had even the aged fool Pietro, the dotard, in whom folly and age wrought, more than enmity or malevolence, to practice and conspire against my peace, – had either of these but opened, I had paused. But it was she the hag, she that brought hell for a dowry with her to her husband's house, she the mock-mother, she that made the match and married me to perdition, spring and source o' the fire inside me that boiled up from heart to brain and hailed the Fury gave it birth, – Violante Comparini, she it was, with the old grin amid the wrinkles yet, opened: as if in turning from the Cross, with trust to keep the sight and save my soul, I had stumbled, first thing, on the serpent's head coiled with a leer at foot of it. *There* was the end! Then I was rapt away by the impulse, one immeasurable everlasting wave of a need to abolish the detested life. 'T was done: you know the rest and how the folds o' the thing, twisting for help, involved the other two more or less serpent-like; how I was mad, blind, stamped on all, the earthworms with the asp."

The self-professed slayer made eye-contact with the judges. "Twenty miles off, sound-sleeping as a child on a cloak i' the straw which promised shelter first, I was my own self, had my sense again, my soul safe from the serpents; I could sleep. Old Pietro, old Violante, side by side at the church Lorenzo, oh, they know it well! So do I. But my wife is still alive, – her breath enough to tell her story yet, her way, which is not mine, no doubt at all. And Caponsacchi, – you have summoned him, – well, he too tells his story, – florid prose as smooth as mine is rough. You see, my lords, the trial is no concern of mine; with me the main of the care is over: I at least recognise who took that huge burthen off, let me begin to live again. I did God's bidding and man's duty, so, breathe free. I am myself and whole now: I prove cured and taking to our common life once more. The willingness to live, what means it else? Clearly my life was valueless, but now I find the instinct bids me save my life; my wits, too, rally round me; I pick up and use the arms that strewed the ground before, unnoticed or spurned aside: I take my stand, make my defence. God shall not lose a life may do Him further service, while I speak and you hear, you my judges and last hope! You are the law: 't is to the law I look. Here, then, I clutch my judges, – I claim law – cry, on what point is it, where either accuse, I fail to furnish you defence? I stand acquitted, actually or virtually, by every intermediate kind of court that takes account of right or wrong in man, each unit in the series that begins with God's throne, ends with the tribunal here. God breathes, not speaks, his verdicts, felt not heard, – till last come human jurists, solidify fluid result: what's fixable lies forged, statute; the residue escapes in fume, yet hangs aloft, a cloud, as palpable to the finer sense as word the legist welds. Look on it by the light reflected thence! What has Society to charge me with? I am Guido Franceschini, am I not? You know the courses I was free to take? I took just that which let me serve the Church, I gave it all my labour in body and soul: so far, there's my acquittal, I suppose. Then comes the marriage itself – no question, lords, of the entire validity of that! Well, let me have the benefit, just so far, o' the fact announced: my wife then is my wife; I have allowance for a husband's right. I am charged with passing right's due bound, – such acts as I thought just, my wife called cruelty, complained of in due form, – convoked no court of common gossipry, but took her wrongs to the Archbishop and the Governor. These heard her charge with my reply and found *that* futile, *this* sufficient: they dismissed the hysteric querulous rebel, and confirmed Authority in its wholesome exercise, they, with directness access to the facts. Do you blast your predecessors? What forbids posterity to trebly blast yourselves who set the example and instruct their tongue? Look to it, – or allow me freed so far!"

Like a wheel rolling down a slope, the plea for liberty gathered momentum. "The wife, you allow so far, I have not wronged, has fled my roof, plundered me and decamped in company with the priest her paramour: and I gave chase, came up with, caught the two at the wayside inn where both had spent the night.

The fault was furtive then that's flagrant now, their intercourse a long-established crime. I did not take the license law's self gives to slay both criminals o' the spot at the time, but held my hand, – preferred play prodigy of patience which the world calls cowardice, rather than seem anticipate the law: so, to your bar I brought both criminals, only contending that the deeds avowed would take another colour and bear excuse. You disregard the excuse, you breathe away the colour of innocence and leave guilt black. True, punishment has been inadequate – 't is not I only, not my friends that joke, my foes that jeer, who echo 'inadequate' for, by a chance that comes to help for once, the same case was judged at Arezzo, in the province of the Court where the crime had beginning but not end. What was it they adjudged as penalty to Pompilia, – the one criminal o' the pair amenable to their judgment, not the priest who is Rome's? Why, just imprisonment for life i' the Stinche. There was Tuscany's award to a wife that robs her husband: you at Rome give gentle sequestration for a month in a manageable Convent, then release. I acquiesce for my part, – punished, though by a pin-point scratch, means guilty; guilty means: what have I been but innocent hitherto? Anyhow, here the offence, being punished, ends."

A big question mark formed on Guido's brow.

"Ends? – for you deemed so, did you not, sweet lords? Well then, – what if I, at this last of all, demonstrate you, as my whole pleading proves, no particle of wrong received thereby one atom of right? – that cure grew worse disease? All along you have nipped away just inch by inch the creeping climbing length of plague breaking my tree of life from root to branch, and left me, after all and every act of your interference, – lightened of what load? At liberty wherein? Mere words and wind! *There* was the reptile that feigned death at first: its aim is now to evoke life from death, make me anew, satisfy in my son the hunger I may feed but never sate, – my son whom, dead, I shall know, understand, feel, hear, see, never more escape the sight … fashioned of soul as featured like in face, first taught to laugh and lisp and stand and go by that thief, poisoner and adulteress I call Pompilia, – he calls ... sacred name, be unpronounced, be unpolluted here! – and last led up to the glory and prize of hate by his foster-father, Caponsacchi's self, the perjured priest, pink of conspirators, tricksters and knaves, yet polished, superfine, manhood to model adolescence by ..."

Then and there Count Guido Franceschini sounded like a man stuck between a rock and a hard place. "Lords, look on me, declare when what I show is nothing more nor less than what you deemed and doled me out for justice. What did you say? Will you not thank, praise, bid me to your breasts for having done the thing you thought to do, and thoroughly trampled out sin's life at last? Absolve, then, me, law's mere executant! Protect your own defender, – save me, Sirs! Give me my life, give me my liberty, my good name and my civic rights again!"

The appeal reached fever pitch. "It would be too fond, too complacent play into the hands o' the devil, should we lose the game here, I for God: a soldier-bee that yields his life, exenterate with the stroke o' the sting that saves the hive. I need that life! For, first thing, there's the mother's age to help – let her come break her heart upon my breast, not on the blank stone of my nameless tomb! The fugitive brother has to be bidden back to the old routine, repugnant to the tread, of daily suit and service to the Church, ay, and the spirit-broken youth at home, the awe-struck alter-ministrant, shall make amends for faith now palsied at the source. Give me – for last, best gift, my son again, whom law makes mine, – I take him at your word, mine be he, by miraculous mercy, lords! Let me lift up his youth and innocence to purify my palace, room by room purged of the memories, lend from his bright brow light to the old proud paladin my sire! Then may we, – strong from that rekindled smile, – go forward, face new times, the better day. And when, in times made better through your brave decision now, – might but Utopia be! – Rome rife with honest women and strong men, manners reformed, old habits back once more, customs that recognize the standard worth, – the wholesome household rule in force again, husbands once more God's representative, wives like the typical Spouse once more, and Priests no longer men of Belial, with no aim at leading silly women captive, but of rising to such duties as yours now, – then will I set my son at my right hand and tell his father's story to this point, adding 'The task seemed superhuman; still I dared and did it, trusting God and Law, and they approved of me. Give praise to both!' And if, for answer, he shall stoop to kiss my hand and peradventure start thereat, – I engage to smile 'That was an accident i' the necessary process, – just a trip o' the torture irons in their search for truth, – hardly misfortune, and no fault at all.'"

It was the last flare in the Count's pyrotechnic display. The artificer regained his seat with a bittersweet smile. The ecclesial judges gazed at him with an air of finality and sedately filed out. Silence fell, in sync with the shadows of a parky early January day quietly drawing to a close.

"Thanks, Sir, but, should it please the reverend Court, I feel I can stand somehow, half sit down without help, make shift to even speak, you see. Not your fault, sweet Sir! Come, you take to heart an ordinary matter. Law is law."

Guido Franceschini's resistance on the strength of a good dose of Velletri wine coupled with a burning desire to escape death has sounded consonant with the contention that 'power, or our capacity to act on others, is ... an ineluctable social fact.'[1] Indeed, the Count has been induced to follow the follow the line of least resistance by a legal authority endowed with social leverage: in the teeth of his noblesse, torture on the rack had been inexorably applied to him. On the other hand, the excruciating method was nothing new under the Italian sun: official records showed that the rack had been a common-or-garden tool in imperial Rome at the expense of slaves under a cloud, but then low-grade freemen as well as upper-class citizens had found it harder and harder to escape extreme physical suffering when charged with heinous crimes. In the Middle Ages some *supplizio* or other had been instrumental in applying the law; even the Holy Inquisition had resorted to extremity in order to retrieve truth and, more *ad hominem*, ensure the salvation of a heretic soul.

At the time of Guido Franceschini's heinous achievement, a couple of pain-inflicting procedures had been sanctioned by the powers that be: one of the two, graphically termed *strappado* in the Spanish manner, consisted in trussing up the victim's hands with a cord at the back of the naked body, then hoisting the limbs and letting the body fall at an aptly chosen point, with the likely result that the arms and/or the shoulders were dislocated. Weights were frequent extras with a view to intensifying the pain. The other modus operandi, aptly called *veglia*, entailed the deprivation of sleep for an unconscionable period of time; whether on its own or combined with the *strappado*, the enforced wakefulness would open the ominous gate of Hell.

In the case against Guido, the authorities had deemed the recourse to torture to be a sine qua non for justice and, in consequence, the Count had been beaten fair and square by a thin rope in full swing; unsurprisingly, he had promptly fainted. In the wake of the efficacious treatment, the noble victim had been taken to the awe-inspiring *Palazzo di Giustizia*.

Standing round-shouldered and sunken-eyed in front of a reverend jury, Guido has begun his testimony by paying homage to the Velletri wine as a sort of *Aqua Vitae* and stating that after being "operated on i' the soul" by his wife Pompilia, her parents, her paramour Caponsacchi and his own fellow citizens, for good measure, he had come to feel that "a trifle of torture to the flesh … while soul is spared such foretaste of hell fire, is naught". Significantly, his assertion calls to mind Sigmund Freud's contention that the soul constitutes the immaterial part of a human being and has to be seen as an entity that, although intangible, exercises a powerful influence on our lives; in fact, it makes us human'[2]. In this connection, it is tempting, in the light of Immanuel Kant's weltanschauung, to think of Guido as a self-declared unified subject entering the realm of metaphysics and claiming to have *a priori* knowledge of the soul.

Taking the whole caboodle into account, it makes sense to temporarily put the religious overtones of the Count's statement in the shade and highlight instead the notion that his utterances have reawakened the old question of mind/body dualism to which they have tried to give an answer on the strength of qualities that provide relief from bodily pain and allow a 'growth of the mind' (as celebrated by William Wordsworth in Romantic times) by one's bootstraps. The noble convict's relevant endeavour has been aided by his belief that the time had come to explain the whys and wherefores of his behaviour; hence his emphatic request to the "gracious Court" to examine his 'irregular deed' in great depth with a view to ascertaining the true facts. "Now for truth!" the detainee has exclaimed, and the impassioned cry has evoked the attitude adopted by Robert Browning qua a poet intrigued by 'the utterance of large and noble truths by the lips of mean and grotesque human beings'[3]. On the other hand, a scrutiny of the Count's oral speech as part of a text[4] may well lead to the conclusion that his demand for truth has implied the use of a metalinguistic code and thus posed an enigma endowed with the quality of an aperitif. The remaining question is whether Guido, as a careful user of words, has employed a sound rhetorical code; in other words, has he been making good use of reason as something of paramount importance for the discovery of truth? Or has his 'growing' mind thwarted the ambition of his 'tortured' soul? It makes sense to assume that an attempt at dialogue has been the name of the game and, as speech act, tentatively made room for positive feedback. Equally significant has been Guido's admission that he, the "representative of a great line", had been under the sway of the Church, – "no mock-mistress, she", – and simultaneously engaged in riding, dancing and gaming in the hope of pleasing the world. Last but not least, he had proved himself subtle enough to understand a joke and taken turns to speak in courteous jest.

At this point, it can reasonably be posited that the image of Guido's selfhood conveys not solely the traits of a latter-day Renaissance character possessed of microcosmic qualities but also the make-up of a modern pragmatist keen on making a validity claim on the basis of social values and beliefs strong enough to cope with a demanding system. On the other hand, the claimant in question could arguably be seen as a peculiar specimen of 'modernity' hankering for a practical truth a long way down the ethical scale and consequently confusing the meaning of 'true' with the criteria that ought to be used when laying claim to the concept at issue. By the same token a recourse to descriptive ethics in lieu of ethics proper has prevented the 'modernist' Guido from reaching satisfactory socio-ethical conclusions – hardly a surprise in view of the fact that he has held a relativistic view of the true and the good.

It ought to be added that the Count's monologue has been enlivened by details about the vicissitudes of his courting life: the judges have been fully apprised of how, after thirty years of service at the feet of *Monsignor* this and *Eminenza* that, he had "felt the tick of time" inside himself and known in his bones that he had "better not press it further, be content with living and dying only a nobleman." For all that, under pressure from the counselling Paolo, he had come to relish the prospect of marrying a young woman blessed with a substantial dowry. "Where was the wrong step?" he has asked the reverend jury; indeed, if the style and state he had given in barter were valueless, well, the "social fabric, pinnacle to base", would fall to the ground, clattering like a house of card."

At this critical juncture, Guido's performatory act appears to have taken a sociological turn; interestingly, his *modus cogitandi* brings to mind Virginia Woolf's *Orlando*'s contention that 'at one and the same time ... society is everything and society is nothing.'[4] In addition, the Aretine speaker has rhetorically made use of metaphor, reinforced by simile, with the aim of provoking an interpretive response from his select audience, and he has put the finishing touches to the picture by ironically descanting on the concept of honour as a privilege "worth the market price, – now up, now down". The demands of the socio-economic market, he has let the judges know, had induced him to weigh "mere rank against mere wealth; some youth beside, some beauty too, thrown into the bargain just as the buyer likes or lets alone"; hence his falling back on falsification and fabrication, notably when compelled to declare his income. But then again, it had all been "mere grace, mere coquetry" in his eyes and nobody had been deceived; in point of fact the ethical balancing act had been upset by the Comparini couple by dint of resorting to shenanigans after joining the smart set and discovering that "all was vanity, vexation, and what Solomon describes".

In connection with the disturbance in the realm of ethics, Guido has denounced the "purblind greed that dog-like still drops bone, grasps shadow, and then owls the case is hard" – an attitude markedly divergent from his own, for whenever he had bought a tree, he had been keen on purchasing "the song o' the nightingale inside." Unfortunately, as far as Pompilia was concerned, the bird had failed to sing.

Sometime later, the likewise blue-bloodied Alec D'Urberville, exasperated with the shillyshallying of Tess, a 'pure woman' evocative of Pompilia's qualities, told her, 'What am I, to be repulsed so by a mere chit like you? For near three mortal months have you trifled with my feelings, eluded me, and snubbed me; and I won't stand it!'[5]

Regrettably, the undulating quality of Guido's speech act has left the question of the veracity of his allegations hanging in the balance: it was at heart a matter of 'how to do things with words'.[6] In truth, the prisoner has done his utmost to hoodwink his captors by engaging in smooth talk and exploring a peculiarly rhetorical avenue in the hope that the significance of both would be properly appreciated; he has even seen himself as the owner of a personal meaning while using a language hopefully conducive to the detection of truth. The mind shifts back to the Renaissance philosopher Paracelsus warning Festus that 'there is an inmost centre in us all, where truth abides in fulness; and around wall upon wall, the gross flesh hems it in. A baffling and perverting carnal mesh blinds it and makes all error.'[7] As a self-styled truth-seeker, Guido has owned up to being economical with the truth about his personal finances as well as inclined to look on marriage as a provider of wifeliness; conversely, his spouse had been playing a conventional feminine role in her quest for love, 'a little word whereof we have not heard one syllable', people were reported to have said.

In this respect it bears fruit to consider how Browning has focused on the picture of the apostle John on the brink of death in a desert cave and reflecting that 'truth, deadened of its absolute blaze, might need love's eye to pierce the o'erstretched doubt.'[8] Unwittingly in tune with Christ's disciple, Guido has declared to be eager for a wholesale marriage agreement just as when he bought a tree he bought the "song o' the nightingale inside'. Regrettably, his ardour had been dampened by the fact that the bird he had secured and taken home, far from being the intended "pigeon, Venus' pet", was a "hawk". Well then, what the frustrated husband has subsequently disclosed in court has brought to the fore a fellow inclined to view marriage as a commodity exchange between man and wife, the latter being morally obliged to give pleasure to the former and submit to his "practice mastery" in compliance with God's will. Admittedly, the purchaser of the hawk may have clumsily mishandled his newly gained property, but then again, was the mismatched bird of prey entitled to "bite and claw to mend the case"? Not for the world! Pompilia ought to have fought against her parents' dislike of her and duly acknowledge that her husband had bravely refused "to become partner with the pair". Granted, she had gone as far as to make Brother Paolo privy to her appreciation of Guido's modus operandi, but her ambivalent impulse had gradually faded. In this connection it helps to recall the growing unease which G. K. Chesterton has identified as one of the motifs that go into making *The Ring and the Book* different from a common-or-garden detective story: 'The whole object of the poem is to show what infinities of spiritual good and evil a current and sordid story may contain.'[9]

A chartaceous bone of contention has been duly provided by the letters allegedly sent by Pompilia to Caponsacchi: her husband has lashed at the correspondence qua being indicative of an ongoing love affair; at the same time, confronted with the accusation that he had traced the signs and his wife merely marked them, he has rejoined that any forged writing on his part might well be justified by the need to teach Pompilia her duty and help her to "see what it behoved her see and say and do": honest to God, he had been "marching in mere marital rectitude!" The ensuing rhetorical question, "And who finds fault here, say the tale be true?" has replaced ambiguity with a parameter of straight ethical standards and on the strength of it has had a knock-on emancipatory effect on the truth which, as a truth-seeker, Guido may well have deemed to be the correspondence of a statement to a situation.

In this regard it is apropos to recall Browning's assertion in the Prologue that "there's nothing in nor out o' the world good except truth"; for his part, he has poetically mixed truth with "something else" and in the end found himself asking, "what's this then, which proves good yet seems untrue?" Without further delay, he has raised the question whether "fiction which makes fact alive is fact too" and in so doing has let the unconscious come out into the open and fulfil a major poetic function.

As for Guido, it is quite conceivable that he has espoused the cause of truth by killing the *spirit* and cottoning to the *letter* as a surrogate for it. If that is the case, he, too, has in all likelihood been urged by the unconscious, – namely by something that, according to a psychoanalytic insight, is structured like a language and therefore contains the letter.[10] On the other hand, he has consciously hinted at a "cup full of bitterness", – redolent, by the way, of the vessel Christ begged his Father to take away from him. Also, Guido has lamented that he was "chin deep in a marsh of misery" just when the feelings experienced by Pompilia and Caponsacchi were blossoming into romantic love. By the same token, the Argus-eyed husband has ironically expressed his appreciation of Caponsacchi's discovery that Pompilia's abode was on the shortest route to his church. And what had the outcome of the detection been? Little more than his awakening with fumes in the brain coupled with fire in the throat and the news that his wife had eloped with the priest. A frantic pursuit of the fugitive couple in the name of morality had led to the sight of Caponsacchi strolling across the courtyard of an inn, "in cape and sword a cavalier confessed", and of his wife scurrying out of her chamber and pleading for a horse.

Qua a 'speech actor', the chasing husband has cottoned to an 'emotive' as well as 'referential' language and made the 'conative' effort of an addresser aiming to act on the addressee. "Is the case complete? Do your eyes here see with mine?" he has asked the jury, thus adding a 'phatic', to use linguistic jargon[11], colour to his question: it is reasonable to think of a speaker eager for interaction and anxious about the impact of his words upon the hearers.

Associated with the above, there has followed the denunciation of the ambivalent attitude adopted by friends towards Guido's murder and then the beating of the drum for Pompilia, in his eyes a lamb resigned to surrendering himself to the wolf: the follow-on had been his bowing to the inevitable and an official censure for the mistiming of his legal action. "Cowardice were misfortune and no crime!" the rebuked plaintiff has rejoined before unwittingly echoing the Preacher's dictum that 'there is a time to keep silence, and a time to speak'. "There's the riddle solved", he has confidently concluded.

Solved forsooth! Arguably operating in the fashion of an Aristotelian 'man of substance', the Count has claimed autonomy when his law-abiding conduct was the issue. While openly talking about his deed and endeavouring to explain the meaning of it, he has striven to avoid individual involvement and, as it were, universalize himself. But then, was he aware that any success in his attempt would largely depend on his being engaged in an act of effective communication? And if he was, did he at some point suspect that the meaning of his utterances, far from being the upshot of a shared system of sense-making notions, would ultimately be determined by the Court's ideological inclinations? Indeed, such leanings would be liable to hinder the judges' comprehension of his 'speech act' and consequently prevent him from creating the conditions necessary for a rightful decision on the validity of his claims.

Guido's ensuing legal step has led him to press charges over an exchange of missives between Pompilia and Giuseppe Caponsacchi. He has, however, conceded that the amorous correspondence could be no more than "a prank o' the pen, flight of the fancy ... or at worst mere exercise of scholar's wit in the courtly Caponsacchi". Come to think of it, had not Catullus written "less seemly once"? For all that, the poet was still regarded as *doctus* and unblemished!

In this respect it does appear that the Count has been prompted to lodge an appeal by his gut attitude towards truth, and the propensity has left the real nature of his concern open to question: his relativism and emotivism have come to the fore and suggested no absolute ground of truth. In the above-mentioned *Orlando*, Purity, Chastity and Modesty try to solve the riddle: 'Truth, come not out from your horrid den. Hide deeper, fearful

Truth, for you flaunt in the brutal gaze of the sun things that were better unknown and undone; you unveil the shameful, the dark you make clear. Hide! Hide! Hide!'[12] The three Sisters' command has conceivably hit the nail on the head, yet a picture of Guido as a character mainly concerned with the nature of truth would be satisfactory only by virtue of a *reductio ad absurdum*, for he was a post-Renaissance aristocrat articulating his onlook on life on the strength of borrowed ethical and metaphysical tenets which have seemingly anticipated the logical positivist contention that a proposition has meaning whenever sense experience is sufficient to decide its truth. To put it another way, the Count's sense experience has proved to be deep enough to justify a view of him as a narcissist erecting obstacles on the road to truth; for the same reasons, his language-structured unconscious has harboured a recognition of desire bound up with a desire for recognition. In the final analysis, it is arguable that this human being's divided Self has repressed his unconscious drive, thus heralding a conscious inability to find the truth and pass it on to fellow humans. In linguistic parlance, the monologist under scrutiny has made good use of *parole*, namely the actual utterance of his native tongue, yet he has failed to attain *langue*, i.e. the totality of language shared by a collective consciousness.[13] Interestingly, he has disclosed a primitivistic streak when he has talked of himself as a human being covered with "sores o' the soul and not the body"; at the same time he has shown signs of a Cartesian dualism of sorts, and it is not difficult to understand why he has expressed his confidence in a divine Nature as well as in a human Law capable of bringing Lazarus back to life and therefore of restoring him to good health. In effect, the seriousness of his latest assertion has shifted the discourse from a positive to a natural religion, and it has done so notably when he has denounced the covert irony of a conciliatory approach to Pompilia's "poison, theft and flight", namely to deeds manifestly inherent in her Machiavellian notion of means justified by a legitimate purpose. In the same vein, he has approved of the priest's "colour charity" as shown by his leaving, "like a provident shepherd, his safe flock to follow the single lamb and strayaway". Then he has poignantly recalled how he had retraced his steps homewards and found himself in his "horrible house once more … marched to the public Square and met the world." His return evokes memories of Homer's *nostos*, i.e. the motif permeating Ulysses' voyage back to Ithaca. For good measure, the home-comer has evinced a juridical frame of mind when he has demanded release from the marital bond in default of a proper contract and, in consequence, reiterated his faith in law, – to little avail though, for in the eyes of Rome his plea would have had a solid basis solely if he, 'taking thought to wed Rachel of the blue eye and golden hair' had instead 'found swarth-skinned Leah cumber couch'. In reality, no Leah had replaced Rachel and, as a consequence, Pompilia was still his legitimate spouse.

While on the subject of legal niceties, it seems fair to take account of the contention that nobody can 'choose the imaginary, the semiotic, the carnival as an alternative to the symbolic, as an alternative to the law; it is set up by the law precisely as its own ludic space, its own area of imaginary alternative, but not as a symbolic alternative.'[14] It seems equally fair to postulate that at this juncture Guido's legal-minded ego has been replaced by a Calvinistic *alter ego* in whose eyes the newly experienced events had been an epiphany of God's will and as such had made him wonder while staying with his family, "Is this, we live on, heaven and the final state, or earth which means probation to the end? Why claim escape from man's predestinate lot of being beaten and baffled?" It was, he has added, "God's decree, in which I, bowing bruised head, acquiesce."

The string of utterances has connoted the plight of a man desperate to find antidotes to a substance liable to poison his moral fibre. But then, his noble line would terminate with his demise and therefore prevent further ominous happenings of the kind. It would and no mistake! Guido's reappraisal has sounded like the speech act of a character in a psychodrama, and, in the light of latter-day linguistic apperceptions, it makes sense to wonder how his articulation might, qua a 'perlocutionary' act, affect a jury concerned with justice as well as truth and consequently inclined, presumably in accordance with an Aristotelian view of human nature, to resist anger, envy, and pity as feelings likely to blur the difference between right and wrong. On the one hand, it is not difficult to detect a streak of candour in a human being hoping against hope that "by some miracle of chance" the newborn baby was indeed his flesh and blood, – that is, the infant he would have "died to see though in a dream"; on the other hand, a dichotomy appears to have torn him apart: "He's the priest's bastard and none of mine!" he has burst out and soon after, desperate for a unifying fatherhood, his Ego has appealed to a providential God and to an oracular Nature, thus adopting an attitude fortuitously consonant with the ethical-minded Spinoza's theory that a love of God entails a grasp of human nature and the universe.

It ought to be added that the plea of the aspiring father has sounded like the expression of a 'primitivist' endowed with "brain and heart and tongue and right-hand too; nay, even with friends in such a cause as this"; also, it has suggested the mind of a morally lethargic man suddenly galvanized by an impulse of life. Amazingly, the Count's primitivist frame has materialised anew whilst he was galloping towards Rome: Guido has recounted how a cloud of horror had lifted and he had "listened to some song in the ear, some snatch of a legend, relic of religion, stray fragment of record very strong and old of the first conscience, the anterior right." Then, in sharp contrast to the previous image of a Holy Infant and a halo around his head, he had watched a face prematurely sunk "into wrinkled ruinous old age, suffering and death" before vanishing into the mist and letting a Cross take centre stage.

The road to Golgotha had reached its end at the Comparini abode: Violante Comparini, the "spring and source o' the fire ...

that boiled from heart to brain and hailed the Fury gave it birth" had given him access to the site of sacrifice and he had stumbled "on the serpent's head coiled with a leer"; immediately after, Pietro and Pompilia, themselves "more or less serpent-like", had come on the scene, only to be blindly stamped on ; Pompilia had suffered the same fate in a flash.

Then the escape, a successful one until the emissaries of justice had caught up with him and his mates. In the teeth of the accident, his mind had regained its balance, his soul had evaded the clutches of the snakes crossing his path, and his frayed nerves had been soothed by sleep.

Guido's account of his felony and the ensuing frantic rush has conveyed the mood of a man convinced that he had crossed the finishing line and was entitled to release for "having truth enough": in truth, he had done "God's bidding and man's duty" and by virtue of that deserved to "breathe free." Well, well, well! Quite a change of tune from the previous assertion that he was "done with, dead now!" The corollary of it all has been his invocation to God, – in the belief that the good Lord "shall not lose a life may do Him further service", – followed by his appeal to judges who, as representatives of the law, were his "last hope". Accordingly, he has declared his firm intention to stick to his creed and the rules of the game.

Unquestionably, the summonsed fellow has been put on his mettle and proved to be a skilled fencer; his claim to be "acquitted, actually or virtually, by every intermediate kind of court that takes account of right or wrong in man" has doubtless been a clever thrust: he has, with questionable conscientiousness, paid tribute to the view that an act consistent with rational nature is morally obligatory and as such prescribed by God qua the creator of Nature. Equally striking has been his request to look at the bigger picture and evaluate his life as a mixture of good and bad: he had been a good servant of the Church through "labour in body and soul till these broke down i' the service."

At this defining stage of his performance, the speaker has adroitly replaced his monologue with a socially interactive discourse and enhanced the latter with the argument that "anyhow, here the offence, being punished, ends." Nevertheless, he has wondered, what if, "at this last of all", the cure grew worse disease?" Upon reflection, had the "sweet lords" left him "at liberty wherein? Mere words and wind!" For good measure, a "reptile … had feigned death at first" and now aimed "to evoke life from death". Distressingly, the serpent in question was his young wife, a creature capable of rising to "heights of hate". As if by magic, Caliban of yore has reappeared in the shape of a 'man-monster' dealing with 'a four-legged serpent he makes cower and couch, now snarl, now hold its breath and mind his eye and says she is Miranda and my wife.'[15]

It is, however, well worth noting that Guido has recalled how Pompilia had given him a son, – viz a creature whom he, once dead, would, "know, understand, feel, hear, see, never more escape the sight, moulded into the image and made one, fashioned of soul as featured like in face". At the same time, the imaginative father has pointed a finger of blame at Caponsacchi, "the perjured priest, pink of conspirators, tricksters and knaves, yet polished, superfine, manhood to model adolescence by"; moreover, he has combined his scornful irony with self-praise for having "thoroughly trampled out sin's life at last" and consequently acted in harmony with "the mood o' the magistrate, the mind of law." From a distance come echoes of the ostracised magician Prospero ruing the day he had trusted his false brother Antonio and laying into him for being 'one who having into truth, by telling of it, made such a sinner of his memory to credit his own lie – he did believe he was indeed the Duke; out o' th'substitution, and executing th'outward face of royalty with all prerogative. Hence his ambition growing'.[16] In this regard, it is apposite to emphasize the fact that Antonio was an actor desirous of reality in lieu of fantasy whereas his self-exiled brother had learned the art of white magic in a bid to defeat falsehood and sin.

As for the Guido, he has acted on the assumption that he has triumphed over falsehood and sin; consequently, he has pleaded with the judges to allow him to regain his former condition: "Protect your own defender; save me, Sirs! Give me my life, give me my liberty, my good name and my civic rights again!" The urgent request has expressed a yearning for liberty and life mainly for the sake of an ageing mother and a fugitive brother, not to mention the offspring who was his own by law and ought to be returned to him as a most precious gift: a reunion between father and son would immensely contribute to the restoration of traditional family values, manners and old habits, "customs that recognize the standard worth, the wholesome household rule in force again: husbands once more God's representative, wives like the typical Spouse once more, and priests no more men of Belial." Most endearingly, one fine day the nipper would sit on his father's right side and hear him tell a tale of woe; then, should he kiss the narrator's hand and start at the sight of sores on it, dear papa' would smile and hint at "an accident i' the necessary process; just a trip o' the torture irons in their search for truth — hardly misfortune, and no fault at all."

Strikingly, the deep-seated father/son tie calls up John Earle's picture in *A Child*: 'We laugh at his foolish sports, but his game is our earnest; and his drums, rattles, and hobbyhorses but the emblems and mocking of man's business. His father has writ him as his own little story … and sighs to see what innocence he has outlived.'[17] Furthermore, Guido's appreciation of convention has sounded in harmony with the postulate that tradition is 'an element of freedom' and as such 'needs to be affirmed, embraced, cultivated.'[18] At first blush, the nobleman has displayed the traits of a refined humanist, but then, on reflection, his metaphorical use of language has betrayed a conceptual distortion as well as a neurotic frame of mind.

Empirical-minded observers have stated that every cloud has a silver lining: Count Franceschini's redeeming quality has been shown by his being prepared to meet his doom: indeed, his personality has come to light as that of a man strong enough to make his mind have priority over his body. Nevertheless, the opposite side of the coin has displayed a 'false self', i.e. a façade attempting 'to hide the 'true Self', which it does by compliance with environmental demands'[19]. We have been presented with a many-sided, chameleon-like, Guido who, after being a supporter of the law and servant of the Church for many years, had found himself adopting a stance typical of a grovelling layman. Hence a question about the consistency and, ultimately, credibility of the cleric at issue: had he been suffering hallucinations engendered by a mental drug? Admittedly, Guido has not minced his words when referring to his allegedly adulterous wife, to a priest living a double life, and to his deceitful in-laws, yet can his testimony taken to be trustworthy? In the process of interacting with the judges he has endeavoured to free himself from previously upheld social norms and begged for salvation instead of clinging to a dignified quest for truth. It does seem as if the torture irons have been successful in their search for the verities of life.

At this closing stage, the bottom line reads like the desire of an individual for interpersonal communication. It is all well and good, but intersubjectivity entails a dialogic engagement: a monologic utterance may be effective to a large extent and yet leave the hearer wondering whether the speaker has been motivated by a true self or prompted by a false one. And here's the rub: an ambivalent utterer is liable to shift from discourse, used as a a means of interaction, to a language that, besides failing to be dialogic, is imbued with a parodic-travestying undertone and a perversely polymorphous meaning imposed on it by a familial and social presence perceived as a central, originating signified. In reality, there is no ultimate signified and the absence of it 'extends the domain and signification of play to infinity'[20]. In the light of all the above, a big question lingers over Count Franceschini's overall performance: has the speaker shown to be endowed with the creative wherewithal to make it a speech act good enough to help him save his noble neck? It is a moot point and no mistake.

1. Michel Foucault, in *Western Philosophy and Philosophers*, p. 112

2. Bruno Bettelheim, *Freud and Man's Soul*, Penguin Books, 1991, p. 78

3. As seen by G. K. Chesterton in *Robert Browning*, Macmillan and Co. 1911, p. 192

4. Virginia Woolf, *Orlando*, Granada Publishing, 1979 p.121

5. Thomas Hardy, *Tess of the D'Urbervilles*, J. M. Dent, 1933, p. 63

6. As propounded by the analytic philosopher John Langshaw Austin

7. Robert Browning, *Paracelsus*, Part 1, ll. 728 ff

8. Robert Browning, *A Death in the Desert*, ll. 320-21

9. G. K. Chesterton, *Op. Cit.* p. 168

10. Jacques Lacan, *Being, the Letter, and the Other*, in *Modern Criticism and Theory*, p. 101 ff.

11. Roman Jakobson, *Linguistics and Poetics*, in *Modern Criticism and Theory, p. 38*
12. Virginia Woolf, *Op. Cit.* p. 85
13. Ferdinand de Saussure, *On Defining a Language*, in *Modern Criticism and Theory*, p. 2 ff
14. Juliet Mitchell, *Femininity, Narrative and Psychoanalysis*, in *Modern Criticism and Theory*, p. 428
15. Robert Browning, *Caliban upon Setebos*, ll. 158-60
16. William Shakespeare, *The Tempest*, Act I, Sc. 2, ll. 99-105
17. As quoted in A. C. Baugh, *A Literary History of England*, 2nd Ed. Routledge & Kegan Paul, p. 604
18. *Western Philosophy and Philosophers*, p. 117
19. D. W. Winnicott, as cited in *Psychoanalytic Theory*, by Anthony Elliott, Blackwell, p. 26
20. Jacques Derrida, as quoted by M. H. Abrams in *Op. Cit.* p. 269

GIUSEPPE CAPONSACCHI

Within the space of a single day, Canon Giuseppe Maria Caponsacchi was summonsed, – six months after his first appearance in court, – and asked by the reverend judges to give a satisfactory answer to their probing questions.

"Answer you, Sirs? Do I understand aright?" he asked in response. "Tell over twice what I the first time told, fronting you same three in this very room? There was the blameless shrug, permissible smirk, the titter stifled in the hollow palm which rubbed the eyebrow and caressed the nose. And now you sit as grave, stare as aghast as if I were a phantom; now 't is – 'Friend, collect yourself!' – no laughing matter more – 'Counsel the Court in this extremity!'"

The rejoinder foreshadowed a 'performative' speech act: "Why does the mirth hang fire and miss the smile? Pompilia is bleeding out her life belike, gasping away the latest breath of all. It seems to fill the universe with sight and sound, – from the four corners of this earth tells itself over, to my sense at least. Well then, let me, the hollow rock, condense the voice o' the sea and wind, interpret you the mystery of this murder, God above!"

The speaker's sonorous voice trailed off for a short while and resonated afresh. "This deed you saw begin – why does its end surprise you? Why should the event enforce the lesson we ourselves learned, she and I, from the first o' the fact, and taught you, all in vain? Law was aware and watching, would suffice, wanted no priest's intrusion, palpably pretence, too manifest a subterfuge! Whereupon I, priest, coxcomb, fribble and fool, ensconced me in my corner, thus rebuked, a kind of culprit, over-zealous hound kicked for his pains to kennel. I gave place to you and let the law reign paramount: I left Pompilia to your watch and ward, and now you point me there and thus she lies! I have paid enough in person at Civita, am free, – what more need I concern me with? Thank you! I am rehabilitated then, a very reputable priest. But she, the glory of life, the beauty of the world, the splendour of heaven, – well, Sirs, does no one move? do I speak ambiguously? – the glory, I say, and the beauty, I say, and splendour, still say I, who, a priest, – trained to live my whole life long on beauty and splendour, solely at their source, God, – have thus recognized my food in one."

The Canon's face grew pale, but a warm smile restored colour to his voice. "You are all struck acquiescent now, it seems: you understand, of a sudden, – gospel too has a claim here, may possibly pronounce consistent with my priesthood, worthy Christ, – that I endeavoured to save Pompilia? Well then, I have a mind to speak, see cause to relume the quenched flax by this dreadful light, burn my soul out in showing you the truth. Let me, in heaven's name, use the very snuff o' the taper in one last spark shall show truth for a moment, show Pompilia who was true. There! I was born, have lived, shall die, a fool. This is a foolish outset: might with cause give colour to the very lie o' the man, the murderer, make as if I loved his wife in the way he called love, – he is the fool there! – the snow-white soul that angels fear to take untenderly. But, all same, I know I too am taintless, and I bare my breast."

The monologuist inhaled deeply and exhaled slowly. "Yes, I am one of your body and a priest. Also, I am a younger son o' the House oldest now, greatest once, in my birth-town Arezzo; I recognize no equal there. Not simply for the advantage of my birth i' the way of the world, was I proposed for priest, was made expect, from infancy almost, the proper mood o' the priest; till time ran by and brought the day when I must read the vows, having gone trippingly hitherto up to the height o'er the wan water. Just a vow to read! So I became a priest. Those terms changed all: I could live thus and still hold head erect. Now you see why I may have been before a fribble and coxcomb, yet, as a priest, break word nowise, to make you misbelieve me now. I need that you should know my truth. Well then, according to prescription did I live, – conformed myself, both read the breviary and wrote the rhymes, was punctual to my place i' the Pieve and as diligent at my post where beauty and fashion rule. I throve apace."

The priest flashed a glance at the ceiling, presumably hoping to detect an ethereal light beyond it, but just as quickly his verdigris eyes descended to the tangible presence in front of him. "Well, after three or four years of this life, in prosecution of my calling, I found myself at the theatre one night with a brother Canon, in a mood and mind proper enough for the place, amused or no: when I saw enter, stand, and seat herself a lady, young, tall, beautiful, strange and sad. It was as when, in our cathedral once, as I got yawningly through matin-song, I saw *facchini* bear a burden up: *there* was Raffaello! I was still one stare when 'Nay, I'll make her give you back your gaze', said Canon Conti, and at the word he tossed a paper-twist of comfits to her lap, nodding from over my shoulder. Then she turned, looked our way, smiled the beautiful sad strange smile. 'Is not she fair? 'T is my new cousin', said he; 'the fellow lurking there i' the black o' the box is Guido, the old scapegrace; she's his wife. He has brought little back from Rome beside, after the bragging, bullying: a fair face and – they do say – a pocketfull of gold. Hallo, *there*'s Guido, the black, mean and small, bends his brows on us – please to bend your own on the shapely nether limbs of Light-skirts there by way of a diversion! I was a fool to fling the sweetmeats. Prudence, for God's love!' "

One long sigh flowed through the narrator's chest. "That night and next day did the gaze endure, burnt to my brain, as sunbeam thro' shut eyes, and not once changed the beautiful sad strange smile. One evening I was sitting in a muse over the opened *Summa,* darkened round by the mid-March twilight, thinking how my life had shaken under me, – broke short indeed and showed the gap 'twixt what is, what should be, – and into what abysm the soul may slip; how utterly dissociated was I, a priest and celibate, from the sad strange wife of Guido, just as an instance to the point; how, when the page o' the *Summa* preached its best, her smile kept glowing out of it. As to mock the silence we could break by no one word, there came a tap without the chamber-door, and a whisper when I bade who tapped speak out; in glided a masked muffled mystery, laid lightly a letter on the opened book. I took the letter, read to the effect that she, Canon Conti flung the comfits to, had a warm heart to give me in exchange and bade me render thanks by word of mouth.

"And you?" I asked. "What may you be?"

'Count Guido's kind of maid. We all hate him, the lady suffers much. What answer may I bring to cheer the sweet Pompilia?'

Then I took a pen and wrote: 'No more of this! That you are fair I know, but other thoughts now occupy my mind. I should not thus have played the insensible once on a time. What made you, – may one ask, – marry your hideous husband? 'T was a fault, and now you taste the fruit of it. Farewell.'

'There!' smiled I as she snatched it and was gone – 'There! Let the jealous miscreant, – Guido's self, whose mean soul grins through this transparent trick, – be baulked so far, defrauded of his aim! There's the reply which he shall turn and twist at pleasure, snuff at, till his brain grow drunk, as the bear does when he finds a scented glove that puzzles him, – a hand and yet no hand, of other perfume than his own foul paw! Last month I had doubtless chosen to play the dupe, accepted the mock-invitation, kept the sham appointment, – cudgel beneath cloak, – prepared myself to pull the appointer's self out of the window from his hiding place: such had seemed once a jest permissible; now I am not i' the mood.'

Pompilia's reluctant correspondent gave the jury a twisted smile. "Back next morn brought the messenger, a second letter in hand: 'You must love someone else; I hear you do. I take the crumbs from table gratefully nor grudge who feasts there. 'Faith, I blush and blaze! Are you determinedly bent on Rome? I am wretched here, a monster tortures me; carry me with you! Come and say you will! I am ever at the window of my room over the terrace, at the *Ave*. Come!'

I wrote: 'In vain do you solicit me: I am a priest and you are wedded wife, whatever kind of brute your husband prove. I have scruples, in short. Yet should you really show sign at the window … but nay, best be good! My thoughts are elsewhere.'

"Take her that!" he had enjoined the go-between then and there.

"And so, the missives followed thick and fast", he went on to recount. "A slip was found i' the door-sill, scribbled word 'twixt page and page o' the prayer-book in my place; a crumpled thing dropped even before my feet as I passed, by day, the very window once. One day, a variation; thus I read: 'You have gained little by timidity. My husband has found out my love at length, will stick at nothing to destroy you. Stand prepared, or better, run till you reach Rome! Anyhow, I beseech you, stay away from the window! He might well be posted there.'

I wrote 'You raise my courage, or call up my curiosity, who am but man. If it should please me pad the path this eve, Guido will have two troubles: first to get into a rage and then get out again. Be cautious, though: at the *Ave*!'

You of the Court! 'I will to the window, as he tempts', said I. 'While the imprisoned lady keeps afar, there will they lie in ambush, heads alert, kith, kin, and Count, mustered to bite my heel. No mother nor brother viper of the brood shall scuttle off without the instructive bruise!' " He nodded emphatically. "So, I went: crossed street and street. The next street's turn, 'Out of the hole you hide in; on to the front, Count Guido Franceschini, show yourself! Hear what a man thinks of a thing like you, and after, take this foulness in your face!' The words lay living on my lip; I made the one turn more, and there at the window stood, framed in its black square length, with lamp in hand, Pompilia; the same great, grave, griefful air as stands i' the dusk, on altar that I know, left alone with one moonbeam in her cell, Our Lady of all the Sorrows. Ere I knelt – assured myself that she was flesh and blood – she had looked one look and vanished. I thought, 'Just so: it was herself; they have set her there to watch. She never dreams they used her for a snare, and now withdraw the bait has served its turn.' And on my lip again was 'Out with thee, Guido!' – when all at once she reappeared, but, this time, on the terrace overhead, while I stood still as stone, all eye, all ear.

She began – 'You have sent me letters, Sir. I have read none, – I can neither read nor write, – but she you gave them to, a woman here, partly explained their sense, I think, to me obliged to listen while she inculcates that you, a priest, can dare love me, a wife, desire to love or die as I shall bid. Such wickedness were deadly to us both, but good true love would help me now so much I tell myself you may mean good and true. That it is only you in the wide world, knowing me nor in thought nor word nor deed, who, all unprompted save by your own heart, come proffering assistance now, were strange but that my whole life is so strange: as strange it is, my husband, whom I have not wronged, should hate and harm me. For his own soul's sake, hinder the harm! But there is something more, and that the strangest: it has got to be somehow for my sake too, and yet not mine, – this is a riddle – for some kind of sake not any clearer to myself than you, and yet as certain as that I draw breath: I would fain live, not die – oh no, not die!' "

Caponsacchi looked at the judges with big soulful eyes and continued recalling Pompilia's words.

'My case is, I was dwelling happily at Rome with those dear Comparini, called father and mother to me, when at once I found I had become Count Guido's wife. He laid a hand on me that burned all peace, all joy, all hope, and last all fear away. My father once, my mother all those years, that loved me so, now say I dreamed a dream and bid me wake, henceforth no child of theirs, never in all the time their child at all. Do you understand? I cannot: yet so it is. Just so I say of you that proffer help: I cannot understand what prompts your soul, I simply needs must see that it is so, only one strange and wonderful thing more. They came here with me, those two dear ones, kept all the old love up, till my husband, till his people, here so tortured them they fled. And now, is it because I grow in flesh and spirit one with him their torturer, that they, renouncing him, must cast off me? The Archbishop said to murder me were sin: my leaving Guido were a kind of death with no sin, – more death, he must answer for. Hear now what death to him and life to you I wish to pay and owe. Take me to Rome where the father and the mother are; and soon they'll will come to know and call me by my name, their child once more; since child I am, for all they now forget me, which is the worst o' the dream – and the way to end dreams is to break them, stand, walk, go: then help me to stand, walk and go! You know how weak the strongest women are. Wake me! The letter I received this morn, said – if the woman spoke your very sense – you would die for me. I can believe it now, for now the dream gets to involve yourself. Though you have never uttered word yet, well, I know, here too has been dream-work, delusion too, and that at no time, you with the eyes here, ever intended to do wrong by me, nor wrote such letters, therefore. It is false, and you are true, have been true, will be true. To Rome then! When is it you take me there? Each minute lost is mortal. When? I ask.'

I answered 'It shall be when it can be. A day's work by to-morrow at this time. How shall I see you and assure escape?'

She replied, 'Pass to-morrow, at this hour.'

'To-morrow at this hour I pass,' said I.

Afterward, – oh! I gave a passing glance to a certain ugly cloud-shape, goblin-shred of hell-smoke hurrying past the splendid moon out now to tolerate no darkness more, and saw right through the thing that tried to pass for truth and solid, not an empty lie: 'So she, by the crystalline soul, knew me, never mistook the signs. Enough of this – let the wraith go to nothingness again, here is the orb, have only thought for her!' "

A knowing smile spread across the priest's strong features. "Thought? Nay, Sirs, what shall follow was no thought: I put forth no thought, – powerless, all that night I paced the city. It was the first Spring: *in* rushed new things, the old were rapt away; alike abolished – the imprisonment of the outside air, the inside weight o' the world that pulled me down. Death meant, to spurn the ground, soar to the sky, – die well and you do that. The very immolation made the bliss: into another state, under new rule I knew myself was passing swift and sure; i' the grey of dawn it was I found myself facing the pillared front o' the Pieve – mine, my church; it seemed to say for the first time: 'But am not I the Bride, the mystic love o' the Lamb, who took thy plighted troth, my priest, to fold thy warm heart on my heart of stone and freeze thee nor unfasten anymore?' Now, when I found out first that life and death are means to an end, that passion uses both, indisputably mistress of the man whose form of worship is self-sacrifice – now, from the stone lungs sighed the scrannel voice 'Leave that live passion, come be dead with me!' As if, i' the fabled garden, I had gone on great adventure, plucked in ignorance hedge-fruit, and feasted to satiety, and scorned the achievement: then come all at once o' the prize o' the place, the thing of perfect gold, the apple's self: and, scarce my eye on that, was 'ware as well o' the seven-fold dragon's watch."

Caponsacchi crossed his wellrounded arms in a hieratic fashion: was he regaining sight of the Edenic apple of his eye? "Sirs, I obeyed. Obedience was too strange, – this new thing that had been struck into me by the look o' the lady, – to dare disobey the first authoritative word. 'T was God's. I had been lifted to the level of her, could take such sounds into my sense. I said, 'It is she bids me bow the head: how true, I am a priest! I see the function here.' So, I went home. Dawn broke, noon broadened, I – I sat stone-still, let time run over me. The sun slanted into my room, had reached the west. I opened book, – Aquinas blazed with one black name on the white page. I looked up, saw the sunset: vespers rang. 'Duty to God is duty to her. I think God, who created her, will save her too some new way, by one miracle the more. She knows it is no fear withholds me: fear? Of what? Suspense here is the terrible thing.'" He unfolded his arms and clenched his fists. "Again the morning found me. 'I will work, tie down my foolish thoughts. Thank God so far!' " He nodded repeatedly, as was his wont. "There she stood – leaned there for the second time, over the terrace, looked at me, then spoke: 'You are again here, in the selfsame mind, I see here, steadfast in the face of you, – you grudge to do no one thing that I ask. Why then is nothing done? You know my need.'

I answered – 'Lady, waste no thought, no word even to forgive me! Care for what I care – only! Now follow me as I were fate! Leave this house in the dark tomorrow night, just before daybreak: – there's new moon this eve; it sets, and then begins the solid black. Descend, proceed to the Torrione, step over the low dilapidated wall. An inn stands; cross to it; I shall be there.'

She answered, 'If I can but find the way. But I shall find it. Go now!'

I know not how the night passed. Morning broke: through each familiar hindrance of the day did I make steadily for its hour and end till, at the dead between midnight and morn, *there* was I at the goal, before the gate, with a tune in the ears, low leading up to loud, a light in the eyes, faint that would soon be flare, ever some spiritual witness new and new, till it was she! *There* did Pompilia come: the white I saw shine through her was her soul's, certainly, for the body was one black, black from head down to foot. She did not speak, glided into the carriage, – so a cloud gathers the moon up. 'By San Spirito, to Rome, as if the road burned underneath!' I said, – then, in another tick of time, sprang, was beside her, she and I alone."

The last detail was enhanced by an otherworldly overtone.

"So it began, our flight thro' dusk to clear, through day and night and day again to night once more, and to last dreadful dawn of all. Blackness engulfed me, – partial stupor, say, – then I would break way, breathe through the surprise. I said to myself – 'I have caught it, I conceive the mind o' the mystery: 't is the way they wake and wait, two martyrs somewhere in a tomb each by each as their blessing was to die; so, through the whole course of the world they wait. No otherwise, in safety and not fear, I lie, because she lies too by my side.' You know this is not love, Sirs; it is faith, the feeling that there's God, he reigns and rules out of this low world: that is all; no harm!" The believer's eyes sparkled with religious fervour.

She said, – a long while later in the day:

'Have you a mother?'

'She died, I was born.'

'A sister, then?'

'No sister.'

Who was it – what woman were you used to serve this way, be kind to, till I called you and you came?'

I did not like that word. Soon afterward:

'Tell me, are men unhappy, in some kind of mere unhappiness at being men, as women suffer, being womanish? Have you, now, some unhappiness, I mean, born of what may be man's strength overmuch, to match the undue susceptibility, the sense at every pore when hate is close and strength may have its drawback, weakness scapes?'

At eve we heard the *angelus*. She turned – 'I told you I can neither read nor write; my life stopped with the play-time. I will learn, if I begin to live again, but you – who are a priest –

wherefore do you not read the service at this hour? Read Gabriel's song, the lesson, and then read the little prayer to Raphael, proper for us travellers!'

I did not like that word, neither, but I read.

We did go on all night; but at its close she was troubled, restless, moaned low, talked at whiles to herself, her brow on quiver with the dream. Once, wide awake, she menaced, at arm's length waved away something – 'Never again with you! My soul is mine, my body is my soul's: you and I are divided ever more in soul and body; get you gone!'

Then I – 'Oh, if the God, that only can, would help! Am I his priest with power to cast out fiends? Let God arise and all His enemies be scattered!'

By morn, there was peace, no sigh out of the deep sleep. When she woke at last, 'No more o' the journey: if it might but last! It is the interruption that I dread, – with no dread, ever to be here and thus! Never to see a face nor hear a voice! Yours is no voice; you speak when you are dumb; nor face, I see it in the dark. I want no face nor voice that change and grow unkind.' *That* I liked, *that* was the best thing she said.

And presently – for there was a roadside-shrine – 'Now, be you candid and no priest but friend – were I surprised and killed here on the spot, a runaway from husband and his home, do you account it were in sin I died? My husband used to seem to harm me, not … not on pretence he punished sin of mine, nor for sin's sake and lust of cruelty, but, as I heard him bid a farming-man at the villa take a lamb once to the wood and there ill-treat it, meaning that the wolf should hear its cries and so come, quick be caught, enticed to the trap, he practised thus with me. Had it been only between our two selves, – his pleasure and my pain, – why, only pleasure him by dying, nor such need to make a coil! But this was worth an effort, that my pain should not become a snare, prove pain threefold to other people – strangers or unborn

... how should I know? I sought release from that. You are a man: what have I done amiss?' This time she might have said, – might, did not say – 'you are a priest.' She said, 'my friend.'" The last two words were accompanied by a friendly smile.

"Day wore, we passed the places, somehow the calm went, she wandered in her mind, – addressed me once 'Gaetano!' – that's not my name: whose name? I grew alarmed, my head seemed turning too: I quickened pace with promise now, now threat; bade drive and drive, nor any stopping more. 'Already Castelnuovo – Rome!' I cried, 'this is where travellers' hearts are wont to beat.' The sky was fierce with colour from the sun setting. She screamed out 'No, I must not die! Take me no farther, I should die. Stay here! I have more life to save than mine!' She swooned."

The narrator fixed the reverend judges with an icy stare and stood akimbo. "We seemed safe: what was it foreboded so? Out of the coach into the inn I bore the motionless and breathless pure and pale Pompilia, – bore her through a pitying group and laid her on a couch, still calm and cured by deep sleep of all woes at once.

The host was urgent: 'Let her stay an hour or two! Leave her to us, all be right by morn!'

I paced the passage, kept watch all night long, found myself throb with fear from head to foot i' the court-yard, roused the sleepy grooms: 'Have out carriage and horse, give haste, take gold!' – said I. 'T was the last minute, – needs must I ascend and break her sleep. I turned to go." The voice turned gravelly. "And *there* faced me Count Guido; there posed the mean man as master, – took the field, encamped his rights, challenged the world: *there* leered new triumph, there scowled the old malice in the visage bad and black o' the scamp. Soon triumph suppled the tongue a little, malice glued to his dry throat:

'My salutation to your priestship! What? Matutinal, busy with book so soon of an April day that's damp as tears that now deluge

Arezzo at its darling's flight? 'The lady, – could you leave her side so soon? You have not experienced at her hands my treatment: you lay down undrugged, I see! Hence this alertness – hence no death-in-life like what held arms fast when she stole from mine. Here is the lover in the smart disguise with the sword: he is a priest, so mine lies still; there upstairs hides my wife the runaway, his leman: the two plotted, poisoned first, plundered me after, and eloped thus far where now you find them. Do your duty quick!' Giuseppe Caponsacchi snorted and stamped his foot. "During this speech of that man, – well, I stood away, as he managed, – still, as near the throat of him, – with these two hands, my own, – as now I stand near yours, Sir, – one quick spring, one great good satisfying gripe, and lo! there had he lain abolished with his lie, creation purged o' the miscreate, man redeemed! I, in some measure, seek a poor excuse for what I left undone, in just this fact that my first feeling at the speech I quote was – not of what a blasphemy was dared, not what a bag of venomed purulence was split and noisome, – but how splendidly mirthful, what ludicrous a lie was launched!" The theatrically inspired fellow chuckled. "The minute, oh the misery, was gone! On either idle hand of me there stood really an officer, nor laughed i' the least. They rendered justice to his reason, laid logic to heart, as 't were submitted them 'twice two makes four.' 'And now, catch her!' – he cried.

Up we all went together; *in* they broke o' the chamber late my chapel. There she lay, composed as when I laid her, that last eve, o' the couch, – still breathless, motionless, sleep's self, wax-white, seraphic, saturate with the sun o' the morning that now flooded from the front and filled the window with a light like blood.

'Behold the poisoner, the adulteress, – and feigning sleep too! Seize, bind!' – Guido hissed.

She started up, stood erect, face to face with the husband: back he fell, was buttressed there by the window all aflame with morning-red, he the black figure, the opprobrious blur against all peace and joy and light and life. 'Away from between me and hell!' – she cried: 'Hell for me, no embracing any more! I am God's, I love God, God – whose knees I clasp, whose utterly most just award I take, but bear no more love-making devils: hence!' She sprung at the sword that hung beside him, seized, drew, brandished it; the sunrise burned for joy o' the blade. 'Die,' cried she, 'devil, in God's name!' No matter for the sword, her word sufficed to spike the coward through and through: he shook, could only spit between the teeth: 'You see? Carry these criminals to the prison house!"

I took the truth in, guessed sufficiently the service for the moment – 'What I say, slight at your peril! We are alien here, my adversary and I, called noble both. I am the nobler, and a name men know. Though in a secular garb, – for reasons good I shall adduce in due time to my peers, – I demand that the Church I serve decide between us, right the slandered lady there. A Tuscan noble, I might claim the Duke; a priest, I rather choose the Church, – bid Rome cover the wronged with her inviolate shield.'

Pompilia's face, then and thus, looked on me the last time in this life: not one sight since. I thought I had saved her. I appealed to Rome: it seems I simply sent her to her death. No, Sirs, I cannot have the lady dead. Let me see for myself if it be so! My punishment had motive that, a priest I, in a laic garb, a mundane mode, did what were harmlessly done otherwise. I never touched her with my fingertip except to carry her to the couch, that eve, as we priests carry the paten: that is why I have told you this whole story over again, have told my tale to the end, – nay, not the end – for, wait – I'll end – not leave you that excuse!"

The Canon's fleshy hands chopped the air. "I was presently brought to Rome – yes, here I stood opposite yonder very crucifix. I showed you how it came to be my part to save the lady. Then your clerk produced papers, a pack of stupid and impure banalities called letters about love – love, indeed, – I could teach who styled them so, better, I think, though priest and loveless both.

'The trusty servant, Margherita's self, even she who brought you letters you confess, and, you confess, took letters in reply: forget not we have knowledge of the facts.'

'Sirs, who have knowledge of the facts, defray the expenditure of wit I waste in vain, trying to find out just one fact of all!' She who brought letters from who could not write and took back letters to who could not read, – who was that messenger, of your charity?'

'Well, so far favours you the circumstance that this same messenger ... how shall we say? ... labours under the imputation of being a quean, – which makes accusation null. We waive this woman's. Nought makes void the next: Borsi, called *Venerino*, he who drove, deposes to your kissings in the coach – frequent, frenetic...'

'When deposed he so?'

'After some weeks of sharp imprisonment...'

'Granted by friend the Governor, I engage.'

'For his participation in your flight! At length his obduracy-melting made the avowal mentioned...'

'Was dismissed forthwith to liberty, poor knave, for recompense. Sirs, give what credit to the lie you can! For me, no word in my defence I speak, and God shall argue for the lady!'

So did I stand question and make answer, still with the same result of smiling disbelief, polite impossibility of faith in such affected virtue in a priest. If I pretended simply to be pure honest and Christian in the case, – absurd! The intrigue, the elopement, the disguise ... well charged! Your apprehension was – of guilt enough to be compatible with innocence, so, punished best a little and not too much. Oh, Sirs, depend on me for much new light thrown on the justice and religion here by this proceeding, much fresh food for thought! Can I assist to an explanation? – Yes, I rise in your esteem, sagacious Sirs, stand up a renderer of reasons, not the officious priest would personate Saint George for a mock

Princess in undragoned days. What, the blood startles you? What, after all the priest who needs must carry sword on thigh may find imperative use for it? Then, there was a Princess, was a dragon belching flame, and should have been a Saint George also? Then, there might be worse schemes than to break the bonds. You blind guides who must needs lead eyes that see! Fools, alike ignorant of man and God! What was there here should have perplexed your wit for a wink of the owl-like eyes of you? How miss, then, – what's now forced on you by this flare of fact, – that he, from the beginning pricked at heart by some lust, letch of hate against his wife, plotted to plague her into overt sin and shame, would slay Pompilia body and soul, and save his mean self miserably caught i' the quagmire of his own tricks, cheats and lies? That when at the last we did rush each on each, – by no chance but because God willed it so, – the spark of truth was struck from out our souls, leaving the show of things to the Lord of Show and Prince o' the Power of the Air? Our very flight, even to its most ambiguous circumstance, irrefragably proved how futile, false…"

An aposiopetic shake of the head proved to be the prelude to a colourful turn of phrase. "Had the liar's lie been true one pin-point speck, were I the accepted suitor, free o' the place, what need of flight, what were the gain therefrom but just damnation, failure or success? What other advantage, – we who led the days and nights alone i' the house, – was flight to find? You did so far give sanction to our flight, confirm its purpose, as hand helping hand; why then could you, who stopped short, not go on one poor step more and justify the means, having allowed the end? not see and say, 'Here's the exceptional conduct that should claim to be exceptionally judged on rules which, understood, make no exception here'? Why play instead into the devil's hands by dealing so ambiguously as gave Guido the power to intervene like me, prove one exception more? I saved his wife against law; against law he slays her now. Deal with him!"

The self-proclaimed saviour's duck-egg blue eyes flashed on and off. "I have done with being judged," he thundered. "I stand here guiltless in thought, word and deed, to the point that I apprise you, in contempt for all misapprehending ignorance o' the human heart, much more the mind of Christ, that I assuredly did bow, was blessed by the revelation of Pompilia. There! Such is the final act I fling you, Sirs, to mouth and mumble and misinterpret: *there*! 'The priest's in love,' have it the vulgar way! Unpriest me, rend the rags o' the vestment, do; remove me from the midst, no longer priest and fit companion for the like of you: there's a crack somewhere, something that's unsound i' the rattle!"

The impassioned plea sounded pre-climactic, and the acme was indeed reached in a twinkling. "For Pompilia – be advised, build churches, go pray! You will find me there. But for Count Guido, you must counsel there! I bow my head, bend to the very dust, break myself up in shame of faultiness: I could have killed him ere he killed his wife, and did not; he went off alive and well and then effected this last feat – through me! Instruct me in procedure! I conceive – in all due self-abasement might I speak – how you will deal with Guido: oh, not death! Let us go away – leave Guido all alone back on the world again that knows him now! I think he will be found – indulge so far! – not to die so much as slide out of life, pushed by the general horror and common hate low, lower, left o' the very ledge of things, and thus I see him slowly and surely edged off all the table-land whence life upsprings aspiring to be immortality. So I lose Guido in the loneliness, silence and dusk, till at the doleful end, lo, what is this he meets, strains onward still? What other man deep further in the fate? Judas, made monstrous by much solitude! The two are at one now! Let them love their love that bites and claws like hate, or hate their hate that mops and mows and makes as it were love! There, let them each tear each in devil's-fun, or fondle this the other while malice aches: the cockatrice is with the basilisk! There let them grapple, denizens o' the dark, foes or friends, but indissolubly bound, – in their one spot out of the ken of God or care of man, for ever and ever more!"

The high-keyed curse ushered in a *gran finale*: "Why, Sirs, what's this? Why, this is sorry and strange! I give you cause to doubt the lady's mind; a pretty sarcasm for the world! I fear you do her wit injustice … all through me! A poor rash advocate I prove myself. My part was just to tell you how things stand, state facts and not be flustered at their fume. But then 't is a priest speaks: as for love, – no! I went too much o' the trivial outside of her face: her brow had not the right line, leaned too much, – painters would say: they like the straight-up Greek, – this seemed bent somewhat with an invisible crown of martyr and saint, not such as art approves. The lips, compressed a little, came forward too: careful for a whole world of sin and pain. That was the face, her husband makes his plea, he sought just to disfigure, – no offence beyond that! Sirs, let us be rational!"

The sensitive observer gave a loud sniff. "Then, here's another point involving law: I use this argument to show you meant no calumny against us by that tile of the sentence, – liars tried to twist it so: what penalty it bore, I had to pay till further proof should follow of innocence. You went through the preliminary form, stopped there, contrived this sentence to amuse the adversary. If the title ran for more than fault imputed and not proved, that was a simple penman's error, else a slip i' the phrase, – as when we say of you, 'Charged with injustice' – which may either be or not be, – 't is a name that sticks meanwhile."

"Another relevant matter: fool that I am! It is not true, – yet, since friends think it helps, – she only tried me when some others failed and when abandoned by them, not before, turned to me: that's conclusive why she turned. Much good they got by the happy cowardice! That's the charge goes to the heart of the Governor. He gets Arezzo to receive, – nay more, gets Arezzo and Rome to receive, – nay more, gets Florence and the Duke to authorize! This is their Rota's sentence, their Granduke signs and seals. Rome for me henceforward – Rome, where better men are, – most of all that man, the Augustinian of the Hospital, who writes the letter, – he confessed, he says, many a dying person, never one so sweet and true and pure and beautiful. A good man! Will you make him Pope one day?" The canon enhanced the question statement with a ceremonious smile. "Sirs, I am quiet again. You see, we are so very pitiable, she and I, who had conceivably been otherwise. Apart from truth's sake, what's to move so much? Pompilia will be presently with God; I am, on earth, as good as out of it. She and I are mere strangers now: but priests should study passion; how else cure mankind, who come for help in passionate extremes? I do but play with an imagined life of who, unfettered by a vow, unblessed by the higher call, – since you will have it so, – leads it companioned by the woman there. To live, and see her learn, and learn by her, out of the low obscure and petty world – or only see one purpose and one will evolve themselves i' the world, change wrong to right: to have to do with nothing but the true, the good, the eternal – and these, not alone in the main current of the general life, but small experiences of every day, concerns of the particular hearth and home: to learn not only by a comet's rush but a rose's birth, – not by the grandeur, God – but the comfort, Christ. All this, how far away! Mere delectation, meet for a minute's dream! Just as a drudging student trim his lamp, opens his Plutarch, puts him in the place of Roman, Grecian; draws the patched gown close, dreams, 'Thus should I fight, save or rule the world!' – then smilingly, contentedly, awakes to the old solitary nothingness. So I, from such communion, pass content …"

The eventually appeased monologist raised his verdigris eyes to the ceiling decorated with a polychrome picture of the deity in the shape of a Holy Ghost. "O great, just, good God! Miserable me!" he cried out. The impromptu expression of self-pity, redolent of Jeremiah's *lament over personal affliction*, was Canon

Caponsacchi's farewell utterance in court as a parky January day drew to a close.

Giuseppe Maria Caponsacchi, a 'young, bold, handsome priest, popular in the city', - in Tertium Quid's words, - has taken a stand in the law-court drama.

The canon has begun his testimony by giving an answer to a formerly mirthful jury in the shape of a question which has enhanced the cryptic features of the slowly unfolding Roman murder story. Without mincing words, the cleric has depicted himself as an erstwhile "coxcomb, fribble and fool" providentially rehabilitated by a vision of "the beauty of the world, the splendour of heaven" as embodied by Pompilia, the angelic woman he has endeavoured to save in the awareness that her husband was a "bad" fellow "bound, for better or worse, to act."

Next, he has gone on to tackle the thorny issue of truth: "I have a mind to speak, see cause to relume the quenched flax by this dreadful light, burn my soul out in showing you the truth", he has boasted and, in the process, evinced a comprehensive code of ethics - which has nonetheless left a couple of questions hanging in the balance. First, the meaning given by him to the word 'truth', even though apparently consistent with the essence of the latter, has raised doubts as to whether he has based the veracity of his deposition on a phenomenological correspondence between a claim to be telling the truth and reality or on a close connection between the events and his interpretation of them. Secondly, his assertion that the jury had better know his personal truth may well be conducive to a perception of him as an empiricist holding a relativist's ethical view of truth itself.

Significantly, the reverend judges have been reminded that he was one of their body and in addition "a younger son of o' the House oldest now, greatest once" in his birth-town. Unquestionably, the dual recollection has conveyed the pride of an aristocratic scion aware of being part and parcel of an institution known for its capacity to bestow a sense of purpose and identity on its members.

As a follow-up, Caponsacchi has recounted how he had been inordinately affected by the sight of Pompilia at the theatre: "That night and next day did the gaze endure, burnt to my brain as sunbeam thro' shut eyes, and not once changed the beautiful strange smile." Suddenly, as if by magic, *la donna angelicata* has metamorphosed into a *Monna Lisa* while a man of the cloth has displayed the traits of an enthralled gallant, even those of a 'courtly spiritual Cupid'. An aura of gracefulness has come to the fore and sounded in tune with the poetic question: 'What vertue is so fitting for a knight or for a Ladie, whom a knight should loue, as Curtesie, to beare themselves aright to all of each degree, as doth behoue?'[1] As a matter of fact, the spiritual Cupid's *amour courteois* has engendered a "gap 'twixt what is, what should be, and into what abyss the soul may slip". In consequence, he appears to have adopted an approach consonant with the descriptive ethics of a lover encumbered with a vision of himself as "a priest and celibate" unable to communicate with a married woman whose enigmatic smile had been flowing out of the *Summa* just when the *Magnum Opus* preached its best. The dichotomy between heavenly bliss and earthly allure has conjured up the image of a True Self thwarted by a False Self, as epitomised by the to-and-fro letters involving the canon and Pompilia. The former has testified that he had written to Guido's wife mainly in compliance with an ethic imperative, but his asseveration has left a cloud of doubt in its wake, notably as regards the young woman's response: had the letters to the priest been written by her, or had they been forged by her husband? Here a case of veracity vs. falsehood has materialised anew and, in that respect, Caponsacchi's discourse has implied an equation of 'true' with something good to believe; by the same token, it has stemmed from the utilitarian premise that truth-seeking is a societal convention. At an educated guess, the speaker has been motivated by his belief that his fellow human beings were capable of a pleasurable interpersonal relationship inside the boundaries of ethics; along similar lines, he has deemed his action to be right for reasons related to Pompilia's pleasure, which he has seen as an absolute good antithetical to evil-engendering pain. In this connection, he has pursued jouissance by aiming at truth not merely for its own sake but for being an idea to be cherished as an end rather than as a means. Interestingly, an approach of this sort has given an ethically inspired man the traits of a hedonist escaping from the fetters of a strictly utilitarian *weltanschauung* on the assumption that an exclusive use of the criteria of utility would hardly lead him to the realm of virtue. Moreover, on the strength of his hedonistic streak, he has managed to spare himself the evil inherent in pain. *All's well that ends well*, then? In Shakespeare's version of Count Bertram's story, the King of France's warns the gentlewoman Helena, 'Thy pains not used must by thyself be paid'[2]. If applied to Caponsacchi's case, the monarch's moral statement raises questions about Caponsacchi's determination to have no truck with the world now that he has played an appreciable role on the local stage. Here close scrutiny is a must in order to establish whether the virtuous-minded guy had a priori considered the consequences of an escape with a lawfully wedded lady. The epistolary exchange fosters the theory that, in virtue of being prompted by a laudable desire to save Pompilia's life, the priest had had a presentiment of Guido's foul play in reaction to his wife's flight in the company of a stranger; hence his decision to cultivate an *artificial* virtue (of the kind propounded, say, by David Hume) obtainable solely by dint of following a path leading to freedom.

The blooming relationship between Giuseppe Caponsacchi and Pompilia Comparini has taken on a new dimension when the young man has recalled how he had knelt in front of the window where the young lady was standing with lamp in hand and a "griefful air" conjuring up the picture of Our Lady of all the Sorrows that stood in the penumbra on the altar he had frequently visited. The *chiaroscuro* in the visual image suggests a soul taking centre stage while a body "stood still as stone, all eye, all ear", and the juxtaposition of the two events intimates a man possessed with a ready spirit and an eager flesh. Pompilia had gazed at the enthralled visitor from a height, but a quasi-mystical experience had been tainted by the ever-present flesh. Matthew Arnold's contention that religion is morality tinged with emotion appears to fit in with the priest's ecstatic moment while being close to Pompilia: what his keen eyes and attentive ears had seen and heard beneath her window had made him conscious of the predicament of a spouse caught in a fire started by an imperfect husband on one side and a perfect stranger on the other. However, she had sounded as if she was struggling with her 'minimal self'[3] and feeling that it was all a riddle, 'for some kind of sake' barely clearer to herself than to him, the newcomer. The inescapable corollary of the enigmatic situation had been, Caponsacchi has added, Pompilia's admission of her inability to understand what had prompted him to offer help. Following the perception, she had looked dispassionately on both hate and love while being quietly confident that the *new man* in her life was fully aware of 'how weak the strongest women are' and had been, was, would always be, true to her.

Elaborating on his testimony, the Pieve-born Canon has pressed home the question of the authorship of the letters: "He wrote, she spoke", he has asserted, and her words had been a miracle made possible by their mutual recognition in the dazzling light of truth.

At this point, the flames of ethics have been reignited by someone who happened to be a man of the cloth: driven by a yearning for truth, he had coped with his duty to God as well as man, successfully dealt with the contest between love and hate, and passed into a state conducive to the vision of his church as "the Bride, the mystic love o' the Lamb". At the end of the canonical day, a religious consciousness had compelled him to live in conformity with the church teachings while being in suspended animation as a priest as well as a friend. By the same token, a categorical imperative had clashed with his hankering for freedom.

When it comes to the depiction of Pompilia over the course of the flight, it is fair to say that the canon has shown a mundane ego hand in glove with a religious one. Consider, for instance, how he has perceived his companion's white soul vis-à-vis the blackness of her body; moreover, think of how he has pondered over the nature of the mystery engulfing him and compared it to the way two martyrs wake up in a tomb and wait in unison for doomsday: surely it was not a matter of love; faith, *that* was the name of the game. Some time after him, a bishop has said something apropos: 'If so when, where and how? Some way must be; once feel about and soon or late you hit some sense, in which it might be, after all. Why not, 'The Way, the Truth, the Life?'[4]

As to Pompilia's pure soul, the priest has told the jury about his belief that it had helped her to accept affliction: 'All pain must be to work some good in the end', she had averred, – echoing, it is worthwhile to recall, the above-quoted King of France's assertion that suffering ought to be turned to good account as a means to a beneficial end. Intriguingly, Pompilia had subsequently asked her fellow fugitive whether men ever found themselves at odds with their masculinity, just as women were liable to feel ill at ease about their femininity. Here a recollection of Arthur Schopenhauer's socio-philosophical postulation that suffering is a universal condition may not come amiss.

Other significant events have occurred in the course of the journey Romewards. Most dramatically, Guido's wife has cried out that her soul belonged to her just as her body belonged to her soul; then, outweighing earthly preoccupations, she has acknowledged Caponsacchi's clerical status and been able to hear his voice even when he was silent; she has also detected his features when darkness reigned supreme. Indeed, the young woman has evinced religious sensibilities while highlighting her feelings of anxiety over the prospect of dying a sinner; furthermore, she has manifested a womanly moral consciousness through refraining from an overstatement of her pain and thinking that her demise could be justified as a fountainhead of pleasure for her consort. Her equitable approach has sounded in tune with the utilitarian view that a balance of pleasures is conducive to further pleasure. Moreover, her inner feelings may well have had their *fons et origo* in the humankind surrounding her: personal experience has prompted her *ego* to enter a realm of patriarchal culture which has replaced her world of imaginary plenitude with the reality of a symbolic conjugal cage; at the same time, her attitude has exposed Guido's *id* as that of as a maladjusted husband subconsciously governed by a Freudian pleasure principle. It should be added that she has provided an instance of feminine insecurity when she has asked Caponsacchi, in her eyes a man and a friend, if she had done anything wrong.

The gallant fellow has responded to Pompilia's misgivings by taking her, a "pure and pale" young woman, into an inn. His action has arguably revivified the literary convention of a damsel in distress rescued by a wight; it has also epitomised the poetic function of a fictional character along the lines suggested by a latter-day theory.[5] To set the record straight, his moral fibre has been revealed by the mention of his worst enemy appearing at the inn with "the old malice in the visage bad and black o' the scamp" who "kept well out o' the way, at arms' length and to spare" while spluttering with rage. Instead of getting hold of the villain and making him lie "abolished with his lie, creation purged o' the miscreate, man redeemed", he has desired to hear more filth and been inclined to recognise not "what a bag of venomed purulence was split and noisome, but how splendidly mirthful, what ludicrous a lie was launched!" Well, well, well, the crux of the matter is shouldn't he have borne, qua a priest, the stamp of care and compassion? Come to think of it, his mock-serious stance calls to mind the reaction of a fellow cleric in a similar situation: 'Till, wholly unexpected, in there pops the hothead husband! Thus I scuttle off to some safe bench behind, not letting go the palm of her, the little lily thing.'⁶ Strikingly, the dithering saviour has been put to shame by the "wax-white, seraphic, saturate with the sun" damsel when she has seized her husband's sword and brandished it to the accompaniment of bloodcurdling cries. There you are: *la donna angelicata* metamorphosing into a female endowed with an "erect form", a "flashing brow" and a "fulgurant eye". As for the knight, he has boasted that Pompilia had called him 'far beyond 'friend' and he had responded by making a desperate attempt to protect her from blatant lies such as the driver Venerino's deposition that he and Pompilia had now and then kissed each other in the coach: alas, his mendacity had been rewarded with liberty.

Caponsacchi's litany of grievances suggests the duality of a sower of wild oats turned "renderer of reason, not the officious priest would personate Saint George for a mock Princess in undragoned days". In this context, he has wondered whether "the priest who needs must carry sword on thigh may find imperative use for it" and the postulate has preceded a stream of invective levelled at the judges as blind guides leading the sighted as well as "fools, alike ignorant of man and God". In close succession, Guido has been described as a guy "miserably caught i' the quagmire of his own tricks, cheats and lies" whereas Pompilia's soul has been depicted as the agent of a change and a quest for truth: "The first glance told me there was no duty patent in the world like daring try be good and true myself, leaving the show of things to the Lord of Show and Prince o' the Power of the Air" – how unlike the 'inordinate culture of the sense made quick by soul, – the lust o' the flesh, lust of the eye, and pride of life, – and consequent on these the worship of that prince o' the power o' the air who paints the cloud and fills the emptiness and bids his votaries, famishing for truth, feed on a lie.'[7]

At this point, Caponsacchi has combined ethics with rhetoric: "What need of flight, what were the gain there from but just damnation, failure or success? What other advantage, – we who led the days and nights alone i' the house, – was flight to find?" Heavens above, the Court ought to shoulder the blame for sanctioning the escape and then failing to justify the means after allowing the end. In effect, the judicial system had played "into the devil's hands" whereas he, as a partner in the flight from marital oppression, had endeavoured to save Pompilia "against law" seraphically and in contrast to her husband who would slay her in contravention of the same law.

In this connection, the priest's hypersensitive consciousness of his exploit has been heightened by his claim to innocence "in thought, word and deed", which has been followed by an ironic exhortation to unfrock him: "There's a crack somewhere", he has stated, unwittingly echoing the sentry Marcellus' suspicion that something was rotten in the State of Denmark.[8] Immediately after that and in a serious vein again, he has requested to build churches and pray for Pompilia, for he has managed to achieve verity primarily thanks to her guidance – conducive, alas, to martyrdom. The religious mood has made Truth take centre stage anew qua *summum bonum* and placed the canon's attitude on a par with the Renaissance philosophical tenet that 'there is an inmost centre in us all, where truth abides in fulness; and around, wall upon wall, the gross flesh hems it in, this perfect, clear perception, which is truth.'[9]

The rhetorical flourish in the middle of a descriptively ethical evaluation has been softened by the orator's deep sense of guilt for failing to prevent Guido from doing violence to Pompilia; moreover, his admission of failure has whimsically been accompanied by a plea for lenience in dealing with the murderous husband on the grounds that, even if spared, the man would "slide out of life, pushed by the general horror and common hate low, lower, left o' the very ledge of things ... in the loneliness, silence and dusk" up to the moment he would come face to face with "Judas, made monstrous by much solitude" and the two of them would become entangled in a love/hate web: "There! Let them each tear each in devil's fun! The cockatrice is with the basilisk! There let them grapple, denizens o' the dark, foes or friends, but indissolubly bound, in their one spot out of the ken of God or care of man, for ever and ever more!" The nightmare scenario sparks a riveting picture of Count Ugolino furiously gnawing the head of a fellow damned in the frozen Lake of Cocytus.[10]

Giuseppe Caponsacchi's fireworks have been dimmed by an ambivalent view of Pompilia's features. Here Lippo Lippi springs to mind afresh: 'Take the prettiest face ... is it so pretty you can't discover if it means hope, fear, sorrow or joy? Won't beauty go with these? ... Can't I take breath and try to add life's flash, and then add soul and heighten them threefold?'[11] Then 'you get about the best thing God invents: that's somewhat, and you'll find the soul you have missed.'[12] Reflections of that ilk have added colour to the priest's extolment of Pompilia's soul vis-à-vis her body.

The canon has subsequently focused on the evidence essential for a proper trial and claimed that unproven fault in his case was the outcome of either a scribe's oversight or a slip of the tongue. Furthermore, what about the stance of the Governor, i.e. the official who had come to regard the runaway couple as "fit to brand and pillory and flog"? How unlike Fra Celestino, the Augustinian who had confessed many moribund faithfuls but "never one so sweet and true and pure and beautiful" as Pompilia; a good man the monk was, doubtless deserving of popedom. As to the incumbent pontiff, he too could be deemed to be full of goodness.

In the final analysis, a new quest for the holy grail of human verity appears to have played a pivotal role in the whydunit at issue. On reaching a climactic stage of his testimony, the Canon has pointed to his hard-won state of mind: "Sirs, I am quiet again", he has let his judges know and then urged them to "forget distemperature and idle heat." It has sounded like an echo of a 'faultless' painter's hushed confession in a 'settled dusk': 'I am grown peaceful as old age tonight. I regret little, I would change still less. Since there my past life is, why alter it?'[13]

Naturally, "priests should study passions; how else cure mankind who come for help in passionate extremes?", but it is reasonable to detect subtle nuances of irony in the cleric's assertion that he had been impelled by his soul-searching to "play with an imagined life" side by side with Pompilia. As a matter of fact, the two of them seem to have learnt from each other and been concerned with the eternal verities of life even while engaged in everyday routines: with the benefit of hindsight, learning "not only by a comet's rush but a rose's birth" had been "mere delectation, meet for a minute's dream." Like a student sitting in reverie close to his Plutarch, the Canon has awoken and found himself alone, as was his wont; his closing appeal to a "great, just, good God", coupled with the pathos of the alliterative "Miserable me!" – reminiscent of Everyman's mood in Allegri's *Miserere*, – has added a finishing touch to the portrait of his self-identity.

At the end of the day, a unifying factor has been provided by Giuseppe Caponsacchi's acknowledgement that he had been playing with an imagined life when in the company of Pompilia: in this respect, he can be credited with clinging to the Truth, – even though one of his own. One may justifiably resist the kind of suspicion engendered by Parson Williams as portrayed by Henry Fielding in *Pamela* and, by the same token, one may take with a pinch of salt Plato's contention in *The Republic* that a lover's attraction to his sweetheart suggests an inferior element of the soul. As the self-conscious canon leaves the scene, Augustine of Hippo comes on it and tells the audience about his sinful youth thank heavens obliterated by his discovery of Truth and lifelong exploration of the latter's redemptive power.

1. *The Faerie Queene*, VI, II, 1
2. *All's Well That Ends Well*, 2,1, l. 140
3. As figured out by Christopher Lasch. See *Psychoanalytic Theory*, by Anthony Elliott, p. 59
4. Robert Browning, *Bishop Blougram*.
5. Roman Jakobson, *Linguistics and Poetics*, in *Modern Criticism and Theory*, Ed. David Lodge, Longman 1988, pp. 37ff.
6. Robert Browning, *Fra Lippo Lippi*, ll. 382ff
7. Robert Browning, *Prince Hohenstiel-Schwangau*, ll. 2117-2023
8. William Shakespeare, *Hamlet*, 1. 4
9. Robert Browning, *Paracelsus*, Part I, ll. 728ff
10. Dante Alighieri, *La Divina Commedia −Inferno*, XXXII, ll. 124ff
11. *Fra Lippo Lippi*, ll. 208ff
12. *Ibid*. ll. 217-20
13. Robert Browning, *Andrea del Sarto*, ll. 244-46

POMPILIA

At the same time as Giuseppe Maria Caponsacchi testified in court, Pompilia lay agonizingly bedridden. A surgeon was in constant attendance while neighbours came and went. Now and again subdued voices raised questions and the distressed young woman gave answers in hushed tones that seemed like a miracle under the circumstances.

"I am just seventeen years and five months old. 'T is writ so in the church's register, *Lorenzo in Lucina*; all my names at length, so many names for one poor child: Francesca Camilla Vittoria Angela Pompilia Comparini. Laughable!" The lavishly named patient gave a nervous little laugh. "Also 't is writ that I was married there. I used to wonder, when I stood scarce high as the bed here, what the marble lion meant, with half his body rushing from the wall, eating the figure of a prostrate man, – an ominous sign to one baptized like me, married, and to be buried there, I hope. And they should add, to have my life complete, he is a boy and Gaetan by name". The mother's voice sank to a whisper. "Oh, how good God is that my babe was born, – better than born, baptized and hid away before this happened, safe from being hurt! Now I shall never see him. What is worse, when he grows up and gets to be my age, he will seem hardly more than a great boy; and if he asks 'What was my mother like?' people may answer 'Like girls of seventeen'. Therefore I wish someone will please to say I looked already old though I was young!"

The appearance-nonchalant mother turned sideways and settled herself, her pupils dilating and displaying their dark hue to the full. "How happy are those who know how to write! Such could write what their son should read in time. But then, how far away, how hard to find will anything about me have become, even if the boy bethink himself and ask! No father that he ever knew at all, nor ever had, – no, never had, I say; that is the truth,

– nor any mother left, fit for such memory as might assist. On second thoughts, I hope he will regard the history of me as what someone dreamed, and get to disbelieve it at the last, – since to myself it dwindles fast to that, sheer dreaming and impossibility. Good Pietro, kind Violante, gave me birth? They loved me always as I love my babe, did for me all I meant to do for him, till one surprising day, three years ago, they both declared, at Rome, before some judge, that really I had never been their child." The disowned offspring tossed and turned. "So with my husband, – just such a surprise, such a mistake, in that relationship! Everyone says that husbands love their wives, guard them and guide them, give them happiness; 'tis duty, law, pleasure, religion: well, you see how much of this comes true in mine!" She unleashed a rueful smile. "Then there is ... only let me name one more! There is the friend, – men will not ask about, but tell untruths of, and give nicknames to, and think my lover – most surprise of all! I am married, he has taken priestly vows; they know that and yet go on, say, the same, 'yes, how he loves you! That was love' – they say, when anything is answered that they ask. Or else, 'No wonder you love him', they say; then they shake heads, pity much, scarcely blame – as if we neither of us lacked excuse, and anyhow are punished to the full, and downright love atones for everything!" The smile turned apologetic. "I touch a fairy thing that fades and fades – even to my babe! I thought, when he was born, something began for once that would not end, nor change into a laugh at me, but stay for evermore, eternally quite mine. Yet thence comes such confusion of what was with what will be, – that late seems long ago, and, what years should bring round, already come, till even he withdraws into a dream." The speaker breathed an ethereal sigh. "Six days ago, when it was New Year's Day, we bent above the fire and talked of him: what he should do when he was grown and great. Oh what a happy friendly eve was that! And, next day, about noon, out Pietro went; he was so happy and would talk so much, until Violante pushed and laughed him forth sight-seeing in the cold: 'So much to see i' the churches! Swathe your throat three times!' she cried, 'and, above all, beware the slippery ways!" He came back late, laid by cloak, staff and hat, powdered so thick with snow it made us laugh, and bade Violante treat us to a flask because he had obeyed her faithfully, gone sight-see through the temples, and found no church to his mind like San Giovanni – 'There's the fold, and all the sheep together, big as cats! And such a shepherd, half the size of life, starts up and hears the angel' – when, at the door, a tap: we started up. You know the rest."

She broke off, though not for long. "Pietro at least had done no harm, I know; nor even Violante, so much harm as makes such revenge lawful. Certainly she erred in telling that first falsehood: buying me from my poor faulty mother at a price, to pass upon Pietro as his child. My father, – he was no one, any one, – was wicked for his pleasure, went his way, and left no trace to track by; there remained nothing but me, the unnecessary life, to catch up or let fall, and yet a thing she could make happy, be made happy with, this poor Violante. Who would frown thereat? Well, God, you see! God plants us where we grow. She thought, moreover, real lies were lies told for harm's sake; whereas this had good at heart, good for my mother, good for me, and good for Pietro who was meant to love a babe, and needed one to make his life of use."

The 'transplanted' daughter glanced at her audience with a flushed face and eyes alight. "Wrong, wrong and always wrong! how plainly wrong! For see, this fault kept pricking, as faults do, all the same at her heart, – this falsehood hatched, she could not let it go nor keep it fast. This it was set her on to make amends; this brought about the marriage – simply this! When Paul, my husband's brother, found me out, heard there was wealth for who should marry me, – so, came and made a speech to ask my hand for Guido, – she, instead of piercing straight through the pretence to the ignoble truth, fancied she saw God's very finger point, designate just the time for planting me in soil where I could strike real root and grow, find nothing , this time, but was what it seemed all truth and no confusion anymore. She meant well; has it been so ill i' the main? My child is safe; there seems not so much pain. It comes, most like, that I am just absolved, purged of the past, – the foul in me washed fair. One cannot both have and not have, you know, – being right now, I am happy and colour things. I know that when Violante told me first *il cavalier* she meant to bring next morn would be at San Lorenzo the same eve and marry me, – which over, we should go home both of us without him as before, – well, I no more saw sense in what she said than a lamb does in people clipping wool; only lay down and let myself be clipped. And when next day *il cavalier* who came, when he proved Guido Franceschini, – old , hook-nosed and yellow in a bush of beard, much like a thing I saw on a boy's wrist, he called an owl and used for catching birds, – and when he took my hand and made a smile, why, the uncomfortableness of it all seemed hardly more important in the case than, – when one gives you, say, a coin to spend, – its newness or its oldness: if the piece weigh properly and buy you what you wish, no matter whether you get grime or glare! Here, marriage was the coin, a dirty piece would purchase me the praise of those I loved: about what else should I concern myself?"

The laud-seeking spouse left the question hanging in the air for a moment and closed her ebony eyes tightly. "So, hardly knowing what a husband meant, I supposed this or any man would serve, no whit the worse for being so uncouth. However, I was hurried through a storm into blank San Lorenzo, up the aisle, my mother keeping hold of me so tight I fancied we were come to see a corpse before the altar which she pulled me toward. There we found waiting an unpleasant priest who proved the brother, not our parish friend: Paul, whom I know since to my cost. And then I heard the heavy church-door lock out help behind us: for the customary warmth, two tapers shivered on the altar. 'Quick – lose no time!' cried the priest. And straightway down from …

what's behind the altar where he hid – hawk-nose and yellowness and bush and all – stepped Guido, caught my hand, and there was I o' the chancel, and the priest had opened book, read here and there, made me say that and this, and after, told me I was now a wife, honoured indeed, since Christ thus weds the Church, and therefore turned he water into wine, to show I should obey my spouse like Christ. Then the two slipped aside and talked apart, and I, silent and scared, got down again and joined my mother who was weeping now."

Pompilia reopened her eyes and leaned forward, flushed with regret. "When we were in the street, the rain had stopped, all things looked better. At our own house-door, Violante whispered 'No one syllable to Pietro! Girl-brides never breathe a word!'" She broke into a smile, which seemed de rigueur. "Madonna saved me from immodest speech." She adjusted her suddenly untidy blanket. "When I saw nothing more, the next three weeks, of Guido – 'Nor the Church sees Christ' thought I. 'Nothing is changed, however: wine is wine and water only water in the house.'" She forced another smile. "Until one morning, – as I sat and sang at the broidery-frame, alone i' the chamber, – loud voices, two, three together, sobbings too, and my name, 'Guido', 'Paolo', flung like stones from each to the other!

In I ran to see. *There* stood the very Guido and the priest with sly face, formal but nowise afraid, while Pietro seemed all red and angry, scarce able to stutter out his wrath in words; and this it was that made my mother sob, as he reproached her – 'You have murdered us, me and yourself and this our child beside!' Then Guido interposed 'Murdered or not, be it enough your child is now my wife!'

I stood mute, – those who tangled must untie the embroilment. Pietro cried 'Withdraw, my child! Go, child, and pray God help the innocent!'"

Absorbingly, the features of the guiltless young woman made up a pale shape against the blackness of her wavy hair. "I did go and was praying God, when came Violante, with eyes swollen and red enough. She bade me sit down by her side and hear: 'You are too young and cannot understand, nor did your father understand at first. I tried to have my way at unaware, obtained him the advantage he refused; but either you have prayed him unperverse or I have talked him into his wits, and Paolo was a help in time of need. A priest is more a woman than a man, and Paul did much to persuade. In short, my scheme was worth attempting and bears fruit, gives you a husband and a noble name, a palace and no end of pleasant things. What do you care about a handsome youth? They are so volatile and teaze their wives! This is the kind of man to keep the house: we lose no daughter, – gain a son, that's all; in good or ill, we share and share alike, and cast our lots into a common lap. '

A brief silence intervened while Pompilia laboriously pulled herself upright. Then, "And so an end! Because a blank begins from when, at the word, she kissed me hard and hot, and said 'Count Guido, take your lawful wife until death part you!' All since is one blank, over and ended; a terrific dream. It is the good of dreams – so soon they go, and when you rub your eyes awake and wide, where's the harm o' the horror? Gone! So here. I know I wake, but from what? Blank, I say! This is the note of evil, for good lasts. I am held up, amid the nothingness, by one or two truths only – thence I hang and there I live; the rest is death or dream. So, what I hold by, are my prayer to God some hand would interpose and save me, – hand which proved to be my friend's hand and, – best bliss, – that thrill of dawn's suffusion through my dark, which I perceive was promise of my child, the light his unborn face sent long before." Her eyes lit up with a seraphic hue. "Don Celestine urged 'But remember more! Other men's faults may help me find your own. I need the cruelty exposed, explained, or how can I advise you to forgive?' He thought I could not properly forgive unless I ceased forgetting, – which is true: for, bringing back reluctantly to mind my husband's treatment of me, by a light that's later than my lifetime, I review and comprehend much and imagine more, and have but little to forgive at last. For now, – be fair and say, – is it not true he was ill-used and cheated of his hope to get enriched by marriage? Marriage gave me and no money, broke the compact so: he had a right to ask me on those terms, as Pietro and Violante to declare they would not give me: so the bargain stood; they broke it and he felt himself aggrieved, became unkind with me to punish them. Echoes die off, scarcely reverberate forever, – why should ill keep echoing ill and never let our ears have done with noise?" The maltreated lass swung her ebony hair from side to side. "Then my poor parents took the violent way to thwart him, – he must needs retaliate, – wrong, wrong, and all wrong; better say, all blind!" She produced a floral tissue and blew her Roman nose. "As I myself was, that is sure, who else had understood the mystery: for his wife was bound in some sort to help somehow there. Thus, when he blamed me, 'You are a coquette, a lure-owl posturing to attract birds; you look love-lures at theatre and church, in walk, at window!' – that, I knew, was false, but why he charged me falsely, whither sought to drive me by such charge, – how could I know? So, unaware, I only made things worse. I tried to soothe him by abjuring walk, window, church, theatre, for good and all, as if he had been in earnest: that, you know, was nothing like the object of his charge. Yes, when I got my maid to supplicate the priest, – whose name she read when she would read those feigned letters I was forced to hear though I could read no word of – he should cease writing, nay, if he minded prayer of mine, cease from so much as even pass the street whereon our house looked, in my ignorance I was just thwarting Guido's true intent, which was to bring about a wicked change of sport to earnest, tempt a thoughtless man to write indeed, and pass the house, and more, till both of us were taken in a crime. It follows, – if I fell into such a fault, he also may have overreached the mark, made mistake, by perversity of brain. I cannot say less; more I will not say. Leave it to God to cover and undo! Must I speak? I am blamed that I forwent a way to make my husband's favour come. That is true: I was firm, withstood, refused ... women as you are, how can I find the words?"

The response of the women encircling her was a knowing smile. "I felt," she continued, "there was just one thing Guido claimed I had no right to give nor he to take; we being in estrangement, soul from soul, even at Arezzo, when I woke and found first ... but I need not think of that again! After the first, my husband, for hate's sake, said one eve, when the simpler cruelty seemed somewhat dull at edge and fit to bear, 'How long is this your comedy to last? Go this night to my chamber, not your own!' At which word I did rush – most true the charge – and gain the Archbishop's house – he stands for God! – and fall upon my knees and clasp his feet, praying him hinder what my estranged soul refused to bear, though patient of the rest. What did he answer? 'Folly of ignorance! Know, daughter, circumstances make or mar virginity, – 't is virtue or 't is vice. Had Eve, in answer to her Maker's speech: "Be fruitful, multiply, replenish earth", pouted "But I choose rather to remain single" – why, she had spared herself forthwith further probation by the apple and snake, been pushed straight out of Paradise! For see – if motherhood be qualified impure, I catch you making God command Eve sin!' Then he pursued, ''T was in your covenant!'"

The virginal-minded descendant of Eve gave a snort. "No! There my husband never used deceit. He only stipulated for the wealth; honest so far. But when he spoke as plain, dreadfully honest also: 'Since our souls stand each from each, a whole world's width between, give me the fleshy vesture I can reach and rend and leave just fit for hell to burn', I did resist; would I had overcome!"

The belated wish was conveyed in a high voice, but the sound abated in the twinkling of an eye. "My heart died out at the Archbishop's smile; it seemed so stale and worn a way o' the world. Then I resolved to tell a frightful thing: 'I am not ignorant, – know what I say, declaring this is sought for hate, not love. My husband sees this, knows this, and lets be. Is it your counsel I bear this beside?'

'Rise up, my child, for such a child you are, the rod were too advanced a punishment! Therefore go home, embrace your husband quick!'

So, home I did go; so, the worst befell: so, I had proof the Archbishop was just man, and hardly that, and certainly no more. My husband's hatred waxed nor waned at all; his brother's boldness grew effrontery soon, and my last stay and comfort in myself was forced from me: henceforth I looked to God only, nor cared my desecrated soul should have fair walls, gay windows for the world. They said, 'No care to save appearance here!' – adding, it all came of my mother's life, my own real mother whom I never knew. The rather do I understand her now, – from my experience of what hate calls love, much love might be in what their love called hate. If she sold … what they call, sold … me her child – I shall believe she hoped in her poor heart that I at least might try be good and pure, begin to live untempted, not go doomed and done with ere once found in fault, as she. Oh and, my mother, it all came to this? Why, since all bound to do me good did harm, may not you, seeming as you harmed me most, have meant to do most good – and feed your child from bramble-bush, whom not one orchard-tree but drew-back bough from, nor let one fruit fall? This it was for you sacrificed your babe? Gained just this, giving your heart's hope away as I might give mine, loving it as you, if … but that never could be asked of me!"

Pompilia's mouth twitched slightly, but a hard-won smile restored it to smoothness. "There, enough! I have my support again, again the knowledge that my babe was, is, will be mine only. Him, by death, I give outright to God without a further care, – what guardianship were safer could we choose? All human plans and projects come to nought; my life, and what I know of other lives, prove that: no plan nor project. God shall care!"

The firm believer turned silent again while laboriously detaching her head from the pillow; her tremulous bosom stood out like a bas-relief whilst she stared vacantly into space, then it fell back and her long eyelids slowly merged, but the doze into which she had sunk ended within a short space of time and her eyes converged on the charitable neighbours still standing at her bedside.

She spoke anew. "And now you are not tired? How patient then all of you, oh yes, patient this long while, – listening and understanding, I am sure! Four days ago, when I was sound and well and like to live, no one would understand. People were kind, but smiled 'And what of him, your friend, whose tonsure, the rich dark-brown hides? Still, he thinks many a long think, never fear, after the shy pale lady lay so light for a moment in his arms, the lucky one!' And so on: wherefore should I blame you much? So are we made, such difference in minds, such difference too in eyes that see the minds! That man, you misinterpret and misprise, – the glory of his nature, I had thought, shot itself out in white light, blazed the truth through every atom of his act with me. Thus it fell: I was at a public play, in the last days of Carnival last March. My thoughts went through the roof and out, to Rome on wings of music, waft of measured words, set me down there, a happy child again! Sudden I saw him; into my lap there fell a foolish twist of comfits, broke my dream and brought me from the air and laid me low. I looked to see who flung them, and I faced this Caponsacchi, looking up in turn. Up rose the round face and good-natured grin of him who, in effect, had played the prank: fat waggish Conti, friend of all the world.

There is a psalm Don Celestine recites, 'Had I a dove's wings, how I fain would flee!' The psalm runs not 'I hope, I pray for wings,' – simply 'How good it were to fly and rest, how well to do what I shall never do!' So I said, 'Had there been a man like that, to lift me with his strength out of all strife into the calm, how I could fly and rest!'

Presently Conti laughed into my ear, 'Cousin, I flung them brutishly and hard!'

That night at supper, out my husband broke, 'Why was that throwing, that buffoonery? 'T was knowledge of you bred such insolence in Caponsacchi; he dared shoot the bolt, using that Conti for his stalking horse. Does he presume because he is a priest? I warn him that the sword I wear shall pink his lily-scented cassock through and through next time I catch him underneath your eaves!' But he had threatened with the sword so oft and, after all, not kept his promise. All I said was, 'Let God save the innocent! I shall go pray for you and me, not him.'

Pompilia's dark eyes lit up with a stoical hue, but the tinge faded away as she recalled how Margherita, her so-called waiting-maid, had come home bearing a poetic message of love from the cleric who was convinced that she loved her husband and hated him. She had promptly refuted the allegation and termed her 'report of Caponsacchi false, folly or dreaming.' By contrast, she was 'speaking truth to the Truth's self' and no doubt God would credit her words.

The stream of words ran on untrammelled. "One vivid daybreak, – light in me, light without me, everywhere change! A broad yellow sunbeam was let fall from heaven to earth, – a sudden drawbridge lay, along which marched a myriad merry motes. On the house-eaves, a dripping shag of weed shook diamonds on each dull grey lattice-square, as first one, then another bird leapt by, and light was off, and lo was back again, always with one voice, – where are two such joys? The blessed building-sparrow! I stepped forth, stood on the terrace, – o'er the roof, such sky! My heart sang, 'I too am to go away: I have my purpose and my motive too, my march to Rome, like any bird or fly! Had I been dead! How right to be alive! Not to live, now, would be the wickedness, – for life means to make haste and go to Rome!'

Now, as I stood letting morn bathe me bright, choosing which butterfly should bear my news, the Margherita, I detested so, in she came – 'The fine day, the good Springtime! No thought of Caponsacchi? – who stood there all night on one leg, like the sentry crane?'

I turned – 'Tell Caponsacchi he may come.'

'Tell him to come? Ah, but, for charity, a truce to fooling! Come? What, – come this eve? What is the message that shall move him now?'

'After the *Ave Maria*. At first dark I will be standing on the terrace, say!'

Off she went –'May he not refuse, that's all – fearing a trick!'

I answered, 'He will come.'

And, all day, I sent prayer like incense up to God the strong, God the beneficent, God ever mindful in all strife and strait, who, for our own good, makes the need extreme, till at the last He puts forth might and saves. And still, as the day wore, the trouble grew whereby I guessed there would be born a star, until at an intense throe of the dusk I started up, was pushed, I dare to say, out on the terrace, leaned and looked at last where the deliverer waited me: the same silent and solemn face, I first descried at the spectacle, confronted mine once more. So was the minute twice vouchsafed me, so the manhood, wasted then, was still at watch! "

The narrator breathed a sigh of relief. "I spoke on the instant, as my duty bade. 'Friend, foolish words were borne from you to me; your soul behind them is the pure strong wind, not dust and feathers which its breath may bear. If by mischance you blew offence my way, the straws are dropped, the wind desists no whit. You serve God specially, as priests are bound, and care about me, stranger as I am, so far as wish my good, – that miracle I take to intimate He wills you serve by saving me; what else can He direct? You go to Rome, they tell me. Take me there, put me back with my people!'

He replied, – the first word I heard ever from his lips, all himself in it, – an eternity of speech to match the immeasurable depths o' the soul that then broke silence: 'I am yours.'

She sounded elated. "So did the star rise, soon to lead my step, and the way was Caponsacchi – 'mine,' thank God! He was mine, he is mine, he will be mine! Next night there was a cloud came, and not he: but I prayed through the darkness till it broke and let him shine. The second night, he came: 'The plan is rash; the project desperate: in such a flight needs must I risk your life, give food for falsehood, folly or mistake, ground for your husband's rancour and revenge' – so he began again, with the same face. I felt that, the same loyalty – one star turning now red that was so white before – one service apprehended newly: just a word of mine and there! the white was back.

'I know you: when is it that you will come?'

'To-morrow at the day's dawn.'

Then I heard what I should do: how to prepare for flight. And this man, men call sinner? Jesus Christ! I did think, do think, in the thought shall die, that to have Caponsacchi for my guide, ever the face turned up to mine, the hand holding my hand across the world, – a sense that reads, as only such can read, the mark God sets on woman, signifying so she should – shall peradventure – be divine. 'Such way the saints work', says Don Celestine. The saints must bear with me, impute the fault to a soul i' the bud so starved by ignorance, stinted of warmth, it will not blow this year nor recognize the orb which Spring-flowers know."

The recipient of Flora's blessing gave a little gasp of delight and extended her arms in the direction of the window: were they reaching for the goddess of flowers and Spring? Her face broke into a wan smile. "Is all told?" she wondered *sotto voce*. "There's the journey: and where's time to tell you how that heart burst out in shine? Towns, flowers and faces, all things helped so well! As I look back, all is one milky way. Him I now see make the shine everywhere as in his arms he caught me and, you say, carried me in, that tragical red eve, and laid me where I next returned to life. in the other red of morning, – two red plates that crushed together, crushed the time between, and are since then a solid fire to me. I did for once see right, do right, give tongue the adequate protest: for a worm must turn if it would have its wrong observed by God. I did spring up, attempt to thrust aside that ice block 'twixt the sun and me, lay low the neutralizer of all good and truth. I am clear it was on impulse to serve God, not save myself, – no – nor my child unborn! If only I was threatened and belied, what matter? I could bear it and did bear. But when at last, all by myself I stood obeying the clear voice which bade me rise, not for my own sake but my babe unborn, and found the old adversary athwart the path, *that* only I resisted! So, my first and last resistance was invincible. Prayers move God; threats, and nothing else, move men. I must have prayed a man as he were God when I implored the Governor to right my parents' wrongs: the answer was a smile. The Archbishop, – did I clasp his feet enough, hide my face hotly on them, while I told more than I dared make my own mother know? The profit was compassion and a jest."

The speaker's deliberate undertone rose by an octave. "Yet, shame thus rank and patent, I struck, bare, at foe from head to foot in magic mail, and off it withered, cobweb-armoury against the lightning. 'T was truth singed the lies and saved me, not the vain sword nor weak speech! A fortnight filled with bliss is long and much: not all women are mothers of a boy. There I lay, then, all my great fortnight long, as it would continue, broaden out happily more and more, and lead to heaven. Christmas before me, – was not that a chance? I never realized God's birth before; this time I felt like Mary, had my babe lying a little on my breast like hers. So all went on till, just four days ago – the night and the tap."

There followed yet another brief silence and then, "Oh, it shall be success to the whole of our poor family! My friends ... nay, father and mother, – give me back my word! They have been rudely stripped of life, disgraced like children who must needs go clothed too fine, carry the garb of Carnival in Lent: if they too much affected frippery, they have been punished and submit themselves, say no word: all is over, they see God who will not be extreme to mark their fault or He had granted respite: they are safe." She breathed a sigh of relief. "For that most woeful man my husband once, I – pardon him? So far as lies in me, I give him for his good the life he takes; let him make God amends, – none, none to me. We shall not meet in this world nor the next, but where will God be absent? In His face is light, but in His shadow healing too; let Guido touch the shadow and be healed! May my evanishment for evermore help further to relieve the heart that cast such object of its natural loathing forth. So he was made; he nowise made himself. His soul has never lain beside my soul; but for the unresisting body, – thanks! He burned that garment spotted by the flesh! Whatever he touched is rightly ruined: plague it caught, and disinfection it had craved still but for Guido; I am saved through him so as by fire; to him – thanks and farewell!"

A touch of forced brightness lent an edge to her voice. "Even for my babe, my boy, there's safety thence – from the sudden death of me, I mean: we poor weak souls, how we endeavour to be strong! The great life; see, a breath and it is gone! Shall not God stoop the kindlier to His work? Why should I doubt He will explain in time what I feel now but fail to find the words? My babe nor was, nor is, nor yet shall be Count Guido Franceschini's child at all – only his mother's, born of love, not hate! So shall I have my rights in after-time. It seems absurd, impossible today; so seems so much else not explained but known."

It sounded as though Pompilia's monologue had reached peroration. "Ah! Friends, thanks and bless you everyone! No more now. I withdraw from earth and man to my own soul, compose myself for God." A brief interlude came to an end as she resumed: "Well, and there is more! Yes, my end of breath shall bear away my soul in being true! 'T is now, when I am most upon the move, I feel for what I verily find – again the heart and its immeasurable love of my one friend, my only, all my own, who put his breast between the spears and me. O lover of my life, O soldier-saint, no work begun shall ever pause for death! Love will be helpful to me more and more i' the coming course, the new path I must tread, – my weak hand in thy strong hand, strong for that!"

The doomed patient fixed her gimlet eyes on the compact assembly. "Tell him that if I seem without him now, that's the world's insight. Oh, he understands! What I see, oh, he sees and how much more! It was the name of him I sprang to meet when came the knock, the summons and the end."

A second octave-leap in the music-like scale resounded. "He is ordained to call and I to come! Say, – I am all in flowers from head to foot. Say, – not one flower of all he said and did, might seem to flit unnoticed, fade unknown at this supreme of moments. He is a priest; I think he would not marry if he could. Marriage on earth seems such a counterfeit, mere imitation of the inimitable; in heaven we have the real and true and sure. Be as the angels rather, who, apart, know themselves into one, are found at length married, but marry never, no, nor give in marriage; they are man and wife at once when the true time is. Here we have to wait not so long neither! Could we by a wish have what we will and get the future now, would we wish aught done in the past undone? So, let him wait God's instant men call years; meantime hold hard by truth and his great soul, do out the duty! Through such souls alone, God stooping shows sufficient of His light for us i' the dark to rise by." She shifted to a forward position and lifted her dark eyes to an immaculate ceiling and the Presence beyond it. "And I rise", she let the audience know with an otherwordly modulation. It was the end of the road. Guido's unready wife was making herself ready for God.

Pompilia Franceschini's testimony has brought more than a modicum of self-awareness to the fore. To start with, the young woman has made a facetious comment on the "so many names for one poor child", thus unwittingly recalling a prestigious *gens Romana* as well as the 14th-century Giulietta Capuleti asking Romeo Montecchi 'What's in a name?' and remarking, 'That which we call a rose by any other word would smell as sweet.'[1] By the same token, Pompilia has recalled San Lorenzo's Church, her 'own particular place', where she had been baptised and, as a little kid, mesmerized by the spectacle of a marble lion intent on devouring a prostrate man. In addition, qua a parent, she has experienced the imaginary child/mother dyadic bond conducive, in her case, to a deep-seated fear of not seeing her son again; also, she has charmingly linked her unpleasant emotion with the hope that people would one day tell her only child that his departed mum had looked already old when she was still in her prime. Concerning her short life, Pompilia has lamented that it had been shot through with "sheer dreaming and impossibility" until her would-be parents' loving care in contrast to her husband's erratic behaviour, not to mention Caponsacchi's empathy, had made her discover the real world. Honest to God, the burgeoning rapport with the cleric had been no liaison, yet suspicious observers had conceded that in a world of sinful humans "downright love atones for everything." However, the experiences of childhood had turned her life into a dwindling "fairy thing": even her flesh-and-blood offspring had withdrawn "into a dream as the rest do."

Looking at her condition from a latter-day critical angle, it could be argued that Gaetano's withdrawal had put paid to her hopes of a play in which absolute affirmation would surrender itself to 'genetic indetermination [and] seminal adventure of the trace'[2]: torn between dream and reality, she has wavered between scorn and appreciation while determined to advocate a disruption of presence and make claims about a world entirely of her own.[3]

Another significant component of Pompilia's character has been brought out by a kind of Freudian realistic stroke when she has maintained to have gained a clear understanding of Pietro's yearning for a son, that is, of the longing that makes a man see the birth of his offspring as a mythic event embodying an unconscious perception of the mystery of the father. The alleged daughter's attitude has produced a strong contrast with the depraved mind of her natural father; similarly, her philosophy of life has made her weigh Violante's benevolent lies vis-à-vis her biological mother's degradation. "Wrong, wrong, and always wrong!" she has exclaimed and then gone as far as to claim that, for her part, she was "absolved, purged of the past". Significantly, the fourth dimension has reappeared in the shape of her husband, graphically depicted as a "hook-nosed and yellow in a bush of beard", ergo endowed with features redolent of those of Antipholus of Syracuse as depicted by the ludicrously erring Adriana, Antipholus of Ephesus' jealous wife.[4]

In Pompilia's eyes her marriage had proved to be a filthy coin which she was expected to put to good use by dint of buying the praise of those she loved. Her unorthodox verbal description in the course of her wedding suggests a desecration of the Cana miracle; moreover, its carnivalesque undertone betrays a tension conducive to a belittlement of the spiritual quality inherent in the liturgical ceremony. As a married woman aware of the fact that the Cana miracle had not repeated itself, she has admitted to nostalgia about the pristine purity of her true self. However, in her mind's eye the tenor of her life had been adequate – at least until Guido had tainted the big picture, that is to say.

Interestingly, Pompilia has proved to have a keen eye far beyond the reach of her years: in this connection, it would be appropriate to consider the way she has dealt with a social factor having a Marxian 'exchange value' as well as with a complex ethical issue.

A small yet crucial step in the right direction has made a highly strung lass enter a Freudian world of dreams and perceive the recent events in her life as an oneiric fleeting experience: "All since is one blank, over and ended; a terrific dream. It is the good of dreams: so soon they go!" – only "good lasts." On awaking, Pompilia has felt like the confessional poet had said, 'Twas beautiful, yet but a dream, and so adieu to it!"[5] Accordingly, after oscillating between an oneiric realm and the real world, she has clung to "one or two truths only" in addition to a plethora of prayers to God: on the one hand, she has forgiven her husband on the grounds that "he was ill-used and cheated of his hope to get enriched by marriage"; on the other hand, she had "but little to forgive" because a man so badly treated "must needs retaliate". A radically feminist critic would probably have no hesitation in maintaining that she has betrayed a concern about her weak ego-boundaries and made an attempt to erect a defensive wall; on the strength of a mental association, her subsequent affirmation that it was "wrong, wrong, and all wrong – better say, all blind!" has not come as a surprise in the light of the fact that her conjugal status has compelled her "in some sort to help somewhere there."

Jealous Adriana springs to mind again: 'Thou art an elm, my husband; I a vine, whose weakness, married to thy strong state, makes me with thy strength to communicate.'[6] The statement suggests a 'weakness of the will', as explored by Socrates, as well as a marital dependence tantamount to a master/slave tie. In this respect, Adriana's sister, Luciana, has come on the scene and declared that men, 'indued with intellectual sense and souls, of more pre-eminence than fish and fowls, are masters to their females, and their lords.'[7] Here's the rub: in more recent times, psychoanalytic feminism has emphasised that 'women's core gender identity (weak ego boundaries, immersion in narcissism etc.) comes to mirror their culturally devalued social position'[8]; accordingly, a bunch of feminists has, amazingly in tune with Adriana and Luciana, put forth that one way out of their lower standing would be for them to deny 'what is needed within, focusing on what is needed by others – particularly the needs of men.'[9]

Interestingly, Pompilia has evinced a leaning towards the above-mentioned women's perspective on the male/female interaction, and the remaining question is whether we ought to see her as a woman 'slydinge of corage' on a par with Chaucer's *Criseide* and, in effect, manipulated by Guido. Amid accusations of failure to win her husband's favour, she has admitted to unwisely spurning a man's overtures. Later in the day, she has asked other women to understand her great difficulty in providing a satisfactory explanation for her modus operandi. Strikingly, her request has sounded in tune with the assertion that "it's a question woman asks herself ... because there is so little place in society for her desire that she ends up by dint of not knowing what to do with it, not knowing where to put it, or if she has any, conceals the most immediate and urgent question: 'How do I experience sexual pleasure?'[10] In this connection, it makes sense to argue symptoms of libidinal economy and point up a metaphor in which a female subject's flesh and function appear to be signifying elements.

Guido and Pompilia have given a clear-cut instance of marital problems when both have mentioned "estrangement, soul from soul." With a difference though: the husband has hankered for a 'fleshy vesture ... just fit for hell to burn' while the wife has put up strong resistance for his" soul's own sake." However, the latter has gone on to express deep regret about not relinquishing her opposition; in saying so, she has betrayed a deep sense of responsibility for an irretrievable loss. It is apposite to recall the similar mood experienced by a male lover in the Roman *campagna*: 'I would that you were all to me; you that are just so much, no more. Nor yours, nor mine, nor slave nor free! Where does the fault lie? What the core o' the wound since wound must be?'[11]

The core of the wound can be found in Pompilia's double self, which has emerged when she has recounted how she felt about the people she had been closely in touch with – folk such as her biblically inspired as well as mundane husband and the awkward Archbishop to whom she had unsuccessfully turned: her double-edged personality was the cause of her love and hate for them taking shape in equal measure. It calls to mind the alchemist Paracelsus' words on the brink of death: 'In my own heart love had not been made wise … to know even hate is but a mask of love's'[12]. The dichotomous compound, redolent of Catullus' *Odi et Amo*, has disfigured the 'wild beauty of a yearning soul' and sounded antithetical to a Tuscan friar's street song, 'Flower o' the clove, All the Latin I construe is, '*amo*', I love!'[13]

Pompilia's equally ambivalent mood has possessed her until, on the strength of a cathartic experience, she has sensed that, concerning her natural mother's motives, there might be much love in what other people called hate. The question is had she overcome her pre-Oedipal complex and succeeded in redirecting her sexual passivity? In any case, she appears to have been guided by an exclusive maternal instinct – witness her forceful statement, "My babe was, is, will be mine only." At the same time, an egocentric motherhood has made her willing to give her own child "outright to God without a further care", while the recognition of an Eternal Father has kept her embryonic feminism within the bounds of a transcendent patriarchal authority. "God shall care!" she has exclaimed, unwittingly echoing a biblical prophet's trust in God's help: 'I will wait for the God of my salvation; my God will hear me.'[14]

A short while later, a philosophical turn of the tide has given special value to her perception of the world as the planet on which Caponsacchi's radiant energy had "shot itself out in white light" and "blazed the truth" in the guise of a quintessentially pure phenomenon. She had heard some juicy gossip about the priest's feelings about her and taken pains to "disperse the stain … about a lustrous and pellucid soul". A janitor called Faunia Farley springs to mind on the strength of her belief that there is a human stain which is 'so intrinsic it doesn't require a mark ... [and] perplexes all explanation and understanding';[in effect], 'all the cleansing is a joke.'[15] The sceptical contention can be associated with Pompilia's depiction of her clerical friend's purity as the nearest thing to a pie in the sky; also, with her own attempt to "be good and pure", – the depiction and the attempt being specimen of hopeless endeavour. By the same token it is highly significant that, echoing Don Celestino's biblical citation 'Had I a dove's wings, how I fain would flee!', the faithful lass has exclaimed, "Had there been a man like that, to lift me with his strength out of all strife into the calm, how I could fly and rest!" It has sounded like the utterance of a distressed damsel yearning for the presence of a chivalric knight.

The reappearance of Margherita has acted as a catalyst for a renewed epiphany centred around Pompilia's and Giuseppe's emotions: when the latter says to the former's waiting-maid 'To her behest I bow myself, whom I love with my body and my soul', his passionate utterance contains echoes of Launcelot of the Lake's profession of *courtly love* for Guinevere; also, it shows traces of the imperfection that had prevented the knight of old from achieving the Grail. For her part, the latter-day Guinevere has mirrored a medieval *chanson de la mal mariée* and in the process restated the complex interaction between between veracity and falsehood by asking "Why, what was all I said but truth, even when I found that such as are untrue could only take the truth in through a lie?" and repeating herself when, on meeting Caponsacchi, she has told him of her conviction that she was in touch with a "strong soul". Interestingly, this 'strong soul' appears to have been a counterpoint to the strength displayed by her through brandishing a sword to protect her soul mate in a fashion recalling, for instance, Britomart's endeavour to save Artegall in *The Faerie Queene*. Nonetheless, she has been in desperate need of help and has been saved solely by the might of a truth that has "singed the lies." At this critical juncture, truth has taken centre stage anew as a means of escape from the claims of a mendacious carnality. As if by a touch of magic, Paracelsus has reappeared as the alchemist heard by Browning to assert that 'there is an immanent centre in us all, where truth abides in fulness; and around, – wall upon wall, – the gross flesh hems it in.'[16] In effect, the Victorian poet has put the metonymic event to good use in *The Ring and the Book* by highlighting the indestructibility of the unconscious desire which has made Caponsacchi's bearing of truth more essential than ever for Pompilia's splendid maternal soul as well as for the salvation of Gaetano, her innocent offspring.

The mother/son bond has been imbued with a mystical hue when, holding her child on her breast, the young mother has felt in harmony with the divinable mood of the Virgin Mary. Then, standing her ground, she has expressed her readiness to give Guido "for his good the life he takes" and "let him make God amends": hatred may have been "the truth of him", but then "so he was made; he nowise made himself". On the other hand, "his soul has never lain beside my soul; but for the unresisting body, – thanks! He burned that garment spotted by the flesh! ... I am saved through him so as by fire; to him – thanks and farewell!"

A mood of the kind suggests that Pompilia has inadvertently made use of the *reductio ad absurdum* method; also, it creates the image of a woman whom Aristotle would probably have regarded as the epitome of virtue. By the same token her attitude calls to mind 'a Nietzschean *affirmation*, the joyous affirmation of the play of the world and of the innocence of becoming'[17].

The young wife has gone on to state that burning a "garment spotted by the flesh" had been a stepping-stone to her babe's salvation and her own. However, Guido had played no part in the parenthood: indeed, she would never identify him as the begetter of her offspring; Gaetano was "only his mother's son, born of love, not hate."

At this advanced phase of a speech act imbued with ethical and religious/overtones, Pompilia has reached a plateau. "Yes, my end of breath shall bear away my soul in being true!" she has exclaimed and gone on to extol the close link between truth and love; even the love/hate dichotomy inherent in her soul has proved a springboard to the panegyric of a soldier/saint/lover whose strong hand had held her weak one and whose name she had sprung to meet "when came the knock, the summons and the end".

At this defining moment, Pompilia has disclosed what has been termed by latter-day theorists 'basic trust' and deemed to be 'a fundamental condition for the subject's handling of unconscious anxiety ... in the network of social relations'.[18] The event has signalled the end of the road for a traveller on her last legs, now decked with flowers "from head to foot" in honour of God and yet still in touch with a man who had sown a seed from which a balsam tree had now grown. As it happened, this man was a clergyman and therefore committed to celibacy, but then she felt sure that "he would not marry if he could."

Now, did her feeling originate from a desire to redress her earlier sense of inadequacy by associating a metaphorically castrated celibate with her virtually virginal motherhood? There are psychoanalytic grounds for making such an assumption: 'Where id was, there ego shall be', Freud has asserted,[19] and the maxim still strikes a chord. Indeed, the next step in Pompilia's ego's progress has been upwards: the floral pattern on the girl's vestment has contrasted planet Earth, where marriage "seems such a counterfeit", with Heaven, where "it is real and true and sure." As for Caponsacchi, he was a man bound to "wait God's instant" and "meantime hold hard by truth and his great soul, do out the duty".

In the final analysis, a summary of Guido' wife's speech act may be of some help in building up a picture of the woman at issue.

While talking of her husband, she has dropped a hint about her willingness to condone his misconduct. Early in her monologue she has pointed out that he had "never used deceit" and only "stipulated for the wealth"; soon after, she has changed tack and quoted Guido's request for her garment so that he might tear it and 'leave just fit for hell to burn.' Mildred Tresham's frame of mind in Browning's *A Blot in the 'Scutcheon* appears to be strikingly similar when she says to her brother Thorold, 'There may be pardon yet; all's doubt beyond. Surely the bitterness of death is past!'[20]. Equally salient are the lines sent by Pamela Andrew's to her parents concerning Mr. B.'s behaviour suspiciously based on 'free principles': 'What sort of creatures must the womenkind be, do you think, to give way to such wickedness? ... What a world we live in!'[21] Association of ideas validates the contention that the forgiving Pompilia has on occasion been ambivalent, if not highly ambiguous, in her relationship with her husband as well as with Caponsacchi. It is tempting to suppose that the young woman has found herself in what has been termed a 'paranoid-schizoid' position and then moved to a 'depressive' position; hence her desire to 'make reparation'.[22]

At such juncture, it is only fitting to cry foul: it has been argued that one type of ambiguity materialises when 'alternative meanings combine to make clear a complicated state of mind in the author'[23] whereas another type suggests 'a division in the author's mind'.[24] If the premise is that Pompilia has been in either state of mind, the conclusion must be that she has been actively engaged in a questionable *modus operandi*. On the other hand, she can be seen catching a glimpse of an ideal world where a liberating experience is within the realms of possibility. On entering an oneiric realm, she has been confronted with the simultaneous presence of a potentially honest husband and a cleric with an aura of sanctity. As to the latter, the conjecture about an amorous affinity between him and her is conducive to the sight of both entering the domain of the *human, all too human*, as conceived by

Nietzsche. Indeed, their victory on the couch can be interpreted as an emblem of erotic lack and of a *modus vivendi* inspired by spirituality. A moment's reflection, inspired by an Aristotelian concept, will show Pompilia's moral goodness as inseparable from her practical wisdom: her aim has been to live agreeably through her short life and there is no denying that, in the teeth of her young age, she has implied familiarity with the name of the game. Simultaneously, she has shown signs of what Aristotle termed 'theoretical wisdom', viz an intuitive appreciation of truth, and her brand of intellectual wisdom has brought her to the fore as a human being still wavering between Heaven and Earth. She has sensed a mystical affinity with the Virgin Mary while holding little Gaetano in her arms, but she has also been suffering from what has been critically described as a distorting 'mirror image' dating back to early childhood. Sadly, the world of imaginary plenitude she has entered has turned out to be a narcissistic illusion of her nostalgic self.

End of story, perchance? Not for all the world. Miraculously, the juxtaposition of truth and soul in the course of Pompilia's deathbed confession has guided her through the three mystical stages experienced by St. Paul, namely *Purgation* by means of sincere repentance, *Illumination* in the wake of surrender to the will of God, and *Contemplation*, i.e. an ecstatic vision of a Divine Presence. The moribund patient has felt that a benevolent God bends towards great souls like that of Caponsacchi and through them "shows sufficient of His light for us i' the dark to rise by". Her final cry of horror, provoked by the monster who had intruded on her domestic sanctuary and left a trail of devastation, has contained echoes of the question raised by Giovanni, the Duke of Brachiano's son, when confronted by 'bloody villains': 'By what authority have you committed this massacre?'[25] The Almighty's readiness to help bedevilled souls find a way out of darkness into light has worked wonders: Pompilia Comparini has risen.

1. 'William Shakespeare, *Romeo and Juliet*, II,1, ll. 85-86
2. Jacques Derrida, *Structure, Sign and Play in the Discourse of the Human Sciences*, in *Modern Criticism and Theory*, Ed. David Lodge, Longman 1992, p. 121
3. *Ibid.*
4. William Shakespeare, *The Comedy of Errors*, IV. 2. ll. 19ff
5. Robert Browning, *Pauline*, ll. 448-450
6. William Shakespeare, *The Comedy of Errors*, II. 2 .ll. 172ff
7. *Ibid*, II, 1, ll. 22-24.
8. Nancy Chodorow, as cited by Anthony Elliott in *Psychoanalytic Theory*, p. 121, Blackwell, 1994
9. *Ibid.*
10. Hélène Cixous, *Sorties*, in *Modern Criticism and Theory*, p. 2
11. Robert Browning, *Two in the Campagna*.
12. Robert Browning, *Paracelsus*, Part V. l. 874
13. Robert Browning, *Fra Lippo Lippi*, ll. 110-
14. *Micah*, 7.7
15. In Philip Roth's *The Human Stain*, Vintage, 2000, p. 242
16. Robert Browning, *Paracelsus, Part I*, ll. 728ff.
17. As mentioned by M. H. Abrams, in *The Deconstructive Angel*, in *Modern Criticism and Theory*, p. 270
18. Erik Erikson, in *Psychoanalytic Theory*, p. 65
19. In *The Ego and the Id.*
20. Act I, Sc. 3
21. Both positions and the consequent desire have been theorised by Melanie Klein. See *Psychoanalytic Theory*, pp. 26-27

22. Samuel Richardson, *Pamela*, W.W. Norton & Company, 1958, p. 68
23. William Empson, *Seven Types of Ambiguity*, as quoted in *The Concise Oxford Companion to English Literature*, OUP, 1986, p. 509
24. *Ibid.*
25. John Webster, *The White Devil*, V, 6, ll. 283-84

MASTER GIACINTO ARCANGELI

The bleak January was drawing to a close when, in the wake of the tragic incident at the Comparini abode, Master Giacinto Arcangeli and Doctor Giovanni Battista Bottini got locked in a forensic battle in their capacity as defender and prosecutor respectively in the Franceschini cause cèlébre. Prevented by the strictures of the Roman procedural rules from uttering their *arringhe* in court, they found themselves performing their roles in the solitude of their *studi*.

Giacinto Arcangeli was the first to speak, – or read his brief for that matter. Gazing at a portrait displaying his male offspring, he clutched the lapels of his dark robe and pitched in. "Ah, my Giacinto, he's no ruddy rogue, is not Cinone? What, today we're eight? Seven and one's eight, I hope, old curly-pate! Branches me out his verb on the slate, *amo-as-avi-atum-are-ans*, up to *-aturus*, person, tense and mood. Look eight years onward, and he's perched, he's perched, dapper and deft on stool beside this chair, Cinozzo, Cinoncello who but he? – trying his milk-teeth on some crusty case like this, *papà* shall triturate full soon to smooth Papinian pulp! It trots already through my head, though noon be now, does suppertime and what belongs to eve. 'Dispose, o Don, o' the play, first work then play!' the proverb bids – and 'then' means: won't we hold our little yearly lovesome frolic feast, Cinuolo's birth-night, Cinicello's own, that makes gruff January grin perforce? Commend me to home joy, the family board, altar and hearth! These, with a brisk career, a source of honest profit and good fame, honouring God and serving man, I say, these are reality and all else fluff, *nil in nuce* – thank Flaccus for the phrase! Why, work with a will, then! Wherefore lazy now? Let Law come dimple Cinoncino's cheek, and Latin dumple Cinarello's chin, the while we spread him fine and toss him flat this pulp that makes the pancake, trim our mass of matter into *Argument the First, Prime Pleading* in defence of our accused, – which, once a-waft on paper wing, shall soar, shall signalize before applausive Rome what study, and mayhap some mother-wit, can do toward making Master fop and Fisc old bachelor Bottinius bite his thumb. Now, how good God is! How falls plumb to point this murder, gives me Guido to defend now, of all days i' the year, just when the boy verges on Virgil, reaches the right age for some such illustration from his sire. The fact is, there's a blessing on the hearth, a special providence for fatherhood!"

A flash of jouissance lit up the lawyer's round face as he focused his attention on the file concerning the Franceschini case. "I defend Guido and his comrades, I! Pray God, I keep me humble: not to me, *not to us, o Lord, but to thee the praise*!" he burst out and then, with a barely biblical inspiration, "Count Guido married – or, in Latin due, what? *Duxit in uxorem*? Commonplace! He underwent the matrimonial torch? In stable bond of marriage bound his own? He wedded, – ah, with owls for augury! – one of the blood Arezzo boasts her best." Guido's defender stifled a smirk. "Out-of-the-way events extend our scope: for instance, when Bottini brings his charge, 'That letter which you say Pompilia wrote, to criminate her parents and herself and disengage her husband from the coil, – *that*, Guido Franceschini wrote, say we: because Pompilia could nor read nor write; therefore, he pencilled her such letter first, then made her trace in ink the same again.' How will you turn this nor break Tully's pate? Her husband outlined her the whole, forsooth? What, she confesses that she wrote the thing, *fatetur eam scripsisse*, – scorn that scathes! – *ita pariter* she seeks to show the same, no voluntary deed but fruit of force, *non voluntate sed coactu scriptam*! That's the way to write Latin, friend my Fisc! Better we lost the cause than lacked the gird at the Fisc's Latin, lost the Judge's laugh!" The *latinista* gave a little chuckle. "How he draws up, ducks under, twists aside! He eludes law by piteous looks aloft, lets Latin glance off as he makes appeal to the saint that's somewhere in the ceiling top. I know he writes as if he spoke: I hear the hoarse shrill throat, see shut eyes, neck shot-forth, – I see him strain on tiptoe, soar and pour eloquence out, nor stay nor stint at all. He'll keep clear of my cast, my logic-throw, let argument slide and then deliver swift some bowl from quite an unguessed point of stand, a plaguy cast, a mortifying stroke. Safer I worked at the new, the unforeseen, the nice bye-stroke, the fine and improvised point that can titillate the brain o' the Bench torpid with over-teaching, by this time! Oh, I was young and had the trick of fence, knew subtle pass-and-push with careless right – the left arm ever quietly behind back with the dagger in 't, not both hands to blade! Puff and blow, put the strength out, Blunderbore!"

A bout of hostility pervaded the advocate's hazel eyes. "Guido must be all gooseflesh in his hole, despite the prison-straw: bad Carnival for captives; no sliced fry for him, poor Count! The old fox takes the plain and velvet path, the young hound's predilection, – prints the dew, do n't he, to suit their pulpy pads of paw? No! Burying nose deep down i' the briery bush, thus I defend Count Guido."

A succession of nods underpinned a breezy mood. "Where are we weak? First, which is foremost in advantage too: our murder, – we call, killing, – is a fact confessed, defended, made a boast of: good! To think the Fisc claimed use of torture here! One may dispute, – as I am bound to do and shall, –validity of process here inasmuch as a noble is exempt from torture which plebeians undergo in such a case, – for law is lenient, lax, remits the torture to a nobleman unless suspicion be of twice the strength attaches to a man born vulgarly: we do n't card silk with comb that dresses wool. Moreover, 'twas severity undue in this case, even had the lord been lout: death on the spot is no rare consequence.

Had the antagonist left dubiety, here were we proving murder a mere myth, and Guido innocent, absent, – ay, absent! He was – why, where should Christians be? – engaged in visiting his proper church, the duty of us all at Christmas time. So, doubtless, had I needed argue here but for the full confession round and sound! So, *Vindicatio*, – here begins the same! – *Honoris causa!* So we make our stand: honour in us had injury, we shall prove; or if we fail to prove such injury more than misprision of the fact, – what then? It is enough, authorities declare, if the result, the deed in question now, be caused by confidence that injury is veritable and no figment: since, what, though proved fancy afterwards, seemed fact at the time, they argue shall excuse result. The casuists bid: man bound to do his best, they would not have him leave that best undone and mean to do the worst, – though fuller light show best was worst and worst would have been best; act by the present light, they ask of man. It is not anyway our business here to prove what we thought crime was crime indeed, *ad irrogandam poenam*, and require its punishment; *sed ad effectum*, but 't is our concern, *excusandi*, here to simply find excuse, *occisorem*, for who did the killing-work, *et ad illius defensionem*, – mark the difference! – and defend the man. Just that. It should be always harder to convict, in short, than to establish innocence. Therefore, we shall demonstrate first of all that Honour is a gift of God to man: therefore, the sensitivest spot of all is, – honour within honour, like the eye centred i' the ball, – the honour of our wife. Touch us o' the pupil of our honour, then, this were our warrant for eruptive fire 'to whose dominium I impose no end'. Virgil, now, should not be too difficult to Cinoncino, – say the early books ... pen, truce to further gambols! I shall sing!"

Arcangeli swung his arms and by so doing inadvertently upset the symmetrical pattern of dots on his gown, but a flick of the wrist restored the array. "Nor can revenge of injury done here to the honour proved the life and soul of us, be too excessive, too extravagant: such wrong seeks and must have complete revenge. Show we this first on the mere natural ground, begin at the beginning and proceed incontrovertibly. Theodoric propounds for basis of all household law 'Bird mates with bird, beast genders with his like; the very insects ... if they wive or no, how dare I say when Aristotle doubts? But the presumption is they likewise wive, at least the nobler sorts; for take the bee as instance, – copying King Solomon, – why that displeasure of the bee to aught that savours of incontinency, makes the unchaste a very horror to the hive? Whence comes it bees obtain the epithet of *castae apes*? Because, ingeniously saith Scaliger, 'Such is their hatred of immodest act, they fall upon the offender, sting to death.' Only cold-blooded fish lack instinct here, nor gain nor guard connubiality. If a poor animal feel honour smart, taught by blind instinct nature plants in him, shall man, – confessed creation's master-stroke, nay, intellectual glory, nay, a god, nay, of the nature of my Judges here, – shall man prove the insensible, the block, the blot o' the earth he crawls on to disgrace?"

A shake of the head enhanced the rhetorical question. "From beast to man next mount we – ay, but, mind, still mere man, not yet Christian, – that, in time! If, with his poor and primitive half-lights, the Pagan, whom our devils served for gods, could stigmatise the breach of marriage-vow as that which blood, blood only might efface, – absolve the husband, outraged, whose revenge anticipated law, plied sword himself, – how with the Christian in full blaze of day? Shall not he rather double penalty, multiply vengeance, than, degenerate, let privilege be minished, droop, decay? Therefore, set forth at large the ancient law: so old a chime, the bells ring of themselves! I point you, for my part, the belfry out, intent to rise from dusk, at dawn, into the Christian day shall broaden next.

First, the fit compliment to His Holiness happily reigning: then sustain the point: all that was long ago declared as law by the early Revelation stands confirmed by Apostle and Evangelist and Saint, – to wit – that Honour is the supreme good, since harder 't is, *quum difficilius sit, iram cohibere*, to coerce one's wrath, *quam miraculum facere*, than work miracles, – Saint Gregory smiles in his First Dialogue. Whence we infer the ingenuous soul, the man who makes esteem of honour and repute, whenever honour and repute are touched, arrives at term of fury and despair, loses all guidance from the reason-check, – not even if he attain the impossible, o'erturn the hinges of the universe."

Guido's defender shook his head anew and ambled to a stylish bay window where he took a gander at the world out there before walking back, his features suffused with the tight smile of a man of the world. "Who recognises not my client's case? Samson in Gaza was the antetype of Guido at Rome: for note the Nazarite! Blinded he was, – an easy thing to bear; intrepidly he took imprisonment, gyves, stripes and daily labour at the mill; but when he found himself, i' the public place, destined to make the common people sport, disdain burned up with such an impetus i' the breast of him that, all of him on fire, *moriatur*, roared he, 'let my soul's self die, *anima mea*, with the Philistines!' So, pulled down pillar, roof, and death and all, and many more he killed thus, *moriens*, dying, *quam vivus*, than in his own life, *occiderat*, he ever killed before. Are these things writ for no example, Sirs? Our Lord Himself, made up of mansuetude, sealing the sum of sufferance up, received opprobrium, contumely and buffeting without complaint, but when He found Himself touched in His honour never so little for once, then outbroke indignation pent before: '*Honorem meum nemini dabo!*' 'No, my honour I to nobody will give!' And, certainly, the example so hath wrought, that whosoever, at the proper worth, apprises worldly honour and repute, esteems it nobler to die honoured man beneath *mannaia* than live centuries disgraced in the eye o' the world. We find Saint Paul no recreant to this faith delivered once: 'Far worthier were it that I died,' cries he, *expedit mihi magis mori*, 'than that anyone should make my glory void', *quam ut gloriam meam quis evacuet!*"

Master Arcangeli set about pacing the floor. "Then, Sirs, this Christian dogma, this law-bud full-blown now, soon to bask the absolute flower of Papal doctrine in our blaze of day, – bethink you, shall we miss one promise-streak, one dew-drop to humanity, now that the chalice teems with noonday wine? The doom of the adulterous wife was death, stoning by Moses' law. 'Nay, stone her not, put her away!' next legislates our Lord; and last of all, 'Nor yet divorce a wife!' ordains the Church, 'she typifies ourself, the Bride no fault shall cause to fall from Christ.' Then, as no jot nor tittle of the Law has passed away – which who presumes to doubt? – where do I find my proper punishment for my adulterous wife, I humbly ask of my infallible Pope who now remits even the divorce allowed by Christ in lieu of lapidation Moses licensed me? The Gospel checks the Law which throws the stone; the Church tears the divorce-bill Gospel grants; the wife sins and enjoys impunity! What profits me the fulness of the days, the final dispensation, I demand, unless Law, Gospel and the Church subjoin 'But who hath barred thee primitive revenge, which, like fire damped and dammed up, burns more fierce? Use thou thy natural privilege of man!"

The religious-minded lawyer's bony face broke into a hieratic smile of sorts. "Law, Gospel and the Church – from these we leap to the very last revealment, easy rule befitting the well-born and thorough-bred o' the happy day we live in, – not the dark o' the early rude and acorn-eating race. Civilization bows to decency, the acknowledged use and wont, the manners, – mild but yet imperative law, – which make the man. What *dictum* doth Society lay down i' the case of one who hath a faithless wife wherewithal should the husband cleanse his way? Be patient and forgive? Oh, language fails, shrinks from depicturing his punishment! For if wronged husband raise not hue and cry, *quod si maritus de adulterio non conqueretur*, he's presumed a – foh! *presumitur leno*: so, complain he must. But how complain? At your tribunal, lords? Far weightier challenge suits your sense, I wot! You sit not to have gentlemen propose questions gentility can itself discuss. Did you not prove that to our brother Paul? In a cause like this, so multiplied were reasons *pro* and *con*, delicate, intertwisted and obscure, that law were ashamed to lend a finger-tip to unravel, readjust the hopeless twine. My lords, my lords, the inconsiderate step was – we referred ourselves to law at all. Twit me not with, 'Law else had punished you!' Each punishment of the extra-legal step, to which the high-born preferably revert, is ever for some oversight, some slip i' the taking vengeance, not for vengeance's self. A good thing done unhandsomely turns ill, and never yet lacked ill the law's rebuke."

A shrug of the shoulders made *Dominus Hyacinthus'* elegant ermine gown lie aslant again, and the wearer's mouth twisted while he readjusted the prescribed garment. "Another fructuous sample," he resumed. See '*De Re Criminali*', in Matthaeus' divine piece": "Another husband, in no better plight, simulates absence, thereby tempts the wife; on whom he falls, out of sly ambuscade, armed to the teeth with arms that law had banned. *Nimis dolose*, overwilily, *fuisse operatum*, was it worked, pronounced the Law: had all been fairly done Law had not found him worthy, as she did, of four years' exile. Why cite more? Enough is as good as a feast – unless a birthday feast for one's Cinuccio: so, we'll finish here. My lords, we rather need defend ourselves inasmuch as for a twinkling of an eye we hesitatingly appealed to law, – rather than deny that, on mature advice, we blushingly bethought us, bade revenge back to the simple proper private way of decent self-dealt gentlemanly death. 'Impunity were otherwise your meed: go slay your wife and welcome,' may be urged, 'but why the innocent old couple slay, Pietro, Violante? You may do enough, not too much, not exceed the golden mean: neither brute-beast nor Pagan, Gentile, Jew, nor Christian, no nor votarist of the mode, were free at all to push revenge so far!'" The speaker's head wagged in denial. "The actual wrong, Pompilia seemed to do, was virtual wrong done by the parents here – imposing her upon us as their child – themselves allow: then, her fault was their fault, her punishment be theirs accordingly! The precious couple you call innocent, – why, they were felons law failed to clutch, – *partum supposuerunt*, feigned this birth. Do you blame us that we turn law's instruments not mere self-seekers, – mind the public weal, nor make the private good our sole concern? We are the over-ready to help Law – zeal of her house hath eaten us up: for which, can it be, Law intends to eat up us, *crudum Priamum*, devour poor Priam raw. Shame! And so, ends the period prettily."

The rhetorician tapped on the restored gown to the accompaniment of a tight smile. "But even: prove the pair not culpable, ours the mistake, is that a rare event? *Non semel*: it is anything but rare, *in contingentia facti*, that by chance, *impunes evaserunt*, go scot-free, *qui*, such well-meaning people as ourselves, *justo dolore moti*, who aggrieved with cause, *apposuerunt manus*, lay rough hands, *in innocents*, on wrong heads. Nor Cyriacus cites beside the mark: Just so, a lady who had taken care, *homicidium viri*, that her lord be killed, – for denegation of a certain debt *matrimonialis* he was loath to pay, – *fuit pecunaria mulcta*, was amerced in a pecuniary mulct, *punita, et ad poenam*, and to pains, *temporalem*, for a certain space of time, *in monasterio*, in a convent. Ay, *in monasterio*! How he manages *in* with the ablative, the accusative! I had hoped to have hitched the villain into verse. Law in a man takes the whole liberty; the muse is fettered, – just as Ovid found."

The tight smile loosened up. "And now, sea widens and the coast is clear. Surely things brighten, brighten, till at length remains – so far from act that needs defence – apology to make for act delayed one minute, let alone eight mortal months of hesitation! 'Why procrastinate?' – out with it, my Bottinius, ease thyself! – 'Right, promptly done, is twice right: right delayed turns wrong. We grant you should have killed your wife, but on the moment, at the meeting her in company with the priest: then did the tongue o' the Brazen Head give licence, "Time is now!" You make your mind up: "Time is past!" it peals. Friend, you are competent to mastery o' the passions that confessedly explain an outbreak, – yet allow an interval, and then break out as if time's clock had clanged. You have forfeited your chance and flat you fall into the commonplace category of men bound to go softly all their days, obeying law.' He curved a hand behind his ear as if he intended to give his adversary a fair hearing. "Now, which way make response? What was the answer Guido gave, himself? That so to argue came of ignorance how honour bears a wound: 'For, wound,' said he, 'my body, and the smart is worst at first; while, wound my soul where honour sits and rules, longer the sufferance, stronger grows the pain, 't is with the passing of time fresh as first.' We did demur, awhile did hesitate, yet husband sure should let a scruple speak ere he slay wife, – for his own safety, lords! Suppose the source of injury a son, – father may slay such son yet run no risk: why graced with such a privilege? Because a father so incensed with his own child, or must have reason, or believe he has, *bonum consilium pro filio*, the best course as what befits his boy, through instinct, *ex instinctu*, of mere love, *amoris*, and, *paterni*, fatherhood; *quam confidentiam*, which confidence, *non habet*, law declines to entertain, *de viro*, of the husband: where has he an instinct that compels him love his wife? Rather is he presumably her foe: so, let him ponder long in this bad world ere do the simplest act of justice."

Cinoncino's besotted begetter extended his arms and waved them in an empty space. "But again – and here we brush Bottini's breast – object you, 'See the danger of delay! Suppose a man murdered my friend last month: had I come up and killed him for his pains in rage, I had done right, allows the law; I meet him now and kill him in cold blood, I do wrong, equally allows the law; wherein do actions differ, yours and mine?'" The lawyer's eyes widened. "Hast thy wits, Fisc? To take such slayer's life, returns it life to thy slain friend at all? Had he stolen ring instead of stabbing friend, – today, tomorrow or next century, meeting the thief, thy ring upon his thumb, thou justifiably hadst wrung it thence: so, couldst thou wrench thy friend's life back again, why, law would look complacent on thy rush. Ere thou hast learned law, will be much to do, as said the rustic while he shod the goose." A quizzical look darkened the sparkle in the man's pupils as he heard Guido Franceschini intervene: "Nay, if you urge me, interval was none! What with the priest who flourishes his blade; the wife who like a fury flings at us; the crowd – and then the capture, the appeal to Rome, the journey there, the journey thence, the shelter at the House of Convertites, the visits to the Villa, and so forth … where was one minute left us all this while to put in execution that revenge we planned o' the instant? – as it were, plumped down a round sound egg, o' the spot, some eight months since, Rome, more propitious than his nest, should hatch! Object not, 'You reached Rome on Christmas Eve and, despite liberty to act at once, waited a week – indecorous delay!' No care for aught held holy by the Church? What, would you have us skip and miss those feasts o' the Natal time? Must we go prosecute secular business on a sacred day? Should not the merest charity expect, setting our poor concerns aside for once, we hurried to the song matutinal and thereby whet our courage if 't were blunt?' He urged his antagonist to picture the enraged Count saying to himself: 'Money? I need none. Friends? The word in null. I see my grandsire, he who fought so well. I see this, I see that.' "See to it all, or I shall scarce see lamb's fry in an hour!" he exclaimed.

The chasm between holiness and profanity, coupled with the prospect of a plate piled with the specialty at issue, gave the soliloquist a pause. He went on pacing the floor while he envisioned a lamb's fry-up made more succulent by the proximity of Cinoncello and, to crown all, a well-earned nocturnal rest. The perusal of the remainder of his harangue could wait till the morrow, and he was ready for it.

DOCTOR JOHANNES-BAPTISTA BOTTINIUS

Giovanni Battista Bottini settled himself at the core of his *studio*. Wrapped, on a par with Arcangeli, in an official ermine gown, the prosecuting attorney cast his eye over the brief intended for the clerical court presiding over the Franceschini trial and cried out, "Had I God's leave, how I would alter thing!" Then, in an inquisitive tone, "Have ye seen, Judges, have ye, lights of law, – when it may hap some painter, much in vogue throughout our city nutritive of arts, ye summon to a task shall test his worth, afford my lords their Holy Family, – hath it escaped the acumen of the Court how such a painter sets himself to paint? Why, first he sedulously practiseth on what may nourish eye, make facile hand: to him the bones their inmost secret yield; on him the muscles turn, in triple tier, ensuring due correctness in the nude. Which done, is all done? Not a wit, ye know! He, – to art's surface rising from her depth, – may simulate a Joseph – happy chance! – limneth exact each wrinkle of the brow, loseth no involution, cheek or chap, till lo, in black and white, the senior lives! Is it a young and comely peasant-nurse that poseth? – be the phrase accorded me! – each feminine delight of florid lip, eyes brimming o'er and brow bowed down with love, marmoreal neck and bosom uberous, – glad on the paper in a trice they go to help the notion of the Mother-Maid, yea, and her babe: that flexure of soft limbs, that budding face imbued with dewy sleep, contribute each an excellence to Christ. Even the poor ass, unpanniered and elate stands, perks an ear up, he a model too; no jot nor tittle of these but in its turn ministers to perfection of the piece. Such prelude ended, pause our painter may, submit his fifty studies one by one, and in some sort boast 'I have served my lords.'"

The *Fisci Advocatus* inhaled and exhaled slowly. "But what? And hath he painted once this while? Or when you cry 'Produce the thing required, thy *Journey through the Desert* done in oils!' – what, doth he fall to shuffling 'mid his sheets, – fumbling for first this, then the other fact, and fasten here a head and there a tail by bits of reproduction of the life? I trow not! do I miss with my conceit the mark, my lords? Not so my lords were served! Rather your artist turns abrupt from these, and preferably buries him and broods on the inner spectrum filtered through the eye, his brain-deposit, bred of many a drop. For in that brain, – their fancy sees at work, could my lords peep indulged, – results alone, not processes which nourish the result, would they discover and appreciate, – life fed by digestion, not raw food itself, not this nose, not that eyebrow, the other fact o' man's staff, woman's stole or infant's clout, but lo, a spirit-birth conceived of flesh, truth rare and real, not transcripts, fact and false!"

The orator hastened to deal with the *corpus sceleris* allocated to him.

"End we exordium, Phoebus plucks my ear! The patriarch Pietro with his wise old wife and juvenile Pompilia with her babe, who, seeking safety in the wilderness, were all surprised by Herod, while outstretched in sleep beneath a palm-tree by a spring, and killed: the very circumstance I paint, moving the pity and terror of my lords, until the glad result is gained, the group demonstrably presented in detail, their slumber and his onslaught, – like as life. Therefore by part and part I clutch my case which, in entirety now, – momentous task, – my lords demand, so render them I must. No more of proof, disproof, – such virtue was, such vice was never in Pompilia, now! Hath calumny imputed to the fair a blemish, mole on cheek or wart on chin, much more, blind hidden horrors best unnamed? Shall I descend to prove you, point by point, never was knock-knee known nor splay-foot found in Phryne? – I must let the portrait go, content with the model, I believe –and what is this tale of Tarquin, how the slave was caught by him, preferred to Collatine? Thou, even from thy corpse-clothes virginal, look'st the lie dead, Lucretia! Thus at least

I, by the guidance of antiquity, – our one infallible guide – now operate, sure that the innocency shown is safe; sure, too, that, while I plead, the echoes cry 'Monstrosity the Phrynean shape shall mar, Lucretia's soul comport with Tarquin's lie, when thistles grow on vines or thorns yield figs, or oblique sentence leave this judgment-seat!'

A wry smile permeated the Fisc's face. "A great theme: may my strength be adequate! For – paint Pompilia, dares my feebleness? First, infancy, pellucid as a pearl; then, childhood – stone which, dew-drop at the first, an old conjecture, sucks by dint of gaze blue from the sky and turns to sapphire so – its milk-white pallor, chastity, suffused with here and there a tint and hint of flame. Pompilia, infant, child, maid, woman, wife – crown the ideal in our earth at last! As Horace prompts, I dare the epic plunge – begin at once with marriage, up till when little or nothing would arrest your love. Oh, the weaker sex, my lords, the weaker sex! To whom, Anacreon teaches us, for gift, not strength, – man's dower, – but beauty, nature gave, 'Beauty in lieu of spears, in lieu of shields!' And what is beauty's sure concomitant, nay, intimate essential character, but melting wiles, deliciousest deceits, the whole redoubted armoury of love?" The ad hoc aesthete extended his arms in a transport of delight. "For lo, advancing Hymen and his pomp! Farewell to dewiness and prime of life! Remains the rough determined day: dance done, to work, with plough and harrow! What comes next? 'Tis Guido henceforth guides Pompilia's step, cries 'No more frisking o'er the foodful glebe, else 'ware the whip!' Accordingly, first crack o' the thong, – we hear that his young wife was barred, *cohibita fuit*, from the old free life. Demur we? Nowise: heifer brave the hind? We seek not there should lapse the natural law, the proper piety to lord and king and husband, – let the heifer bear the yoke, – only, I crave he cast not patience off, this hind; for deem you she endures the whip, nor winces at the goad, nay, restive, kicks? What if the adversary's charge be just and all untowardly she pursue her way with groan and grunt, though hind strike ne'er so hard? If petulant remonstrance made appeal when silence more decorously had served for protestation; if Pompilian plaint wrought but to aggravate Guidonian ire, why, such mishaps, ungainly though they be, ever companion change, are incident to altered modes and novelty of life. The philosophic mind expects no less, smilingly knows and names the crisis, sits waiting till old things go and new arrive: therefore, I hold a husband but inept who tuns impatient at such transit-time, as if this running from the road would last!"

The socio-philosophical view was enhanced by an assertive shake of the head. "Success awaits the soon-disheartened man: the parents turn their backs and leave the house; the wife may wail but none shall intervene; old things are passed and all again is new, over and gone the obstacles to peace, and forth from plain each pleasant herb may peep, each bloom of wifehood in abeyance late – compare a passage in the Canticles! But what if, as 't is wont with plant and wife, flowers, – after a suppression to good end, still, when they do spring forth, – sprout here, sprout there, anywhere likelier than beneath the foot o' the lawful good-man gardener of the ground? The lady, foes allege, put forth each charm and proper floweret of femininity to whosoever had a nose to smell or breast to deck. What if the charge be true? The fault were graver had she looked with choice, but, first come was first served, the accuser saith. Which butterfly of the wide air shall brag 'I was preferred to Guido' – when 't is clear the cup, he quaffs at, lay with olent breast open to gnat, midge, bee and moth as well? One chalice entertained the company." The prosecutor's pupils flashed with mischief. "Nay, even so, he shall be satisfied! Concede we there was reason in his wrong, grant we his grievance and content the man! For lo, Pompilia, she submits herself. No longer shall he blame 'She none excludes,' but substitute 'She laudably sees all, searches the best out and selects the same.' For who is here, long sought and latest found, waiting his turn unmoved amid the whirl, calm in his levity, – indulge the quip! – since 't is a levite bears the belle away? Priest, ay, and very phoenix of such fowl, well-born, of culture, young and vigorous, comely too, since precise the precepts points: nor mole nor scar nor blemish, lest the mind come all uncandid through the thwarting flesh! But ah, the faith of early days is gone! Alas, ancient faith! Nothing died in him save courtesy, good sense and proper trust. Guido, left high and dry, shows jealous now! Have I to teach my masters what effect hath jealousy and how, befooling men, it makes false true, abuses eye and ear, turns the mist adamantine, loads with sound silence, and into void and vacancy crowds a whole phalanx of conspiring foes? The man grows insane; threat succeeds to threat, and blow redoubles blow, – his wife, the block. But, if a block, shall not she jar the hand that buffets her? The injurious idle stone rebounds and fits the head of him who flung. No, dictates duty to a loving wife. Far better that the unconsummated blow, adroitly baulked by her, should back again, correctly admonish his own pate!"

Bottini nodded his head sympathetically. "Crime then, – the Court is with me? – she must crush. How crush it? By all efficacious means; and these, why, what in woman should they be? 'With horns the bull, with teeth the lion fights; to woman', quoth the lyric Anacraeon, 'nor teeth, nor horns, but beauty, Nature gave.' Pretty i' the Pagan! Who dares blame the use of the armoury thus allowed for natural, exclaim against a seeming-dubious play o' the sole permitted weapon, – spear and shield alike, – resorted to i' the circumstance by poor Pompilia? Grant she somewhat plied arts that allure, the magic nod and wink, the witchery of gesture, spell of word, whereby the likelier to enlist this friend, yet stranger, as a champion on her side: such, being but mere man, 't was all she knew – must be made sure by beauty's silken bond, the weakness that subdues the strong, and bows wisdom alike and folly. Grant the tale o' the husband, which is false, for proved and true to the letter, – or the letters, I should say, the abominations he professed to find and fix upon Pompilia and the priest; allow them hers, for though she could not write, in early days of Eve-like innocence that plucked no apple from the knowledge-tree, yet, at the Serpent's word, Eve plucks and eats and knows, especially how to read and write, – so she, through hunger after fellowship, may well have learned, though late, to play the scribe: 'You thought my letters could be none of mine,' she tells her parents –'mine, who wanted skill; but now I have the skill, and write, you see!' This letter nowise 'scapes the common lot, but lies i' the condemnation of the rest, found by the husband's self who forged them all."

Doctor Bottini gave a little chuckle and continued unabated. "Yet, for the sacredness of argument, for this once an exemption shall it plead: being in peril of her life – "my life, not an hour's purchase", as the letter runs, – and having but one stay in this extreme, and out of the wide world a single friend – what could she other than resort to him? Shall she propose him lucre, dust o' the mine, or pearl secreted by a sickly fish? Scarcely! She caters for a generous taste. 'T is love shall beckon, beauty bid to breast, because, permit the end, permit therewith means to the end!"

The Machiavellian contention was fittingly elaborated. "To such permitted motive, then, refer all those professions, else were hard explain, of hope, fear, jealousy, and the rest of love! He is *Myrtillus*, *Amaryllis* she: she burns, he freezes, – all a mere device to catch and keep the man may save her life, whom otherwise nor catches she nor keeps! Hence, beyond promises, we praise each proof that promise was not simply made to break, no moonshine-structure meant to fade at dawn: would such external semblance of intrigue demonstrate that intrigue must lurk perdue? Does every hazel-sheath disclose a nut? Pompilia took not Judith's liberty, no faulchion find you in her hand to smite, no damsel to convey the head in dish, of Holophernes, – style the Canon so – or is it the Count? If I entangle me with my similitudes, – if wax wings melt and earthward down I drop, not mine the fault: blame your beneficence, O Court, O sun, whereof the beamy smile affects my flight! What matter, so Pompilia's fame revive i' the warmth that proves the bane of Icarus?"

The recourse to the Scriptures and to myth was supported by an air of quiet confidence. "Yea, we have shown it lawful, necessary Pompilia leave her husband, seek the house o' the parents; and because 'twixt home and home lies a long road with many a danger rife, lions by the way and serpents in the path, to rob and ravish, – much behoves she keep each shadow of suspicion from fair fame, for her own sake much, but for his sake more, the ingrate husband! Evidence shall be, some witness to the world, how white she walks i' the mire she wanders through ere Rome she reach. And who so proper witness as a priest? Gainsay ye? Let me hear who dares gainsay! I hope we still can punish heretics!" The orthodox speaker's eyes sparkled with missionary zeal. "Therefore the agent, as prescribed, she takes: a priest, juvenile, potent, handsome too. How boldly would Pompilia and the priest march out of door, spread flag at beat of drum, but that inapprehensive Guido grants neither premiss nor yet conclusion here, and, purblind, dreads a bear in every bush! For his own quietude and comfort, then, means must be found for flight in masquerade at hour when all things sleep."

'Save jealousy!' he felt himself hearing. "Right, judges!" he promptly cried out. "Therefore shall the lady's wit supply the boon thwart nature baulks him of, and do him service with the potent drug – Helen's nepenthe, as my lords opine – shall respite blessedly each frittered nerve o' the much-enduring man; accordingly, there lies he, duly dosed and sound asleep, relieved of woes or real or raved about. While soft she leaves his side, he shall not wake nor stop who steals away to join her friend, nor get himself raw head and bones laid bare in payment of his apparition!"

Pearly beads of sweat wet Bottini's forehead, but they were wiped up forthwith with the help of a serviceable handkerchief. "Thus would I defend the step, were the thing true that Guido slept, – who never slept a wink, – through treachery, an opiate from his wife, who not so much as knew what opiates mean." A chain of approving nods materialised. "Now she may start: but hist, – a stoppage still. A journey is an enterprise which costs, – money, sweet Sirs! And were the fiction fact, she helped herself thereto with liberal hand from out the husband's store, – what fitter use was ever husband's money destined to? With bag and baggage thus did Dido once decamp, – for more authority, a queen!

So is she fairly on her route at last, prepared for either fortune: nay, and if the priest, now all aglow with enterprise, cool somewhat presently when fades the flush o' the first adventure, clouded o'er belike by doubts, misgivings how the day may die, vanquished by tedium of a prolonged jaunt in a close carriage o'er a jolting road, shall not Pompilia haste to dissipate the silent cloud that, gathering, bodes her bale, prop the irresoluteness may portend suspension of the project, check the flight, bring ruin on them both? use every means, since means to the end are lawful? What i' the way of wile should have allowance like a kiss sagely and sisterly administered? Such was the remedy her wit applied to each incipient scruple of the priest, if we believe, – as, while my wit is mine I cannot, – what the driver testifies, Borsi, called Venerino, the mere tool of Guido and his friend the Governor: 'The journey was one long embrace,' quoth he. Still, though we should believe the driver's lie, – nor even admit as probable excuse that what the owl-like eyes, at the back of head, o' the driver, drowsed by driving night and day, supposed a vulgar interchange of love, this was but innocent jog of head 'gainst head, cheek meeting jowl as apple may touch pear from branch and branch contiguous in the wind when Autumn blusters and the orchard rocks, – say she kissed him and he kissed her again, such osculation was a potent means, a very efficacious help, no doubt! This with a third part of her nectar did Venus imbue: why should Pompilia fling Horace's declaration in his teeth?"

The classics-imbued assertion was fleshed out with a straight face and further oscillations of the head. "Ah, Nature – baffled she recurs, alas! Nature imperiously exacts her due, spirit is willing, but the flesh is weak: Pompilia needs must acquiesce and swoon, give hopes alike and fears a breathing-while. The innocent sleep soundly: sound she sleeps. So let her slumber, then, unguarded save by her own chastity, a triple mail! Nay, what and if he gazed rewardedly on the pale beauty prisoned in embrace, stooped over, stole a balmy breath perhaps for more assurance sleep was not decease? How can the priest but pity whom he saved? And pity is how near to love, and love how neighbourly to unreasonableness! So, sleep thou on, secure whate'er betide! For thou, too, hast thy problem hard to solve – how so much beauty is compatible with so much innocence!"

Pompilia's admirer rubbed his forehead. "Fit place, methinks, to treat of and repel objection here: 'Lie not at all,' the exacter precept bids. 'Each least lie breaks the law, – is sin', ye hold. I humble me, but venture to submit: what prevents sin, itself is sinless, sure; and sin, which hinders sin of deeper dye, softens itself away by contrast so. Now, what is greatest sin of womanhood? That which unwomans it, abolishes the nature of the woman? Impudence. Now, what is taxed as duplicity, feint, wile and trick, – admitted for the nonce, – what worse do one and all than interpose, hold, as it were, a deprecating hand, statuesquely, in the Medicean mode, before some shame which modesty would veil? Who blames the gesture prettily perverse? Thus, – lest ye miss a point illustrative, – admit the husband's calumny; allow that the wife, having penned the epistle fraught with horrors, charge on charge of crime, she heaped o' the head of Pietro and Violante, – still presumed her parents, – and despatched the thing to their arch-enemy Paolo, through free choice and no sort of compulsion in the world – put case that she discards simplicity for craft, denies the voluntary act, declares herself a passive instrument i' the hands of Guido; duped by knavery, she traced the characters, she could not write, and took on trust the unread sense which, read, were recognized but to be spurned at once. Allow this calumny, I reiterate! Who is so dull as wonder at the pose of our Pompilia in the circumstance? Who sees not that the too-ingenuous soul, stung to the quick at her impulsive deed, and willing to repair what harm it worked, she – wise in this beyond what Nero proved, who, when needs were the candid juvenile should sign the warrant, doom the guilty dead, 'Would I had never learned to write', quoth he, – Pompilia rose above the Roman, cried, 'To read or write I never learned at all!' O splendidly mendacious!" The final cry sounded like the prelude to a disquisition on her ambivalent attitude towards Caponsacchi, but a gander at the clock on the wall engendered the perception that it was about time for his regular visit to the posh coffee-house round the corner; hey presto, the professional ermine gown fell off his obliging shoulders.

MASTER GIACINTO ARCANGELI

Twelve hours after his unfinished harangue, the *Pauperum Procurator* returned to the task on his hands and focused without delay on the 'six qualities' which his opponent Bottini would see as 'parasite-growth upon mere murder's back.' "A fico for your aggravations, Fisc!" he ejaculated before enumerating them.

"Therefore, first aggravation: we made up a regular assemblage of armed men. Unluckily it was the very judge who sits in judgment on our cause to-day that passed the law as Governor of Rome: 'Four men armed,' – though for lawful purpose, mark; much more for an acknowledged crime, – 'shall die.' We five were armed to the teeth, meant murder too? Why, that's the very point that saves us, Fisc! Let me instruct you. Crime nor done nor meant, – you punish still who arm and congregate: for why have used bad means to a good end? Crime being meant not done, – you punish still the means to crime, you haply pounce upon, though circumstance have baulked you of their end; but crime not only compassed but complete, meant and done too? Why, since you have the end, be that your sole concern, nor mind those means no longer to the purpose! Murdered we? Of many crimes committed with a view to one main crime, you overlook the less, intent upon the large. Suppose a man, having in view commission of a theft, climb the town wall: 't is for the theft he hangs, suppose you can convict him of such theft, remitted whipping due to who climbs wall for bravery or wantonness alone, just to dislodge a daw's nest and no more. So I interpret you the manly mind of him the Judge shall judge both you and me, – o' the Governor, who, being no babe, my Fisc, cannot have blundered on ineptitude!"

The inquisitive mood generated further articulation.

"Next aggravation, – that the arms themselves were specially of such forbidden sort through shape or length or breadth, as, prompt, law plucks from single hand of solitary man and makes him pay the carriage with his life: such are the poignard with the double prong, and all of brittle glass – for man to stab and break off short and so let fragment stick fast in the flesh to baffle surgery." The verbal sound intensified. "Fisc, thy objection is a foppery! Thy charge runs, that we killed three innocents; killed, dost see? Then, if killed, what matter how? – By stick or stone, by sword or dagger, tool long or tool short, round or triangular – poor folks, they find small comfort in a choice. Means to an end, means to an end, my Fisc! Nature cries out 'Take the first arms you find!' Well then, how culpably do we gird loin and once more undertake the high emprise, unless we load ourselves this second time with handsome superfluity of arms, since better say 'too much' than 'not enough', and *plus non vitiat*, too much does no harm, – except in mathematics, sages say. And, while we speak of superabundance, fling a word by the way to fools that cast their flout on Guido – 'Punishment exceeds offence: you might be just but you were cruel, too!' If so you stigmatise the stern and strict, still, he is not without excuse – may plead transgression of his mandate, overzeal o' the part of his companions: all he craved was, they should fray the faces of the three and hew, i' the customary phrase, his wife. If his instructions then be misconceived, nay, disobeyed, impute you blame to him? Cite me no Panimollus to the point: how certain noble youths of Sicily, having good reason to mistrust their wives, killed them and were absolved in consequence, while others who had gone beyond the need by mutilation of the paramour – these were condemned to the galleys, as for guilt exceeding simple murder of a wife. But why? Because of ugliness, and not cruelty, in the said revenge, I trow. Pray, grant to one who meant to slit the nose and slash the cheek and slur the mouth, at most, a somewhat more humane award than these. Your plan abysmally failed, flat you fall, My Fisc! I waste no kick on you but pass!"

The heated argument progressed apace. "Third aggravation: that our act was done – not in the public street, where safety lies, not in the bye-place, caution may avoid, wood, cavern, desert, spots contrived for crime, – but in the very house, home, nook and nest, o' the victims, murdered in their dwelling-place. All three were housed and safe and confident; moreover, the permission that our wife should have at length *domum pro carcere*, her own abode in place of prison – why, we ourselves granted, by our other self and proxy Paolo: did we make such grant, meaning a lure? – elude the vigilance o' the jailor, lead her to commodious death, while we ostensibly relented? Ay, just so did we, nor otherwise, my Fisc!" He gave a corroborative nod. "Is vengeance lawful? We demand our right, but find it will be questioned or refused by jailor, turnkey, hangdog, – what know we? Pray, how is it we should conduct ourselves? To gain our private right – break public peace, do you bid us? Trouble order with our broils? endanger … shall I shrink to own … ourselves? Would you give man's abode more privilege than God's? – for in the churches where He dwells, *ex justa via delinquens*, whoso dares to take a liberty on ground enough, is pardoned, *excusatur*, – that's our case, – delinquens through befitting cause. You hold, to punish a false wife in her own house is graver than, what happens every day, to hale a debtor from his hiding place in church protected by the Sacrament? To this conclusion have I brought my Fisc? Foxes have holes, and fowls o' the air their nests; shall falsewife yet have where to lay her head?" A vigorous shake of the head enhanced the probing questions.

"Fourth aggravation, that we changed our garb, and rusticized ourselves with uncouth hat, rough vest and goatskin wrappage; murdered thus *mutatione vestium*, in disguise, whereby mere murder got complexed with wile, turned wickedly *homicidium*. Fisc, how often must I round thee in the ears – all means are lawful to a lawful end? The Count indulged in a travesty; why? That on her he might lawful vengeance take *commodius*, with more ease, *et tutius*, and safelier: wants he warrant for the step? Read to thy profit how The Apostle once for ease and safety, when Damascus raged, was let down in a basket by the wall to 'scape the malice of the Governor?" The recollection of Saul of Tarsus' peculiar adventure was accompanied by a knowing smile.

"Fifth aggravation, that our wife reposed *sub potestate judicis*, beneath protection of the judge: her house was styled a prison, and his power became its guard in lieu of wall and gate and bolt and bar. This is a tough point, shrewd, redoubtable: the cards are all against us; make a push, kick over table, as our gamesters do! We, do you say, encroach upon the rights, deny the omnipotence o' the Judge forsooth? We, who have only been from first to last intent on that his purpose should prevail, nay, more, at times, anticipating both at risk of a rebuke?" The tone of voice ushered in a thrilling phase of the speech.

"But wait awhile! Cannot we lump this with the sixth and last of the aggravations – that the Majesty o' the Sovereign here received a wound, to wit, *Laesa Majestas*, since our violence was out of envy to the course of law? Yes, here the eruptive wrath with full effect! How – did not indignation chain my tongue – could I repel this last, worst charge of all! Our stomach ... I mean our soul, is stirred within, and we want words. *We* wounded Majesty? Fall under such a censure, we who yearned so much that Majesty dispel the cloud and shine on us with healing on its wings? who prayed the Pope, *Majestas*' very self, to anticipate a little the tardy pack, grant there assemble in our own behoof a Congregation, a particular Court, a few picked friends of quality and place, to hear the several matters in dispute, bred of our marriage like a mushroom-growth? 'What, take the credit from the Law?' you ask? Indeed, we did! Law ducks to Gospel here: why should Law gain the glory and pronounce a judgment shall immortalize the Pope? We venerate the father of the flock, whose last faint sands of life, the frittered gold, fall noiselessly, yet all too fast, o' the cone and tapering heap of those collected years; never have these been hurried in their flow, though Justice fain would jog reluctant arm, in eagerness to take the forfeiture of guilty life: much less shall Mercy sue in vain that thou let innocence survive, precipitate no minim of the mass o' the all-so precious moments of thy life, by pushing Guido into death and doom! The Fisc will find himself forestalled, I think, though he stand, beat till the old ear-drum break! The boy of my own bowels, Hyacinth, wilt ever catch the knack, – requite the pains of poor *papà*, become proficient too i' the how and why and when – the time to laugh, the time to weep, the time, again, to pray, and all the times prescribed by Holy Writ? Well, well, we fathers can but care, but cast our bread upon the waters!"

The besotted father with an eye for the Scriptures advanced on to a major issue: "In a word, these secondary charges go to ground, since secondary, so superfluous, – motes quite from the main point: we did all and some, little and much, adjunct and principal, *causa honoris*. Is there such a cause as the sake of honour? By that sole test try our action, nor demand if more or less, because of the action's mode, we merit blame or may-be deserve praise. The Court decides. Is the end lawful? It allows the means: what we may do we may with safety do, and what means 'safety' we ourselves must judge. Taunt us not that our friends performed for pay! For us, enough were simple honour's sake: give country clowns the dirt they comprehend, the piece of gold! Our reasons, which suffice ourselves, be ours alone; our piece of gold be, to the rustic, reason and to spare! We must translate our motives like our speech into the lower phrase that suits the sense o' the limitedly apprehensive: let each level have its language! Heaven speaks first to the angel, then the angel tames the word down to the ear of Tobit; he, in turn, diminishes the message to his dog, and finally that dog finds how the flea shall learn its hunger must have holiday, – how many varied sorts of language here, each following each with pace to match the step, yet not with equal steps!" The *langue*-concerned fellow chuckled.

"Talking of which flea reminds me I must put in special word for the poor humble following, the four friends, *sicarii*, – our assassins in your charge. Ourselves are safe in your approval now, yet must care for our companions, plead the case o' the poor, the friends – of old-world faith – who are in tribulation for our sake. *Pauperum Procurator* is my style: I stand forth as the poor man's advocate: and when we treat of what concerns the poor, *pietas* ever ought to win the day because those very paupers constitute *thesaurus Christi*, all the wealth of Christ. One of them falls short, by some months, of age fit to be managed by the gallows; two may plead exemption from our law's award, being foreigners, subjects of the Granduke, – and they, at instance of the rack, confessed all four unanimously did resolve, behind the back of Guido as he fled, that, since he had not kept his promise, paid the money for the murder on the spot, – and, reaching home again, might even ignore the pact or pay it in improper coin, – they would inaugurate the morrow's light by killing Guido as he lay asleep pillowed by wallet which contained their fee. I thank the Fisc for knowledge of this fact: what fact could hope to make more manifest their rectitude, Guido's integrity? For who fails recognise apparent here that these poor rustics bore no envy, hate, malice, nor yet uncharitableness against the people they had put to death? All done was to deserve their simple pay, while he the Count, the cultivated mind, he, wholly rapt in his serene regard of honour, – as who contemplates the sun and hardly minds what tapers blink below, – would he so desecrate the deed, vulgarise vengeance, as defray its cost by money dug out of the dirty earth? The deed done, those coarse hands were soiled enough, he spared them the pollution of the pay."

All of a sudden, the protector of the destitute perceived that his valuable headgear was askew and briskly restored it to its orthodox position. Soon after, his attention shifted from poor rustics to Rome's wealthy ruler. "And now, thou excellent the Governor! *Enixe supplico*, I strive in prayer, *ut dominis meis*, that unto the Court *perpendere placeat*, it may please them weigh, *quod dominus* Guido, that our Count, *occidit*, did the killing in dispute, *ut eius honor tumulatus*, that the honour of him buried fathom-deep in infamy, *in infamia*, might arise. *Occidit*, I repeat he killed the clan lest peradventure longer life might trail, *viveret*, link by link his turpitude. *Occidit*, and he killed them here in Rome, the appropriate theatre which witnessed once *matronam nobilem*, Lucretia's self, wash off the pots of her pudicity *sanguine proprio*, with her own pure blood; *quae vidit*, and which city also saw, *patrem*, Virginius, *undequaque*, quite, *impunem*, with no sort of punishment, imbrue his hands with butchery, *filiae*, of chaste Virginia, to avoid a rape; *occidit* – killed them, I reiterate – *in propria domo*, in their own abode moreover, dreading lest within those walls the opprobrium peradventure be prolonged, and that the domicile which witnessed crime, *esset et poenae*, might watch punishment; *occidit*, killed, I round you in the ears, *quia alio modo*, since by other mode, there was no possibility his fame *ducere cicatrices*, might be healed: that he, please God, might creditably live, *sin minus*, but if fate willed otherwise, *proprii honoris*, of his outraged fame, *offensi*, by Mannaja, if you please, the pitiable victim he should fall!"

The emotional outburst, inspired by events of yore and sprinkled with the speaker's Ciceronian Latin, was boosted by his finely embroidered handkerchief mopping his fleshy face.

"Done! I' the rough, i' the rough! But done! And, lo, landed and stranded lies my very own, my miracle, my monster of defence – Leviathan into the nose whereof I have put fish-hook, pierced his jaw with thorn, and given him to my maidens for a play! It's hard: you have to plead before these priests and poke at them with Scripture, – or you pass for heathen and, what's worse, for ignorant o' the quality o' the Court and what it likes by way of illustration of the law – regularize the whole, next emphasize, then latinize and lastly Cicero-ize, giving my Fisc his finish." His forefinger jerked to the tip of his nose. "And where's my fry, and family and friends? Hail, ye true pleasures, all the rest are false! Oh, the old mother; oh, the fattish wife! Rogue Hyacinth shall put on paper toque, and wrap himself around with mamma's veil done up to imitate papa's black robe, and call himself the Advocate o' the Poor, mimic Don father that defends the Count, and for reward shall have a small full glass of manly red *rosolio* to himself, – always provided that he conjugate *bibo*, I drink, correctly – nor be found make the preterite, *bipsi*, as last year! How the ambitious do so harden heart as lightly hold by these home sanctitudes, to me is a matter of bewilderment." The family man pushed out the underlip. "Am I refused an outlet from my home to the world's stage? – whereon a man should play the man in public, vigilant for law, zealous for truth, a credit to his kind, nay, – through the talent so employed as yield the Lord his own again with usury, – a satisfaction, yea, to God himself! Well, I have modelled me by Agur's wish, 'Remove far from me vanity and lies, feed me with food convenient for me!' What i' the world should a wise man require beyond? Correct that clause in favour of a boy to pledge a memory when poor papa Latin and Law are long since laid at rest. The wife should get a necklace for her pains, the very pearls that made Violante proud; her bosom shall display the big round balls, no braver should be borne by wedded wife! With which Horatian promise I conclude. Into the pigeonhole with thee, my speech! Off and away, first work then play, play, play! Bottini, burn your books, you blazing ass! Sing '*Tra-la-la*, for, lambkins, we must live!'"

Master Giacinto Arcangeli's forensic performance had reached its exodus. The lawyer slapped his hands down on the desk and padded along with his head slightly bent, uncomfortably aware that the Fisc would shortly regale the reverend judges with further display of his casuistry. Would it be music to a lambkin's sensitive ears? It was a moot point.

DOCTOR JOHANNES-BAPTISTA BOTTINIUS

Did Giovambattista Bottini burn his books? Far from it. Hot on the heels of Master Arcangeli, the 'blazing ass' set about completing his *arringa*.

"Let us not linger: hurry to the end, since end does flight and all disastrously. Beware ye blame desert for unsuccess, call failure folly! Man's best effort fails. After ten years' resistance Troy fell flat; could valour save a town, Troy still had stood."

The recollection of Ilion's heroic defiance and pathetic surrender conjured up a defining moment in Pompilia's and Guido's conjugal life: "Pompilia came off halting in no point of courage, conduct, the long journey through, but nature sank exhausted at the close. Who bursts upon her chambered privacy? 'T is decent horror, regulated wrath, befit our dispensation: have we back the old Pagan licence? Shall a Vulcan clap his net o' the sudden and expose the pair to the unquenchable universal mirth? Count Guido Franceschini, what were gained by publishing thy shame thus to the world? Were all the precepts of the wise a waste? Why, say thy wife – admonish we the fool, – were false, and thou bid chronicle thy shame, much rather should thy teeth bite out thy tongue, dumb lip consort with desecrated brow, but virtue, barred, still leaps the barrier, lords! Surprised, then, in the garb of truth, perhaps, Pompilia, thus opposed, breaks obstacle, springs to her feet and stands Thalassian-pure, confronts the foe, – nay, catches at his sword and tries to kill the intruder, he complains. Why, so she gave her lord his lesson back, crowned him, this time, the virtuous woman's way, with an exact obedience; he brought sword, she drew the same, – since swords are meant to draw. It was the husband chose the weapon here. Why did not he inaugurate the game with some gentility of apophthegm still pregnant on the philosophical page, some captivating cadence still a-lisp o' the poet's lyre? Such spells subdue the surge, make tame the tempest, much more mitigate the passions of the mind, and probably had moved Pompilia to a smiling blush. No, he must needs prefer the argument o' the blow: and she obeyed, in duty bound, for wife must follow whither husband leads, vindicate honour as himself prescribes, save him the very way himself bids save, – anything to content a wilful spouse. And so he was contented – one must do justice to the expedient which succeeds. Forthwith the wife is pronounced innocent: what would the husband more than gain his cause, and find that honour flash in the world's eye, his apprehension was lest soil had besmirched?"

A shade of irony coloured the speaker's voice. "So, happily the adventure comes to close whereon my fat opponent grounds his charge preposterous: at mid-day he groans 'How dark!' Listen to me, thou Archangelic swine! Where is the ambiguity to blame, the flaw to find in our Pompilia? Safe she stands, see! Does thy comment follow quick 'Safe, inasmuch as at the end proposed, but thither she picked way by devious path. What, had Pompilia gained the right to boast "No devious path, no doubtful patch was mine, I saved my head nor sacrificed my foot"? Why, being in a peril, show mistrust of the angels set to guard the innocent? Why rather hold by obvious vulgar help of stratagem and subterfuge, excused somewhat, but still no less a foil, a fault, since low with high, and good with bad is linked? The trick succeeds, but 't is an ugly trick, where needs have been no trick!'" He shook his head in disbelief. "My answer? Faugh! *Nimis incongrue*! Too absurdly put. Trick, I maintain, had no alternative. Gentle and simple, here the Governor, there the Archbishop, everywhere the friends, shook heads and waited for a miracle or went their way, left Virtue to her fate. Just this one rough and ready man leapt forth; he only, Caponsacchi, 'mid a crowd, caught Virtue up, carried Pompilia off thro' the gaping impotence of sympathy, did yeoman's service, cared not where the gripe was more than duly energetic: bruised, she smarts a little, but her bones are saved a fracture, and her skin will soon show sleek. *Quid vetat*, what forbids, I aptly ask with Horace, that I give my anger vent? Just so the Archbishop and all good like him went to bed meaning to pour oil and wine i' the wounds of her next day, – but long ere day, they had burned the one and drunk the other; while just so, again, contrariwise, the priest sustained poor Nature in extremity by stuffing barley-bread into her mouth, saving Pompilia – grant the parallel – by the plain homely and straightforward way taught him by common-sense. Let others shriek, 'Oh what refined expedients did we dream proved us the only fit to help the fair!' Caponsacchi's advocate adopted an air of gravitas. "Back to beseemingness and gravity! For Law steps in: Guido appeals to Law, demands she arbitrate, – does well for once. O Law, of thee how neatly was it said by that old Sophocles: thou hast thy seat i' the very breast of Jove, no meanlier throned! Here is a piece of work now, hitherto begun and carried on, concluded near, without an eye-glance cast thy sceptre's way; and, lo, the stumbling and discomfiture! Guido would try conclusions with his foe: instead of asking Law to lend a hand, what pother of sword drawn and pistol cocked, what peddling with forged letters and paid spies, politic circumvention! – all to end as it began – by loss of the fool's head, first in a figure, presently in a fact. It is a lesson to mankind at large. How other were the end, would men be sage and bear confidingly each quarrel straight, o Law, to thy recipient mother-knees! No foolish brawling murders any more! Peace for the household, practice for the Fisc, and plenty for the exchequer of my lords! Too much to hope, in this world: in the next, who knows? Since, why should sit the Twelve enthroned to judge the tribes, unless the tribes be judged? And 't is impossible but offences come: so, all's one lawsuit, all one long leet-day!"

Bottini rolled his sleeves and expatiated on the cause célèbre under scrutiny.

"Forgive me this digression – that I stand entranced at Law's first beam, outbreak o' the business, when the Count's good angel bade 'Put up thy sword, born enemy to the ear, and let Law listen to thy difference!' And Law does listen and compose the strife, settle the suit, how wisely and how well! On our Pompilia, faultless to a fault, Law bends a brow maternally severe, implies the worth of perfect chastity, by fancying the flaw she cannot find. 'Quit the gay range o' the world,' I hear her cry. 'Enter, in lieu, the penitential pound: exchange the gauds of pomp for ashes, dust: – leave each mollitious haunt of luxury, the golden-garnished silken-couched alcove; for the warm arms, were wont enfold thy flesh, let wire-shirt plough and whip-cord discipline!'

A flush of excitement enhanced the rhetorical flow. "And so, our paragon submits herself, goes at command into the holy house and, also at command, comes out again: she may betake her to her parents' place, and she is domiciled in house and home as though she thence had never budged at all. And thither let the husband, joyous – ay, but contrite also – quick betake himself, proud that his dove which lay among the pots hath mued those dingy feathers, – moulted now, shows silver bosom clothed with yellow gold. O let him not delay! Time fleets how fast, and opportunity, the irrevocable, once flown will flout him! Is the furrow traced? Already – hist – what murmurs 'monish now the laggard? – doubtful, nay, fantastic bruit of such an apparition, such return, now and then, of Caponsacchi's very self! 'T is said when nights are lone and company is rare, his visitations brighten winter up." Bottini raised his eyebrows. "If so they did – which nowise I believe – he, too, must need his recreative hour. And thus, nocturnal taste of intercourse – which never happened, but suppose it did – may have been used to dishabituate by sip and sip this drainer to the dregs o' the draught of conversation, – heady stuff, and must we marvel if the impulse urge to talk the old story over now and then, the hopes and fears, the stoppage and the haste? *'Forsan et haec olim'*… such trifles serve to make the minutes pass in winter-time."

The Advocate of the Fisc poured an abundant dose of his legitimate ruby wine into a goblet and quaffed the content with gusto. Smacking his lips, he carried on with his prosecutorial performance.

"What is the hap of the unconscious Count? O admirable, there is born a babe, a son, an heir, an infant for the apple of his eye, core of his heart, and crown completing life, the *summum bonum* of the earthly lot! 'We,' saith ingeniously the sage, 'are born solely that others may be born of us.' O faith, where art thou flown from out the world? Already on what an age of doubt we fall! Whose the babe? '*Cuium pecus?*' Guido's lamb? '*An Meliboei?*' Nay, but of the priest! '*Non, sed Aegonis!*' Someone must be sire: and who shall say, in such a puzzling strait, if there were not vouchsafed some miracle to the wife who had been harassed and abused more than enough by Guido's family for non-production of the promised fruit of marriage? What if Nature, I demand, touched to the quick by taunts about her sloth, had roused herself, put forth recondite power, bestowed this birth to vindicate her sway? Spontaneous generation: need I prove were facile feat to Nature at a pinch? Let whoso doubts, steep horsehair certain weeks, in water: there will be produced a snake; a second product of the horse, which horse happens to be representative – now that I think on 't – of Arezzo's self the very city our conception blessed! Note, further, as to mark the prodigy, the babe in question neither took the name of Guido, from the sire presumptive, nor Giuseppe, from the sire potential, but Gaetano – last saint of the hierarchy, and newest namer for a thing so new: what other motive could have prompted choice? Therefore be peace again: exult, ye hills! Ye vales rejoicingly break forth in song!"

It sounded sweetly bucolic, but a change of expression followed instantly: "In vain! The perverse Guido doubts his eyes, distrusts assurance, lets the devil drive; his fate is sealed, his life as good as gone, on him I am not tempted to waste word. Yet though my purpose holds, – which was and is and solely shall be to the very end, to draw the true *effigiem* of a saint, do justice to perfection in the sex, – by painting saintship I depicture sin; beside the pearl, I prove how black the jet, and through Pompilia's virtue, Guido's crime.

Back to her then, – with but one beauty more, end we our argument, – one crowning grace pre-eminent 'mid agony and death. For to the last Pompilia played her part, used the right means to the permissible end, and, wily as an eel that stirs the mud thick overhead, so baffling spearman's thrust, she, while he stabbed her, simulated death, delayed, for his sake, the catastrophe, obtained herself a respite, four days' grace, whereby she gave her version of events and, by a full confession, saved her soul."

A laboured sigh of relief pervaded the speaker's sturdy body. Then, words flowed freely once more. "Far better had Pompilia died o' the spot than found a tongue to wag and shame the law, shame most of all herself, – did friendship fail, and advocacy lie less on the alert. Do I credit the alleged narration? No! Lied our Pompilia then, to laud herself? Still, no; – clear up what seems discrepancy? The means abound, – art's long, though time is short, so, keeping me in compass, all I urge is – since confession at the point of death, *nam in articulo mortis*, with the Church passes for statement honest and sincere, – 't was charity, in one so circumstanced, to spend her last breath in one effort more for universal good of friend and foe, and, by pretending utter innocence, reintegrate not solely her own fame but do the like kind office for the priest whom the crude truth might treat less courteously, indeed, expose to peril, abbreviate the life and long career of usefulness presumably before him: while her lord, whose fleeting life is forfeit to the law, – what mercy to the culprit if, by just the gift of such a full certificate of his immitigable guiltiness, she stifled in him the absurd conceit of murder as it were a mere revenge! Whereas, persuade him he has slain a saint who sinned not in the little she did sin, you urge him all the brisklier to repent! Next, – if this view of mine content ye not, Lords, nor excuse the genial falsehood here, we fall back on the inexpugnable, submit you, – she confessed before she talked! The sacrament obliterates the sin: what is not, – was not, in a certain sense. *Solvuntur tabulae*? May we laugh and go?" There was a tinge of mock-epic in the utterance. "We take on us to vindicate Law's self, for – yea, Sirs, – curb the start, curtail the stare! Remains that we apologize for haste i' the Law, our lady who here bristles up 'And my procedure? Did the Court mistake? Did not my sentence in the former stage o' the business bear a title plain enough? *Decretum*' – I translate it word for word – ' "Decreed: the priest, for his complicity i' the flight and deviation of the dame, as well as for unlawful intercourse, is banished three years": crime and penalty, declared alike. If he be taxed with guilt, how can you call Pompilia innocent? If they be innocent, have I been just?'"

The Aristotle-based question was voiced in a smooth sustained manner. "Gently, O mother, judge men! – whose mistake is in the poor misapprehensiveness. Title is one thing, arbitration's self, *probatio*, quite another possibly. All is tentative, till the sentence come, mere indication of what men expect, and nowise an assurance they shall find!"

The verdict was pronounced with a steady intonation. "Lords, what if we permissibly relax the tense bow, as the law-god Phoebus bids, relieve our gravity at close of speech? I traverse Rome, feel thirsty, need a draught, look for a wineshop, find it by the bough projecting as to say, 'Here wine is sold!' So much I know, – 'sold': but what sort of wine? That much must I discover by myself. 'Wine is sold', quoth the bough, 'but good or bad, find, and inform us when you smack your lips!' Exactly so, Law hangs her title forth, to show she entertains you with such case about crime: come in! she pours, you quaff. You find the Priest good liquor in the main, but heady and provocative of brawls. Remand the residue to flask once more, lay it low where it may deposit lees, i' the cellar: thence produce it presently, three years the brighter and the better!"

The self-proclaimed wine connoisseur repeated himself by refilling his long-stemmed glass, imbibing the delicious content and smacking his lips anew to the accompaniment of a wide grin. "Thus, Law's son, have I bestowed my filial help, and thus I end, *tenax proposito*; point to point as I purposed have I drawn Pompilia, and implied as terribly Guido: so, gazing, let the world crown Law – able once more, despite my impotence, and helped by the acumen of the Court, to eliminate, display, make triumph truth! What other prize than truth were worth the pains?" A momentary pause for breath was superseded by "*There*'s my oration – much exceeds in length that famed Panegyric of Isocrates they say it took him fifteen years to pen … but all those ancients could say anything! He put in just what rushed into his head, while I shall have to prune and pare and print. This comes of being born in modern times with priests for auditory. Still, it pays."

The rhetoric-conscious *Fisci Advocatus* wound up his performance by bowing down before prospective cassocked judges who would be, he surmised, agog to bring down the curtain on the gory Roman drama presented to them.

Master Giacinto Arcangeli and Doctor Giovanni Battista Bottini have had their haranguing say: performing in the relative seclusion of their *studi*, both have come up with a speech act replete with its 'locutionary, illocutionary, and perlocutionary' elements.[1]

First in line for a brief, Master Arcangeli has played the role of *Procurator Pauperum*, even though he happened to be the advocate of a reputedly well-off Count. By the same token he has created an image of exceedingly paternal care for tender-aged Giacinto – alias Cinone, Cinozzo, Cinoncello, Cinuciattolo etc. For good measure, he has made him the beneficiary of a classical education; in much in the same vein, he has enthused over "home joy, the family board, altar and hearth" for being moral values consonant with "honest profit and good fame ... honouring God and serving man" and at variance with the "fluff, nil *in nuce*" exposed by the satirical Horace as a common-or-garden source of deception.

Such has been the overture of a fellow rich in legal pronouncements and delighted to see "law come dimple Cinoncino's cheek and Latin dumple Cinarello's chin; to his eye, "there's a blessing on the earth, a special providence for fatherhood!" In this connection, Arcangeli has endeavoured to put pristine Latin to good use while dealing with Guido's marriage as well as with the vexed question of the identity of the person responsible for the exchange of letters between the nobleman's young wife and the canon Caponsacchi; unquestionably, he has maintained, prosecutor Bottini's efforts to "break Tully's pate" was a different kettle of fish! One is reminded of a 16th-century Bishop's evaluation of the Latin inscription on his predecessor Gandolfo's tombstone in *Santa Prassede*'s Church: 'Tully, my masters? Ulpian serves his need.'[2] It is indeed fair to remark that the ability to use a refined idiom has been of paramount importance to Master Arcangeli and Dr Bottini. The question is has either of them succeeded in making a mockery of 'Tully's pate'?

At the end of the day, the two layers have, to all appearances, put on a show reminiscent of Horace's view of the ridicule as a test of truth. A moment's reflection may well lead to the conclusion that both have availed themselves of sources provided by Renaissance scholars and managed to turn classical Latin into a dexterously updated jargon. In this context, it is worth bearing in mind that it was barely feasible in those days to sustain the classic Ciceronian purity of Latin whilst using a language tainted with unrefined *heteroglossia*, i.e. with words of another tongue: the use of idiomatic Latin could be tantamount to the employment of a scientific code – as it is, for instance, in the textual analysis of *La Vérité sur le Cas de M Valdemar in articulo mortis*[3], – but then any emotive element in a speech act would be liable to contravene the dicta of linguistic science, and the re-establishment of Latin classical purity would restrict its area of application to essentially the sphere of stylization alone: it was as though the old language was being measured against a new world and the former could not be stretched to fit the latter.[4] In that respect, it makes sense to suspect that the author of *The Ring and the Book* has spiced a dough moulded in earnest with an ample dose of parody/travesty, and, in this connection, it *has* been held that 'a certain seriousness is cause for amusement from the standpoint of veracity.'[5] In the light of this evaluation, the lawyers' feat appears to have been a thought-provoking language-imbued exercise.

Take Giacinto Arcangeli's boast, "We'll garnish law with idiom, never fear! Out-of-the way events extend our scope": a reasoned argument is likely to justify the assumption that the gentleman's bold commitment has anticipated the linguistic theory about an '*event*' in language related to 'the preserving of time and being and thereby of the particular ways in which being as a whole is revealed'.[6]

For his part, Giovambattista Bottini has adopted the attitude of a painter depicting the soul as a substitute for physical details, – a far cry from, say, Lippo Lippi, the Renaissance painter who had highlighted the beauty of the natural environment as well as its ethical connotations: 'If you get simple beauty and nothing else, you get about the best thing God invents. That's somewhat, and you'll find the soul you have missed within yourself when you return him thanks ... this world's no blot for us, nor blank; it means intensely and means good; to find its meaning is my meat and drink.[7] At first blush the latter's assertion has struck a happy note, but there's the rub: far from being definite, the meaning of the world may well turn out to be an amalgam of endlessly changing 'signifiers' only arbitrarily connected with the 'signified'. In consequence, there appears to be a need to go beyond the structuralist quest for the "signified" advocated by Browning at the outset of the poem at issue: such a move would lead to the apperception of language as a play of meaning and therefore integral to a polysemous discourse. If that is the case, a post-structuralist approach would validate the conjecture that the Florentine painter has obliquely acknowledged that his "meat and drink" was barely helping him to keep the wolf from the door.

A renewed focus on Arcangeli's forensic 'menu' reveals that a blend of law and language has made up a second course, – which, it is well worth noting, has been offered with a flourish: "Better we lost the cause than lacked the gird at the Fisc's Latin, lost the Judge's laugh." In the *Procurator Pauperum*'s eyes, Bottini "eludes law by piteous looks aloft, lets Latin glance off as he makes appeal to the saint that's somewhere in the ceiling top". In this context, it is not difficult to see how Arcangeli has, on the strength of being a devotee of Cicero's decorous Latin, highlighted the link between rhetoric and philosophy of mind, in respect of which his platonically rhetorical approach has made him strive after clarity by means of a dialectical investigation of verbal meanings. By the same token he has, qua an aspiring philosopher of mind, contrasted his little son's discernment with the authorities' indiscriminate recourse to torture. Regrettably, the duress that had made the Count admit to killing was now hindering him, as his defender, from proving "murder a mere myth and presenting Guido as an innocent, ignorant, absent" and religiously engaged fellow whilst the canon Caponsacchi was hell-bent on covering up his unwelcome paternity with the help of the Comparini household. Until then, the law had consistently sanctioned the presumption of innocence as prior to suspicion of guilt; alas, the offended husband had accidentally "arrived i' the nick of time to catch the charge o' the killing".

On taking centre stage again, Arcangeli's opponent has donned the philosophical mantle of Aristotle and conveyed absolute confidence that his *arringa* would cathartically instil pity and terror into the reverend judges; in a similar fashion, he has, qua an Aristotelian rhetorician, aimed at clarity by means of words endowed with their ordinary meanings. Accordingly, in the process of negatively evaluating Guido's deed, he has "searched out, pried into, pressed the meaning forth of every piece of evidence in point"; however, to set the record straight, he has been assisted in his painstaking quest and final stance by authorities willing to resort to excruciating torture in order to extract a confession from the hapless victim. As to Pompilia, he has worked on the assumption that she was utterly innocent about "blind hidden horrors best unnamed"; in harmony with that, he has confidently stated that, in tune with leading ladies of yore, the latter-day heroine could be charged with monstrosity or mendacity solely when, to paraphrase Luke, 'thistles would grow on vines or thorns yield figs', or if the judges now in session came up with an "oblique sentence". At this juncture, past and present have joined in giving a helping hand to a lawyer who, as a visual artist, has intimated a penchant for gemstones and depicted Pompilia as a bejewelled "infant, child, maid, woman, wife".

Concerning Guido, Arcangeli has put forward a well-argued case for exempting him from condemnation on the grounds of honour: the concept was a gift of God as well as a basic moral ingredient leading to revenge if ignored; furthermore, an act in reprisal for injury to somebody's dignity ought to be justified in the light of Nature's set of rules, for a fierce defence of the territory reserved for honour was inherent in the natural law of animals. As a corollary, Master Arcangeli has come up with a naturalistic definition of the moral concept at issue: a good show, but he has exposed himself to dangers inherent in the casting aside of subtle nuances of meaning in a moral term such as Good. And the next move in the attack? Immunity for the sake of honour was a must: it had not only been codified by pagan legislators but even sanctioned by Jesus. *'My honour I to nobody will give!'* the Son of God had asserted and, in harmony with him, Christians had extolled self-respect as 'the supreme good'. In that regard, the "infallible Pope" had better explain why, when it comes to a woman's adultery, "the Gospel checks the Law which throws the stone, the Church tears the divorce bill God grants, the wife sins and enjoys impunity". In the wake of the whole kit and caboodle, Count Franceschini was in no position to see the light at the end of the tunnel he was in.

At this advanced stage of the drama, Arcangeli has put his finger on a major strand of the argument inherent in the 'whydunit' set in motion by a nobleman keen on salvaging his battered prestige. The defender has entered the domain of philosophy, notably that of normative ethics: on dealing with a wife's alleged adultery and a husband's sense of honour, he has made a descriptive ethical statement and then moved on to a prescriptively moral one on the assumption that the meaning of words such as 'the supreme good' calls for a normative ethical investigation into what makes self-respect a guiding principle. A relevant question would be whether, by sharing the Count's egocentric attitude, he has upheld a relativist's contention that a moral criterion used by an individual is valid only as the corollary of adhesion to it; if that is the case, he has espoused a far-from naturalistic moral doctrine and, by unconsciously adhering to Protagoras' relativistic view of 'man as the measure of all things', he has opened the door to the unorthodox conclusion that Guido and Pompilia could both be right in their own ways.

Pursuing his line of defensive attack, Master Arcangeli has put forth the case of Leonardo, a Sicilian gentleman who had made history through slaying his wife 'with commodity' and had been sent to labour on the galleys mainly because of his offensive *modus operandi*. Interestingly, the mention of the peculiar episode appears to have turned the *whydunit* into a *howdunit*, and it is worthwhile to add that to mention that by association of ideas it conjures up the figure of the upper-class Francesca da Rimini, daughter of Guido's namesake, telling Dante in the *Inferno* how the noble *game of love* played by her and her socially equal Paolo Malatesta had been brought to a deadly end by Gianciotto, who was her consort and Paolo's brother. The lady's confession, 'The way of it leaves me still distressed'[9], implies that to her mind the "how" was more important than the "what".

In the Franceschini cause célèbre the above-mentioned 'what' has reasserted itself when the advocate has pointed the finger of blame at the Comparini couple for pretending to be Pompilia's parents: "Her fault was their fault; her punishment be theirs accordingly!" In parallel with them, the Count had gone through "eight mortal months of hesitation" which could be explained by the grievous wound in his soul, that is, "where honour sits and rules"; but then again, a "husband sure should let a scruple speak ere he slay wife", and Guido's Yuletide week-long wait only a stone's throw from the Comparini household had been motivated by his "care for aught held holy by the Church".

At this critical juncture, Arcangeli has played a hazardous chess-like game: eager for a checkmate, he has shifted his chessmen from an objective position grounded on natural law to an ego-based one, and the move has made his moral judgement tantamount to a purely descriptive ethical statement. Admittedly, he has subsequently reached the thoroughly ethical position essential to convey the meaning of the moral terms he had been using so far, yet he has failed to checkmate the king because, on a par with Bottini's *modus ludendi*, he has availed himself of moral terms such as 'right' and 'wrong' within the context of semantics utterly incongruous under the circumstances; consequently, he has been unable to pass from the meaning of his moral statement to conclusions of substance as far as his moral questions were concerned. In the final analysis, he has not been successful in endorsing Guido's philosophy of life qua a matter of substance; in fact, he has inadvertently shared Bottini's standpoint on that score.

In this respect, a comparison between the two lawyers leads to the conclusion that the Fisc's philosophical approach has been grounded in a mixture of ethics and aesthetics. Ergo his appreciation of Pompilia's exploitation of the looks allotted to her by Mother Nature "in lieu of spears, in lieu of shields": the young woman had put her comeliness to good use by dint of "melting wiles, deliciousest deceits" and resorted to the "armoury of love" while simultaneously feeling "the proper pity for lord and king and husband". In the prosecutor's eyes she had behaved like a heifer bearing the yoke yet wincing at the goad and kicking from time to time: "the philosophical mind expects no less", Bottini has pointed out, thus mingling the rules of Nature with the precepts of philosophy and showing a streak of ethical emotivism conducive to duality. Lo and behold, the image of a Provencal *jeune fille mal mariée* making a stand against her unloved husband comes to the fore – with a difference, though: unlike the medieval spouse, Pompilia has submitted to Guido's sway: "He hath attained his object; groom and bride partake the nuptial bower no soul to see; old things are passed and all again is new, over and gone the obstacle to peace", Bottini has jubilantly remarked. Well, well, well, it would not come amiss to cry out in response, 'So much for the emancipation of the female sex!', for the conception of male dominance has been, somewhat paradoxically, revivified.

At this point, it is well worth highlighting Guido's combative spouse acceptance of solely a provisional coexistence: to her husband's mind, she had been searching for an outstanding specimen of male gender and identified it with the personable Giuseppe Maria Caponsacchi. As a corollary, in contrast to the priest's flawlessness, "courtesy, good sense and proper trust" have deserted Guido and jealousy has held sway. In this connection, the Moor Othello's *honest* adviser Iago springs to mind as the one who described jealousy as a 'green-eyed monster which doth mock the meat it feeds on'[10]. For his part, Bottini has contemplated telling the judges how jealousy "makes false true, abuses eye and ear, turns the mist adamantine, loads with sound silence, and into void and vacancy crowds a whole phalanx of conspiring foes". In that respect, it does appear that the conflation of descriptive ethics and metaphor has served the purpose, and the real nub of the matter has been the presence of Caponsacchi as a major factor in Pompilia's rebellion and recourse to feminine wiles in self-defence and out of a "laudable wish to live and see good days".

The lawyer's subsequent reiteration of Pompilia's attributes and tactics has ushered in a *coup de théâtre*: in harmony with the young woman's disclosure to her self-styled parents that she had acquired the writing skill and availed herself of it, he has, through a *reductio ad absurdum*, acknowledged her literacy. However, she had never written to the priest, but even conceding, for the sake of argument, that she had secretly dropped him a line, well, what of it? Caponsacchi was her only friend and her only hope; she "was bound to proffer nothing short of love to the man whose service was to save her.'

At this point, Bottini, now a probing conjurer on an ad hoc basis, has pulled a rabbit out of the hat and completed the trick with a Machiavellian flourish: Pompilia's modus operandi had simply been a means to a legitimate end; her human desire to escape death had made her feign love, allure her saviour, and embark on a flight of fancy. She had sounded like a passionate Amaryllis declaiming her love, versus a Caponsacchi reminiscent of the coldly analytical Myrtillus': in other words, a *chanson courtoise* had been heard once again.

In respect of that, Bottini's 'perlocutory' act deserves recognition for being engendered by a resolve to prove Guido's duplicity and enhanced by a refutal of the theory that Pompilia had not only drugged her consort but also "helped herself thereto with liberal hand from out the husband's store": the truth of the matter was that the newly wedded spouse was entitled to "use every means, since means to the end are lawful".

In step with the resurrection of Amaryllis' and Myrtillus' feelings, rhetoric has gained momentum: the chauffeur Venerino has come to the fore with his testimony that the journey had been 'one long embrace"; in reality, the prosecutor has averred, the amorous picture had been no more than the upshot of a "back-eyed" driver's hallucination caused by his driving for a long spell. Anyway, a validation of the testimony would incline any unbiased observer to see the repeated osculation as a token of Caponsacchi's deep humanity to be associated with the evangelist Matthew's dictum the "spirit is willing, but the flesh is weak". Arguably, Pompilia's fellow traveller had only stolen "a balmy breath perhaps for more assurance sleep was not decease", and any jaundice-free person would detect the presence of compassion for a woman in need of help. In conclusion, the whole kit and caboodle had been "how near to love, and love how neighbourly to unreasonableness!

As for Pompilia, "Now, what is the greatest sin of womanhood?" Bottini has asked the prospective judges, and his own reply has been: "That which unwomans it, abolishes the nature of woman; impudence". Having said that, he has hastened to add, "Whatever friendly fault may interpose to save the sex from self-abolishment, is three-parts on the way to virtue rank". The female fugitive's one-off impudence had reached breaking point when, contradicting herself, she had stated, 'To read or write I never learned at all'. "O splendidly mendacious!" the layer has commented and in so doing brought to the fore more than one of the seven types of ambiguity singled out by a literary theorist, namely the third if the statement is interpreted as a pun, and the seventh if it is deemed to be a symptom of a 'division in the author's mind'[11]. A directly related question would be whether the latter has been soliciting his listeners' assent with a view to provoking dissent.

Returning to Giacinto Arcangeli's *arringa*, it is not difficult to notice how the lawyer has availed himself of his pyrotechnic skills while grappling with aggravations of Guido-and-co.'s crime – "*our* crime", he has specified, thus implying some sort of identification with the culprits while presumably ruminating on an effective line of defence. The orator has highlighted six aggravations qua *exempla* liable to bring into existence "parasite growth upon mere murder's back"; at the same time, he has artfully made major concessions with a view to strengthening his own argument.

On mentioning the first aggravation Arcangeli has related how five armed men had hatched a wicked plan, and four of them had been sentenced to death by the Governor of Rome because of complicity in somebody else's murder. The official-in-chief had presumably intended to punish the use of means qua an end in itself, but then, what about a "crime not only compassed but complete, meant and done too?" Replacing the focus on the means with a scrutiny of somebody else's ends would have been highly appropriate in the lawyer's eyes: the bottom line was that if more than one crime had been committed with the aim of transgressing no more than once, the dictates of ethical logic demanded that only the foremost violation ought to be taken into consideration.

Reader, what a *modus concludendi*! A moment's reflection will suffice to spark off the thought that Arcangeli's subtle argumentation has a sophistic quality, even though not of the kind opposed by, say, Plato and Aristotle, but one germane to the sophistry associated with rhetoric and the art of making headway in an argument. Regarding that, the defender's fiery contention hardly cuts any ice: on the contrary, it feels flimsy, if not twisted, and as such is conducive to rejection for being tainted with paralogism and consequently providing an instance of rhetorical fallacy.

Second aggravation: strictly forbidden tools had been used to commit the murder of three innocent human beings. "Fisc, thy objection is a foppery!" Arcangeli has ejaculated. "Killed, dost see? If killed, what matter how? ... poor folks, they find small comfort in a choice! Means to an end, means to an end, my Fisc! Nature cries out, 'Take the first arms you find!'" The runaway couple had escaped injury only because the pursuer lacked the means to achieve his goal, the lawyer has remarked. For all that, had he gone too far and sunk into cruelty? Not for the world. His accomplices had disobeyed his reasonable instructions, and how could he be blamed for that? To be fair, the Count deserved a "somewhat more humane award than these!"

The whole statement has a Machiavellian flavour: Arcangeli has fleshed out his sophistic outlook with an avowed respect for Mother Earth and an appreciation of Guido's shrewd plans, but on the other hand he has sounded ambivalent while dealing with the intercourse between the Count and the not-so-noble Comparini family as well as with the former's rapport with his henchmen. In effect, his request for a "more humane award" has sounded somewhat preposterous and therefore caused a precipitous descent from the highly serious to the ridiculous.

Third aggravation: Guido's heinous crime had been perpetrated not in the open but inside the victims' house. The exacerbation was, of course, mere twaddle: the choice of the place did in truth not intensify the offence, because any assertion that "to punish a false wife in her own house" was ethically worse than, say, to drag a debtor out of a church would treat man's abode better than the house of God and therefore paradoxically justify the theory that an untruthful wife had right to find sanctuary in her house as if it was a holy place.

A critical eye's response to Arcangeli's argument may well be that only a *reductio ad absurdum* can give substance to it: a crime is a crime, regardless of where it has occurred; even an unbeliever would find it implausible to think more highly of a secular dwelling than of a sacred building.

A fourth aggravation, viz Guido's attempt at disguise, has been peremptorily dismissed by the lawyer with further help from Machiavelli: "All means are lawful in order to reach a lawful end", he has stated, echoing the philosopher's words. Furthermore, ages before the latter's advisory compendium, a providential cloak had given the Apostle Paul means of escape from a malicious Governor.[12] All things considered, indulging in a travesty had been the safest way for Guido to take honourable vengeance.

Now, it would be unfair to gainsay the logicality of the thesis: unquestionably, a Count admittedly devoid of a lofty aim could be given the benefit of the doubt even when opting for tactics, including an ingenious disguise, conducive to a spuriously lawful end. In that respect, it is worthwhile to quote the Stoic Cato's reaction to an utterly novel project: '*Cui bono?*'[13], for it was his philosophical way of expressing doubts about anyone profiting from the project and, by association of ideas, about the virtues of the very idea.

Fifth aggravation: Pompilia was under judicial protection. In response, Arcangeli has accentuated the fact that it was "a tough point, shrewd, redoubtable" and then heightened the game by making a stand against any enfeeblement of order and justice. Well played! Suffice to say by way of comment that, in underscoring Themis' sovereignty and by the same token praising his paternal instinct to the skies, the ardent supporter of legalism and fatherhood has sounded too clever by half.

The sixth and final aggravation, one somewhat related to the previous increase in intensity and bound up with the burning issue of *Laesa Majestas*, – has prompted the counsel for the defence to remind the Court how he had "prayed the Pope, *Majestas*' very self, to anticipate a little the tardy pack". As it happened, Guido Franceschini had been left in the hands of secular judges, and he had begged the latter to furnish him with a pronouncement on the Count's civil rights. In the absence of a positive response, he had appealed to the Pope, i.e. the Father of the flock, – for a final say on the celebrated trial in progress.

'Praise be!': Master Arcangeli does appear to have magisterially shifted the focus from the temporal to the spiritual realm. Furthermore, his attachment to the offspring of his bowels has urged him to express his hopes that one day Cinuccino would "become proficient too i' the how and why and when – the time to laugh, the time to weep, the time again to pray, and all the time prescribed by Holy Writ". Intriguingly, the dedicated father has made rationalism join forces with theocracy and genetics; in addition, his professionalism has prompted him to see rhetoric as the name of the game.

At this juncture, the question is how Arcangeli's approach stands vis-à-vis Bottini's evaluation of Pompilia's code of conduct? Well, the short answer is that the latter has seen her succumb in a fashion evocative of ancient Troy's fall after a decade of epic defiance: her nature had sunk "exhausted at the close". Soon after, and echoing Hamlet's statement: 'Frailty, Thy Name is Woman', he has acknowledged that Guido's wife had failed to preserve the necessary strength of character. On the other hand, her husband had equally failed by being unable to keep his emotions within bounds: by exposing the fugitive pair, he had resorted to the old Pagan licence as epitomised by the god Vulcan. Yet "virtue, barred, still leaps the barrier", Bottini has tagged on: by drawing Guido's sword, Pompilia had hurdled the fence in the shape of a *Thalassian*-pure female specimen and proved to be a wife duty bound to take a leaf out of her husband's book. "Anything to content a wilful spouse", the lawyer has wryly commented; those who knew her would understand her predicament only too well, he has suggested.

In the wake of the above standpoint, the classically minded Bottini has forestalled Arcangeli's questions about Pompilia's flawless nature and Caponsacchi's moral fibre: in fact he has come up with an answer by bringing in a quick-witted Hesione and an unmanly Hercules. Then, with the help of metaphor, he has given an account of how the compassionate Caponsacchi had stepped in and saved the young woman by stuffing barley bread in her mouth, whereas the Governor and the Archbishop had seen fit to apply a blend of oil and wine over her wounds and then burn the former while imbibing the latter. Now then, what about Guido? Well, well, well, the Count – in harmony, say, with Sophocles' vision of Justice proclaiming eternal laws alongside Zeus – had appealed to a kind of divinely inspired Law, only to turn his back on the legislating divinities without much ado and resort to violence. Right now, the upshot of his abrupt change of heart would in all likelihood be the severance of his head, – an utterly avoidable event if only he had persevered in his legal action. Alas, "too much to hope in this world", the prosecutor has philosophically concluded, but "in the next, who knows?"

Delving into the above-mentioned issue, Doctor Bottini has trodden a well-known path when he has eulogised Pompilia's submission to the wishes of the court and her acceptance of house arrest at her parents' dwelling even though a reunion with her husband was on the cards. "Quick, he shall tempt her to the perch she fled, bid to domestic bliss the truant back!" the lawyer has remarked. As to Caponsacchi's conduct, he has emphasised the canon's stoic acceptance of relegation, but then any evidence to the contrary would not detract from his need of a short time-out in order to prevent malaise and muse about the future. On that score, it is safe to say that the concomitance of offended husband and allegedly offending lover has been illustrated by the prosecutor in a felicitous rhetorical manner.

A bird's-eye view of Guido's and Pompilia's vicissitudes of fortune has led Bottini to emphasize the fact that she had turned out to be "the apple of his eye, core of his heart, and crown completing life, the *summum bonum* of the earthly lot!" Furthermore, she had put her husband in a position to claim fatherhood: by law, their wedding had made the ascription of paternity something beyond dispute.

Guido Franceschini's moral standards have likewise attracted Master Arcangeli's attention and he has promptly associated them with honour: "*Causa honoris*. Is there such a cause as the sake of honour?" he has rhetorically asked and come up with an answer by virtue of linking the high principle on the tapis with Machiavelli's dictum that the end justifies the means, – most forcibly when the perpetrator of highly motivated violence joins with 'lesser mortals' in employing the means/end link. In respect of that, Guido had supplied his less articulate partners in crime with gold as a means to an end and they had responded in their native tongue. "Let each level have its language!" Arcangeli has exclaimed, thus giving a linguistic property to a difference in status. Furthermore, the four rustics deserved pity because they lacked the wherewithal. But then again, they made up "all the wealth of Christ", the *Procurator Pauperum* has added, artfully interpreting Jesus' socio-economic tenets, and then he has embellished his bravura piece with an *exemplum* supporting the view that, when an honourable man acts in tune with his principles, 'who helped him in the right can scarce be wrong'. There was no gainsaying the helpers had plotted to bump off their employer for fear that he might refrain from giving them the badly needed money, but it was also true that their very scheme proved that they had nursed neither a grudge against the slain family nor a particular hate of the murderer. Far from it. The four henchmen had been impelled by the only too human expectation of a reward consonant with "the absolute instinct of equity in rustic souls", while the Count's cultivated mind had been prepossessed by the conviction that "those fair-minded souls" ought to be spared "the pollution of the pay."

Reader, what an instance of dialectical sleight of hand! Guido has been portrayed as an equable city dweller impressed by the "instinct of equity in rustic souls", whereas his defender has made statements imbued with a strong flavour of irony while providing a barely credible alternative to the postulation of criminal intent issuing from Bottini's "cogitative brain".

Arcangeli's ensuing peroration has stressed the extenuating circumstances of the case and underpinned them with *exempla* taken from the *veteros mores* of the Eternal City; honour has been pinpointed for the umpteenth time as the provider of an incentive for an upper-class fellow who had found himself the "pitiable victim" of a disastrous event. Right-ho! The picture of Guido as a humiliated human being is instrumental in awaking a feeling of compassion, but at the same time it would be unreasonable to deny further nuances of Machiavel-imbued cunning.

The lawyer's next move has brought up the biblical Leviathan as the monster whom he had miraculously pierced and given to his own maidens for a play, – one up on old Job by the look of it, – but by the same token the religiously inspired lawyer has expressed doubts about a positive outcome of his efforts and humbly promised to prune his luxuriant speech as a way of paying tribute to the Holy Writ as well as to the judges, not to mention the linguistically faultless Cicero and, to crown all, his kith and kin, especially the "rogue" Giacinto who would one fine day "mimic Don father that defends the Count" and would be rewarded with a glass of "manly red *rosolio*" on condition that he conjugated "*bibo*, I drink" the way the Romans had done. Then, echoing the words of Agur of old, 'Don father' has expressed a desire that he should get rid of conceit as well as of mendacity and be fed only with convenient food.

Master Arcangeli's end-all fireworks have shed light on his little son in the act of receiving a gift from his grandpa after "poor papa Latin and law" had been "laid at rest". While still alive, the "poor papa" has seen himself as deserving of a pat on the back for generating an offspring that was the source of a sound 'investment', and the sentiment may be taken to be a symptom of the pathological narcissism that, it has been aptly held, is 'fundamentally the outcome when the family, so to speak, is not merely centred on children but collapses upon them as well, crushing them beneath its weight.'[14] In an ambience of the kind, Giacinto Arcangeli has had a vision of his "fat little wife" sporting a necklace given to her for her pains: "her bosom shall display the big round balls", he has promised, quoting from Horace though not without a Freudian slip, and in this ludic context he has made himself ready for "play, play, play!" The tail end of the lawyer's harangue has taken the shape of a firecracker: "Sing 'Tra-la-la, for, lambkins, we must live!' he has exclaimed, and the Parthian shot at Bottini seen as a "blazing ass" suggests a detection of faint-heartedness in his adversary's moral fibre. In days of old, a youth called Lucian had been transmogrified into a 'golden ass' and abused by magistrates of all people. Centuries later, did the lawyer suspect that the donkey had regained his humanity and made an excellent use of it? The metamorphosis might well give the 'archangelic swine' some food for thought.

Giambattista Bottini has indeed given Giacinto Arcangeli some food for thought when, the day after the latter's harangue, he has re-entered his *studio* and emitted rhetorical brays. The *Fisci Advocatus* has declared Guido as arguably responsible for the paternity of Gaetano, albeit, come to think of it, parthenogenesis was not to be ruled out: "Spontaneous generation, – need I prove were facile feat to Nature at a pinch?" he has submitted before paying tribute to Pompilia's virginal status while en route for sainthood vis-à-vis her sinful husband: "By painting saintship, I depicture sin; beside the pearl I prove how black the jet, and through Pompilia's virtue, Guido's crime". Then, making artful use of amplification and antithesis, Bottini has underscored how the young woman had "played her part, used the right means to the permissible end ... obtained herself a respite, four days' grace, whereby she told her story to the world ... and, by a full confession, saved her soul". It had been "perfect in the end, perfect i' the means, perfect in everything": Pompilia had conducted herself impeccably and therefore in no need of excuses despite all the malicious talk, chatter and gossipry: her disclosure had, from all accounts, connoted a charitable effort to help a priest in the lurch and at the same time pave the way for a murderer's repentance. Moreover, in the eyes of Mother Church, confession on the verge of death was an utterly credible testimony and, qua a sacrament, wiped out sin. '*Solvuntur tabulae?* May we laugh and go?' Bottini has finally asked, taking his cue from the satirical Horace; the judicial system had admitted being on the horns of a dilemma, and the dilemma was: if Caponsacchi had been found complicit in the flight, how could Pompilia be presumed innocent? Moreover, if both of them were innocent, had the trial been a fair process?

There was, however, a way out of the impasse by seeing things in a lighter vein, Bottini has gone on to contend, and it could be found with a little help from wine: most people would agree that the quality of the stuff sold at a wine shop could be ascertained solely by dint of having a taste of the alcoholic drink, and in that respect the priest's nature had been duly tested and found good albeit wanting maturation; the remaining question was closely related to the truth about Pompilia's and Guido's role in the drama enacted by them, and it would come out in the wash thanks to the "acumen of the Court". Needless to add, it was going to be a laborious task, but then "what other prize than truth were worth the pains?"

The concluding rhetorical question has heralded the end of Bottini's lengthy *arringa*. Come to think of it, the so-called brief had turned out to be lengthier than Isocrates's celebrated Panegyric; hence, a good deal of pruning and paring was a must, the lawyer has remarked. But then again, "this comes of being born in modern times with priests for auditory", he has stated in self-defence and, reader, the inherent sting in the tail has sounded quite consistent with the pungency of his discourse *tout ensemble*. "Still, it pays", the grandiloquent prosecutor has concisely concluded.

When all is said and done, Master Giacinto Arcangeli and Doctor Giovanni Battista Bottini have, to all appearances, yielded to the allure of sophism and done so in their own idiosyncratic ways: interestingly, they have shared a penchant for ambiguous rhetoric spiced with crumbs of good-humoured irony and, often, parody; in addition, they have evinced an irrepressible urge to take a leaf out of some learned ancestor's book, notably if couched in Latin.

At this point, if the question is how their efforts can be properly evaluated, a vital clue may be provided by the critical contention that an author is in constant dialogical contact with his/her characters and, far from being neutral about the way they use language, 'argues with it ... interrogates it ... but also ridicules it, paradoxically exaggerates it ... represents this language, carries on a conversation with it, and the conversation penetrates into the interior of this language-image and dialogizes it from within.'[15] What's more, it is 'in the light of another potential language or style that a given straightforward style is parodied, travestied, ridiculed.'[16] In this connection, Arcangeli's and Bottini's frequent recourse to Cicero's language may be justified by the lawyers' awareness of the bilingual Roman literary consciousness. It has cogently been said that 'only polyglossia fully frees consciousness from the tyranny of its own language and its own myth of language. Parodic-travestying forms flourish under these conditions.'[17]

Taking account of the polyglottic factor, it is not difficult to detect an undertone of amusement in Robert Browning's exposure of the recurrent hyperbolic tone of the lawyers' utterances, but by the same token the *raison d'être* of their playfulness as well as of their propensity to magnify can be identified with the assumption they have been giving voice to the linguistic leanings of the poet who has made them characters in his work. If that is the case, the undercurrent of tease in their performances has not disturbed the flow of the narrative; on the contrary, it has enhanced it. After due consideration, there is good reason to maintain that the author of *The Ring and the Book* has aimed at depicting a rhetorical style designed to be grand, middle, low, or plain according to the context of the speech; in other words, a linguistic approach has shaded into a stylistic one. In stylistic terms, the lawyers' use of laughter and ridicule has been a leitmotif in harmony with the local tradition, and their parodic/travestying approach has pointed to the linguistic consciousness that has been the *fons et origo* of their rhetorical phrasing. In this connexion, Browning's poetic diction appears to be in tune with Arcangeli's and Bottini's witty eloquence – witness, for instance, the latter's choice of a painter's method while in the process of portraying the Comparini family. Bottini's option calls to mind the philosophical assertion that 'words are but the images of matter; and except they have life of reason and invention, to fall in love with them is to fall in love with a picture'[18]. Arguably, Cicero and Quintilian would have appreciated Arcangeli's and Bottini's adherence to their guidelines.

If the issue is approached from a psychoanalytic angle, the idiom that has afforded *jouissance* to the two lawyers may well be seen as an expression of the imaginary and/or symbolic dimensions of psychical life. Consider apropos the narcissistic bond between the patriarchal Giacinto senior and the rebellious Giacinto junior: the former has impressively made use of rhetoric with a view to helping the latter to enter a man's world – with the proviso that the child, called to negotiate the niceties of the Latin grammar (sic), should comply with *papà*'s linguistic know-how. The remaining question is what about his *mamma*? Clearly, the father at issue has failed to recognise what latter-day feminists have identified as the child/mother bond.[19]

Undeniably, Arcangeli's and Bottini's performances have shown an intriguing melange of rhetoric, devotion to duty, and élan; on the other hand, if we turn from form to substance, a different pattern will emerge: both lawyers have failed to score the clincher while skirmishing with each other about the reasons for having Guido and his accomplices either acquitted or charged. Their infatuation with words, whether vernacular or Latin, has forbidden the Aristotelian use of a 'substance' prior to all other categories and turned the twosome into conveyors of paralogism, viz of a fallacious sophistry conducive to lack of logic in an otherwise rational argumentation. When all is said and done, Guido Franceschini's defender as well as his accuser have not been able to clarify the real nature of the culpable characters under scrutiny. Regrettably, their language game has come to grief and, as a result, their postulations have left a big question mark hanging over the unfolding whydunit.

1. As propounded by J. L. Austin, *Western Philosophy and Philosophers*, Unwin Hyman, 1991, p. 35
2. Robert Browning, *The Bishop Orders His Tomb at Saint Praxed's Church*, l. 79
3. Roland Barthes, *Textual Analysis: Poe's 'Valdemar'*, in *Modern Criticism and Theory*, p. 182
4. Franz Brentano, as cited by Bakhtin in *Op. Cit*, p. 154.
5. Jacques Lacan, *The Insistence of the Letter in the Unconscious*, in *Op. Cit*, p. 81
6. Martin Heidegger, in *Western Philosophy and Philosophers*, p. 130
7. Robert Browning, *Fra Lippo Lippi*, ll. 217-20 and 313
8. Cicero had dealt with the concept of decorum in *De Oratore*.
9. Dante Alighieri, *La Divina Commedia – Inferno*, Canto V, l. 102

10. William Shakespeare, *Othello*, Act3, Sc3,
11. 164-65
    11. William Empson, *Seven Types of Ambiguity*, 1930, rev. 1947, 1953
12. Paul, 2 *Corinthians* 11. 33
13. As cited in Brewer's *Dictionary of Phrase and Fable*, Chambers Harrap Publishers, 2012
14. Joel Kovel, *Narcissism and the Family*. in *Psychoanalytic Theory*, by Anthony Elliott, Blackwell, 1994, p. 57
15. Mikhail Bakhtin, in *Modern Criticism and Theory*, p. 129
16. Mikhail Bakhtin, in *Op. Cit.*, p. 139
17. Mikhail Bakhtin, *Op. Cit.*, p. 140
18. Francis Bacon, in *Western Philosophy and Philosophy*, p. 39
19. See *Psychoanalytic Theory*, pp. 42-43

THE POPE

Sedately ensconced in his austere chamber at the core of the Holy See, Pope Innocent XII gave his undivided attention to the Franceschini case: in accordance with the laws in force, the Church supremo was in the privileged position of having the last word about the Count's *casus horribilis*.

"I will begin, – as is, these seven years now, my daily wont", he said to himself, "and read a History of all my predecessors, Popes of Rome. Being about to judge, as now, I seek how judged once, well or ill, some other Pope: so, do I find example, rule of life."

The first pontifical event on his list was related to the medieval Formosus: in wake of a posthumous "ghastly trial", the pontiff's cadaver had been exhumed and made sit, "clothed in pontific vesture now again, upright on Peter's chair as if alive." Not for too long, though: 'those same three fingers which he blessed withal', his head and his trunk, had been thrown in 'Tiber that my Christian fish may sup', as the succeeding Pope Stephen had put it. End of story? Far from it. One year after the rather peculiar treatment, the remains of Formosus' body had been snatched back from the 'Christian fish' and laid anew in Peter's burial-place while Pope Stephen was being strangled by the mob. Sometime later, Pope Sergius had 'reaffirmed the right of Stephen, cursed Formosus, nay cast out, some say, his corpse a second time ... here is the last pronouncing of the Church, her sentence that subsists unto this day. Yet constantly opinion hath prevailed i' the church, Formosus was a holy man.'

The grotesque sequence of events had deserved a mention in the Curia Records and now he, the latest pontiff in a long line, was finding himself wondering which of the judgments had been infallible and which of his predecessors had spoken for God. Furthermore, to what extent had the alternation of cursing and blessing affected Formosus? In the Scriptures Christ had urged his disciples, 'Fear ye not those whose power can kill the body and not the soul, but rather those can cast both soul and body in hell!'. One and a half millennia later, he, qua the Vicar of Christ, strongly sensed that he was duty bound to square up to the past and face the moment of truth. He got hold of his walking cane and plodded across the historiated room. "In God's name!" he exclaimed. "Once more on this earth of God's I take His staff with my uncertain hand, and forthwith think, speak, act in place of Him – the Pope for Christ. Once more appeal is made from man's assize to mine: I sit and see another poor weak trembling human wretch pushed by his fellows, who pretend the right, up to the gulf which, where I gaze, begins from this world to the next, – gives way and way, just on the edge over the awful dark: with nothing to arrest him but my feet. He catches at me with convulsive face, cries 'Leave to live the natural minute more!' while hollowly the avengers echo 'Leave? We yet protest against the exorbitance of sin in this one sinner, and demand that his poor sole remaining piece of time be plucked from out his clutch: put him to death, punish him now! As for the weal or woe hereafter, God grant mercy! Man, be just!' And I am bound, the solitary judge, to weigh the worth, decide upon the plea; the case is over, judgment at an end, and all things done now and irrevocable. I have worn through this sombre wintry day, with winter in my soul beyond the world's, over these dismalest of documents, pleadings and counter-pleadings, figure of fact beside fact's self, these summaries to-wit, – how certain three were slain by certain five and how the chief of them preferred excuse; what argument he urged by wary word, and what the unguarded groan told, torture's feat when law grew brutal, outbroke, overbore and glutted hunger on the truth, at last. All's a clear rede and no more riddle now. Truth, nowhere, lies yet everywhere in these – not absolutely in a portion, yet evolvable from the whole: evolved at last painfully, held tenaciously by me. Therefore there is not any doubt to clear when I shall write the brief presently and chink the hand-bell, which I pause to do." The truth-seeker's eyes ran over a brazen crucifix hanging on his chest. "Irresolute? Not I more than the mound with the pine-trees on it yonder! Some surmise, perchance, that, since man's wit is fallible, mine may fail here? Suppose it so, what then? What other should I say than 'God so willed, mankind is ignorant, a man am I: call ignorance my sorrow not my sin!' For I am ware it is the seed of act, God holds appraising in His hollow palm, not act grown great thence on the world below, leafage and branchage, vulgar eyes admire. Therefore I stand on my integrity, nor fear at all: and if I hesitate, it is because I need to breathe awhile, rest, as the human right allows, review intent the little seeds of act, the tree, – the thought, to clothe in deed, and give the world at chink of bell and push of arrased door."

The soul-baring soliloquist shot a glance at the colourful tapestry hanging from the ceiling and depicting a batch of God's four-legged creatures. "Two men are in our city this dull eve", he went on to utter in an undertone; "one doomed to death, – but hundreds in such plight slip aside, clean escape by leave of law which leans to mercy in this latter time; moreover in the plenitude of life is he, with strength of limb and brain adroit, presumably of service here: beside, the man is noble, backed by nobler friends. Again, there is another man, – weighed now by twice eight years beyond the seven-times-ten, – trying one question with true sweat of soul: 'Shall the said doomed man fitlier die or live?' The aged man stroked his forehead thoughtfully, "Not so! Expect nor question nor reply at what we figure as God's judgment bar! None of this vile way by the barren words which, more than any deed, characterize man as made subject to a curse: no speech – that still bursts o'er some lie which lurks inside, as the split skin across the coppery snake, and most denotes man! since, in all beside, in hate or lust or guile or unbelief, out of some core of truth the excrescence comes, and, in the last resort, the man may urge

'So was I made, a weak thing that gave way to truth, to impulse only strong since true, and hated, lusted, used guile, forwent faith.' Therefore this filthy rags of speech, this coil of statement, comment, query and response, tatters all too contaminate for use, have no renewing: He, the Truth, is, too, the Word. We men, in our degree, may know there, simply, instantaneously, as here after long time and amid many lies, that I am I, as He is He, – what else? But be man's method for man's life at least! Wherefore, Antonio Pignatelli, – thou my ancient self, who wast no Pope so long but studied God and man, the many years i' the school, i' the cloister, in the diocese domestic, legate-rule in foreign lands, – thou other force in those old busy days than this grey ultimate decrepitude, – yet sensible of fires that more and more visit a soul, in passage to the sky, – wilt though, the one whose speech I somewhat trust, question the after-me, this self now Pope, hear his procedure, criticize his work?"

Innocent XII's "ancient self" sighed deeply. "Wise in its generation is the world. This is why Guido is found reprobate. I see him furnished forth for his career: body and mind in balance, a sound frame, a solid intellect: the wit to seek, wisdom to choose, and courage wherewithal to deal with whatsoever circumstance should minister to man, make life succeed. Oh, and much drawback! What were earth without? Is this our ultimate stage, or starting-place to try man's foot, if it will creep or climb? So, Guido, born with appetite, lacks food, is poor, who yet could deftly play-off wealth, – with less monition, fainter conscience-twitch than nature furnishes the main mankind, making it harder to do wrong than right. Wherein I see a trial fair and fit for one else too unfairly fenced about by a great birth, traditionary name, diligent culture, choice companionship, above all, conversancy with the faith which puts forth for its base of doctrine just 'Man is born nowise to content himself but please God." He accepted such a rule, professed so much of priesthood as might sue for priest's-exemption where the layman sinned, – got his arm frocked which, bare, the law would bruise. This is the man proves irreligiousest of all mankind, religion's parasite!" The ejaculation came out of Antonio Pignatelli's novel self and was followed by "I find him bound, then, to begin life well; fortified by propitious circumstance, great birth, good breeding, with the Church for guide. How lives he? Cased thus in a coat of proof, in and out, now to prey and now to skulk. Armour he boasts when a wave breaks on beach, the man of rank, the much-befriended man. Do tides abate and sea-fowl hunt i' the deep? Already is the slug from out its mew, ignobly faring with all loose and free, – a naked blotch no better than they all: Guido has dropped nobility, slipped the Church, plays trickster if not cut-purse, body and soul prostrate among the filthy feeders – faugh! And when Law takes him by surprise at last, catches the foul thing on its carrion-prey, behold, he points to shell left high and dry, pleads 'But the case out yonder is myself!' Low instinct, base pretension, are these truth? Then, that aforesaid armour, probity he figures in, is falsehood scale on scale; honor and faith, – a lie and a disguise, probably for all livers in this world, certainly for himself! All say good words to who will hear, all do thereby bad deeds to who must undergo; so thrive mankind! See this habitual creed exemplified most in the last deliberate act; as last, so, very sum and substance of the soul of him that planned and leaves one perfect piece, the sin brought under jurisdiction now, even the marriage of the man: this act I sever from his life as sample, show for Guido's self, intend to test him by, as, from a cup filled fairly at the fount, by the components we decide enough or to let flow as late, or staunch the source. The best he knew and feigned, the worst he took."

The pontiff's lips touched the pectoral cross *con amore*. "Not one permissible impulse moves the man: all is the lust for money; to get gold, why, lie, rob, – if it must be, murder! Make body and soul wring gold out, lured within the clutch of hate by love, the trap's pretence! To get this good, – with but a groan or so, then, silence of the victims, – were the feat. He foresaw, made a picture in his mind, – of father and mother stunned and echoless to the blow, as they lie staring at fate's jaws, plundered to the last remnant of their wealth, hunted forth to go hide head, starve and die, so leave the pale awe-stricken wife, past hope of help i' the world now, mute and motionless, his slave, his chattel, to use and then destroy: all this, he bent mind how to bring about, put this in act and life, as painted plain, have success, the crown of earthly good, in this particular enterprise of man, a marriage – undertaken in God's face with all those lies so opposite God's truth, for ends so other than man's end." Another deep sigh seeped down the highest priest's regalia and insignia. "Thus schemes Guido, and thus would carry out his scheme: but when an obstacle first blocks the path, when he finds there is no monopoly of lies and trick i' the tricking lying world, – that sorry timid natures, even this sort o' the Comparini, want nor trick nor lie proper to the kind, – that as the gor-crow treats the bramble-finch so treats the finch the moth, and the great Guido is minutely matched by this same couple, – whether true or false the revelation of Pompilia's birth, which in a moment brings his scheme to nought, – then, he is piqued, advances yet a stage, leaves the low region to the finch and fly, soars to the zenith whence the fiercer fowl may dare the inimitable swoop. I see. He draws now on the curious crime, the fine felicity and flower of wickedness; determines, by the utmost exercise of violence, made safe and sure by craft, to satiate malice, pluck one last arch-pang from the parents, else would triumph out of reach, by punishing their child, within reach yet, who nowise could have wronged, thought, word or deed, i' the matter that now moves him. So plans he, always subordinating – note the point! – revenge, the manlier sin, to interest: such a plan as, in its completeness, shall ruin the three together and alike, yet leave himself in luck and liberty, while they, with all their claims and rights that cling, shall forthwith crumble off him every side, scorched into dust, a plaything for the winds. So did his cruelty burn life about, and lay the ruin bare in dreadfulness, try the persistency of torment so o' the wife that, at some fierce extremity, the patient stung to frenzy should break loose, fly anyhow, find refuge anywhere, even in the arms of who might front her first! Hence this consummate lie, this love-intrigue, unmanly simulation of a sin, these letters false beyond all forgery – not just handwriting and mere authorship, but false to body and soul they figure forth. – whereby the man so far attains his end that strange temptation is permitted, – see! Pompilia, wife, and Caponsacchi, priest, are brought together as nor priest nor wife should stand, and there is passion in the place, power in the air for evil as for good, promptings from heaven and hell, as if the stars fought in their courses for a fate to be. Such was this gift of God who showed for once how He would have the world go white: it seems as a new attribute were born of each champion of truth, the priest and wife I praise, – as a new safeguard sprang up in defence of their new noble nature: so a thorn comes to the aid of and completes the rose – courage to-wit, no woman's gift nor priest's, i' the crisis; might leaps, vindicating right."

The last clause was enhanced by a twinkle in the senescent gentleman' eye. "There quails Count Guido, armed to the chattering teeth, cowers at the steadfast eye and quiet word o' the Canon at the Pieve! *There* skulks crime behind law called in to back cowardice, while out of the poor trampled worm the wife, springs up a serpent!" The twinkling eyes focused on the animated image. "But anon of these! Him I judge now, – of him proceed to note, failing the first, a second chance befriends Guido, gives pause ere punishment arrive. The law he called, comes, hears, adjudicates, nor does amiss i' the main, secludes the wife from the husband, respites the oppressed one, grants probation to the oppressor, – could he know the mercy of a minute's fiery purge! The lost be saved even yet, so as by fire? Let him, rebuked, go softly all his days, meditate on a man's immense mistake who, fashioned to use feet and walk, deigns crawl, may sin, but must not needs shame manhood so: since fowlers hawk, shoot, nay and snare the game, and yet eschew vile practice, nor find sport in torch-light treachery or the luring owl. But how haunts Guido? Why, the fraudful trap: here he picks up the fragments to the least. Craft, greed, and violence complot revenge as though the elements whom mercy checked had mustered hate for one eruption more, one final deluge to surprise the Ark cradled and sleeping on its mountain-top: the outbreak-signal – what but the dove's coos back with the olive in her bill for news sorrow was over? 'T is an infant's birth. Guido cries 'Soul, at last the mire is thine! These parents and their child my wife, – touch one, lose all! Their rights determined on a head I could but hate, not harm, since from each hair dangled a hope for me: now – change and change! No right was in their child but passes now to that child's child and through such child to me!"

Streaks of light and shade crisscrossed the Father of the flock's features. "Wherefore should mind misgive, heart hesitate? He calls to counsel, fashions certain four colourless natures counted clean till now, – rustic simplicity, uncorrupted youth. The courtier tries his hand on clownship here, speaks a word, names a crime, appoints a price, – just breathes on what, suffused with all himself, is red-hot henceforth past distinction now i' the common glow of hell – and thus they break and blaze on us at Rome, Christ's Birthnight-eve. So is the murder managed, sin conceived to the full: and why not crowned with triumph too? I note how, within hair's-breadth of escape, Guido's must needs trip on a stumbling-block too vulgar, too absurdly plain i' the path! Why, the first urchin tells you, to leave Rome, get horses, you must show the warrant, just the banal scrap, clerk's scribble, a fair word buys, – or foul one, if a ducat sweeten word, – and straight authority will back demand, give you the pick o' the post-house! In such wise, the resident at Rome for thirty years, Guido instructs a stranger and himself forgets just this poor paper-scrap, wherewith armed, every door he knocks at opens wide! So, tired and footsore, those blood-flustered five went reeling on the road through dark and cold, and so were caught and caged – all through one trip, touch of the fool in Guido the astute! Thy comrades each and all were of one mind straightaway, thy murder done, to murder thee in turn, because of promised pay withheld. So, to the last, greed found itself at odds with craft in thee, and, proving conqueror, had sent thee, the same night that crowned thy hope, thither where, this same day, I see thee not, nor, through God's mercy, need, tomorrow, see. Such I find Guido, midmost blotch of black; around him ranged, now close and now remote, prominent or obscure to meet the needs o' the mage and master, I detect each shape subsidiary i' the scene nor loathed the less, all alike coloured, all descried akin by one and the same pitchy furnace stirred at the centre. See, they lick the master's hand, – this fox-faced horrible priest, this brother-brute the Abate, – why, mere wolfishness looks well. Guido stands honest in the red o' the flame, beside this yellow that would pass for white, twice Guido, all craft but no violence, armed with religion, fortified by law, a man of peace, who trims the midnight lamp. While Guido brings the struggle to a close, Paul steps back the due distance, clear o' the trap he builds and baits. Guido I catch and judge, Paul is past reach in this world and my time." The pontiff's bony fingers pattered on the pectoral cross with a touch of frustration. "Pass to the next, the boy of the brood, the young Girolamo, priest, Canon and – what more? – nor wolf nor fox, but hybrid, neither craft nor violence wholly, part violence part craft. Such cross tempts speculation: will both blend one day, more than a match for yellow and red? Once more, a case reserved. Why should I doubt?"

The reassuring question was followed by additional taps on the crucifix. "Then comes the gaunt grey nightmare in the furthest smoke, unmotherly mother and unwomanly woman, that near turns motherhood to shame, womanliness to loathing: no one word, no gesture to curb cruelty a whit more than the shepard thwarts her playsome whelps trying their milk-teeth on the soft o' the throat o' the first fawn, flung, with those beseeching eyes, flat in the covert! How should she but couch, lick the dry lips, unsheathe the blunted claw, catch 'twixt her placid eyewinks at what chance old bloody half-forgotten dream may flit, the while she lets youth take its pleasure." A deep sense of aversion materialised in cerulean eyes. "Last, these God-abandoned wretched lumps of life, these four companions, – country-folk this time, not tainted by the unwholesome civic breath. How greet they Guido with his final task? Demur? As cattle would, bid march or halt! Is it some lingering habit, old fond faith i' the lord o' the land, instructs them, – birthright-badge of feudal tenure claims its slaves again? Not so at all, thou noble human heart! All is done purely for the pay, – which, earned, and not forthcoming at the instant, makes religion heresy, and the lord o' the land fit subject for a murder in his turn."

His Holiness rose from his chair and, bending his tiaraed head, plodded to a marble stoup. His right hand touched the holy water filling it and, on emerging, traced the sign of the cross on his time-worn body.

As he traipsed away, his eyes fell on a drawing of the chief priest who had touched the case that revolved round Guido and Pompilia Franceschini. "Ah, but I save my word at least for thee, Archbishop, who art under me in the Church, as I am under God," he murmured, "thou, chosen by both to do the shepherd's office, feed the sheep – how of this lamb that panted at thy foot while the wolf pressed on her within crook's reach? Wast thou the hireling that did turn and flee? A bolt from heaven should cleave roof and clear place, transfix and show the world, suspiring flame, the main offender, scar and brand the rest hurrying, each miscreant to his hole; then flood and purify the scene with outside day to the despair of hell."

Keeping his head bent, Christ's vicar regained the exclusive chair. "First of the first, such I pronounce Pompilia, then as now perfect in whiteness – stoop thou down, my child, give one good moment to the poor old Pope heart-sick at having all his world to blame – let me look at thee in the flesh as erst, let me enjoy the old clean linen garb. I see in the world the intellect of man, the knowledge which defends him like a shield – everywhere; but they make not up, I think, the marvel of a soul like thine, earth's flower she holds up to the softened gaze of God! It was not given Pompilia to know much, be memorized by who records my time, yet if in purity and patience, if in faith held fast despite the plucking fiend, if there be any virtue, any praise, then will this woman-child have proved – who knows? – just the one prize vouchsafed unworthy me, ten years a gardener of the untoward ground: at least one blossom makes me proud at eve born 'mid the briers of my enclosure, still spreads itself, one wide glory of desire to incorporate the whole great sun it loves from the inch-height whence it looks and longs! My flower, my rose, I gather for the breast of God, this I praise most in thee, where all I praise: dutiful to the foolish parents at first, submissive next to the bad husband, – nay, tolerant of those meaner miserable that did his hests, eked out the dole of pain, – thou, patient thus, couldst rise from law to law, sublime in new impatience with the foe! Thou didst … how shall I say … receive so long the standing ordinance of God on earth, what wonder if the novel claim had clashed with old requirement, seemed to supersede too much the customary law? But, brave, thou at first prompting of what I call God, and fools call Nature, didst hear, comprehend, accept the obligation laid on thee, mother elect, to save the unborn child, to worthily defend that trust of trusts, life from the Ever Living; didst resist, anticipate the office that is mine."

Pompilia's eulogist twisted his head slightly, and glanced at a wooden panel displaying Byzantine Christ Pantocrator, the Ruler of all things. Next, he addressed the cassocked fellow who had hurried to Pompilia's side "for visible providence": "And surely not so very much apart need I place thee, my warrior-priest, – in whom what if I gain the other rose, the gold, we grave to imitate God's miracle? Irregular noble scapegrace – son the same! Faulty

— and peradventure ours the fault who still misteach, mislead, throw hook and line thinking to land leviathan forsooth, tame the scaled neck, play with him as a bird. What if an idol took it? Ask the Church why she was wont to turn each Venus here into Madonna's shape and waste no whit of aught so rare on earth as gratitude! Nay, Caponsacchi, much I find amiss, blameworthy, punishable in this freak of thine, this youth prolonged though age was ripe, this masquerade in sober day, with change of motley too, – now hypocrite's disguise, now fool's-costume which lie was least like truth, which the ungainlier, more discordant garb with that symmetric soul inside my son, the churchman's or the worldling's, – let him judge, our Adversary who enjoys the task! Men mulct the wiser manhood, and suspect no veritable star swims out of cloud: bear thou such imputation, undergo the penalty I nowise dare relax, – conventional chastisement and rebuke. Where are the men-at-arms with cross on coat? Aloof, bewraying their attire: whilst thou in mask and motley, pledged to dance not fight, sprang'st forth the hero! In thought, word and deed, how throughout all thy warfare thou wast pure, I find it easy to believe: and if at any fateful moment of the strange adventure, the strong passion of that strait, fear and surprise, may have revealed too much, – as when a thundrous midnight, with black air that burns, rain-drops that blister, breaks a spell, draws out the excessive virtue of some sheathed, shut, unsuspected flower that hoards and hides immensity of sweetness, – so, perchance, might the surprise and fear release too much the perfect beauty of the body and soul thou savedst in thy passion for God's sake, He who is Pity: was the trial sore? Temptation sharp? Thank God a second time! Why comes temptation but for man to meet and master and make crouch beneath his foot? Thou, whose sword-hand was used to strike the lute, whose sentry-station graced some wanton's gate, thou didst push forward and show mettle, shame the laggards, and retrieve the day. Well done! Be glad thou hast let light into the world, learning anew the use of soldiership, self-abnegation, freedom from all fear, loyalty to the life's end! Ruminate, deserve the initiatory spasm, – once more work, be unhappy but bear life, my son!"

A wave of empathy swept over the holder of the Holy See as he focused his mind on the Comparini couple. "And troop you, somewhere 'twixt the best and worst, where crowd the indifferent product, all too poor makeshift, starved samples of humanity! Father and mother; huddle there and hide! A gracious eye may find you! Foul and fair, sadly mixed natures: self-indulgent, yet self-sacrificing too: how the love soars, how the craft, avarice, vanity and spite sink again! So, they keep the middle course, slide into silly crime at unaware, slip back upon the stupid virtue, stay nowhere enough for being classed, I hope and fear. Accept the swift and rueful death, taught, somewhat sternlier than is wont, what waits the ambiguous creature – how the one black tuft steadies the aim of the arrow just as well as the wide faultless white on the bird's nay.

Nay, you were punished in the very part that looked most pure of speck, – the honest love betrayed you, – did love seem most worthy pains, challenge such purging, as ordained survive when all the rest of you was done with? Go! Never again elude the choice of tints! White shall not neutralise the black, nor good compensate bad in man, absolve him so: life's business being just the terrible choice."

All of a sudden the speaker's white *zucchetto* slid across the crown of his thin-haired head and covered his eyes, but the wearer restored the headgear to its orthodox position by dint of a little jiggling before resuming his speech act. "So do I see, pronounce on all and some grouped for my judgment now, – profess no doubt while I pronounce: dark, difficult enough the human sphere, yet eyes grow sharp by use. I find the truth, dispart the shine from shade, discern and dare decree in consequence. Whence, then, this quite new quick cold thrill, – cloud-like, this keen dread creeping from a quarter scarce suspected in the skies I nightly scan? What if a voice deride me, 'Perk and pry! Brighten each nook with thine intelligence! What if thyself adventure, now the place is purged so well? Leave pavement and mount roof, look round thee for the light of the upper sky, the fire which lit thy fire which finds default in Guido Franceschini to his cost! What if, above in the domain of light, thou miss the accustomed signs, remark eclipse? Shalt thou still gaze on ground nor lift a lid, – steady in thy superb prerogative?'" The questioner pursed his lips in denial. "Yet my poor spark had for its source, the sun; thither I sent the great looks which compel light from its fount: all that I do and am comes from the truth, or seen or else surmised, remembered or divined, as mere man may. I know just so, nor otherwise; as I know, I speak, – what should I know, then, and how speak, were there a wild mistake of eye or brain in the recorded governance above? I, who in this world act resolvedly, dispose of men, – the body and the soul, as they acknowledge or gainsay this light I show them, – shall I too lack courage? - leave I, too, the post of me, like those I blame? Refuse, with kindred inconsistency, grapple with danger whereby souls grow strong? I am near the end; but still not at the end; all till the very end is trial in life: at this stage is the trial of my soul danger to face, or danger to refuse? Shall I dare try the doubt now, or not dare?"

The soul-searching man of the cloth turned once more to the All-powerful towering him from the wall. "O thou, – as represented here to me in such conception as my soul allows, – under Thy measureless my atom with! Man's mind – what is it but a convex glass wherein are gathered all the scattered points picked out of the immensity of sky, to reunite there, be our heaven on earth, our known unknown, our God revealed to man? Existent somewhere, somehow, as a whole in the absolute immensity, the whole appreciable solely by Thyself, – here, by the little mind of man, reduced to littleness that suits his faculty. It is who have been appointed here to represent Thee, in my turn, on earth; incomprehensibly the choice is Thine: I therefore bow my head and take Thy place. There is, beside the works, a tale of Thee in the world's mouth which I find credible. I love it with my heart; unsatisfied, I try it with my reason, nor discept from any point I probe and pronounce sound. Mind is not matter nor from matter, but above; leave matter then, proceed with mind: man's be the mind recognised at the height. Leave the inferior minds and look at man: ay, is he strong, intelligent and good up to his own conceivable height? Nowise. Enough o' the low, – soar the conceivable height, find cause to match the effect in evidence, conjecture of the worker by the work. Is there strength there? Enough. Intelligence? Ample. But goodness in a like degree? Not to the human eye in the present state, this isoscele deficient in the base." The pontiff shook his head. "What lacks, then, of perfection fit for God but just the instance which this tale supplies of love without a limit? So is strength, so is intelligence; then love is so, unlimited in its self-sacrifice: then is the tale true and God shows complete. Beyond the tale, I reach into the dark, feel what I cannot see, and still faith stands: I can believe this dread machinery of sin and sorrow, would confound me else, devised, – all pain, at most expenditure of pain by Who devised pain, – to evolve, by new machinery in counterpart, the moral qualities of man – how else? – to make him love in turn and be beloved, creative and self-sacrificing too, and thus eventually God-like, ay. Nor do I much perplex me with aught hard, dubious in the transmitting of the tale, – no, nor with certain riddles set to solve. This life is training and a passage; pass, – still, we march over some flat obstacle we made give way before us; solid truth in front of it, were motion for the world? The moral sense grows but by exercise. 'T is even as man grew probatively initiated in Godship, set to make a fairer moral world than this he finds, guess now what shall be known hereafter. Thus, o' the present problem: as we see and speak, a faultless creature is destroyed, and sin has had its way i' the world where God should rule. Pompilia lost and Guido saved: how long? For his whole life: how much is that whole life? We are not babes, but know the minute's worth and feel that life is large and the world small, so, wait till life have passed from out the world." The waiting man nodded repeatedly. "Life is probation and this earth no goal but starting-point of man; compel him strife, which means, in man, as good as reach the goal, – why institute that race, his life, at all? But this does overwhelm me with surprise, touch me to terror, – not that faith, the pearl, should be let lie by fishers wanting food, – but that, when haply found and known and named by the residue made rich for evermore, these, – ay, these favoured ones, should in a trice turn, and with double zest go dredge for whelks, mud-worms that make the soup." He gave a wry smile. "Enough o' the disbelievers, see the faithful few! How do the Christians here deport them, keep their robes of white unspotted by the world? What is this Aretine Archbishop, this man under me as I am under God, this champion of the faith, I armed and decked? Pompilia cries, 'Protect me from the fiend!' Have we misjudged here, over-armed the knight, given gold and silk where the plain steel serves best, enfeebled whom we sought to fortify, made an archbishop and undone a saint? Well then, descend these heights, this pride of life, sit in the ashes with the barefoot monk who long ago stamped out the worldly sparks. Fasting and watching, stone cell and wire scourge, he meets the first cold sprinkle of the world and shudders to the marrow, 'Save this child? Who was it dared lay hand upon the ark his better saw fall nor put finger forth? Great ones could help yet help not: why should small? I break my promise: let her break her heart!' These are the Christians not the worldlings, not the sceptics, who thus battle for the faith! If foolish virgins disobey and sleep, what wonder? But the wise that watch, this time sell lamps and buy lutes, exchange oil for wine, the mystic Spouse betrays the Bridegroom here."

The grave observer of human frailty got hold of his crosier, took measured steps to the window and gazed at the verdant oasis directly below.

"To our last resource, then! Since all flesh is weak, bind weaknesses together: we get strength; the individual weighed, found wanting, try some institution, honest artifice whereby the units grow compact and firm: each props the other, and so stand is made by our embodied cowards that grow brave. The monastery called of Convertites, meant to help women because they helped Christ? Pompilia is consigned to these for help. They do help, they are prompt to testify to her pure life and saintly dying days. She dies, and lo, who seemed so poor proves rich. What does the body that lives through helpfulness to women for Christ's sake? The kiss turns bite, the dove's note changes to the crow's cry: judge! Christ must give up his gains then! They unsay all the fine speeches, – who was saint is whore. Why, Scripture yields no parallel for this: the soldiers only threw dice for Christ's coat! Is such effect proportioned to cause? This terrifies me, thus compelled perceive, whatever love and faith we looked should spring at advent of the authoritative star; these have leapt forth profusely in old time, these still respond with promptitude today at challenge of … what unacknowledged powers o' the air, what uncommissioned meteors, warmth by law, and light by law, and light by rule should supersede?"

The ad hoc Manichaean-minded pontiff turned away from the window and regained his chair. He inclined his forehead and let his skinny hand encompass it.

"For see this priest, this Caponsacchi, stung, strike any foe, right wrong at any risk, all blindness, bravery and obedience! Blind? Ay, as a man would be inside the sun, delirious with the plenitude of light. How can I but speak loud what truth speaks low, 'Or better than the best, or nothing serves!' What if the sun crumble, the sands encroach, while he looks on sublimely at his ease? Where is the gloriously-decisive change, the immeasurable metamorphosis of human clay to divine gold, we looked should, in some poor sort, justify the price? Well, is the thing we see, salvation? I put no such dreadful question to myself, within whose circle of experience burns the central truth, Power, Wisdom, Goodness, – God: I must outlive a thing ere know it dead. When I outlive the faith there is a sun; when I lie, ashes to the very soul. How can I speak but as I know? My speech must be, throughout the darkness, 'It will end: the light that did burn, will burn!' Clouds obscure – but for which obscuration all were bright? Too hastily concluded! Sun-suffused, a cloud may soothe the eye made blind by haze, – better the very clarity of heaven: the soft streaks are the beautiful and dear. What but the weakness in a faith supplies the incentive to humanity, no strength absolute, irresistible, comports? How can man love but what he yearns to help? And that which men think weakness within strength, what were it else but the thirst things made new, but repetition of the miracle, the divine instance of self-sacrifice that never ends and aye begins for man? So, never I miss footing in the maze, no, – I have light nor fear the dark at all."

The undaunted assertion betokened the mood of a man emboldened by the wisdom that comes with age, yet it left one or two questions hanging in the air: "But are mankind not real, who pace outside my petty circle, the world measured me? And when they stumble even as I stand, have I a right to stop ears when they cry, as they were phantoms, took the clouds for crags, tripped and fell, where the march of man might move? Beside, the cry is other than a ghost's, when out of the old time there pleads some bard, philosopher, or both, and – whispers not but words it boldly.

'The inward work and worth of any mind, what other mind may judge save God who only knows the things He made, the veritable service He exacts? It is the outward product men appraise. I was born, not so long before Christ's birth, under conditions, nowise to escape, whereby salvation was impossible – as if the insect, born to spend his life soaring his circles, stopped them to describe some "Know thyself" or "Take the golden mean!", forwent his happy dance and the glad ray, died half an hour the sooner and was dust. I, born to perish like the brutes, why not live brutishly, obey my law? But I, of body as of soul complete, adopted virtue as my rule of life, waived all reward, and, what my heart taught me, I taught the world. Witness my work, – plays that should please, forsooth! "They might please, they may displease, they shall teach, for truth's sake," so I said, and did, and do! Five hundred years ere Paul spoke, Felix heard, – how much of temperance and righteousness, judgment to come, did I find reason for, corroborate with my strong style that spare no sin, nor swerved the more from branding brow because the sinner was called Zeus and God? I saw that there are, first and above all, the hidden forces, blind necessities, named Nature, but the thing's self unconceived: then follow, – how dependent upon these, we know not, how imposed above ourselves, we well know, – what I name the gods, a power various or one; for great and strong and good is there, and little, weak and bad there too, wisdom and folly: say, these make no God, – what is it else that rules outside man's self? A fact then, – always, to the naked eye, – and, so, the one revealment possible of what was unimagined else by man. Therefore, what gods do, man may criticise, applaud, condemn, – how should he fear the truth? – but likewise have in awe because of power, venerate for the main munificence, and give the doubtful deed its due excuse from the acknowledged creature of a day to the Eternal and Divine. Thus, bold yet self-mistrusting, should man bear himself, most assured on what now concerns him most – the law of his own life, the path he prints, – which law is virtue and not vice, I say. What could I paint beyond a scheme like this out of the fragmentary truths where light lay fitful in a tenebrific time? You have the sunrise now, joins truth to truth, shoots life and substance into death and void; themselves compose the whole we made before: the forces and necessities grow God, – the beings so contrarious that seemed gods, prove just His operation manifold and multiform, translated, as must be, into intelligible shape so far as suits our sense and sets us free to feel. So much, no more, two thousand years have done! Pope, dost thou dare pretend to punish me for not descrying sunshine at midnight, me who crept all-fours, found my way so far – while thou rewardest teachers of the truth, who miss the plain way in the blaze of noon, – though just a word from that strong style of mine, had pricked them a sure path across the bog, that mire of cowardice and slush of lies wherein I find them wallow in wide day?'"

The ancient tragedian's Weltanschauung goaded the listener into a prompt rejoinder: "How should I answer this Euripides? Paul, – 't is a legend, – answered Seneca, but that was in the day-spring; noon is now we have got too familiar with the light. Shall I wish back once more that thrill of dawn? When the whole truth-touched man burned up, one fire? Was this too easy for our after-stage? Was such a lighting-up of faith, in life, only allowed initiate, set man's step in the true way by help of the great glow? A way wherein it is ordained he walk, bearing to see the light from heaven still more and more encroached on by the light of earth, till at last, who distinguishes the sun from a mere Druid fire on a far mount? More praise to him who with his subtle prism shall decompose both beams and name the true, – so hard now that the world smiles 'Rightly done! It is the politic, the thrifty way, will clearly make you in the end returns beyond our fool's-sport and improvidence: we fools go thro' the cornfield of this life, pluck ears to left and right and swallow raw, – nay, tread, at pleasure, a sheaf underfoot, well aware we shall have so much wheat less in the eventual harvest: you meantime waste not a spike, – the richlier will you reap!'"

A dignified shake of the head signalled the questioner's ethics-tinged reluctance to share the world's view. "Is it not this ignoble confidence, cowardly hardihood, that dulls and damps, makes the old heroism impossible? Unless … what whispers me of times to come? What if it be the mission of that age, my death will usher into life, to shake this torpor of assurance from our creed, re-introduce the doubt discarded, bring the formidable danger back, we drove long ago to the distance and the dark? As we broke up that old faith of the world, have we, next age, to break up this the new – faith, in the thing, grown faith in the report – whence need to bravely disbelieve report through increased faith in thing report belie? Must we deny, – do they, these Molinists, – recognized truths, obedient to some truth unrecognized yet, but perceptible? Correct the portrait by the living face, man's God, by God's God in the mind of man? Then, for the few that rise to the new height, the many that must sink to the old depth, the multitude found fall away! A few, e'en ere the new law speak clear, keep the old, preserve the Christian level, call good 'good' and evil 'evil', – even though, razed and blank, the old titles stand thro' custom, habitude, and all they may mistake for finer sense o' the fact than reason warrants, – as before, they hope perhaps, fear not impossibly. Surely some one Pompilia in the world will say 'I know the right place by foot's feel, I took it and tread firm there; wherefore change?' But what a multitude will fall, perchance, quite through the crumbling truth subjacent late, rest upon human nature, take their stand on what is fact, the lust and pride of life! Those who, with all the aid of Christ, lie thus, how, without Christ, whither, unaided, sink? The impatient antimasque treads close on kibe o' the very masque's self it will mock, – on me, last lingering personage, the impatient mime pushes already. Will I block the way? Will my slow trail of garments ne'er leave space for pantaloon, sock, plume and castanet?"

The 'last lingering personage' coughed a short cough and gazed out of the window. "Here comes the first experimentalist in the new order of things, – he plays a priest; does he take inspiration from the Church, directly make her rule his law of life? Not he: his own mere impulse guides the man: he has danced, in gaiety of heart, i' the main the right step in the maze we bade him foot. Will he repeat the prodigy? Perhaps. Such is, for the Augustine that was once, this Canon Caponsacchi we see now.

'And my heart answers to another tune,' puts in the Abate, second in the suite, 'I have my taste, too, and tread no such step!

I live for greed, ambition, lust, revenge; attain these ends by force, guile: hypocrite, to-day, perchance to-morrow recognized the rational man, the type of common sense.'" There was a low and bitter laugh. "*There*'s Loyola adapted to our time! Under such guidance Guido plays his part, he also influencing in due turn these last clods where I track intelligence by any glimmer, these four at his beck ready to murder any, and, at their own, as ready to murder him, – these arethe world! And, – first effect of the new cause of things, – there they lie also duly, – the old pair of the weak head and not so wicked heart, and the one Christian mother, wife and girl, – which three gifts seem to make an angel up, – the first foot of the dance is on their heads!"

A slap on the brow preceded another move to the cleansing water and a return to the chair.

"Still, I stand here, not off the stage though close on the exit: and my last act, as my first, I owe the scene, and Him who armed me thus with Paul's sword as with Peter's key. I smite with my whole strength once more, then end my part, ending, so far as many may, this offence. And when I raise my arm, what plucks my sleeve? What is the last word I must listen to? Is it 'Spare yet a term this barren stock, till he repent and bring forth fruit even yet?' Is it 'So poor and swift a punishment shall throw him out of life with all that sin? Let mercy rather pile up pain on pain till the flesh expiate what the soul pays else?' Nowise! Remonstrance on all sides begins instruct me there's a new tribunal now higher than God's, – the educated man's! Nice sense of honour in the human breast supersedes here the old coarse oracle – confirming handsomely a point or so wherein the predecessor worked aright by rule of thumb, as when Christ said, – when, where? – 'All other wrongs done, patiently I take, but touch my honour and the case is changed! I feel the due resentment, – *nemini honorem trado* is my quick retort.' Right of Him, just as if pronounced today! At last we have the instinct of the world ruling its household without tutelage, and while the two laws, human and divine, have busied finger with this tangled case, *in* the brisk junior pushes, cuts the knot, pronounces for acquittal. How it trips silverly o'er the tongue! 'Remit the death! Forgive … well, in the old way, if you please, decency and the old routine respected, – let the Count go free as air! The minor orders help enough for that. It proves a pretty loophole of escape moreover, that, beside the patent fact of the law's allowance, there's involved the weal o' the Popedom: a son's privilege at stake. Methinks we see the Golden Age return! One Emperor then, as one Pope now: meanwhile She anticipates a little to tell thee, "Take Count Guido's life, and sap society, whereof the main prop was, is, and shall prove – supremacy of husband over wife!" Shall the man rule i' the house, or may his mate because of any plea dispute the same? Oh, pleas of all sorts shall abound, be sure, and there's but one short way to end the coil, – by giving right and reason steadily to the man and master: then the wife submits. Moreover, if this breed a qualm in thee, give thine own feelings play for once, – deal death? Thou, whose own life winks o'er the socket-edge, wouldst thou it went out in such ugly snuff as dooming sons to death, though justice bade? Mercy is safe and graceful. How one hears the howl begin, scarce the three little taps o' the silver mallet ended on thy brow, – "His last act was to sacrifice a Count and thereby screen a scandal of the Church. Guido condemned, the Canon justified of course, – delinquents of his cloth go free!" But no impunity to any friend so simply over-loyal as these four who made religion of their patron's cause, believed in him and did his bidding straight, as these were times when loyalty's a drug, and zeal in a subordinate too cheap and common to be saved when we spend life. The pardon, Holy Father! Spare grimace, shrugs and reluctance! Are not we the world? Reply is apt. Our tears on tremble, hearts big with a benediction, wait the word shall circulate thro' the city in a trice, set every window flaring, give each man o' the mob his torch to wave for gratitude. Pronounce it, for our breath and patience fail!'

The wait for the official announcement was over in a trice. "I will, Sirs", said the pope, "for a voice other than yours quickens my spirit: '*Quis pro Domino*? Who is upon the Lord's side?' asked the Count. I, who write – 'On receipt of this command, acquaint Count Guido and his fellows four they die to-morrow: could it be to-night, the better, but the work to do, takes time. Set with all diligence a scaffold up, – not in the customary place, by Bridge Saint Angelo, where die the common sort; but since the man is noble, and his peers by predilection haunt the People's Square, there let him be beheaded in the midst, and his companions hanged on either side: so shall the quality see, fear and learn. Let there be prayer incessant for the five!"

The sentencer's bright-blue eyes grew wide as he knelt and rested on his legs in the guise of a praying mantis. "For the main criminal", he added in a soft hushed tone, "I have no hope except in such a sadness of fate." His eyes closed. "I stood at Naples once, a night so dark I could have scarce conjectured there was earth anywhere, sky or sea or world at all: but the night's black was burst through by a blaze – thunder struck blow on blow, earth groaned and bore, through her whole length of mountain visible: *there* lay the city thick and plain with spires, and, like a ghost dis-shrouded, white the sea." The reminiscing Parthenopean's eyelids fluttered. "So may the truth be flashed out by one blow, and Guido see, one instant, and be saved. Else I avert my face, nor follow him into that sad obscure sequestered state where God unmakes but to remake the soul He else made first in vain; which *must not be*." He gave a sniff. "Enough, for I may die this very night and how should I dare die, this man let live?"

Innocent XII rose sedately to his feet, reached for the bell and made it ring out. His closest aide emerged pronto and, bowing his head, got hold of a sealed parchment. "Carry this forthwith to the Governor!" the Church Supremo enjoined in a gravelly voice.

Prompted by the awesome task of giving his definitive verdict on Guido's Franceschini case, Pope Innocent XII has delved into historical Church records, descanted on his philosophy of life, and moved from the known to the unknown.

The senescent investigator has been provided with an unorthodox starting point for his religious journey by a couple of his predecessors' bizarre desecration and reconsecration of the coeval Pope Formosus. However, a way out of the darkness caused by the double-edged event could be found in Jesus' exhortation to fear only the power of those capable of casting both body and soul into hell. For good measure, the disconcerting behaviour of more than one pontiff had raised the vexed question of their infallibility qua the voice of God on earth.

Duty-bound to tackle the twofold issue, Innocent XII has taken God's staff with his uncertain hand and undertaken to think, speak, and act "in place of Him – the Pope for Christ". It has been clear from the outset that he would not refrain from taking drastic measures if need be, and it is tempting to assume that he might have drawn some comfort from the recollection of how, like Formosus, the Puritan Oliver Cromwell had been subjected to a posthumous unholy humiliation for an unconscionable length of time.

A change of scene has brought to light Arezzo and, at the forefront, the native Count Franceschini, a "poor weak trembling human wretch", on whose criminal offence he was about to unalterably adjudicate. Accordingly, on a "sombre wintry day, with winter in my soul", the pontiff has given painstaking attention to "figure of fact beside fact's self" and reached the conclusion that truth lay "not absolutely in a portion, yet evolvable from the whole"; therefore, it had been "evolved at last painfully, held tenaciously" by him. In respect of that, the truth was that man's understanding of the meaning of life was likely to engender delusion, for mankind frequently suffered from lack of knowledge. In consequence, all he could do was to nibble at ideas like reality, truth, and fallibility.

At this early stage of what promised to be a 'dramatic monologue' the utterer's sentiments may well be scrutinised in the light of the theory that 'true' means correspondence with the facts and, as a corollary, it makes sense to posit that, because there are no easy answers to the question of the relation between a fact and a statement about it, the truth that has been "tenaciously held" by the pope on the grounds of a correspondence between fact and theory can be justified solely on the synecdochic basis of the substitution of a whole for a part.

In this connection, the truth-seeker at issue appears to have upheld the concept that truth can be explored solely with the help of a limited number of data that are doubtless legitimate yet unable to constitute the whole[1]. Furthermore, he has intriguingly anticipated the poststructuralist warning against the illusion that it is possible to achieve the absolute truth while a perpetual sliding of the 'signified' under the 'signifier' is taking place.[2] As a matter of fact he has kept a deeply questioning mind in the hope of clearing the haze created by the dogmatism of yesteryear.

If the remaining question is whether the pontiff has displayed the 'theoretical wisdom' that, according to Aristotle, is of help in dealing with what cannot be otherwise, the honest answer is that the former has doubtless worked on achieving that brand of wisdom and, in the process, denoted possession of the kind of intuitive knowledge of truth that the Stagirite had seen pointing to the divine quality of the erring man's soul. Similarly, it helps to remember that Paul the Apostle wrote to the Corinthians that humankind could do very little against the truth and a good deal more in favour of it[3].

As the dramatic monologue unfolds, we learn that Innocent XII has juxtaposed the image of Guido "doomed to death" while still "in the plenitude of life" with the self-portrait of a mortal approaching the natural boundary of life and yet showing the determination of a human being keen on defying death. Arguably, Aristotle would have deemed his response to be indicative of 'practical wisdom'.

As a follow-on from his appraisal of the Count's mode of being, the pope has mulled over his own 'infallible' decision while acknowledging that "this filthy rags of speech, this coil of statement, comment, query and response, tatters all too contaminate for use, have no renewing"; consequently, he has turned to his former self in the hope that quondam Antonio Pignatelli would "question this after-me, this self now Pope, hear his procedure, criticize his work." As luck would have it, *there was* a silver lining, for "wise in its generation is the world"; for his part, he had refrained from shaking the bell that would herald death penalty solely and had done so mainly because he needed "to breath awhile"; in point of fact he was fully conscious of his integrity and devoid of any fear.

Next, the pontiff's evaluation of Guido Franceschini's personality has placed the latter's talents and flaws side by side: a "body and mind in balance, a sound frame, a solid intellect, the wit to seek, wisdom to choose" had conflicted with a gradual loss of wealth and "less monition, fainter conscience twitch"; in a similar fashion, a devout compliance with the Church guidelines had been belittled by a partial consecration with an eye to getting one's arms "frocked which, bare, the law would bruise": at the end of the day, on the strength of being a practically wise man, the part ordained cleric had espoused a means-end philosophy of life. Bearing the whole caboodle in mind, the pontiff has subjected the would-be priest's code of conduct to close scrutiny: "Guido has dropped nobility, slipped the Church, plays trickster if not cutpurse, body and soul prostrate among the filthy feeders – faugh! Honor and faith – a lie and a disguise": the man's "last deliberate act" had been a synthesis of the "very sum and substance of the soul of him that planned and leaves one perfect piece, the sin brought under jurisdiction now, even the very marriage of the man".

A key factor in the reaching of the conclusion has been the association of the Count's falsehood with a flair for deception and highlighted his duplicitous features. In this respect, it is worthwhile to recall that Aristotle had put substance at the top of all the other categories and seen the term 'being' as capable of being used both for substance and essence[4]. A thousand years later, the Parthenopean pope has emphasised that the Arezzan nobleman had come into the picture as a human being committing a sin substantially recognised by the judicial authorities: "Low instincts, base pretensions, are these truths … the best, he knew and feigned, the worst he took."

The heat has been on, and no mistake! Well ahead of Karl Marx's tenets, the pondering ecclesiastic has recognised the 'divine power of money' on alienated human beings: "All is lust for money: to get gold, why, lie, rob, if it must be, murder!" In some respects, Pietro and Violante Comparini could be seen as victims for having been "edged in a month by strenuous cruelty from even the poor nook whence they [had]watched the wolf feast on their heart, the lamb-like child his prey". Being by nature sorrowfully timid, "this sort o' the Comparini" wanted "no trick nor lie proper to the kind", and not before time Guido had found out that there was "no monopoly of lies and tricks i' the tricking lying world". Galled by the discovery, the 'wolf' had left "the low region to the finch and fly" and soared "to the zenith whence the fiercer fowl may dare the inimitable swoop." 'How unlike', one feels like remarking, 'the god Setebos who had looked up and perceived that he could not soar to a sphere where quiet and happiness reigned supreme!'[5] Conversely, the human Guido had taken drastic measures concerning Pompilia and in so doing subordinated "revenge, the manlier sin, to interest, the meaner". On similar grounds, he had planned to goad his wife into a revolt that would turn her alleged parents into "a plaything for the winds"; furthermore, he had raged on seeing Caponsacchi come on the scene, – "hence this consummate lie, this love intrigue, unmanly simulation of a sin … these letters false beyond all forgery", – doubtless a despicable conduct, yet to be linked with the fact that, to all appearances, Pompilia and Caponsacchi had stood together "as nor priest nor wife should stand", and there had been "passion in the place, power in the air for evil as for good."

At this point of no return, *Veritas* has trodden on the boards which have been the epitome of a "tricking lying world". Finding himself face to face with Truth, the pope has asked himself: "What does the world, told truth, but lie the more?" Guido's was a case in point: there he was, a fellow arguably trained to inflict punishment, tainted by "craft, greed and violence" and, *dulcis*[sic] *in fundo*, a self-indulgent lie-prone sinner. Yet, "Why must the sin, conceived thus, bring forth death?" There was still some light in a world darkened by sin, – witness the golden curls of Pompilia's Gaetano – but the glint had been obliterated by the dusky figures of the Count's brothers, that is, Paolo who had displayed "all craft but no violence" and Girolamo who had been "part violence part craft". To cap it all, the picture had been tarnished by Guido's henchmen, "God-abandoned wretched lumps of life" acting purely for the sake of money. It is all very sad, but there it is: if ever they were cognizant of the Bible, they might have taken heed of Timothy's dictum that 'the love of money is the root of all evils.'

In the light of the above, it makes sense to point out that the pontiff's brickbat, plausibly indicative of a light-vs-darkness Manichaean conflict, has led to a moral judgement tinged with an ironic naturalistic hue, on the strength of which the analyst has bypassed descriptive ethics and entered the realm of ethics proper. Within the latter, a phase of relative stability has materialised when the clerically-robed citizen of the world has entreated Pompilia, a woman "perfect in whiteness", to "give one good moment to the poor old Pope heartsick at having all his world to blame". Interestingly, the Church dignitary has been experiencing his moment of truth, – which, enhanced by an intuitional flash of inspiration, has contrasted Pompilia's healthy frame of mind with his malaise and made him entreat her for a quantum of solace. An admittedly mawkish mood has enabled the supplicant's super ego to bridge the gap between the unconscious and the conscious regions of his self-contained entity; furthermore, the plea has shifted the emphasis from a judgement of ethical merit to aesthetic appraisal: Pompilia's "purity and patience", reminiscent of a medieval damsel, have been a great boon to him, "a gardener of the untoward ground", and one blossom has grown into the rose he has culled "for the breast of God."

Reader, watch this space. A very young woman "dutiful to the foolish parents first, submissive next to the bad husband" will abruptly metamorphose into a fighter able to "plant firm foot on neck of man, tread man into the hell meet for him" and do so in answer to the prodding of the God called Nature by fools". The last words, suggestive of a pantheistic approach, can be associated with the future poetic assertion that 'Nature is but a name for an effect, whose cause is God.'[6] By the same token the twist in the plot has brought to the fore the emotion of a man purposing to awaken similar sentiments in the hearts of those receiving his authoritative appraisal. In this connection, a merely naturalistic explanation of the pontiff's frame of mind would be inappropriate, not least because the assumption that an emotive impulse is safely conducive to a significant moral statement smacks of unwarranted rhetoric. It would not go amiss to see Pompilia as a married woman unwittingly following in the footsteps of St. Juliana, videlicet the virgin who had suffered from the Diocletian persecution and held the devil in her clutches until the fiend had begged her to have mercy on him and let him return to hell[7]: the crux of the matter is that the Roman mother-to-be was desperate to save her unborn child, and it is remarkable how she has managed to outdo the pope in charisma and humanity.

At this point, Giuseppe Maria Caponsacchi has stepped into the spotlight and shown the features of a guy determined to win Pompilia's heart by virtue of being a "warrior priest". In the Holy Father's mind's eye the canon had been an "irregular noble scapegrace" and yet a "son the same" of an aged fellow who was willing to admit that he had been in the wrong when he had boasted of having a knack for capturing the *leviathan*! There was no denying that the militant churchman had sometimes been economical with the truth and even prone to foolishness, but most of the time he had been keen on wearing a gladiator's cuirass. Naturally enough, "men mulct the wiser manhood", and in that respect the young priest, undoubtedly deserving of "conventional chastisement and rebuke", had, even when "in mask and motley, pledged to dance not fight, been an admirable foil for all the elusive "men-at-arms with cross on coat". This man still in the prime of life had, in all likelihood, been subjected to temptation, but surely God ought to be thanked for allowing the lure of fleshly desires to beset someone "who dared fight that so he may do battle and have praise". Indeed, Giuseppe Maria Caponsacchi was a fearless soldier of the Church! "Work, be unhappy but bear life, my son!" his spiritual father has finally exclaimed, thus corroborating the familial position of a member of the Church equipped with a fighting spirit and blessed with a rose-like complexion, – in the final analysis, a man endowed with a psyche not all that different from his own. To put it in another way, the pontiff has obliquely conveyed the idea that the goodness or badness of anything hinges upon the circumstances, – thus echoing the pre-Socratic Protagoras' dictum that 'man is the measure of all things'[8]. Leaving that aside, a sense of deep-seated paternity has strengthened the link between an old celibate and a young one.

Following Caponsacchi, the Comparini duo have come under review as middle-of-the-road folk hovering between a minor form of misbehaviour and a ludicrous code of conduct, presumably unaware that the conflict between black and white, or good and bad, is part and parcel of a life whose business is "just the terrible choice." It does seem that Pompilia's putative parents had no utilitarian disposition; had they had one, they would have made choices inspired by a consideration of the probable consequences of their actions as well as by an assumption that their sociability would be enhanced by a respect for conventions conducive to the happiness of a whole community: in this connection, it does help to remember that the remarkably utilitarian Jeremy Bentham has maintained that the measure of right and wrong is the happiness of the greatest number[9].

Keeping utilitarianism in mind, it is arguable that the pontiff has also disclosed an inclination towards the kind of ethical hedonism which Epicurus had espoused in days of old for being a help in making the difficult decisions demanded by life. The former's fear of an eclipse causative of darkness has been counterpoised by his firm belief to be able to "find the truth, disport the shine from shade" and in the light of his achievement issue a decree. However, before making the final decision, the Church supremo has fallen prey to doubt: "I, who in this world act resolvedly, dispose of men, the body and the soul, as they acknowledge or gainsay this light I show them, shall I lack courage? Leave, I, too, the post of me, like those I blame? Shall I dare try the doubt now, or not dare?"

Indeed, self-identity has proved to be the name of the game, and it is worthwhile to recall that an unquestionably notable quest for certainty had recently been crowned with the positive assertion, 'I am thinking, therefore I exist'[10]. If the question is whether the pope has rightly made sounds consonant with the philosophical dictum, an honest answer is provided by the assumption that, despite his fears about the disappearance of the light, his deep conviction that he was approaching the truth might well put doubt to flight. Nevertheless, an objection could be raised on the strength of the latter-day contention that the 'I' who does the enunciation is not unified and therefore cannot claim to constitute the entire being of the subject; therefore, the *cogito ergo sum* dictum ought to be turned into 'I am not where I think, and I think where I am not'.[11] If that is the case, the modern-day philosophical argumentation warrants the syllogistic conclusion that the 'being', arguably the pope's main concern, had become 'non-being'.

The musing ecclesiastic's next step has made him aware of his "atom width" in an immense divine universe – an acknowledgement in harmony with the logical view of a world made of atomic facts directly corresponding to elementary propositions[12], but at the same time an appreciation at odds with the concept of an infinite space and an atomic unit, even though indestructible monads, conceived as the basic cause of reality, can be deemed to be part of an infinite series of monads unfolding in pre-established harmony[13].

"Mind is not matter nor from matter", the analytical pope has gone on to state, yet man is not "strong, intelligent and good up to his own conceivable height": in truth, mankind forms an "isoscele deficient in the base" and is consequently unable to unable to grasp the meaning of the divine tale about "love without a limit". As to himself, the pope has gone on to say, he has by God's grace been spared the epistemological failure: cocking his ear, he has entered the realm of darkness and, strengthened by love, has kept his faith. Amen to that! The self-assured pontiff has sounded like the celebrated Renaissance painter echoing a *stornello* sung in the streets of Florence: 'Take away love and our earth is a tomb!'[14]

In the wake of his stand, the self-confessed 'atom-sized' yet sturdy clergyman has associated pleasure with the pain devised by God to enhance "the moral qualities of man", and in doing so he has given a metaphysical dimension to a sort of Freudian 'pleasure principle'; in fact, he has championed the tenet as "a common heritage to all eternity" conducive to the realisation that "the moral sense grows but by exercise" and ultimately achieves a limited perception of eternal truths which only the Almighty Father, as a perfect being, knows in their entirety.

There you go. Descriptive ethics have once more been put to good use with the aim of reaching conclusions about the meanings of moral terms, and a link with ethics proper has thus been set up. To the pope's mind it was morally perplexing to assume that Pompilia was lost in her confined space while her husband would live in a safe environment and could "wait till life have passed from out the world"; as a matter of fact, life was only "a probation and this earth no goal but starting point of man"; if so, why oblige man to strive after the goal, "why institute that race, his life, at all?" A monk, confronted with Pompilia's ordeal, had told the world, 'I break my promise: let her break her heart'; alas, his words had given more than an inkling of the possible attitude of Christians when dealing with wise virgins busy selling lamps to buy lutes and exchanging oil for wine. "The Mystic Spouse betrays the Bridegroom here", the pontiff has sadly inferred: the truth was that "all flesh is weak" and "stand is made by our embodied cowards that grow brave" by propping up one another.

A shift from descriptive ethics to ethical intuitionism has suddenly taken place, and general principles have been invoked in order to pinpoint the moral characteristics of a particular act and the agent of it. The cynical monk and the descriptively ethical Christians have been cases in point and the intuitionist pontiff has by deductive reasoning made the blanket statement that the flesh is weak and mutual support is vital for the salvation of the soul of cowards. Concerning the Convent's claim on Pompilia's property, the demand has raised the issue about the proportionality of the effect to the cause; as such, it prompts the conjecture that an antidote to the nuns' bite might have been provided by a conjunction of reason and emotion in tune with the harmony of the cosmos. Interestingly, a split between Reason and Faith had been hypostatised by Thomas Aquinas and obviated by means of subordination, without subservience, of Reason to Faith. For his part, Immanuel Kant has postulated that Ideas of Reason are integral to a specious metaphysics. In this connection, has the 17th-century Vicar of Christ fallen prey to self-deception while using his intellect? An ad hoc analysis of the man's weltanschauung leaves the thorny question open to debate.

Next item on the menu, Giuseppe Caponsacchi's modus vivendi has attracted the pope's attention for being that of a fellow blinded by the "plenitude of light" vis-à-vis panoplied Christians skulking in a corner. "Well, is the thing we see, salvation?" the Holy Father has queried, and his answer has been a juxtaposition of salvation with "the central truth, Power, Wisdom, Goodness, God" on the assumption that neither required absolute clarity, for "a cloud may soothe the eye made blind by blaze". A weak faith may be an incentive, and the "divine instance of self-sacrifice" may well help the humans once more, the hopeful theologian has put forth. "I have light nor fear the dark at all", he has swiftly declared, – one up on the patriarchal Job who had prepared himself for a land 'where light is as darkness'[15]. From a critical angle, it would be fitting to adopt a hermeneutic approach to the assertion and posit that, by seizing the light of the day and dispelling the shadows of the night, the pontiff has anticipated the thrust of a blurred 'I' at the sun, namely the modus operandi ascribed to futuristic-minded poets.[6]

Innocent XII's claim that he understood the meaning of concepts like Truth, Power, Wisdom, Goodness, God has been corroborated by his contention that a cloud may be a balm for sun-struck eyes and an unsteady faith may turn out to be a blessing in disguise. After referring to the Manichaean vision of a primeval conflict between light and darkness, he has boasted that he had seen the light and was no longer afraid of the dark. It has been a dramatic moment in, and it has raised the question as to whether the Holy Father was claiming to be a son of light. He presumably was averring something of the kind, and it is helpful to recall that none other than Jesus had bid the crowd to believe in the light so that they might become sons of light.[17]

An equally dramatic moment has occurred when a "bard, philosopher, or both" has made himself heard and cried out how he had lived 'under conditions, nowise to escape, whereby salvation was impossible'; notwithstanding that, he had practised virtue, loved, recognised 'the hidden forces, blind necessities called Nature', and the might of gods whom humans had 'in awe because of power'. At the end of the day, what could he 'paint beyond a scheme like this out of the fragmentary truths where light lay fitful in a tenebrific time?' He was fully conscious that sunrise 'joins truth to truth, shoots life and substance into death and void'. Consequently, he, a man of the theatre, had been able to make all the pieces of a jigsaw-puzzle fall into place in his groundbreaking plays. At the end of the day, would the Pope condemn him 'for not descrying sunshine at midnight' and absolve those who 'miss the plain way in the blaze of noon', even though the playwright's 'strong style' had 'pricked them a sure path across the bog, that mire of cowardice and slush of lies'?

Caught on the hop by the bold attestations and claims of the pre-Christian playwright, unseen yet unerringly identified, the cultured listener has asked himself: "How should I answer this Euripides? Shall I wish back once more that thrill of dawn when the whole truth-touched man burned up, one fire? Was this too easy for our after-stage?" The naked truth was that he was bound to cope with a radiance from heaven dimmed by earthly shadows. Was therefore the heroism of old no longer possible and would the next age "re-introduce the doubt discarded"? Would it "disbelieve report through increased faith in thing reports belie?" and "correct the portrait by the living face, mans' God, by God's God in the mind of man?"

The pope's bunch of questions has made Past, Present and Future contiguous entities and, in the process, reawakened the dormant Doubt at the expense of Faith. To some avail though: used as a method of inquiry, uncertainty may well be conducive to sureness provided that the one and the other interrelate; if they do, inquiring mortals will be able to find a point of contact with God. Immanuel Kant springs to mind again qua the thinker who has held that an act of faith in the existence of God is far better than a fallacious proof of it.[18] Moreover, the pope's invocation to *Veritas* has been a far cry from the sceptic Pyrrho's assertion that *ataraxia*, viz. peace of mind, could be achieved solely after abandoning the frustrating search for truth[19]. In modern times, fuel to the flames has been added by the claim that 'the search for truth, especially for the truth about ourselves, is not a pure path for freedom'[20].

Innocent XII has dealt with pertinent ethical issues when he has disclosed his deep anxiety about human beings who were paying lip service to God's commandments and tumbling "worm-like into the mud light now lays bare". Honest to God, "the impatient antimasque" was treading "close on kibe o' the very mask's self it will mock" as well as on him, "last lingering personage". "I did renounce the world, its pride and greed", the pontiff has boasted, unwittingly echoing the above-mentioned Fra Lippo Lippi[21]; then, "will I block the way?" he has asked himself.

At this juncture, the "lingering personage" has come on the scene and danced in step with the saintly Augustine, albeit not with the Abate who had frankly admitted to being a greedy, ambitious, lustful, and revengeful man, a specimen of hypocrisy today and presumably an exemplar of common sense tomorrow. "There's Loyola adapted to our time!", the pontiff has mockingly commented on the Abate's modus vivendi. In a similar fashion, Guido and his helpmates have played their part: "These are the world", the Roman Catholic commander-in-chief has remarked.

An unbiased observer will probably feel inclined to say that the Papal world resembled the Jacobean mad one submitted by Thomas Middleton to the consideration of his masters: indeed, the feeble-minded but not evil-hearted Comparini duo as well as their severely tested daughter have had "the first foot of the dance ... on their heads"; to add insult to injury, the rhythmical movement of their bodies has fitted a dramatic performance redolent of Euripides' theatrics, and in the pontiff's eyes the show has been tantamount to a mock adaptation of Ignatius Loyola's *Spiritual Exercises* to the proclivities of 17th-century churchgoers: the 'impatient antimasque' had set the scene and it was only fitting that the play should end with a bang. "The facts being proved and incontestable", the Vicar of Christ has gone in search of the truth and found out that he was hearing voices crying out in tune with that of Christ categorically defending his sense of honour: it did appear that the educated man's tribunal was manifestly in favour of mercy and legal authorities were urging the need for forgiveness on the grounds of a priest's immunity, not to mention "the weal o' the Popedom'. Furthermore, the voices were saying, the imperative spirit of Civilization, presumably ushering in the return of the Golden Age, had sanctioned the supremacy of man over wife as the bedrock of society. In the light of the above premises, Innocent XII has felt that, should he decide to condemn Guido to death, people would lament that a Count had been sacrificed and the Church scandalised. In addition, he expected the Luthers and the Calvins of this world to put in an appearance and protest that a death sentence on Guido and his accomplices vis-à-vis impunity for Caponsacchi would be discriminatory in the extreme; they would in all likelihood plead, 'the pardon, Holy Father!' and proclaim that a word of mercy issuing from his lips would "give each man o' the mob his torch to wave for gratitude."

And how has the pontiff responded to the suppliant chorus? Here Guido's question, 'Who is upon the Lord's side?' has made an auspicious starting point and led to the dramatic recollection of a dark night illuminated by lightning and resonant with thunderclaps and groans of the earth while the sea shone brightly in the distance! Antonio Pignatelli, as he was then, had witnessed the spectacle in his native Naples. Many years later, as Innocent XII, he has expressed the hope that the truth would "be flashed out by one blow and Guido see, one instant, and be saved." One is reminded of the mystical poet Emily Dickinson's assertion that 'A single screw of flesh/ Is all that pins the soul that stands for Deity, to Mine, upon my side of the Veil' and contextually of the deconstructionist Geoffrey Hartman's comment that 'her homely metaphor keeps the hope open that, on the other side of the *Vail* or *Gauze* of the body, her soul could enter into its freedom and see God'[22]. Soon afterwards, the pontiff has reflected that Death might well visit him in the dead of night and how could he "dare die, let this man live? Strikingly, the ancient aphorism *Mors Tua Vita Mea*, i.e. 'your death safeguards my life', has been dusted off for the benefit of a pontiff "close on the exit". But then again, has he shown to be an out-and-out sage? Take his recollection of pronouncements made by popes of yore and his final question, "Which of the judgments was infallible? Which of my predecessors spoke for God?" Has he spoken faultlessly and indeed spoken for God? In the biblical land of Ůz, the 'blameless and upright' Job had wondered, 'Where shall wisdom be found? And where is the place of understanding?"[23] Centuries later, the wisdom-seeking Pope has echoed the patriarch by declaring that only 'God understands the way to it, and he knows its place.'[24] Augustine of Hippo has pronounced on the subject and held that anyone searching for Truth was *ipso facto* searching for wisdom. But then, how can anyone graduate from imprudence to sagacity? Augustine's answer had been exquisitely fideistic: the quest for Truth begins with an act of faith, which intimates a desire to know and therefore raises the possibility of loving the Known while encapsulating the reality of the Unknowable and thus making room for a love that is still desire and consequently far from beatitude conceived as *gaudium de veritate*, viz enjoyment of Truth[25]. Enveloped in the silence of the *sanctum*, Innocent XII has endeavoured to achieve wisdom, and the remaining question is as to whether he has been successful either on a theoretical or on a practical level. Of the two possibilities, the former seems more likely because the Pope has been able to discern 'what could not be otherwise' (in Aristotle's terms) and on the strength of that has brought the divine power in his soul to the fore. It appears also to be true that, as an analyst of the human condition, he has carefully evaluated the various factors in Franceschini's crime and given a final answer which has proved him skilful at deliberating and imbued with the moral goodness that is an integral part of 'practical wisdom'. It may appear paradoxical that his hopes for Guido's salvation by dint of a sudden twist of fate have made him opt for a negative response, but it would be difficult to deny that his condemnatory decree has stemmed from a yearning for a truth revealed by another flash of light, namely truth as 'clearing of being', – to put it in Martin Heidegger's existentialist terms. For his part, the ancient Aristotle had opined that an intellectually virtuous human being is in a position to deal satisfactorily with practical issues of conduct, for a severance of the ties between moral goodness and practical wisdom would be out of place. By virtue of such interaction, Innocent XII has projected an image of himself as a good and wise man skilfully steering clear of Arcangeli's and Bottini's casuistry while pursuing timeless truths. A quest of the kind points up admirable enterprise, but it is reasonable to wonder whether the pursuer was in possession of the key to the Eternal Verities. Well, there's no denying that the pontiff has resisted the lure of a metaphorical discourse capable of hindering the pursuit of those imperishable truths. And yet. Could his closing peremptory injunction be taken to be an infallible one? It is a highly debatable point, mainly because a clear-cut distinction between accuracy and fallacy cannot easily be drawn. A modern-day novelist has argued that 'you can't know anything. The things you know you don't know. Intention? Motive? Consequence? Meaning? All that we don't know is astonishing. Even more astonishing is what passes for knowing.'[26] Admittedly, knowledge may be conducive to a preposterous idea of infallibility, but it helps to remember that Augustine declared, thus anticipating Descartes' dictum albeit with a difference, *Si fallor, sum*, that is, 'If I am wrong, I am'.[27]

It is likewise true that Innocent XII has dealt with a complex epistemological issue and, although not immune from misapprehensions, done his utmost to steer clear of them by reasoning, in tune with Blaise Pascal's approach, *more geometrico*. On that score, the religious 'geometer' has plausibly scrutinized Guido's moral conduct. Educated by a lifelong training and practice, he has learnt how to play his pastoral role and intuit the significance of Everyman's journey on earth. As a seasoned traveller himself, he has fathomed out the meaning of murder and reached the conclusion that Guido was a murderer who could still be saved by a blaze of truth. The former's Stoic stance, it would appear, has been in harmony with the age-old belief that Evil is necessary because it gives meaning to Good by being its complete opposite and, in addition, is ethically acceptable as a test because it contributes to the eventual triumph of Evil. At this epistemological juncture, Innocent XII has overcome himself, adopted the attitude of a Nietzschean *übermensch* and moved beyond Good and Evil in a last-ditch effort to act as a creator would. In the innermost depths of the Holy See the *dark night of the soul* has drawn to a close and a morning coloured by Fate has broken.

1. F. R. Bradley, in *Western Philosophy and Philosophers*, p. 54
2. *The Insistence of the Letter in the Unconscious*, in *Modern Criticism and Theory*, p. 79ff
3. *Cor* 13.8
4. *Western Philosophy and Philosophers*, p. 24
5. Robert Browning, *Caliban upon Setebos*, ll. 144-45
6. William Cowper, *The Task*, Book VI, ll. 198-261
7. Cynewulf, *Juliana*, Section IV
8. René Descartes, as quoted in *Western Philosophy and Philosophers*, p. 267
9. *Op. Cit.* p. 42
10. In *Discourse on the Method*, 1637, Pt. IV
11. Jacques Lacan, in *Modern Criticism and Theory,* pp. 96-97
12. Bertrand Russell in *Western Philosophy and Philosophers*, p. 285
13. Gottfried Leibnitz in *Op. Cit.* p. 167ff
14. Robert Browning, *Fra Lippo Lippi*, l. 5414.
15. *The Book of Job*, 10. 21-22
16. Julia Kristeva in *The Struggle between Poet and Sun*, in *Modern Criticism and Theory*, p. 233ff
17. *John,* 12. 36
18. In *Western Philosophy and Philosophers*, p. 162
19. In *Op. Cit.* p. 291
20. Michel Foucault in *Op. Cit.* pp. 112
21. Robert Browning, *Fra Lippo Lippi.* l. 98
22. See Geoffrey Hartman, *The Interpreter's Freud*, in *Modern Criticism and Theory*, p. 416

    Robert Browning, *Pippa Passes*, Pt IV
23. *The Book of Job*, 28.12

24. *Op. Cit.* 28.23
25. See Augustine in *Western Philosophy and Philosophers*, p. 33
26. Philip Roth, *The Human Stain*, Vintage, p. 209.

GUIDO

The sombre light of a wintry daybreak was on the verge of streaming in when a pair of high-ranking prelates visited Guido Franceschini in the *Prigione Nuova* close to *Castel Sant Angelo*. Wearing a dark shirt underneath a goats-hair coat, his gaunt face studded with stubble, the detainee rose laboriously to his feet and addressed the visitors.

"You are the Cardinal Acciaiuoli, and you, Abate Panciatichi – two good Tuscan names. Sirs, I beseech you by blood-sympathy, if there be any vile experiment in the air, – if this your visit simply prove, when all's done, just a well-intentioned trick that tries for ruth truer than truth itself. You have my last word, – innocent am I as Innocent my Pope and murderer, innocent as a babe, as Mary's own, as Mary's self, – I said, say and repeat. Whoever owned wife, sister, daughter, – nay, mistress, – had any shadow of any right, approved. I being for Rome, Rome was for me! Then, there's the point reserved, the subterfuge my lawyers held by, kept for last resource, the knaves! One plea at least would hold, they laughed, and hook my cause on to the Clergy's; plea which, even if law tipped off my hat and plume, would show my priestly tonsure, save me so. Thank the good Pope! Now, is he good in this, never mind, Christian, – no such stuff's extant, – cannot I live if he but like? 'The law!' Why, just the law gives him the very chance, the precise leave to let my life alone, – a life to take and hold and keep: but no! He sighs, shakes head, refuses to shut hand, motions away the gift they bid him grasp, nullifies and ignores, – reverts in fine to the good and right, in detriment of me! He's sick of his life's supper, – swallowed lies: so, hobbling bedward, needs must ease his maw just where I sit o' the door-sill."

Holding his head high, the Count fixed his eyes on Panciatichi. "Sir Abate, can you do nothing? Friends, we used to frisk: were not we put into a beaten path, bid pace the world, we nobles born and bred, the body of friends with each his scutcheon full of old achievement and impunity, – taking the laugh of morn and Sol's salute? Still Sol salutes me and the morning laughs. A trot and a trample! Only I lie trapped, writhe in a certain novel springe just set by the good old Pope: I am first prize."

The speaker's stare extended to Acciaiuoli. "Warn me? Why? Apprize me that the law o' the game is changed? What is your visit but my lure to talk? You have a something to disclose? – a smile, at the end of the forced sternness, means to mock the heart-beats here? I call your two hearts stone! How could I spill this overplus of mine among those hoar-haired, shrunk-shanked, odds and ends of body and soul, old age is chewing dry! How the life I could shed yet never shrink, would drench their stalks with sap like grass in May! Is it not terrible, I entreat you, Sirs, such manifold and plenitudinous life? terrible so to be alive yet die?"

The poignant utterance sounded in sync with the clump of shoes unaccustomed to the place and the shake of a straggly-haired head. "Lucidity of soul unlocks the lips: how I see all my folly at a glance! 'A man requires a woman and a wife': *there* was my folly! I believed the saw: I knew that just myself concerned myself, yet needs must look for what I seemed to lack, in a woman, – why, the woman's in the man! Fools we are, how we learn things when too late! Overmuch life turns round my woman-side; the male and female in me, mixed before, settle of a sudden: I'm my wife outright in this unmanly appetite for truth, this careless courage as to consequence, this instantaneous sight through things and through this voluble rhetoric, if you please, – 't is she! Here you have that Pompilia whom I slew, also the folly for which I slew her! Fool!" The transgendered, avowedly unhinged, murderer produced a handkerchief embroidered with a coat of arms and a collared dog inanely leaping off a tree, wiped his nose, and replaced the noble piece of cloth in his coat. "And, fool-like, what is it I wander from? I chanced to stroll forth, many a good year gone, one warm Spring eve in Rome, and unaware looking, mayhap, to count what stars were out, came on your huge axe in a frame, that falls and so cuts off a man's head underneath, at the Mouth-of-Truth o' the riverside, you know. *There* the man-mutilating engine stood at ease, both gay and grim, like a Swiss guard; *there* stood the twelve-foot-square of scaffold, railed considerably round to elbow-height, all of it painted red. Red, in the midst, ran up two narrow tall beams barred across; tight you are clipped, whiz, there's the blade on you, out trundels body, down flops head on floor, and where's your soul gone? That, too, I shall find!" He sighed heavily. "There's no such lovely month in Rome as May —May's crescent is no half-moon of red plank, and came now tilting o'er the wave i' the west, one greenish-golden sea, right 'twixt those bars of the engine – I began acquaintance with, understood, hated, hurried from before, to have it out of sight and cleanse my soul! Here it is all again, conserved for use, and here's the silver cord which … what's your word? depends from the gold bowl, which loosed – not 'lost' – lets us from heaven to hell, – one chop, we're loose! Such 'losing' is scarce Mother Nature's mode."

The narrator closed his eyes as if he was trying to dispel fears of demonic red engulfing his soul in the nether regions. " Oh, if men were but good! They are not good, nowise like Peter: people called him rough, but if, as I left Rome, I spoke the Saint, – '*Petrus, quo vadis?*' doubtless I should hear: 'To free the prisoner and forgive his fault!' If Innocent succeeds to Peter's place, let him think Peter's thought, speak Peer's speech! Concede I be all one blood-guiltiness and mystery of murder in the flesh, why should that fact keep the Pope's mouth shut fast? He execrates my crime, – good! – sees hell yawn. How does a Pope proceed that knows his cue? Why, leaves me linger out my minute here, since close on death come judgment and the doom. Tender for souls are you, Pope Innocent! Christ's maxim is: one soul outweighs the world. Respite me, save a soul, then, curse the world!"

The outburst was accompanied by an emphatic shake of the head.

'No,' venerable sire, I hear you smirk, 'No: for Christ's gospel changes names, not things, renews the obsolete, does nothing more. Our fire-new gospel is retinkered law, our mercy, justice, Jove's rechristened God, – nay, whereas, in the popular conceit, 't is pity that old harsh Law somehow limps, lingers on earth, although Law's day be done, – else would benignant Gospel interpose. Law is all harshness, Gospel were all love! We like to put it, on the contrary: Gospel takes up the rod which Law lets fall; Mercy is vigilant when Justice sleeps. Does Law let Guido taste the Gospel-grace? Yes, you do say so, – else you would forgive me, whom Law dares not touch but tosses you! Dear my friends, do but see! A murder's tried; there are two parties to the cause: I'm one, – defend myself, as somebody must do; I have the best o' the battle: that's a fact, simple fact, – fancies find no place beside. What though half Rome condemned me? Half approved; all Rome, in the main, acquits me. Whereupon what has the Pope to ask but 'How finds Law?'

'I find', replies Law, 'I have erred this while: guilty or guiltless, Guido proves a priest, no layman; he is therefore yours, not mine. I bound him; loose him, you whose will's Christ's.'" A couple of nods took form. "And now, what does this Vicar of the Lord, shepherd o' the flock, one of whose charge bleats sore for crook's help from the quag wherein it drowns? Law suffers him put forth the crumpled end, – his pleasure is to turn staff, use the point, and thrust the shuddering sheep he calls a wolf, back and back, down and down to where hell gapes!

'Guiltless,' cries Law.

'Guilty' corrects the Pope! 'Guilty', for the whim's sake! 'Guilty', he somehow thinks, and anyhow says: 't is truth; he dares not lie! Others should do the lying. That's the cause brings you both here: I ought in decency confess to you that I deserve my fate, am guilty, as the Pope thinks, – ay, to the end keep up the jest, lie on, lie ever, lie i' the last gasp of me. What reason, Sirs? I die an innocent and murdered man! You two come here, entreat I tell you lies and end, the edifying way. I end, telling the truth! Your self-styled shepherd thieves! A thief – and how thieves hate the wolves we know: the red hand is sworn foe of the black jaw! That's only natural, that's right enough, but why the wolf should compliment the thief with the shepherd's title, bark out life in thanks, and, spiteless, lick the prong that spits him, – eh, Cardinal? My Abate, scarcely thus! There! Let my sheepskin garb, a curse on't, go – leave my teeth free if I must show my shag!"

The pointed plea, evocative of a classical meta morphosis, engendered no palpable token of appreciation. The harangue went on.

"Repent? What good shall follow? If I pass twelve hours repenting, will that fact hook fast the thirteenth at the horrid dozen's end? If I fall forthwith at your feet, gnash, tear, foam, rave, to give your story the due grace, will that assist the engine half-way back into its hiding-house? boards, shaking now, bone against bone, like some old skeleton bat that wants, now winter's dead, to wake and pray! Will howling put the spectre back to sleep? Since I want new life like the creature, – life being done with here, begins i' the world away: I shall next have 'Come, mortals, and be judged!' Hear the truth, you, whatever you style yourselves, civilization and society! Dying in cold blood is the desperate thing; the angry heart explodes, bears off in blaze the indignant soul, and I'm combustion ripe. Why, you intend to do your worst with me! That's in your eyes! You dare no more than death and mean no less. I must make up my mind! Why grant me respite who deserve my doom? I knew that if I chose sin certain sins, solace my lusts out of the regular way prescribed me, I should find you in the path, have to try skill with a redoubted foe; you would lunge, I would parry, and make end. This incidental hurt, this sort of hole i' the heart of me? I stumbled, got it so, fell on my own sword, as as a gambler may! Law had assayed the adventure, – but what's Law? Morality exposed the Gorgon-shield! Morality and Religion conquer me. If Law sufficed, would you come here, entreat I supplement law and confess forsooth? Did not the Trial show things plain enough?" There was an intimation of a legal disquisition in the question. "I say that, long ago, when things began, all the world made agreement, such and such were pleasure-giving, profit-bearing acts, but henceforth extra-legal, nor to be: you must not kill the man whose death would please and profit you, unless his life stop yours plainly, and need so be put aside: get the thing by a public course, by law, only no private bloodshed as of old! All of us, for the good of everyone, renounced such licence and conformed to law: who breaks law breaks pact, therefore, helps himself to pleasure and profit over and above the due, and must pay forfeit, – pain beyond his share: for pleasure is the sole good in the world; anyone's pleasure turns to someone's pain. So, let law watch for everyone, say we. Punishment? quite right! thus the world goes round."

The professedly law-abiding citizen rubbed his chin and locked his gaze on the visitors' gaze: the latter connoted a demand for further utterances. He did not miss his cue: "I, being well aware such pact there was, who in my time have found advantage too in law's observance and crime's penalty, – who, but for wholesome fear law bred in friends, had doubtless given example long ago, furnished forth some friend's pleasure with my pain, I could not, for that foolish life of me, help risking law's infringement: I broke bond and needs must pay price, – wherefore, here's my head, flung with a flourish! But, repentance too? Cardinal, no! Abate, scarcely thus! Is 't the fault, not that I dared try a fall with Law and straightway am found undermost, but that I fail to see, above man's law, God's precept you, the Christians, recognize? Colly my cow! Do n't fidget, Cardinal; Abate, cross your breast and count your beads and exorcise the devil, for here he stands and stiffens in the bristly nape of neck, daring you drive him hence! You,

Christians both? I say, if ever was such faith at all born in the world, by your community suffered to live its little tick of time, 't is dead of age now, ludicrously dead; honour its ashes, if you be discreet, in epitaph only! For, concede its death, allow extinction, you may boast unchecked what feats the thing did in a crazy land at a fabulous epoch, – treat your faith that way; not otherwise, your faith is shrined and shown and shamed at once: you banter while you bow! Come, thus I wave a wand and bring to pass in a moment, in the twinkle of an eye, what but that – feigning everywhere grows fact in Rome, – faith's flow set free at fountain-head! Now, you'll own, at this present when I speak, before I work the wonder, there's no man woman or child in Rome, faith's fountain-head, but might, if each were minded, realize conversely unbelief, faith's opposite – set it to work on life unflinchingly, yet give no symptom of an outward change: why should things change because men disbelief? What's incompatible, in the whited tomb, with bones and rottenness one inch below? Look in your own heart, if your soul have eyes! You shall see reason why, though faith were fled, unbelief still might work the wires and move man, the machine, to play a faithful part. Praise, blame, sit, stand, lie, or go! – all of it, in each of you, purest unbelief may prompt, and wit explain to who has eyes to see. But, lo, I wave wand, make the false the true! What an explosion, how the fragments fly of what was surface, mask and make-believe! I call such difference 'twixt act and act sheer lunacy unless your truth on lip be recognized a lie in heart of you. Contort your brows! You know I speak the truth: gold is called gold, and dross called dross, i' the Book; gold you let lie and dross pick up and prize! I, being the unit in creation now, double or quits, I play, but all or nought exceeds my courage: therefore, I descend to the next faith with no dubiety. I've had my life, whate'er I lose: I'm right? I've got the single good there was to gain: entire faith, or else complete unbelief, – aught between has my loathing and contempt, mine and God's also, doubtless."

The prisoner stepped to the exit door and tapped on it repeatably: was he taking the line of least resistance? Then he shuffled back and fixed Acciaiuoli with an icy stare. "Ask yourself, Cardinal, where and how you like a man you promised trudge behind through fair and foul yet leave i' the lurch at the first spit of rain. Who holds to faith when rain begins? Where's the obedience that shall edify? We have the prodigal son of heavenly sire, turning his nose up at the fatted calf, fain to fill belly with the husks we swine did eat by born depravity of taste!"

The haranguer's stare encompassed both visitors.

"Enough of the hypocrites. But you, Sirs, you who never budged from litter where I lay, and buried snout i' the draff-box while I fed, cried amen to my creed's one article: 'Get pleasure, 'scape pain, give your preference to the immediate good, for time is brief, and death ends good and ill and everything: what's got is gained, what's gained soon is gained twice, and, inasmuch as faith gains most, feign faith!' – you now, like bloody drunkards but half-drunk, o' the sudden you must needs reintroduce solemnity, must sober undue mirth by a blow dealt your boon companion here who, using the old licence, dreamed of harm no more than snow in harvest: yet it falls! You check the merriment effectually by pushing your abrupt machine i' the midst, making me Rome's example: blood for wine! The general good needs that you chop and change! I may dislike the hocus-pocus, – Rome, the laughter-loving people, won't they stare chap-fallen while serious natures sermonize 'The magistrate, he beareth not the sword in vain; who sins may taste its edge, we see'? – Why my sin, drunkards? Where have I abused liberty, scandalized you all so much? I knew my own mind, meant to live my life, take my own part and sell you my life dear. But it was 'Fie! No prejudice in the world to the proper manly instinct! Cast your lot into our lap: one genius ruled our births, we'll compass joy by concert. Take with us the regular irregular way i' the wood; you'll miss no game through riding breast by breast in this preserve, the Church's park and pale, rather than outside where the world is waste!'"

The utterer's gravelly voice, now higher by a semitone, flowed freely as he hissed, "Come, if you said not that, did you say this? Give plain and terrible warning, 'Live, enjoy? Such life begins in death and ends in hell! Dare you bid us assist you to your sins?' Had you so warned me, – not in lying words but veritable deeds with tongues of flame, – that had been fair; that might have struck a man, silenced the squabble between soul and sense. But you as good as bade me wear sheep's wool over wolf's skin, suck blood and hide the noise by mimicry of something like a bleat. Oh, were it only open yet to choose, should not you get a growl through the white fangs in answer to your beckoning! Cardinal, Abate, managers o' the multitude, I'd turn your gloved hands to account, be sure! You should manipulate the coarse rough mob: 't is you I'd deal directly with, not them. Oh, it had been a desperate game, but game wherein the winner's chance were worth the pains to try conclusions: at the worst, what's worse than this *mannaia-*machine each minute's talk helps push an inch the nearer me? Fool, fool!"

Guido' face had now darkened, but it lit up anew quick as a flash. "You understand me and forgive, sweet Sirs? I blame you, tear my hair and tell my woe – alls but a flourish, figure of rhetoric! One makes fools look foolisher fifty-fold by putting in their place the wise like you to take the full force of an argument would buffet their stolidity in vain. If you should feel aggrieved by the mere wind o' the blow that means to miss you and maul them, that's my success! Is it not folly, now, to say with folks, 'A plausible defence – we see through notwithstanding, and reject?' I praise the wisdom of these fools and straight tell them my story – 'plausible, but false!' False, to be sure! What else can story be that runs: a young wife, tired of an old spouse, found a priest whom she fled away with; both took their full pleasure in the two-days' flight, which a grey-haired greyer-hearted pair helped for the love they bore all liars. Oh, here incredulity begins! Indeed? Allow then, were no one point strictly true, there's that i' the tale might seem like truth at least to the unlucky husband, jaundiced patch: jealousy maddens people, why not him? Say, he was maddened, so, forgivable! Jealousy! I have known a score of plays wherein the husband, mad as a March hare, suspected all the world contrived his shame. What did the wife? The wife kissed both eyes blind, explained away ambiguous circumstance, crowned his head, – you know what's the mockery! All those eyes of all husbands in all plays, at stare like one expanded peacock-tail, are laughed at for pretending to be keen while horn-blind; but the moment I step forth – oh, I must needs o' the sudden prove a lynx and look the heart, that stone-wall, through and through! Such an eye, God's may be, – not yours nor mine".

The cutely patterned handkerchief resurfaced and was put to good use out of civilized custom.

The Count resumed. "Yes, presently ... what hour is fleeting now? Away with man! What shall I say to God? This, if I find the tongue and keep the mind – 'Do Thou wipe out the being of me, and smear this soul from off Thy white of things I blot! I am one huge and sheer mistake. Whose fault? Not mine at least, who did not make myself!' Grind your teeth, Cardinal! Abate, writhe! What else am I to cry out in my rage, unable to repent one particle of the past? Oh, how I wish some cold wise man would dig beneath the surface which you scrape, deal with the depths, pronounce on my desert groundedly! I want simple sober sense, that asks, before it finishes with a dog, who taught the dog that trick you hang him for? You both persist to call that act a crime sense would call ... yes, I do assure you, Sirs, ... a blunder! At the worst, I stood in doubt on crossroad, took one path of many paths: it leads to the red thing, we all see now. Put me back to the crossroad, start afresh! Give me my wife: how should I use my wife, love her or hate her? Prompt my action now! There she stands; *there* she is alive and pale, Pompilia Comparini, as at first, held only by the mother's fingertip – struck dumb, for she was white enough before! She eyes me with those frightened balls of black, – the amazed look all one insuppressive prayer might she but be set free as heretofore, so but alone, so but apart from me!" The spurned husband narrowed his eyes, and was he trying to visualize a female figure communing with him?

"You are touched? So am I, quite otherwise, if 't is with pity. I resent my wrong, being a man: we only show man's soul through man's flesh; she sees mine, it strikes her thus! I am past the prime; I scare the woman-world. In vain the mother nods, winks, bustles up 'Count, girls incline to mature worth like you! As for Pompilia, what's flesh, fish or fowl to one who apprehends no difference?' Well, I resent this: I am young in soul, nor old in body, – thews and sinews here, – though the vile surface be not smooth as once; I am the steel man worth ten times the crude, – would woman see what this declines to see, declines to say 'I see', – the official word that makes the thing, pricks on the soul to shoot new fire into the half-used cinder, flesh!" The "steel man" riveted the visitors with soulful eyes. "Therefore 't is she begins with wronging me, who cannot but begin with hating her. Our marriage follows: there we stand again! Take notice we are lovers in a church, waiting the sacrament to make us one and happy! Just as bid, she bears herself, comes and kneels, rises, speaks, is silent, – goes. Yes, I do gain my end and have my will." He gave a peremptory nod. "Pass the next weeks of dumb contented death, she lives, – wakes up, installed in house and home, is mine, mine all day-long, all night-long mine." A fake smile warmed his face and froze. "Good folks begin at me with open mouths: 'Now, at least, reconcile the child to life! Study and make her love … that is, is, endure the … hem! The … all of you though somewhat old, till it amount to somewhat old, till it amount to something, in her eye, as good as love, better a thousand times, – since nature helps the woman in such strait, makes passiveness her pleasure: failing which, what if you give up boys' and girls' fools'-play and go on to wise friendship all at once? Those boys and girls kiss themselves cold, you know, toy themselves tired and slink aside full soon to friendship, as they name satiety: thither go you and wait their coming!'

The recipient of the good folks' recommendations wagged his head. "Thanks, considerate advisers, – but, fair play! Had you and I but started fair at first, we, keeping fair, might reach it, neck by neck, this blessed goal, whenever fate so please: but why am I to miss the daisied mile the course begins with, why obtain the dust of the end precisely at the starting-point? Why quaff life's cup blown free of all the beads? Foolish, the love-fit? Let me prove it such like you, before like you I puff things clear! Go preach that to your nephews, not to me who, tired i' the midway of my life, would stop and take my first refreshment in a rose! What is this coarse woolly hip, worn smooth of leaf, you counsel I go plant in garden plot in confidence the seed shall germinate, grow big, and blow me out a dog-rose bell? This bloom, whose best grace was the slug outside and the wasp inside its bosom, call you 'rose'? Claim no immunity from a weed's fate for the horrible present! What you call my wife I call a nullity in female shape, vapid disgust, soon to be pungent plague, when mixed with, made confusion and a curse by two abominable nondescripts: that mother with her cunning and her cant; the eyes with first their twinkle of conceit, then, dropped to earth in mock-demureness, – now, the smile self-satisfied from ear to ear, now, the prim pursed-up mouth's protruded lips, – that owl-like screw of lid and rock of ruff! As for the father, Cardinal, you know the kind of idiot: rife are such in Rome, but they wear velvet commonly. Such fools, at the end of life, can furnish forth young folk who grin and bear with imbecility, but what say we to the same solemn beast wagging his ears and wishful of our pat? Sir Dignity i' the dumps? Pat him? We drub self-knowledge, rather, into frowzy pate, teach Pietro to get trappings or go hang! Fancy this quondam oracle in vogue; the ends obtained, or else shown out of reach, he goes on, takes the flattery for pure truth: 'You love and honour me, of course; what next?' What, but the trifle of the stabbing, friend? Which taught you how one worships when the shrine has lost the relic that we bent before." The utterance overflowed with vital passion. "Angry? And how could I be otherwise? 'T is plain: this pair of old pretentious fools meant to fool me; it happens I fooled them. Miscalculation has its consequence; but when the shepherd crooks a sheep-like thing and, meaning to get wool, dislodges fleece and finds the veritable wolf beneath, does he, by way of being politic, pluck the first whisker grimly visible? Or rather grow in a trice all gratitude? Ay, thus, with chattering teeth and knocking knees, would wisdom treat the adventure; these, forsooth, tried whisker-plucking, and so found what trap the whisker kept perdue: two rows of teeth – sharp, as too late the prying fingers felt. What would you have? The fools transgress, the fools forthwith receive appropriate punishment. They first insult me, I return the blow, there follows noise enough: four hubbub months, now hue and cry, now whimpering and wail, a perfect goose-yard cackle of complaint! I have enough of noise, ope wicket wide, sweep out the couple to go whine elsewhere, and am just taking thought to breathe again, taste the sweet sudden silence all about, when, there they are at it, the old noise I know! Triumph it sounds and no complaint at all. And triumph it is! My boast was premature: the creatures, I turned forth, clapped wing and crew, fighting cock-fashion, – they had filched a pearl from dung-heap and might boast with cause enough!" Guido tittered a low and bitter laugh. "I was defrauded of all bargained for: my dowry was derision, my gain muck, my wife – the Church declared my flesh and blood! – the nameless bastard of a common whore; my old name turned henceforth to … shall I say 'he that received the ordure in his face'? And they who planned this wrong, performed this wrong, rounded myself in the ears with my own wrong, – too simple to distinguish wrong from right, – these two ambiguous insects changing name and nature with the season's warmth or chill, anon, – with lusty June to prick their heart,

— soared i' the air, winged flies for more offence and stunk me dead with fetor in the face until I stopped the nuisance. *There's* my crime! *Here's* a coil raised, a pother, and for what? Because strength, being provoked by weakness, fought and conquered, – the world never heard the like! Pah, I spend my breath on them, as if 't was their fate troubled me, too hard to range among the right and fit and proper things!"

The speaker moved closer to the dignitaries and, lowering his voice, drew attention to his wife's role in the tragic story. "Ay, but Pompilia, – I await your word, – she, unimpeached of crime, unimplicate in folly, one of alien blood to these I punish … why extend my claim, exact her portion of the penalty? Yes, friends, I go too fast: the orator's at fault. I ought to step back, lead her by degrees, recounting at each step some fresh offence, up to the red bed, – never fear, I will! Gaze at her, where you place her, to begin, confound me with her gentleness and worth! The horrible pair have fled and left her now; she has her husband for her sole concern, his wife, the woman fashioned for his help, flesh of his flesh, bone of his bone, the bride to groom as is the Church and Spouse, to Christ: there she stands in his presence, – 'Thy desire shall be to the husband, o'er thee shall he rule!" The doctrinal tenet was crowned with a knowing smile. "She sits up, she lies down, she comes and goes, kneels at the couch-side, overleans the sill o' the window, cold and pale and mute as stone. 'Speak!' she obeys, 'Be silent!' she obeys, counting the minutes till I cry "Depart!" Departed, just the same through door and wall I see the same stone strength of white despair. Before, the parents' presence lent her life: she could play off her sex's armoury, intreat, reproach, be female to my male, try all the shrieking doubles of the hare and yield fair sport so: but the tactics change, the hare stands stock-still to enrage the hound! But is there no third party to the pact? What of her husband's relish or dislike for this new game of giving up the game, this worst offence of not offending more? I'll not believe but instinct wrought in this. The long black hair was wound now in a wisp; no more soiled dress, 't is trimness triumphs now; the frayed silk looked the fresher for her spite! There was an end to springing out of bed, praying me, with face buried on my feet! Now, mine she is if I please wring her neck: a moment of disquiet, working eyes, protruding tongue, a long sigh, then no more. This self-possession to the uttermost, how does it differ in aught, save degree, from the terrible patience of God?"

'All which just means she did not love you', the Cardinal abruptly interposed. "Again the word is launched, and the fact fronts me!" he rejoined. "What, you try the wards with the true key and the dead lock flies ope? No, it sticks fast and leaves you fumbling still! You have some fifty servants, Cardinal, – which of them loves you? Which subordinate but makes parade of such officiousness that, – if there's no love prompts it, love, the sham, does twice the service done by love, the true. We calculate on word and deed, nor err, – bid such a man do such a loving act just as we bid a horse, with cluck of tongue, stretch his legs archwise, crouch his saddled back to foot-reach of the stirrup – all for love, and some for the memory of the smart of switch on the inside of the foreleg – what care we? Yet where's the bond obliges horse to man like that which binds fast wife to husband? God laid down the law: gave man the brawny arm and ball of fist – woman the beardless cheek and proper place to suffer in the side. Can she feel no love? Let her show the more! This wife of mine was of another mood – would not begin the lie that ends with truth, nor feign the love that brings real love about: wherefore I judged, sentenced and punished her. Say that I hated her for no one cause beyond my pleasure so to do, – what then? Just on as much incitement acts the world! Why should you master natural caprice? Lay the fault elsewhere, since we must have faults: I see not where the fault lies. *That*'s the truth!" A cascade of nods took shape. "I ought ... oh, ought in my own interest have let the whole adventure go untried, this chance by marriage, – or else, trying it, ought to have it turned to account some one o' the hundred otherwises? Ay, my friend, easy to say, easy to do, – step right now you've stepped left and stumbled on the thing, – the red thing! Doubt I any more than you that practise makes man perfect? Give again the chance, – same marriage and no other wife, be sure I'll edify you! That's because I'm practised, grown fit guide for Guido's self. You proffered guidance, – I know, – none so well, – you laid down law and rolled decorum out, from pulpit corner on the gospel-side, – wanted to make your great experience mine, save me the personal search and pains so. Thanks!"

The well-guided detainee's eyebrows flicked upwards. "What do you know o' the world that's trodden flat and salted sterile with your daily dung, leavened into a lump of loathsomeness? I tried chaff, found I famished on such fare, so made this mad rush at the mill-house door, buried my head up to the ears in dew, browzed on the best, for which you brain me, Sirs! Be it so! I conceived of life that way and still declare: 'Life, without absolute use of the actual sweet therein, is death, not life'. Make sure reward, make certain punishment, entice me, scare me, – I'll forego this life." The eyebrows fell. "The fulness of revenge here – blame yourselves for this eruption of the pent-up soul you prisoned first and played with afterward; *you*, whose stupidity and insolence I must defer to, soothe at every turn, whose swine-like snuffling greed and grunting lust I had to wink at or help gratify. I, boast such passions? 'T was, 'Suppress them straight. Or stay, we'll pick and choose before destroy. Here's wrath in you, – a serviceable sword, – but sword used swordwise, spear thrust out as spear? Anathema! Suppression is the word!' My nature, when the outrage was too gross, widened itself an outlet overwide by way of answer? Sought its own relief with more of fire and brimstone than you wished? All your own doing: preachers, blame yourselves!"

The accused turned accuser pointed out a timepiece awkwardly confined to a nook. "'Tis I preach while the hourglass runs and runs! The letter kills, the spirit keeps alive in law and gospel: there be nods and winks instruct a wise man to assist himself in certain matters nor seek aid at all. Sirs, tell me free and fair! Had things gone well at the wayside inn: had I surprised asleep the runaways, as was so probable, and pinned them each to other partridge-wise, would you have interposed to damp the glow applauding me on every husband's cheek? If you had, then your house against itself divides, nor stands your kingdom anymore. Oh, why, why was it not ordained just so? Why fell not things out so nor otherwise? Being incomplete, the act escaped success. Easy to blame now! Every fool can swear to hole in net that held and slipped the fish. But, treat my act with unjaundiced eye, what was there wanting to a masterpiece except the luck that lies beyond a man? My way with the woman, now proved grossly wrong, just missed of being gravely grandly right and making critics laugh o' the other side."

The maladroit performer let out a nervous little laugh. "I march to the abode, and my men with me, that evening, and we reach the door and stand. I say ... no, it shoots through me lightning-like while I pause, breathe, my hand upon the latch, 'Let me forebode! Thus far, too much success. Of three that are to catch, two should go free, one must: all three surprised? Impossible! Beside, I seek three and may chance on six. It cannot be but I surprise my wife; if only she is stopped and stamped on, good! That shall suffice, more is improbable."

The narrator waved a dismissive forefinger and gave a tight smile. "The impossible was effected: I called king, queen and knave in a sequence, and cards came, – all three, three only! So, I had my way, did my deed: so, unbrokenly lay bare each taenia that had sucked me dry of juice. No doubt the fine delirium flustered me, turned my brain with the influx of success as if the sole need now were to wave wand and find doors fly wide, – wish and have my will, – the rest o' the scheme would care for itself. Escape? Easy enough were that, and poor beside: a ducat slid discreetly into palm o' the mute postmaster while you whisper him how you the Count and certain four your knaves have just been mauling who was malapert, therefore want horses in a hurry, – that and nothing more secures you any day the pick o' the stable. Yet I try the trick, double the bribe, call myself Duke for Count and say the dead man only was a Jew, – and for my pains find I am dealing just with the one scrupulous fellow in all Rome! Just this immaculate officer stares, shrugs shoulder, puts my hand by, gold and all, stands on the strictness of the rule o' the road. He dares not stop me, – we five glare too grim, – gives me some twenty miles of miry road more to march in the middle of that night. We gave in ere we reached the boundary and safe spot out of this irrational Rome, Tuscans once more in blessed Tuscany, where the laws make allowance, understand civilized life and do its champions right! All this, that all but was, might all have been, yet was not! baulked by just a scrupulous knave! What say you to the spite of fortune? Well, the worst's in store: thus hindered, haled this way to Rome again by hangdogs, whom find I here, still to fight with, but my pale frail wife, riddled with wounds by one not like to waste the blows he dealt, knowing anatomy? She too must shimmer through the gloom o' the grave, come and confront me, – not at judgment seat where I could twist her soul, as erst her flesh, and turn her truth into a lie, – but there, o' the death bed, with God's hand between us both, striking me dumb and helping her to speak, tell her own story her own way and turn my plausibility to nothingness. When destiny intends you cards like these, what good of skill and preconcerted play? Had she been found dead, as I left her dead, I should have told a tale brooked no reply – you scarcely will suppose me found at fault with that advantage: 'What brings me to Rome? Necessity to claim and take my wife; better, to claim and take my newborn babe. I seek my wife and child; I find no child but wife, in the embraces of that priest who caused her to elope from me: these two, backed by the pander-pair who watch the while, spring on me like so many tiger cats, glad of the chance to end the intruder. I ... what should I do but stand on my defence, strike right, strike left, strike thick and threefold, slay, – not all, because the coward priest escapes. Last, I escape, in fear of evil tongues, and having had my taste of Roman law.' What's disputable, refutable here? Save by just this one ghost-thing half on earth, half out of it, – as if she held God's hand while she leant back and looked her last at me while fixing fast my head beneath your knife! 'T is fate not fortune! All is of a piece!"

The high-ranking listeners nodded ever so slightly, and did they so out of sympathy with the deterministic viewpoint? Visibly gratified, the aristocratic speaker resumed.

"What was it you informed me of my youths? My rustic four o' the family, soft swains, what sweet surprise had they in store for me, those of my very household? What did Law twist with her rack-and-cord-contrivance late from out their bones and marrow? What but this: had no one of these several stumbling blocks stopped me, they yet were cherishing a scheme, – all of their honest country homespun wit, – to quietly next day at crow of cock cut my own throat too, for their own behoof, seeing I had forgot to clear accounts and somehow never might find memory. Well, being the arch-offender, I die last, – may, ere my head falls, have my eyesight free, nor miss them dangling high on either hand, like scarecrows in a hemp-field – for their pains!"

The self-confessed arch-offender rolled his eyes and stared vacantly into space. "And then my Trial, – 't is my Trial that bites like a corrosive, so the cards are packed, dice loaded, and my life-stake tricked away! Look at my lawyers: lacked they grace of law, Latin or logic? Were not they fools to the height, fools to the depth, fools to the level between, o' the foolishness set to decide the case? They feign, they flatter; nowise does it skill, everything goes against me: deal each judge his dole of flattering and feigning, – why, he turns and tries and snuffs and savours it, as an old fly the sugar-grain, your gift; then eyes your thumb and finger, brushes clean the absurd old head of him, and whisks away, leaving your thumb and finger dirty. Faugh!" He inhaled and exhaled slowly.

"And finally, after this long-drawn range of affront, failure, failure and affront, – this path, twixt crosses leading to a skull, paced by me barefoot, bloodied by my palms from the entry to the end. There's light at length, a cranny of escape: appeal may be to the old man, to the father, to the Pope, for a little life from one whose life is spent. Still the same answer, still no other tune from the cicala perched at the tree-top than crickets noisy round the root: 't is 'Die!' bids Law; 'Be damned!' adds gospel – nay, no word so frank; 't is rather 'Save yourself!' – the Pope subjoins – 'Confess and be absolved! So shall my credit countervail your shame, and the world see I have not lost the knack of trying all the spirits. Yours, my son, wants but a fiery washing to emerge in clarity! Come, cleanse you, ease the ache of these old bones, refresh our bowels, old boy!'

The 'adopted' son's arms joined into the shape of a cross. "Do I mistake your mission from the Pope? I do get strength from being thrust to wall, successively wrenched from pillar and from post by this tenacious hate of fortune, hate of all things in, under, and above earth. Warfare, begun this mean unmanly mode, does best to end so, – gives earth spectacle of a brave fighter who succumbs to odds that turn defeat to victory. Stab? I fold my mantle round me! Rome approves my act. Why is it that I make such suit to live?" He opened his arms and wagged his head. "Cardinal, if the Pope had pardoned me, and I walked out of prison through the crowd, it would not be your arm I should dare press. I go my old ways and find things grown grey. What new leap would a life take, checked like mine i' the spring at outset? Where's my second chance?" Doubt appeared to have taken centre stage, and then "Ay, but the babe ... I had forgot my son, my heir!" he exclaimed in an urgent tone, "now for a burst of gratitude! Old, I renew my youth in him, and, poor, possess a treasure, – is not that the phrase? Why, here's my son and heir in evidence, who stronger, wiser, handsomer than I by fifty years, relieves me of each load. Contrariwise, does the blood-offering fail? There's an ineptitude, one blank the more added to earth in semblance of my child? Then, this has been a costly piece of work, my life exchanged for his! – why he, not I, enjoy the world, if no more grace accrue? Dwarf me, what giant have you made of him? No, nothing repays youth expended so. It is the will runs the renewing nerve through flaccid flesh, would faint before the time. Therefore no sort of use for son have I: a man may have an appetite enough for a whole dish of robins ready cooked, and yet lack courage to face sleet, pad snow, and snare sufficiency for supper."

Gaetano's ambivalent father set about pacing the floor, keeping his hands clasped behind his back, but soon came to a stand and faced the prelates with renewed interest. "Thus the time's arrived when, ancient Roman-like, I'm bound to fall on my own sword, – why not say – Tuscan-like, more ancient, better still? Will you hear truth can do no harm nor good? I think I never was at any time a Christian, as you nickname all the world; name me a primitive religionist, one sprung, – your frigid Virgil's fieriest word, – from fauns and nymphs, trunks and the heart of oak. When the sky darkens, Jove is wroth; say prayer! When the sun shines and Jove is glad, – sing psalm! Learned Abate, no one teaches you what Venus means and who's Apollo here. I spare you, Cardinal, – but, though you wince, you know me, I know you, and both know that! The rationale of your scheme is just 'Pay toll here, there pursue your pleasure free.' Irrational bunglers! So, the living truth revealed to strike Pan dead ducks low at last, prays leave to hold its own and live good days provided it go masque grotesquely, called Christian not Pagan? Oh, you purged the sky of all gods save the One, the great and good, clapped hands and triumphed! But the change came fast: life, – you may mulct and minish to a grain out of the lump, so the grain left but live, – laughed at your substituting death for life, keeping the while unspotted from the world! Let the law stand: the letter kills, what then? The spirit saves as unmistakeably, Omniscience sees,

Omnipotence could stop, All-mercifulness pardons, – it must be, frown law its fiercest, there's a wink somewhere."

The excursus was topped with a broad smile, which intimated the sentiments of a member of the chosen people on entering the Promised Land.

"Such was the logic in this head of mine: I, like the rest, wrote 'poison' on my bread; but broke and ate: – said 'those that use the sword shall perish by the same'. Why then this pother? – all because the Pope, doing his duty, cries: 'A foreigner, you scandalize the natives: here at Rome, *Romano vivitur more*; wise men, here, put the Church forward and efface themselves. The fit defence had been, – you stamped on wheat, intending all the time to trample tares, – were fain extirpate, then, the heretic, and now find, in your haste you slew a fool: whence you are duly contrite. Not one word of all this wisdom did you urge! – which slip death must atone for!' So, let death atone!"

Guido's allusive smile brought on a mythically inspired metamorphosis. "*Byblis in fluvium*, let the weak soul end in water, *sed Lycaon in lupum*, but the strong become a wolf for evermore! Change that Pompilia to a puny stream fit to reflect the daisies on its bank! Let me turn wolf, be whole, and sate, for once, – wallow in what is now a wolfishness coerced too much by the humanity that's half of me as well! Grow out of man, glut the wolf-nature, – what remains but grow into the man again, be man indeed and all man? Do I ring the changes right? Deformed, transformed, reformed, informed, conformed! The honest instinct, pent and crossed through life, let surge by death into a visible flow malignant and maligned, thro' stone and ore, till earth exclude the stranger: vented once, it finds full play, is recognized a-top some mountain as no such abnormal birth. Fire for the mount, the streamlet for the vale!"

The unwittingly Heraclitean-minded fellow appeared to be engulfed in waves of egotism. "Ay, of the water was that wife of mine. Again, how she is at me with those eyes! Away with the empty stare! Be holy still, dare follow not another step I take, not with so much as those detested eyes; no, though they follow but to pray me pause on the incline, earth's edge that's next to Hell! None of your abnegation of revenge! There's God, go tell Him, testify your worst!" He shook his head. "Not she! There was no touch in her of hate: and it would prove her hell, if I reached mine, – I who, with outlet for escape to heaven, would tarry if such flight allowed my foe to raise his head, relieved of that firm foot had pinned him to the fiery pavement else! So am I made, 'who did not make myself' … how dared she rob my own lip of the word?"

The plagiarised husband closed his eyes: was he trying to recapture the picture of his "liquid" wife? Within seconds, his eyes were wide open anew.

"She maundered, 'All is over and at end: I go my own road, go you where God will! Forgive you? I forget you!' *There*'s the saint that takes your taste, you other kind of men! Why could not she come in some heart-shaped cloud, rainbowed about with riches, royalty rimming her round, as round the tintless lawn guardingly runs the selvage cloth of gold? I would have left the faint fine gauze untouched, let her bleach unmolested in the midst: purity, pallor grace the lawn no doubt when there's the costly bordure to unthread and make again an ingot, but what's grace when you want meat and drink and clothes and fire? O those Olimpias bold, those Biancas brave, that brought a husband will worth Ormuz' wealth! O thou Lucrezia, is it long to wait yonder where all the gloom is in a glow with thy suspected presence? – virgin yet, I come to claim my bride, – thy Borgia's self not half the burning bridegroom I shall be! Cardinal, take away your crucifix! Abate, leave my lips alone, they bite! 'T is vain you try to change, what should not change, and cannot. I have bared, you bathe my heart – it grows the stonier for your saving dew! You steep the substance, you would lubricate, in waters that but touch to petrify!" The accuser stretched out a pointed forefinger. "You too are petrifications of a kind. I thought you had a conscience. Cardinal, you know I am wronged! – 'wronged', say, and 'wronged' maintain. Was this strict inquisition made for blood when first you showed us scarlet on your back? Does memory haunt your pillow? Not a whit. Feel you remorse about that damsel-fly which buzzed so near your mouth and flapped your face you blotted it from being at a blow? It was a fly, you were a man, and more, lord of created things; so, took your course. Manliness, mind, – these are things fit to save, fit to brush fly from: why, because I take my course, must needs the Pope kill me? Mind you! Because this instrument he throws away is strong to serve a master: it were yours to have and hold and get such good from out! Cardinal, I adjure you in God's name: save my life, fall at the Pope's feet, set forth things your own fashion, not in words like these made for a sense like yours who apprehend: translate into the court-conventional 'Count Guido must not die, is innocent! Fair, be assured! But what an he were foul? He has friends who will avenge him; enemies who hate the Church now with impunity missing the old coercive. Would you send a soul straight to perdition, dying frank an atheist?' Go and say this, for God's sake!"

The prelate's reaction to the vehement request was the lifting of his eyes to the faint light of the lamp hanging from the ceiling and then, presumably, to the everlasting Presence beyond it. Quietude permeated the cell, but it was quickly dispelled by the prisoner's gravelly voice. "Come, I am tired of silence. Pause enough! You have prayed; I have gone inside my soul and shut its door behind me: 't is your torch makes the place dark, – the darkness let alone grows tolerable twilight, – one may grope and get to guess at length and breadth and depth. God takes his own part in each thing he made, gives each its proper instinct of defence. My lamblike wife could neither bark nor bite: she bleated, bleated, till for pity pure the village roused it, ran with pole and prong to the rescue … and, behold, the wolf's at bay!

Shall he try bleating? – or take turn or two, since the wolf owns to kinship with the fox, and failing to escape the foe by these, give up attempt, die fighting quietly? While fighting quietly, the jaws enjoy their re-embrace in mid back-bone they break, after their weary work thro' the foes' flesh – that's the wolf-nature. Do n't mistake my trope: my fight is figurative, blows i' the air, brain-war with powers and principalities, spirit-bravado, no real fisticuffs! The appropriate drunkenness of the death-hour creep on my sense, the work o' the wine and myrrh, – I know not; I begin to taste my strength, careless, gay even: what's the worth of life? I see you all reel to the rock, you waves – some crested, brilliantly with heads above, some in a strangled swirl sunk who knows how, but all bound whither the main-current sets, rockward, an end in foam for all of you! What if I am o'ertaken, pushed to the front by all you crowding smoother souls behind, and reach, a minute sooner than was meant, the boundary, whereon I break to mist? Go to! The smoothest safest of you all will rock vertiginously in turn, and reel, and, emulative, rush to death like me. Be the act harsh and quick! Undoubtedly the soul's condensed and, twice itself, expands to burst thro' life, in alternation due, into the other state whate'er it prove."

Presumably affected by the metaphor, Guido covered his face with his hands for a short time. Then, "You never know what life means till you die: even throughout life 't is death that makes life live, gives it whatever the significance. For see, on your own ground and argument, suppose life had no death to fear, how find a possibility of nobleness in man, prevented daring any more? What's love, what's faith without a worst to dread? Lack-lustre jewelry; but faith and love, with death behind them bidding do or die – put such a foil at back, the sparkle's born! Is there a new rule in another world? Be sure I shall resign myself: as here I recognized no law I could not see, there, what I see I shall acknowledge too; on earth I never took the Pope for God, in heaven I shall scarce take God for the Pope. Unmanned, remade: I hold it probable

– with something changeless at the heart of me to know me by, some nucleus that's myself. Accretions did it wrong? Away with them – you soon shall see the use of fire!"

The prophetic statement sounded like a climactic blast in a pyrotechnic display. A shower of coruscating sparks fell in its wake. "Till when, all that was, is, and must for ever be. Nor is it in me to unhate my hates; I use up my last strength to strike once more old Pietro in the wine-house-gossip-face, to trample underfoot the whine and wile of that Violante, – and I grow one gorge to loathingly reject Pompilia's pale poison my hasty hunger took for food. A strong tree wants no wreaths about its trunk, no cloying cups, no sickly sweet of scent, but sustenance at root, a bucketful. How else lived that Athenian who died so, drinking hot bull's-blood, fit for men like me? I lived and died a man, and take man's chance, honest and bold: right will be done to such."

Themistocles' counterpart raised his hand to his head and doffed the large-brimmed hat still covering his straggly hair. In that very same instant, cloaked men made their presence felt from the top of the stairs and sedately walked down, intoning a sacred song. On reaching the cell gate they stopped and stood motionless. The doomed nobleman stared at them in horror and then flung a hunted look at the Cardinal and the Abate. "Who are these you have let descend my stair?" he burst out. "Ha, their accursed psalm! Lights at the sill! Is it 'Open' they dare bid you? Treachery! Sirs, have I spoken one word all this while out of the world of words I had to say? Not one word! All was folly; I laughed and mocked! Sirs, my first true word, all truth and no lie, is: 'Save me notwithstanding. Life is all!' I was just stark mad, – let the madman live, pressed by as many chains as you please pile."

The plea paved the way for a desperate sense of belonging and an anguished cry for help: "Do n't open! Hold me from them! I am yours, I am the Granduke's – no, I am the Pope's! Abate, – Cardinal, – Christ, – Maria, – God, … Pompilia, will you let them murder me?"

Alas, the young woman to whom Guido Franceschini had *in extremis* turned for salvation was lying alongside her parents on the black-and-white marble floor in the family church of *San Lorenzo in Lucina*. As to her husband, he was, to all appearances, on the brink of meeting the *mannaia* still sitting aloof in *Piazza del Popolo*. Would his noble neck be severed before the eyes of the two Halves of Rome and Tertium Quid? Sadly, it was no moot point.

"Sirs, I beseech you by blood-sympathy, if there be any vile experiment in the air, – if this your visit simply prove, when all's done, just a well-intentioned trick that tries for truth truer than truth itself". The convict Guido Franceschini has fired the opening salvo at a Cardinal and an Abate visiting him, to his mind, with a view to getting at truth on their own terms, regardless of any correspondence with reality: in reality, he was as innocent as Innocent, his "Pope and murderer".

Well then, has the Count been in deadly earnest, or has he been indulging in a play on words? Also, has he been unconsciously extending the notion of "murder" to himself, thus obliterating the innocence he has claimed?

Arguably, a plausible conclusion rests on the premiss that the speaker has made use of a language inadvertently supported by the fantasy at the heart of selfhood. Contextually, the psychoanalytic suggestion that 'the Unconscious is the discourse of the Other'[1] may well help to understand how, by giving voice to the Other within himself, the prisoner has been able to maintain that he could have been set free by a sympathetic Rome as well as by Law if favourably applied to his case by the pontiff; on the strength of both, he would have been relieved of the weight made up by the combination of mountainous lies. Consonant with that, a note of sincerity has been struck by his assertion that it is "terrible so to be alive yet die", and it is worth recalling by contrast the mood of the Renaissance bishop whispering to his nephews: "'Dying by degrees, hours and long hours in the dead night, I ask 'do I live? Am I dead? Peace, peace seems all.' "[2] Along similar lines, the hedonist Epicurus has held that death 'is nothing to us, since so long as we exist death is not with us, but when death comes then we no longer exist.'[3] By the look of it, the juxtaposition of life and death makes room for an Aristotelian *differentia*: the Roman bishop had ordered a tomb inside *Santa Prassede* in the hope of securing a quiet place whereas the Aretine fellow has felt that his cell was giving him no hope of peace. On the other hand, the former and the latter have shared a fit of pique: 'For ye have stabbed me with ingratitude to death – ye wish it – God, ye wish it! Stone, gritstone, a-crumble'[4], the bishop has cried to his son while, unwittingly echoing him, the Count has yelled at smile, at the end of the forced sternness, means to mock the heart beats here? I call your two hearts stone!' Strikingly, in either case a piece of rock has been at the core of the problem. Along similar lines, W.B. Yeats has, on recalling a tragic Easter, detected a 'stone in the midst of all'[5].

At this point, folly has taken centre stage: Guido has seen his erstwhile self as a fool who had stoically aimed at virtue and wisdom by giving credence to the saying that 'a man requires a woman and a wife' in order to make up for his lack. "Why, the woman's in the man!" he has exclaimed before recognizing in the same breath that his leaning towards improvidence, intuition, and voluble rhetoric had made him blend in with his wife and in the process dream up a peculiar scheme to develop a unified selfhood on whose strength he had placed her feminine self simultaneously inside and outside his masculine world. To put it another way, his male identity had subconsciously developed a 'game strategy' and succeeded in doing what happens when one manages to deceive an adversary: the success of the self has been achieved by dint of betrayal of an Other acting in good faith.'[6] In this respect, Pompilia has come up as the epitome of a definable Self and at the same time the signifier of an elusive Other, whereas her husband has presented himself as being capable of unifying his male/female duality, i.e. of identifying with his wife by dint of a Freudian 'incorporation'. Irresistibly, Catherine Earnshaw springs to mind for being the one who in the fullness of time says about her beloved Heathcliff, 'He's more myself than I am'[7]: as the Moorland story goes, the death of both engendered the coalescence of foster siblings qua bisexuals-in-embryo longing for oneness. Here a good argument can be made for comparing the spectral event on the 'wuthering heights' with the Arezzan Count's deed and seeing the latter as a bid to appease the *id* by rejecting the feminine streak in a masculine make-up. The remaining question is as to whether, by taking heed of the Unconscious, Guido has managed to come to terms with himself. In respect of that, it can be argued that the development of the man's false ego has led to the demolition of his ethical self, alas, with dire consequences; nevertheless, it makes sense to opine that his decentred selfhood has, while endeavouring to cover up the split created by an unconscious desire, denoted a yearning for a symbiosis with the spurned Other. "'T is she!" he has exclaimed", and it is semiotically tempting to describe his cry about the Other as well the language he has used as 'a mask covering over the impossibility of desire.'[8]

A touch of the here-and-now as against the here-after has added weight to the Count's duality: standing in full view of the general public, a "both gay and grim" *mannaia* has evoked the image of a Swiss guard and brought the destination of mankind's spirit into question: "And where's your soul gone? That, too, I shall find!" Guido has mock-seriously predicted. Meanwhile, the contours of the guillotine with its silver cord and the gold bowl which "lets us from heaven to hell" have made him aware of its significant divergence from "Mother Nature's mode". "Oh, if men were but good!" he has ethically sighed and in the next breath emphatically stated that "Christ's maxim is: one soul outweighs the world". Accordingly, "Respite me, save a soul, then, curse the world!" he has pleaded and in response heard, 'No, for Christ's gospel changes names, not things, renews the obsolete, does nothing more. Gospel takes up the rod which Law lets fall. Mercy is vigilant when Justice sleeps'. As a counter-thrust, he has put forth, "I have the best o' the battle: that's a fact. All Rome, i' the main, acquits me: whereupon what has the Pope to ask but 'How finds Law?' Law had considered that, guilty or guiltless, he was a priest and therefore it was a matter for the Pope to decide. With debatable logic, the 'Vicar of the Lord' had signalled that he was not unwilling to 'thrust the shuddering sheep he called a wolf, back and back, down and down to where Hell gapes.'

At this crucial stage, reading between the lines is likely to reveal Guido's aversion to the temporal power of the pontiff, – a barely surprising attitude given that the Count hailed from a Ghibelline city. A similar mood has come to the fore when he has accused the Cardinal and the Abate of coming to him in the hope of hearing a mendacious admission of just deserts, – only to be confronted with the naked truth. In reality, they were assisting the Pope as a "self-styled shepherd" of souls, and consequently it would be perfectly reasonable for him, a sheep in the eyes of the secular world, to discard the sheep's clothing and offer the wolf's shag to the pontiff.

Perfectly reasonable, and no mistake! The mythical-minded Ovid would probably have been delighted to see a metamorphosis take shape in papal Rome. Guido's archetypal *shadow*, *anima*, and *persona* (Carl Gustav Jung's terms, for the record) have come under scrutiny: the quondam cleric has rebuked the Church for repressing the wolf's instinct in spite of the fact that it was inherent in a nature-based legal system; nevertheless, after allowing, by dint of a *reductio ad absurdum*, for the possibility of "one blood guiltiness and mystery in the flesh", he has acted in compliance with the dictum imposed by his spiritual Mother. Intriguingly, the mention of a mystery has pointed up the plight of a murderer subconsciously grappling with the issues raised by his horrific misdeed. It has also served as a reminder that, as the age-old simile goes, 'a degenerate Noble, or One that is proud of his birth, is like a turnip: there is nothing good of him, but that which is under-ground.'[9]

In this connection, Guido's soul, qua 'the form of body and the power of life'[10] – as Aristotle would put it – has made him ask Innocent XII not to forget Christ's maxim that 'one soul outweighs the world'; by associative thinking, the degenerate aristocrat has begged the Vicar of Christ to curse the world and save a soul. As to the secular court, Guido has pointed to its confession of unsound judgement and subsequent handing of judicial control over to the Church Supremo. As a result, the latter's final decree might well ignore his ovine candour and have him slaughtered qua a wolf in sheep's clothing. Worst of all, he had not been given sufficient time to repent – witness the *mannaia* sitting quietly and conjuring up the image of a hideous death! Against this background, echoes of the anonymous fifteenth-century lyricist's lament, *Timor mortis conturbat me* would not come amiss.

Truth has stepped into the spotlight anew when the distressed prisoner has invoked it as a saviour of the soul. Lying would be of no use to him: it was only too fair that he should meet his doom, for he had fought his opponents by hook or by crook.

The confession, it can be argued, adumbrates a sense of guilt leading to the disclosure of a warped self and an acceptance of the authority of the Law. The German Sebald's words to his paramour Ottima spring to mind: 'Do you think I fear to speak the bare truth once for all? All we have talked of, is, at bottom, fine to suffer; there's a recompense in guilt.'[11] Guido's *modus operandi* is a case in point: the convergence of his conscious will and his unconscious desire – 'Where *id* was, there *ego* shall be', Freud has stated in *The Ego and the Id* – has made him resort to legal procedures before finding them inadequate. After quarrelling with kith and kin, Morality and Religion have got the better of him, or so he has contended, with the result that his existentialist pursuit of absolute freedom has been supplanted by a compliance with the ethical demand that he ought to concern himself with the needs and desires of fellow humans. Accordingly, he has made ample room for a legal system that condemned pleasurable, as well as profitable, deeds associated with murder; in addition, he has stoically, as it were, relinquished control of his personal liberty to the State with a view to being prevented from enjoying exorbitant pleasure: even though "pleasure is the sole good in the world, anyone's pleasure turns to someone's pain", he has reflected. Hence his pragmatic conclusion: "Let law watch for everyone."

At this critical stage it does seem that, as a law-abiding citizen, Guido Franceschini has taken the legal system to be a valid reference point. "What's Law?" he has wondered, thus unknowingly echoing his contemporary Thomas Hobbes and subscribing to his theory of a social contract between a benevolent ruler and death-fearing subjects. Regrettably, he has broken the agreement and consequently found himself duty-bound to suffer the consequences. More grievously, albeit professedly allured by Morality and Religion, he has failed to comply with God's commandments, namely with precepts well above man's law. At the same time, he appears to have been acutely aware that Faith was dead and that its demise was, as 'love of money' has been termed in a bible verse, the 'root of all evil'.[12] On the other hand, he has been able to see that every cloud has a silver lining: "Unbelief still might work the wires and move man, the machine, to play a faithful part", he has remarked and, in doing so, made a statement redolent of Augustine of Hippo's contention that truth and wisdom are achievable solely by belief in the Word of God, i.e. by virtue of a feeling capable of removing the stain caused by guilt, hubris and insubordination. The Cardinal and the Abate had discarded gold and picked up dross whereas he, compelled to choose between "entire faith, or else complete unbelief" had opted for the former, notwithstanding the pain inherent in the choice – to little avail though, for the visiting prelates had left him "i' the lurch at the first spit of rain."

But then again, Guido has subsequently put forth, "who holds to faith whenever rain begins? No case but has its conduct, faith prescribes: where's the obedience that shall edify?" Indeed, he had insisted on seeking pleasure because "Time is brief, and death ends good and ill and everything"; furthermore, since faith was likely to produce the best results, there was nothing wrong with feigning it if ever the occasion arose.

Nothing philosophically wrong, that's for sure. At an educated guess Guido's utterance has sounded in tune with the utilitarian tenet that if it is probable that the a probably good pretence will is morally acceptable.

The ensuing topic has revolved around a touch of heartedness in the broader context of dullness: laughter had been credited over the centuries with having therapeutic value, the speaker has recalled, and it was a crying shame that both secular and religious hypocrites should have halted the merriment by bringing a guillotine into the open. Regrettably, laughter-loving Romans had been castigated by would-be serious-minded individuals, the likes of the Cardinal and the Abbot who had enjoined him, a pleasure-loving high-born gentleman, to cover his wolf-like skin with ovine wool. As a corollary, he had become engaged in playing "a desperate game, but game wherein the winner's chance were worth the pains to try conclusions" in the hope of mitigating the effects of an evil deed; at the end of the day, nothing was worse than a fast-approaching "*Mannaia*-machine".

'All's but a flourish, figure of rhetoric! One must try each expedient to save life", Guido has commented on the above as a Ciceronian way out of a *mea culpa*. In truth he was a jaundiced fool maddened by jealousy and expected to "prove a lynx and look the heart, the stone wall, through and through"; in effect, no one other than God had such an eye, and all he would be saying to the

Almighty in due course was that, yes, he was one huge and sheer mistake, yet not a culpable human being: come to think of it, he had not been the begetter of himself.

The concluding biologically significant has followed a linguistic oscillation between metaphor and metonymy, namely between figures of speech deemed to be paradigmatic tokens of the way in which discourse gets organized:[13] Guido has been too clever by half in justifying his rhetorical seesawing as a desperate effort to save his own skin; in addition, he has reneged on his previous acceptance of full responsibility by reminding God that he had not made himself and telling the Cardinal and the Abbot that what they had called a crime was little more than a blunder. On the other hand, it can be argued that his urgent request to the visitors to put him "back to the crossroad" and allow him to "start afresh" has provided a dramatic instance of applied ethics. But here's the rub: anyone believing that God's creatures have been fully responsible for their actions since Adam's and Eve's Edenic transgression has reason to deduce that, philosophically speaking, Guido has failed to set up a link between descriptively ethical premises and the meaning of moral words.

An ambivalent act of introspection has subsequently taken place: the Cardinal and the Abate, confessors by trade, have been told that he, admittedly a domineering husband, had been moved by a wife's dark eyes fraught with fright; by the same token he had resented her wincing at the contact with his body, for he was "young in soul nor old in body", a "steel man worth ten times the crude" even though "good folks" had made remarks about 'the ... hem! the ... all of you though somewhat old' being offered to a woman who was making her gender-specific "passiveness her pleasure"; the impudent onlookers had made him think of a female sex unable to defy maleness, and he had wondered why he should be content with "the dust of the end precisely at the starting point." In connection with the gender issue, he has referred to his wife as "a nullity in female shape" and added that, in consequence, he had been compelled to banish her from his domain, – a drastic measure, it should be noted, which has thrown into sharp relief the image of a man unable to perceive that, by the very virtue of her absence, Pompilia had impaired the substructure of gender asymmetry.

As an extra precaution, the Count has put his disagreeable spouse on a par with Violante, a veritable Chimaera, and Pietro, a "Sir Dignity i' the dumps"; in effect, he has, by making cruel remarks about *Signor* and *Signora* Comparini, turned the tables on them: the "old pretentious fools" had brought to light the teeth of a wolf disguised as a sheep as the same time as they had deprived him of a dowry and nipped in the bud the life he had embarked on; in addition, they had proved oblivious to the difference between right and wrong and been utterly unconcerned about the prospect of divine retribution. To add insult to injury, the "two ambiguous insects" had buzzed him deaf, stung him blind and stunk him with fetor in the face until he had felt morally bound to put an end to his ordeal. Heavens above, had he really felt so? One is reminded of how, in a strikingly similar manner, a hypersensitive Duke of Ferrara had felt obliged to stop all the smiles provoked by the conduct of his 'last duchess painted on the wall'.[14]

At this advanced stage of the encounter in the secluded cell, the prisoner's apologetic diatribe has given an insight into the subtleties of the Roman murder case: the speaker has denoted moral emotions as well as a desire to arouse similar emotions in hopefully sympathetic hearers. To put it in linguistic terms, he has fulfilled a *conative* function of verbal communication by virtue of aiming, as an addresser, at a *phatic* contact with the addressee. Moreover, his selfish, gloom-ridden nature has been lightened by a streak of religiously tinged hedonism when he has seen Pompilia as "flesh of his flesh, bone of his bone, the bride to groom as is the Church and Spouse to Christ". As such, she had been urged to submit to him in compliance with God's command in the wake of the disobedience in the garden of yore. She had obliged, but then again, "strong as stone", she had been playing a "new game of giving up the game", – a positive game in the face of his sentiments, – and in the process had committed "this worst offence of not offending more". In this respect, it has been argued that '*game* in the positive sense – the ludic disportings of disruption and desire – plays itself out … in an endless conflict and collusion'.[15]

In addition, Guido has gone on to recount how Pompilia had made him reach the point where he had wondered to what degree her apparent self-possession differed from "the terrible patience of God." Had she been feeling not a jot of love for him? "Let her show the more, sham the worse, damn herself praiseworthily", he has propounded. In effect, she had refused to tell a lie that could pave the way for the truth and declined to "feign the love that brings real love about"; therefore, he had passed judgement and punished her.

If Guido's expostulations are anything to go by, punishment has been the very name of the game, but could the 'game' be justified? It may if one accepts the view that 'punishment is by its nature retributive, yet it can be validated along utilitarian lines.'[16] In this connection, it would be hard to ignore Paracelsus' question: 'what use were punishment, unless some sin be first detected?'[17] Sin can meet with forgiveness, to be sure, but, as Paul wrote to the Hebrews, 'without the shedding of blood there is no forgiveness of sins.'[18] In the light of the aforementioned, there may be some justification for Guido's punitive deed. A relevant question would be did he, as a utilitarian fellow, hate Pompilia merely for the sake of pleasure? A matter of "pure nature", her husband has stated. Honest to God, he had searched his soul for any fault of his and found none. That and no other was the naked truth! .

At this juncture, an ethics-related crack has shown up in the Count's shield against condemnation: the moral foundations of his marriage have been shaken by his belief that falsehood coupled with a pretence of love might well be the lesser evil – an endorsement of the utilitarian acceptance of an amoral stance whenever it is probable that the outcome of it will be more beneficial than the upshot of an ethical stance. That's all well and good, but it's worth mentioning that latter-day mathematicians have suggested that the probability of an event is the ratio of limited possibilities and unlimited ones, and it is therefore far from easy to delineate a stretch of clear blue water between the realm of the possible and that of the probable.

Guido has sleepwalked, as it were, into a logical trap and on awaking has boldly asked to be given a second chance now that, as a grown-up, he was capable of defying social tyranny and therefore "fit guide for Guido's self". The paronomastic juxtaposition of a first name and a common noun smacks of dramatic irony and connotes a desire enmeshed in a constricting social fabric. Such being the case, the nobleman at issue has, by virtue of a distorted mirror image, paradoxically seen himself as an autonomous, self-legislating individual. Here we go again! Not much later his harangue has taken a bitter tone: the two churchmen had caused, in virtue of their stupidity and insolence, the eruption of a "pent-up soul" which they had "prisoned first and played with afterward", and the soul's volcanic nature had reacted by producing more fire and sulphur than either could have wished for. As a result, the Cardinal and the Abate had been beaten at their own game and, honest to God, had better blame themselves for the debacle – an extravagant brickbat, it's fair to say, which, interestingly, recalls the pre-Freudian doctrine that desire is perfectly natural and therefore beyond the control of manipulative spiritual leaders.

Elaborating on the vicissitudes of his life, Guido Franceschini has recounted how he had played the legal and political game, donned a clerical collar, and in the end found himself echoing the apostle Paul's assertion that the letter kills, but the spirit gives life.[19] A contrary viewpoint springs to mind pronto: 'the letter can produce all the effects of truth in man without involving the spirit at all.'[20] Has Guido stuck to the letter or acted in accordance with the spirit? It is an open question: significantly, this perpetrator of murderous violence has voiced the conviction that his failure to produce a masterstroke had been engendered by mere misfortune. "The impossible was effected", he has bragged: the entire Comparini household had been caught unawares in their den and swiftly disposed of; the priest was with them and had survived the ordeal by sheer luck. At this point, the description of the dire event does sound inconsistent with the previous sworn testimony.

Within the space of a few words, Guido has recalled how the force of destiny had made him bump, while plodding along the road to safety, into "the one scrupulous fellow in all Rome" who had taken no notice of his offer of a double bribe, presentation of himself as a Duke, and mention – in an antisemitic mood, arguably – that "the dead man was only a Jew". Then, a quirk of fate had allowed his pale frail wife to live long enough "to tell her own story her own way and turn [his] plausibility to nothingness" – an ironic twist, because, in all frankness, he had travelled to Rome mainly to claim his wife and, more importantly, his newborn baby.

By the sound of it, a family member has gone through an intimate moment and revealed ambivalent feelings created by a subliminal concern with the 'mystery of the father'. Similarly, the subsequent assertion that "'t is fate, not fortune. All is of a piece!" calls to mind the mood of a thinker torn between a belief in free will and the acceptance of forces that are outside human control – a chasm bridgeable by sharing the latter-day view that determinism is compatible with the freedom of the will without fear of contradiction.

Next, an iota of sarcasm has been suggested by the mention of the four rustics complicit in the murder and then "cherishing a scheme all of their honest country homespun wit" to cut the Count's throat solely because he had forgotten to give them their due. In response, he cherished the hope that he would finally "see them dangling high on either hand, like scarecrows in a hemp-field; for their pains!"

The feeling, redolent of a master-slave relationship, has preceded the claim, – presumably motivated by a sense of having been hurt like hell by the violence of friends and foes, – that lawyers and judges had rubbed salt into their victim's wound by making him set forth on a trudge along a "path twixt crosses leading to a skull ... bloodied by [his] palms" – a biblical picture arguably inspired by Guido's priestly background.

There was, however, "a cranny of escape" from crucifixion, the prisoner has let the visitors know: the senescent Pope might be touched by pity and absolve him after full confession; surely His Holiness could deal with him as a father would with a son, and just as surely he was the kind of offspring that gets "strength from being thrust to the wall ... a brave fighter who succumbs to odds that turn defeat to victory".

On the other hand, there was a dark side to the matter: success could easily make him go his "old ways and find things grown grey". Now, did the change of colour signify no "second chance"? Not really, for a silver lining was being supplied by himself and his son as they swapped lives with each other. Even so, as a father still in his prime, he was under no moral obligation to relinquish the benefits of youth to his offspring: at the end of the day, he was a man desirous of a dish of robins yet unwilling to trudge through sleet and snow in pursuit of the little songbirds.

At this juncture, Guido's subconscious grasp of the 'mystery of the father' has brought to the fore the duality of a mind under the sway of a biological imperative. In this connection, his bloodlust has been alleviated by a streak of religiosity compounded of Christianity and Paganism: "Name me a primitive religionist ... one sprung ... from fauns and nymphs, trunks and the heart of oak", he has theosophically stated. Qua a believer in a natural environment, he has contrasted the limitations of humanity with the limitless expanse of nature and expressed his approval of any "rite the fancy may demand", thus admitting the significance of the ritualistic death depicted in biblical as well as in pagan stories. He has also suggested a gradual awareness of unknown modes of being in a manner redolent of Wordsworth's *The Prelude*, videlicet the working of an animistic universe on the mind. In Guido's case the sustained phenomenon has led to murder and significantly provided a brand-new clue as to the motives behind the murderer's deed.

In a similar fashion, the close link between the natural world and that of mankind has been turned to good account: the Christian masque worn as a substitute for the pagan one has not ignored "the inexorable need in man for life"; consequently, the pristine martyrdom has been superseded by Eros, namely the instinct for self-preservation and enjoyment of life. "The letter kills, what then? The spirit saves us unmistakeably", the primitive religionist has averred, echoing again Paul's letter to the Corinthians, and boasted of his inherited unified strength whilst he battled with loss of confidence.

A focus on his divided self helps put the interrelation between the Count and his family into perspective: the threshold of security has been lowered by his fear of being engulfed by the implosive presence of kith and kin. The evolution of religion has compounded the inner split in so far as it has sanctioned his attachment to life and perpetuated the conflict between a damning *letter* and a redeeming *spirit*. He has got to the bottom of the conundrum and discovered that he was standing "on solid earth, not empty air". At the same time, he has felt as though he was on the horns of a dilemma: if he decided to "turn wolf, be whole, and sate, for once" to the detriment of his incomplete humanity, he would nonetheless be liable to return to the state of a "deformed, transformed, reformed, informed, conformed" human being. Alas, he has been caught up in what has been described by a radical feminist as 'an ideological theatre where the multiplications of representations, images, reflections, myths, identifications constantly transforms, deforms, alters each person's imaginary order and, in advance, renders all conceptualization null and void.'[21] The condition would be on a par with 'the healthy spontaneous amnesia of the animal who has wilfully repressed its own sordid determinations and so is free.'[22] Intriguingly, the combination of a touch of Pauline philosophy of life and a flavour of Nietzschean ethics has spawned the vision of a "honest instinct, pent and crossed through life" strong enough to ascend in the shape of fire to the mountain peaks and perceptive enough to leave "the streamlet [Pompilia] for the vale".

The Pre-Socratic Heraclitus saw fire as inherent in the *Logos*, the latter being a controlling primordial element capable of bringing about the 'strife' essential for the unification of opposites such as fire and water. Pompilia, in Guido's eyes a watery frame with "no run o' the red thread through that insignificance", has not appeared to possess the wisdom necessary for perceiving the *Logos* as a rational principle existing in her soul and an integral, as well as fiery, element on earth. Ditto Guido, for all his vision of "the fiery pavement" of hell. By way of comment, it may be said that both the Aretine husband and the Roman wife have not managed to realize their oneness.

The physical reality investigated by the Pre-Socratics has taken centre stage anew when the Cardinal and the Abate have been accused of hardening the Count's heart with their dew and then soaking the solid stuff "in waters that but touch to petrify"; but then, they themselves were "petrifications of a kind", not to put too fine a point on it.

Et voila! The metaphor has conjured up the image of a mind keen on denying the autonomy of the owner of it. The accuser has aimed for somebody else's depersonalisation, even reification, and, ironically, been himself petrified by a dreadful feeling underlying the effort: his *anima* has come out into the open and revealed the Self sporting a Medusa-like head while being eager for a reassuring response from the Other. Pompilia has flashed a watery glance at her incandescent husband and, by an amazing twist of fate, her moisture has quenched his raging flames. In contrast to the man's ontological insecurity, the young woman has displayed a confident personality; her parents have done likewise and, last in line, so have the Cardinal and the Abbot, whereas he, in the teeth of his "implacable, persistent in revenge" ego, has been engulfed, petrified, depersonalised. At this defining moment, his state of mind has corroborated the psychoanalytic assertion that 'when aggression is projected outwards, and deflected onto others through identification, it rounds back upon itself in a persecutory manner, and the typical defence against persecutory anxi-ety … is schizoid splitting.'[23] In this connection, it helps to take account of the theory that 'the paranoid-schizoid position … is essentially a preparation for psychic integration'[24]. On the strength of it, Guido Franceschini's subsequent line of argument has sounded like a frantic bid for emotional and moral recovery, unwittingly along the lines of the Greek king who had declared that "God's most lordly gift to man is decency of mind."[25] Dismally torn apart, the Count has imploded and felt impelled to beg the Cardinal to intercede with the Pope on his behalf, for he was entitled to freedom and, in the absence of it, powerful friends of him and foes of the Church would avenge him; more importantly, would the Holy Father "send a soul straight to perdition, dying frank an atheist?" At this moment in time, the duality in his psyche has re-emerged: a mundane menace of revenge has become intertwined with an avowed atheist's yearning for salvation; significantly, he has recognised his agnostic soul as an integral part of his personality and a great help to him in the darkness created by the crass stupidity of people like the two prelates. A patriarch's plangent remark is here apropos: the wicked 'do not know the light. For deep darkness is morning to all of them'[26]. Furthermore, the mind goes to the Manichaean conflict between darkness and light, i.e. between good and evil, and to how Guido has placed the Church in the shadows. Conversely, a celebrated alchemist has been made to say at death's door, 'If I stoop into a dark tremendous sea of cloud, it is but for a time; I press God's lamp close to my breast; its splendour, soon or late, will pierce the gloom. I shall emerge one day'.[27] For his part, the self-proclaimed primitivist has maintained that "the darkness let alone grows tolerable twilight; one may grope and get to guess at length and breadth and depth". Then, without taking a break, he has professed himself victimized and turned the tables on the visiting priests for being active participants in a blatant violation of human rights. Death was hanging above his head like the sword of Damocles, he has lamented, yet he saw himself as a wolf fighting sedately, while Pompilia bleated, and as a man beginning to savour his "strength, careless, gay even". For all that, "what's the worth of life?" he has wondered, and here is where Guido has sounded like a man reassured by his animal instincts and resolved to bridge the dichotomy between his conflicting selves even though his wondering about the worth of life has left the desired unification hanging in the balance.

In conclusion, dynamics appears to have been part and parcel of Guido's stance in so far as he has gone on to depict the clergymen he is facing as waves ending in foam and himself as an undulating line of water "o'ertaken, pushed to the front" and turning into mist. In the broader context of life and death, the impressionist Virginia Woolf has made the imaginative Bernard spread his wings and state, 'Yes, this is eternal renewal, the incessant rise and fall and fall and rise again. And in me too the wave rises. It swells; it arches its back. I am aware once more of a new desire, something rising beneath me ... against you I will fling myself, unvanquished and unyielding, O Death!'[28] In the Count's eyes the lemming-like rush to death has reached the moment of truth: the floating clerics "will rock vertiginously in turn, and reel, and emulative, rush to death". However, the 'game' will not have come to an end, for the dead and the living are intertwined: "You never know what life is till you die; even throughout life", the doomed fellow has added; "'t is death that makes life live, gives it whatever the significance", for "what's love, what's faith without a worst to dread?"

At the end of the line 'the waves broke on the shore', the narrator finally recalls in *The Waves*. For his part, Guido has brought up a cosmic element when he has confidently averred: "unmanned, remade; I hold it probable. You soon shall see the use of fire!" Here Heraclitus' primary substance has, to all appearances, been put to good use by virtue of being related to other basic elements such as the water and the air, and the conjunction intimates a sudden awareness of the *Logos*. On the strength of being a connecting factor, the rational principle has helped the Count perceive that "all that was, is, and must for ever be", but at the same time his necessitarian view of events has prompted him to deny the freedom of the will. Unable to get rid of his hateful disposition, he has laid with a vengeance into Pietro, Violante and Pompilia while maintaining by contrast that he was going to "take man's chance, honest and bold: right will be done to such." Clearly, the inner division of a productive as well as destructive human being has come to the fore anew and it is worthwhile to recall the psychoanalytic concept that creation and destruction 'are both answers to the same need for transcendence.'[29] At the eleventh hour, the foxed blue-blooded gentleman has promised to live henceforth as an "honest and bold" man, but, oh my! his oath has been made hollow by the appearance of the "Frightful Brotherhood of Death". A sudden panicky mood has made him yell: "Treachery!" and then, reaching a crescendo: "All was folly; I laughed and mocked! Sirs, my first true word, all true and no lie, is … life is all! Let the madman live … I am yours; I am the Granduke's – no, I am the Pope's! Abate, Cardinal, Christ, Maria, God … Pompilia, will you let them murder me?"

The anguished appeal has arguably been the manifestation of an acute sense of belonging caused by the self/other juxtaposition coupled with a feeling engendered by the stirrings of moral consciousness: Guido's self-proclaimed inner fire – how unlike Aristotle's and Thales' appreciation of the cosmic element![30] – has filled him with dread of being made a thing stripped of its identity. By nullifying his wife, he has endeavoured to destroy her petrified subjectivity and ended up with a severely diminished sense of security alongside a loss of ontological autonomy; in other words, the intrusion of 'alien' people has made his 'false self' dream of being a free man living in a prison without bars. At the end of the day, the proximity of Death has made his 'true self' realise that all the previous laughing and mocking had been the token of a conflictual interaction between mind and body. At this climactic moment he has refuted his own credo and confessed to mendacity, – alas, a tad late in the day: his overall attitude has corroborated a philosopher's contention that 'the quest for truth, especially perhaps for the truth about ourselves, is not a sure path to freedom.'[31] Ironically, the *moriturus*' cry, "Life is all!" has connoted a sense of belonging to some of the people with whom he had had social intercourse, and the perception has made him turn to them as sorely needed saviours. Paradoxically, the ill-starred gentleman has betrayed a crying need for corroborative evidence from his former foes that he was a real, unified human being, and it is psychologically feasible to make sense of the need by recalling the cogent assertion that 'a mature and creative psychic organization depends upon an open, revisable sense of self-identity and a willingness to embrace emotional support and change'.[32] Guido Franceschini's trial is a case in point: a man motivated by a reductive ego primarily concerned with survival has sensed that, instead of showing his true self, he has been wearing a *persona* and, as it has been pertinently noted down, '*personare* meant, originally, to "speak through" another, usually by way of an ancestral mask'[33]. Ultimately, qua a 'normal' human desirous of speaking *proprie*, – that is to say, exclusively for himself, – the Count has experienced an overwhelming urge to uncover his face and reject his 'false self'. In this respect, his poignant entreaty to Pompilia has encircled his young spouse's head with a halo as a substitution for the ring with which he had mockingly associated her in the past. "'T is a figure, a symbol, say', Browning has stated early in his poem and Pompilia has made the symbol come to the fore. The appeal to her for a way out of the 'treachery' personified as a Company of Death has pointed to salvation as the name of the game. One is reminded of the fifteenth-century Earl Thorold Thresham declaiming, while referring to his sister Mildred, 'Would she, or could she, err, much less confound, all guilts of treachery, of craft … Avert, oh God, only this woe from me!'[34] At the end of the day, there is good reason to suspect a touch of psychosis in the character of the 'normal' Guido, for he has wreaked havoc on natural cycle of life, notably on the social, notably familial, element in it. Nonetheless his dying plea can be deemed to be a balancing act of faith performed by a psychopath who has finally come to his senses and, guilt-ridden, has vowed to "take man's chance, honest and bold"; to put it in another way, his self-denigrating supplication has intimated the presence of a narcissistic ego capable of critical self-reflection. Regrettably, the flip side of the fellow's positive attitude is that his anarchic desire appears to have been tragically at odds with a consciousness of impotence engendered by duality and disorientation. It has been aptly observed in this respect that his frame of mind irresistibly evokes the state of Man described as 'chaos of thought and passion, all confused', the epitome of a 'great lord of all things, yet a prey to all; sole judge of truth, in endless error hurled; the glory, jest, and riddle of the world!'[35] Engulfed in the shadows of an endless night, Guido Franceschini has let out the strident call of a diminutive *Homo sapiens* frantically attempting to solve a conundrum while staring into an abyss.

"The somehow may be thishow", Robert Browning has put forth in his presentation of *The Ring and the Book*. Along similar lines, it has been maintained that 'actual distinctness or the physical existence with which we are acquainted is finally accounted for by a form of "thisness" or *haecceitas*'.[36]

'Be it so. Amen!'[37]

1. Jacques Lacan, in *Psychoanalytic Theory*, p. 92
2. Robert Robert Browning, *The Bishop Orders His Tomb at St. Praxed's Church.*
3. *Western Philosophy and Philosophers*, p. 93
4. Robert Browning, *The Bishop Orders His Tomb at St. Praxed's Church.*
5. W. B. Yeats, *Easter 1916*
6. Jacques Lacan, in *Modern Criticism and Theory*, p. 102
7. Emily Brontë, *Wuthering Heights*, Ch. 9
8. Jacques Lacan, as referred to in *Psychoanalytic Theory*, p. 96
9. Samuel Butler, as quoted in *Literary History of England*, Routledge & Kegan Paul, 3rd Ed. p. 814
10. As quoted in *Western Philosophy and Philosophers*, p. 28

11. Robert Browning, *Pippa Passes*, Part I, ll. 134-36
12. 1 *Timothy* 6.10
13. Roman Jakobson, in *Modern Criticism and Theory*, pp. 57ff
14. Robert Browning, *My Last Duchess*, ll. 1 & 4
15. Terry Eagleton, *Capitalism, modernism and postmodernism*, in *Modern Criticism and Theory*, p. 389
16. Thomas Hobbes, as referred to in *Western Philosophy and Philosophers*, p. 136
17. Robert Browning, *Paracelsus*, Pt. 2, ll. 278-79
18. *Letter to the Hebrews*, 9. 22
19. *Cor.* 3.6
20. Jacques Lacan, *The Insistence of the Letter in the Unconscious*, in *Modern Criticism and Theory*, p. 91
21. Hélène Cixous, *Sorties*, in Modern Criticism and Theory, p. 292
22. Terry Eagleton, *ibid.*
23. Melanie Klein, in *Psychoanalytic Theory*, p.78
24. Melanie Klein, in *Op. Cit.* p. 79
25. Aeschylus, *Agamemnon*, ll. 927-28
26. *Job*, 24. 16-17
27. Robert Browning, *Paracelsus*, Pt.4, ll.899ff
28. *The Waves*, Granada Publishing 1979, p. 200
29. Eric Fromm, in *Psychoanalytic Theory*, p. 45
30. *Western Philosophy and Philosophers*, p. 261
31. Michel Foucault, as referred to in *Op. Cit.* p. 112
32. Anthony Elliott, in *Psychoanalytic Theory*, p. 156
33. Geoffrey Hartman, *The Interpreter's Freud*, in *Modern Criticism and Theory*, p. 423

34. Robert Browning, *A Blot in the 'Scutcheon*, Act 2, ll. 128-133
35. Alexander Pope, *An Essay on Man*, Epistle II, ll. 13ff
36. John Duns Scotus, as referred to in *Western Philosophy and Philosophers*, p. 295
37. Gonzalo, in William Shakespeare's *The Tempest*, Act 5, Scene 1, l. 215

THE BOOK and the RING

Standing full erect within the walls of his Paddington abode, Robert Browning tapped his fingers on the cover of his faded yellow book. "Here were the end, had anything an end," he uttered in an undertone; "thus, lit and launched, up and up roared and soared a rocket, till the key o' the vault was reached, and wide heaven held, a breathless minute-space. The act, over and ended, falls and fades, a tinge the less in every fresh transmission; till it melts, trickles in silent orange or wan grey across our memory, dies and leaves all dark ... and presently we find the stars again!" The soliloquist reached for his antique cabinet and focused on a thin batch of glossy missives waiting for a reader. He grasped the nearest to him and murmured, "A letter from a stranger, man of rank, Venetian visitor at Rome" before breaking the seal and letting his piercing eyes run through the lines.

'Here we are at our end of Carnival; prodigious gaiety and monstrous mirth. The old Pope totters on the verge o' the grave. A week ago, the sun was warm like May and the old man took daily exercise along the riverside: he loves to see that custom house he built upon the bank, for Naples-born, his tastes are maritime. They say, the trust that keeps his heart alive is that, by lasting till December next, he may hold Jubilee a second time and, twice in one reign, ope the Holy Doors.'

A blank led to the following paragraph: 'Now, from such matters to divert awhile, hear of today's event which crowns the week. Tell Dandolo I owe him fifty drops of heart's blood in the shape of old *zecchini*! The Pope has done his worst: I have to pay for the execution of the Count, by Jove! Two days since, I reported him as safe, re-echoing the conviction of all Rome: who could suspect the one deaf ear – the Pope? But prejudices grow insuperable; these fairly got the better in the man of justice, prudence, and *esprit de corps*, and he persisted in the butchery.

Also, 't is said that in his latest walk to the Dogana-by-the-Bank, he built, the crowd, – he suffers question, unrebuked, – asked whether murder was a privilege only reserved for nobles like the Count, and he was ever mindful of the mob. The substituting, too, the People's Square for the out-o'-the-way old quarter by the Bridge, was meant as a conciliatory sop to the mob; it gave one holiday the more.'

There was another empty space and then: '*Palchetti* were erected in the Place, and houses, at the edge of the Three Streets, let their front windows at six dollars each. Now for the thing: no sooner the decree gone forth, – 't is four-and-twenty hours ago, – than Acciaioli and Panciatichi, old friends, indeed compatriots of the man, were closeted ere cock-crow with the Count. They both report their efforts to dispose the unhappy man for ending well were crowned at last with a complete success: and when the company of Death arrived, the Count was led down, hoisted up on car, last of the five, as heinousest, you know. His intrepidity, nay, nonchalance, struck admiration in those who saw. Then the procession started, took the way from the New Prisons by the Pilgrim's Street and so debouched thence at *Mannaia*'s foot in *Piazza del Popolo*. As is evident, we had the titillation as we sat: now did a car run over, kill a man just opposite a pork-shop numbered Twelve, – and bitter were the outcries of the mob against the Pope: for, but that he forbids the Lottery, why, twelve were Tern Quatern! – now did a beggar by Saint Agnes, lame from his youth up, recover use of leg through prayer of Guido as he glanced that way: so that the crowd near crammed his hat with coin. Thus was kept up excitement to the last, and so all ended ere you well could wink! We hardly noticed how the peasants died: they dangled somehow soon to right and left, and we remained all ears and eyes, could give ourselves to Guido undividedly. He begged forgiveness on the part of God, and fair construction of his act from men, whose suffrage he entreated for his soul; which said, he turned to the confessor, crossed and reconciled himself with decency, and, with the name of Jesus on his lips, received the fatal blow. The headsman showed the head to the populace. Must I avouch we strangers own to disappointment here? Indeed, it was no face to please a wife! So died the man, and so his end was peace; whence many a moral were to meditate.'

The philosophical reflection made Browning refrain from further reading. "You've sputtered into sparks" he murmured while folding the Venetian visitor's missive. "What streak comes next? he wondered as he returned the item to the cabinet. A second postal item fell into his hands. He quickly realised that it had been composed by Don Giacinto Arcangeli, "the virtuous sire, the valiant for the truth" for the benefit of Cencini, an advocate himself, "knit up with the bowels of the case" and a friend of Franceschini. "To this Cencini's care I owe the Book", the poet said to his invisible listener, "the yellow thing I take and toss once more, whence came the other stuff, went, you know how, to make the ring that's all but round and done. He unsealed the epistle without delay and set about reading.

"Late they arrived, too late, egregious Sir, those same justificative points you urge might benefit His Blessed Memory Count Guido Franceschini now with God. I, with expenditure of pains enough, obtained a respite, leave to claim and prove exemption from the law's award, – alleged the power and privilege o' the Clericate: to which effect a courier was despatched. But ere an answer from Arezzo came, the Holiness of our Lord the Pope (prepare!) saw fit, by his particular chirograph, to derogate, dispense with privilege, and wink at any hurt accruing thence to Mother Church through damage of her son. So that all five, to-day, have suffered death with no distinction save in dying, – he, decollated by way of privilege, the rest hanged decently and in order. Thus came the Count to his end of gallant man, defunct in faith and exemplarity, nor shall the shield of his great House lose shine, nor its blue banner blush to red thereby! He had commiseration and respect in his decease from universal Rome, the nice and cultivated everywhere. Needs must I groan o'er my debility, attribute the untoward event o' the strife to nothing but my own crass ignorance which failed to set the valid reasons forth, find fit excuse: such is the fate of war!'

The reader unleashed a knowing smile and turned a page. 'On the next leaf – '*Hactenus senioribus*! There, old fox, show the clients t' other side and keep this corner sacred, I beseech! What was the good of twenty Clericates when Somebody's thick headpiece once was bent on seeing Guido's drop into the bag? How these old men like giving youth a push! Much good I get by my superb defence!" A wry smile supplanted the previous one. "But thou, Cencini, brother of my breast; o fox, whose home is 'mid the tender grape, whose couch in Tuscany by Themis' throne, subject to no such … but I shut my mouth or only open it again to say, – this pother and confusion fairly laid, my hands are empty and my satchel lank. *Reliqua differamus in crastinum*! "My boy, your godson, fat-chaps Giacinto, enjoyed the sight while Papa plodded here. I promised him, the rogue, a month ago, – the day his birthday was, of all days, – that if I failed to save Count Guido's head, Cinuzzo should at least go see it chopped. Accordingly he sat there, bold in box, proud as the Pope behind the peacock-fans. He's long since out of Caesar, – eight years old – and as for tripping in Eutropius … well, reason the more that we strain every nerve to do him justice, mould a model-mouth, a Bartolus-cum-Baldo for next age: for *that* I purse the pieces, work the brain. Cinuzzo will be gainer by it all!'

The letter had reached its last line. The reader sedately put it back on the cabinet and picked up the third and last message. It transpired that it had been written by the "tall blue-eyed Fisc whose head [was] clapped with cloud", Doctor Bottini, and intended for "no matter who". It gave cause for a quick comment. "Now shall the honest championship of right, crowned with success, enjoy at last, unblamed, moderate triumph! Now shall eloquence pour forth in fancied floods for virtue's sake! Here has been truth at issue with a lie; let who gained truth the day have handsome pride in his own prowess!" A puzzled expression suddenly crossed the poet's face. "Eh? What ails the man?" A perusal of the text was a must.

'Well, it is over, ends as I foresaw: easily proved, Pompilia's innocence! I had, as usual, the plain truth to plead. I always knew the clearness of the stream would show the fish so thoroughly, child might prong the clumsy monster: with no mud to splash, small credit to lynx-eye and lightning spear! This Guido, – much sport he contrived to make! – finished, as you expect, a penitent, fully confessed his crime and made amends, died like a saint, poor devil! That's the man the gods still give to my antagonist: imagine how Arcangeli claps wing! What with the plain truth given me to uphold, and, should I let truth slip, the Pope at hand to pick up, steady her on legs again, my office turns a pleasantry indeed! I knew Arcangeli would grin and brag: but what say you to one impertinence might move a man? That monk, you are to know, that barefoot Augustinian whose report o' the dying woman's words did detriment to my best points it took the freshness from, – that meddler preached to purpose yesterday. Out comes his sermon smoking from the press: its text: "Let God be true, and every man a liar" – and its application, this, the longest-winded of the paragraphs, I straight unstitch, tear out and treat you with. Remember it, as I engage to do!'

"God, who seems acquiescent in the main with those who add "So will He ever sleep", flutters their foolishness from time to time, puts forth His right hand recognizably. Because Pompilia's purity prevails, conclude you, all truth triumphs in the end? How many chaste and noble sister-fames wanted the extricating hand, and lie strangled, for one Pompilia proud above the welter, plucked from the world's calumny, stupidity, simplicity, – who cares?"

A short hiatus followed, and then "Romans! An elder race possessed your land long ago, and a false faith lingered still, as shades do, though the morning-star be out. Doubtless, some pagan o' the twilight day has often pointed to a cavern-mouth and said, – nor he a bad man, no, nor fool, – only a man, so, blind like all his mates, – 'Here skulk in safety, lurk, defying law, the devotees to execrable creed. What rites obscene – their idol-god, an Ass!' So went the word forth, so acceptance found, so century re-echoed century. Do you continue in the old belief? Where blackness bides unbroke, must devils be? Is it so certain, not another cell o' the myriad that make up the catacomb, contains some saint a second flash would show? Will you ascend into the light of day and, having recognized a martyr's shrine, go join the votaries that gape around each vulgar god that awes the marketplace? Be these the objects of your praising? See! Each statue of a god were fitlier styled demon and devil. Glorify no brass that shines like burnished gold in noonday glare, for fools! Be otherwise instructed, you! And preferably ponder, ere you pass, each incident of this strange human play privily acted on a theatre, was deemed secure from every gaze but God's, – till, of a sudden, earthquake lays wall low and lets the world see the wild work inside, and how, in petrifaction of surprise, the actors stand, – raised arm and planted foot, – despairing shriek, triumphant hate, – transfixed, both he who takes, and she who yields the life."

Another compact blank space led to "As ye become spectators of this scene, watch obscuration of a fame pearl-pure in vapoury films, enwoven circumstance, – a soul made weak by its pathetic want of just the first apprenticeship to sin, – as ye behold this web of circumstance deepen the more for every thrill and throe, convulsive effort to disperse the films and disenmesh the fame o' the martyr, – mark how all those means, the unfriended one pursues, to keep the treasure trusted to her breast, each struggle in the flight from death to life, how all, by procuration of the powers of darkness, are transformed: no single ray shot forth to show and save the inmost star, but passed as through hell's prism, proceeding black to the world that hates white. As ye watch, I say, hear Law, appointed to defend the just, submit, for best defence, that wickedness was bred of flesh and innate with the bone borne by Pompilia's spirit for a space, and no mere chance fault, passionate and brief. Finally, when ye find, – after this touch of man's protection which intends to mar the last pinpoint of light and damn the disc, – one wave of the hand of God amid the worlds bid vapour vanish, darkness flee away and leave the vexed star culminate in peace of the true instinct of an old man who happens to hate darkness and love light, – all this well pondered, I demand assent to the enunciation of my text in face of one proof more that 'God is true and every man a liar' – that who trusts to human testimony for a fact gets this sole fact: himself is proved a fool, – man's speech being false, if but by consequence that only strength is true while man is weak and, since truth seems reserved for heaven not earth, should learn to love what he may speak one day."

A third break in the inky blackness of the text ushered in further black marks. "I have long since renounced your world, ye know, yet weigh the worth of worldly prize foregone, disinterestedly judge this and that good ye account good: but God tries the heart. Still, if you question me of my content at having put each human pleasure by, I answer, at the urgency of truth, as this world seems, I dare not say I know whether I have not failed to taste some joy. For many a dream would fain perturb my choice, but, for one prize, best meed of mightiest man, repute o' the world, the flourish of loud trump, the softer social fluting, – oh, for these, no, my friends! Fame? That bubble which worldwide each blows and bids his neighbour lend a breath, that so he haply may behold thereon one more enlarged distorted false fool's-face? No, in renouncing fame, the loss was light; choosing obscurity, the chance was well!"

Such was the last of the 'longest-winded paragraphs' that made up Fra Celestino's sermon still 'smoking from the press'. Doctor Bottini was game for a snappy rejoinder.

'Didst ever touch such ampollosity as the man's own bubble, let alone its spite? What's his speech for, but just the flame he flouts? How he dares reprehend both high and low? If law be an inadequate machine, and advocacy so much impudence, we shall soon see, my blatant brother! That's exactly what I hope to show your sort! That Monastery of the Convertites – whereto the Court consigned Pompilia first, and whither she was late returned to die – claims every paul whereof may die possessed each sinner in the circuit of its walls. But here's the capital mistake: the Court found Guido guilty but pronounced no word about the innocency of his wife; it follows that Pompilia, unrelieved by formal sentence from imputed fault, remains unfit to have and to dispose of property, which law provides shall lapse: wherefore the Monastery claims its due. And whose, pray, whose the office, but the Fisc's? Who but I institute procedure next against the person of dishonest life, Pompilia, whom last week I sainted so? I, it is I, teach the monk what Scripture means! *Astraea redux*! I've a second chance before the self-same Court o' the Governor who soon shall see volte-face and chop, change sides! No adequate machinery in law? No power of life and death i' the learned tongue? Methinks I am already at my speech, startle the world with "Thou, Pompilia, thus? How is the fine gold of the Temple dim!" How like the heartlessness of the old hunks Arcangeli! His Count is hardly cold, his client whom his blunders sacrificed, when somebody must needs describe the scene – how the procession ended at the church that boasts the famous relic: quoth our brute, "Why, that's just Martial's phrase for 'make an end': *Ad umbilicum sic perventus est*!" He cuts a joke, and cares no more than so! I think my speech shall modify his mirth.'

The boast wrapped up the letter. The reader shook his head and countered, "Alack, Bottini, what is my next word but death to all that hope? The Instrument is plain before me, print that ends my Book with the definitive verdict of the Court 'in restitution of the perfect fame of dead Pompilia, *quondam* Guido's wife.' And so an end of all i' the story. Strain never so much my eyes, I miss the mark there lived or died that Gaetano, child of Guido and Pompilia; only find, immediately upon his father's death, a public attestation to the right o' the Franceschini to men's reverence. Apparently because of the incident o' the murder, there's no mention made of crime, but what else caused such urgency to cure the mob, just then, of chronic greediness for scandal, love of lying vanity, and appetite to swallow crude reports that bring annoyance to their betters? Bane which, here, was promptly met by antidote. There! Would you disbelieve stern History, trust rather to the babble of a bard?"

The poet made the letters disappear inside the cabinet and ambled back to the window. There he stood, motionless and wondering, his eyes glued to space. "Well, proving of such perfect parentage, our Gaetano, born of love and hate, did the babe live or die? – one fain would find! What were his fancies if he grew a man? Was he proud, – a true scion of the stock, – of bearing blazon, shall make bright my Book? Or did he love his mother, the base-born, and fight i' the ranks, un-noticed by the world?"

A valedictory utterance flowed freely through the questioner's lips. "Such, then, the final state o' the story. So did the Star Wormwood in a blazing fall frighten awhile the waters and lie lost; so did this old woe fade from memory, till after, in the fulness of the days, I needs must find an ember yet unquenched, and, breathing, blow the spark to flame. It lives, if precious be the soul of man to man. So, British Public, who may like me yet – marry and amen! – learn one lesson hence of many which whatever lives should teach: this lesson, that our human speech is naught, our human testimony false, our fame and human estimation words and wind. Why take the artistic way to prove so much? Because, it is the glory and good of Art, that Art remains the one way possible of speaking truth, to mouths like mine, at least. Which truth, by when it reaches him, looks false, seems to be just the thing it would supplant, nor recognizable by whom it left – while falsehood would have done the work of truth. But Art, – wherein man nowise speaks to men, only to mankind, – Art may tell a truth obliquely, do the thing shall breed the thought, nor wrong the thought, missing the mediate word. So may you paint your picture, twice show truth beyond mere imagery on the wall, – so, note by note, bring music from your mind, deeper than ever the *Andante* dived, – so write a book shall mean, beyond the facts, suffice the eye and save the soul beside." A deep sigh of relief floated down the quiet enclosed space. "And save the soul! If this intent save mine, – if the rough ore be rounded to a ring, render all duty which good ring should do, and, failing grace, succeed in guardianship, – might mine but lie outside thine, *Lyric Love*, thy rare gold ring of verse – the poet praised – linking our England to his Italy!"

The ecstatic epilogue echoed the prefatory assertion that the square old yellow book, "pure crude fact secreted from man's life" was "restorative i' the touch and sight"; as for the ring, "the rondure brave, the lilied loveliness, gold as it was, shall be evermore". The bard pricked up his ears: was a golden bell lyrically pealing out in the distance, he wondered?

"Here were the end, had anything an end"; the memory of an act may fade into obscurity and be engulfed in darkness until "*we find the stars again.*" On reflection, Robert Browning's concluding statement has sounded in harmony with Dante Alighieri's recollection of how he had surfaced at the end of his accidental trek through the *Inferno* and looked '*once more upon the stars*'.

Contrastingly, Guido Franceschini's wanderings through a Hell largely of his own making have not ended with 'the son of perdition' finally reaching Paradise and therefore 'the Love that moves the sun and the other stars'.

The impulse buyer of the Yellow Book dealing with the Arezzan aristocrat's unhappy vicissitudes has left Florence and regained his Paddington abode. Here he has succumbed to temptation and given undivided attention to a batch of letters sitting on his cabinet.

The first of the written messages, penned by a distinguished visitor from Venice, has mentioned the prodigiously gay and monstrously mirthful *Carnevale* celebrated in his lagoonal city and given serious attention to a presumably not too distant demise of the senescent Pope. In passing, he has touched on the wager he had placed on the outcome of the Franceschini case and lost primarily because the prejudiced and butchery-prone pontiff had persisted in being a butcher. Indeed, should the question arise as to whether the blunt reference to the Monarch-like, *most serene* Head of the Church has intimated a sizeable dose of animosity and secularism, an honest answer would take account of the fact that the visitor hailed from a *Serenissima* Republic.

In this context, a string of lines has focused on Guido Franceschini's "intrepidity, nay, nonchalance" in the face of death and then, in an ambivalent vein, on his sudden healing powers, not to mention his moving valedictory speech to the voyeuristic crowd and his devout acceptance of the fatal blow. By a touch of magic, King Charles has been brought into the dismal light of Whitehall and seen assuming a dignified posture prior to his beheading. In addition, lo and behold, the angelic-faced Christian protomartyr Stephan, has been praying God to forgive the crowd pelting him with stones at a Jerusalem gate. As for the Venetian witness to the Count's execution, it is safe to assume that a touch of shared class consciousness has gone hand in hand with an appreciation of how Guido's selfhood, unified at the eleventh hour, has connoted the Christian resignation of a pagan sinner.

Isaiah's message sounds peculiarly relevant: "Those who dwelt in a land of deep darkness, on them has light shined."[1]

The other side of the coin has shown Guido's severed head as something hideous enough to engender the scathing remark that 'it was no face to please a wife'. Despite that, the distinguished spectator has commented that 'his end was peace' and added, 'whence many a moral may meditate', thus making descriptive ethics play a key role in the scrutiny of an ontologically insecure, even fragmented, human being. Interestingly, Browning has remarked that the foreign "man of rank" had "sputtered into sparks."

The second letter waiting for a reader had appeared to be the brainchild of Don Giacinto Arcangeli, "the virtuous sire, the valiant for truth", – as Browning at an educated guess has mock-seriously apposed, – and intended for his colleague Cencini, the very fellow towards whom Browning has hastened to express his gratitude for helping him with the yellow book, unquestionably a key factor in the making of the ring that was now "round and done". A tribute to Guido, a 'gallant man defunct in faith and exemplarity', has been a noticeable feature of Arcangeli's message, and the homage has been followed by a *mea culpa* for failing 'to set the valid reasons forth'. However, the acknowledgement of guilt has been ironically contradicted by the lawyer's braggadocio about his 'superb defence' and, in its wake, by his dig at Innocent XII, an aged man keen on 'giving youth a push'. Then the sender has taken great pleasure in recounting how his little son Giacinto – aka Cinuzzo, Cintino, Cinone – had been gazing at the Count's execution 'proud as the Pope behind the peacock fans'. Clearly, the father/son bond has here reasserted itself and conveyed the notion of a determined complementarity: Cinuzzo has been seen by his *papà* as a diminutive creature prematurely conscious of his dad's patriarchal attitude; at the same time, the nipper has looked at himself through a mirror and detected the image of a unified Self in harmony with that of the loquacious Other. However, it makes sense to postulate that Giacinto's sense of plenitude has been little more than a narcissistic misrecognition and his ego may well have grown aware of the difference between his imaginary world and the reality of a law coupled with his father's language.[2] Along similar lines, it is tempting to visualize the child as a lad coming to terms with his new consciousness, moving away from the 'mirror stage' and joining his parent's 'symbolic order', videlicet the familial network of vessels in the social body. If the premiss is correct, it is possible to conclude, in harmony with the view that patriarchal culture encapsulates language, that in the fullness of time Gaetano entered the metonymic world of his father's language as well. When all is said and done, it has come as no surprise when Master Arcangeli, the ingenious user of a language peppered with *exempla* of the Latin idiom, has finally predicted that his son would "be gainer by it all." In conclusion, the whole caboodle has provided an instance of language used as a 'game'.[3]

On picking up the third letter demanding attention, – a message from the 'tall blue-eyed Fisc whose head [was] capped with cloud' and addressed 'to no matter who', – Browning has remarked *ante litteram*, "Here has been truth at issue with lie", thus suggesting the insight of a Victorian observer obsessed by the idiosyncrasies of a freak. Sure enough, the missive has dealt with the truth about the innocence of a young wife and the conduct of a not so young husband who had repented and "died like a saint, poor devil!" All at once, the juxtaposition of contrasting attitudes has given prominence to a touch of irony reminiscent of that relished by Arcangeli, as against the earnestness of a pontiff eager to ascertain the truth.

Concerning the latter, the lawyer has implied that something is true only if it corresponds to the facts, and in so doing he has associated facts like Pompilia's innocence and Guido's saintly death with his own statement that he "had, as usual, the plain truth to plead." *QED*. It has been held from an empiricist point of view that 'since everything lies open to view, there is nothing to explain … the aspects of things that are most important for us are hidden because of their simplicity and familiarity.'[4]

At this point in time, Fra Celestino's meddling sermon has intervened, "still smoking from the press", and constituted a significant digression: 'God who seems acquiescent in the main … puts His right hand recognizably', yet 'because Pompilia's purity prevails, conclude you, all truth triumphs in the end?' The columbine young woman had been plucked from the jumble, but how many dove-like sisters were having their names dragged through the mire?

Next, Brother Celestine has inveighed against the Romans for espousing a pagan faith. In days of yore, 'an idol-god, an Ass' had been worshipped in some cavern or other and, as 'century re-echoed century', the people of Rome had accepted the worship. Later, lightning had revealed the contours of a Christian martyr in a cell, and yet the multitude was inclined to believe that not 'another cell o' the myriad that make up the catacomb' contained 'some saint a second flash would show'. Would the Romans 'join the votaries that gape around each vulgar god that awes the market-place?'

In connection with the aforesaid belief, a Manichaean view of the world, tinged with an Augustinian hue, has prompted Fra Celestino to see Pompilia's whiteness blackened by a dark world. Not for long though: in the eyes of the Law the young woman's spirit exemplified the shortcomings of a soul tainted with an inborn albeit temporary disposition towards evil, but then the providential 'right hand' of God had 'bid vapour vanish, darkness flee away and leave the vexed star culminate in peace.' Praise be! The reinstatement of light had proved anew that "God is true, and every man is a liar", and weak men had better learn to love the truth they might be able to tell in the future.

In conclusion, Fra Celestino has disclosed that he had turned his back on the world: despite temptations and doubts, he had, urged by truth and enlightened by an otherworldly weltanschauung, resisted the lure of fame and opted for obscurity. Intriguingly, spiritual values of the kind recall a more recent poet's yearning for a life out of the limelight and a nameless gravestone: 'Thus let me live, unseen, unknown//Thus unlamented let me die//Steal from the world, and not a stone//Tell where I lie.'[5]

The inevitable corollary of the barefoot Augustinian's piece of religious instruction has been a vitriolic rejoinder from Doctor Bottini. He has poured scorn on "the man's own bubble, let alone its spite" and then cast doubts on his disdain for renown as well as underscored his glaring omission of the Pope as an exception to the rule established by mendacious mankind. Then, tackling the issue of the troubles incurred by the Franceschini household, he has belittled Guido for contravening the law and refrained from coming come to Pompilia's defence; at the same time he has upheld the Convertites' claim to her funds in default of a court judgement, – a baffling stance if compared with his previous extolling of the young woman's virtues, – but then he was fully aware that every cloud had a silver lining: to his mind there was "adequate machinery in law", and, for his part, he was working hard on his legal address, which would commence with something like 'Thou, Pompilia, thus? How is the fine gold of the Temple dim!'

Now, how is *that* for a speech act? It is only too fair to posit that the question echoing Julius Caesar's '*Et tu, Brute?*' and the exclamation redolent of a biblical expression of sorrow[6] denote a sophisticated way of ending a lawyer's oration.

"Alack, Bottini, what is my next word but death to all that hope?" Browning has rhetorically asked by way of comment on the Fisc's letter, and the question has echoed the 'Lay down all hope, you that go in by me' – that is to say, the warning inscribed on the gate of Hell and detected by Dante Alighieri at the outset of his peregrination in the Underworld[7]. On the other hand, the Victorian poet has stated that he was in possession of the 'definitive verdict of the Court' clearing Pompilia's name." For good measure, the Priors of Arezzo had recognised 'the right o' the Franceschini to men's reverence' and the populace had been seen by its 'betters' as a bunch of mere onlookers in need of a cure for their "chronic greediness for scandal, love of lying vanity, and appetite to swallow crude reports". In this context, a dichotomy between a plebeian penchant for trivialities and bourgeois orthodoxy has reasserted itself along with the official rehabilitation of Guido Franceschini.

At the end of the day, a juxtaposition of Poetry and History is likely to bring about another dichotomy: from a historicist angle it is tempting to subscribe to the theory that history makes for a harmonic continuum and, by virtue of being 'the conversation that we are', fully deserves credit[8], but at the same time it appears to be more creditable to follow an antitraditional route and conclude that history is 'rent by conflict and domination'[9]. If the latter is the case, it makes sense to infer that 'the dialogue of human history is as often as not a monologue by the powerful to the powerless'[10] and the chatter of a poet is not inevitably more erratic than the "stern" discourse of history.

Dulcis in fundo, Robert Browning's preoccupation with Gaetano's fortunes has made the former wonder whether the baby "born of love and hate" had survived the ordeal. In this case, had Gaetano been proud of his inherited coat of arms? More importantly, had he nursed a grudge against his mother, or had he managed to cherish memories of her? A tentative hypothesis with a little help from Freud inspires the conjecture that if the low-born child was ever successful in sublimating the mother/child libidinal bond and moving from the 'pleasure principle' to the 'reality principle', he may well have succeeded on the strength of the latter in detaching himself from his female parent and being "proud, a true scion of the stock, of bearing blason". If that is what happened, it is safe to postulate that Gaetano was able to prove his manhood in the fullness of time.

---

1. *Isa*, 9. 2
2. A conjecture in keeping with Jacques Lacan's views, as decribed in *Psychoanatytic Theory*, by Anthony Elliott, pp. 91ff
3. Ludwig Wittgenstein, in *Western Philosophy and Philosophers*, p. 329
4. Ludwig Wittgenstein, as quoted in *Op. Cit.*, pp. 33-34
5. Alexander Pope, *Ode on Solitude*
6. *Lamentations*, 4.1
7. *Inferno*, Canto III
8. Hans Gadamer, as quoted in *Literary Theory – An Introduction*, by Terry Eagleton, Blackwell, 1993, pp. 72-73
9. Terry Eagleton in *Op. Cit.* p. 73
10. *Ibidem*

THE ROUNDING OF THE RING

"Such, then, the final state o' the story. So did the Star Wormwood in a blazing fall frighten awhile the waters and lie lost. So did this old woe fade from memory till after, in the fulness of the days, I needs must find an ember yet unquenched and, breathing, blow the spark in flames. It lives, if precious be the soul of man to man. So, British Public, who may like me yet – marry and amen! – learn one lesson hence of many which whatever lives should teach: this lesson, that our human speech is naught, our human testimony false, our fame and human estimation words and wind." Robert Browning's chancing on the "ember" and his bedimming ethical statement have highlighted the issue of human fallibility and given prominence to the question: is there a need to "take the artistic way to prove so much"? It may well be true that, as Johnny Nash has singingly told the world, there are more questions than answers and the more one learns the less one knows, but it is also true that the author of *The Ring and the Book* has come up with an answer: "Art remains the one way possible of speaking truth … may tell a truth obliquely, do the thing shall breed the thought". It follows that the pursuit of truth with the help of art may tangentially bear fruit: "So may you paint your picture, twice show truth beyond mere imagery on the wall …; so, write a book shall mean, beyond the facts, suffice the eye and save the soul beside."

It has been held along similar lines that 'it is in art alone that … phenomenological truth is able to manifest itself; … art, like language, is not to be seen as the expression of an individual subject: the subject is just the place or medium where the truth of the world speaks itself, and it is this truth which the reader of a poem must attentively hear.'[1] Furthermore, it has been argued that 'once we have discovered how truth can happen in art …

we can begin to see how understanding…works.'² In conclusion, truth can be attained solely by those who possess wisdom and transcendent insight.

To put the above in philosophical terms, truthfulness has established itself as a metaphysical entity: in a bygone era, Aristotle conceived of metaphysics as an investigation into the range of the intellect, while in modern times Wittgenstein has compared a 'metaphysical suggestion to the invention of a new kind of song.'³ Moreover, a metaphysical system has been deemed to be the foundation stone of a construct made of reality rather than appearance and as such allowing transcendental-minded people to eventually get to know things not as they seem to be but as they are, even though 'we see things in a mirror dimly'.⁴

When all is said and done, an open-ended reading of *The Ring and the Book* may well engender the view of Browning as a metaphysical poet implicitly advocating a change in how we think of, and look at, the world. In this context, the bard has pointed out Hope Road to cognitively sceptical empiricists and consequently made the land of salvation appear on the horizon in the shape of Ultima Thule. At this point, there is every reason to posit that it took a considerable space of time for Browning's poetic genius to achieve its full potential, and here's the rub: the Scottish essayist Thomas Carlyle is on record as infamously asserting that Browning's extensive tour de force had stemmed from an old Bailey story which might have been told in ten lines and then forgotten without compunction. Heavens above! Was the distinguished historian ignoring the oneiric as well as factual significance of a ring? Conversely, would it not be more reasonable to maintain that a tendentially absolutist poet has chosen to play a relativist's trump card? It's well worth remembering that a ring has been a source of magical power from time immemorial: in Wagner's *Nibelungenlied,* for instance, Siegfried gives a cursed ring to Brunnhilde as a token of his passion, but later he snatches it back from her. By a touch of magic, she regains the talisman and returns it to the Rhyne-maids, thus obliterating the bane. It is enticing to suggest that, following in Brunnhilde's footsteps, Pompilia has made Guido's tarnished ring shine anew by offering it to God on her deathbed. "Gold as it was, is, shall be evermore: prime nature with an added artistry; no carat lost, and you have gained a ring": this much Browning has confidently stated early in the poem, and the ring has sparkled, – just as the 'goodly golden chaine, wherewith yfere the vertues linked are in lovely wize' had glittered in the chivalric times of the Virgin *Gloriana*.[5] In this connection, a celebrated psychiatrist has told the world that one of his patients, a hypersensitive young woman, was fully convinced that 'if one could go deep into the depth of the dark earth, one would discover the bright gold'.[6] For his part, the Victorian poet has descended, holding his *yellow book*, into a deep pit and re-emerged sporting a gold ring in the hope that, as he finally says, it would lie outside the "rare gold ring of verse" created by his *Lyric Love*". It could be argued that the concluding utterance has made *The Ring and the Book* shine with *élan vital* by virtue of two juxtaposed signifiers, – one of which has taken the place of the signifying chain; in some respects, the substitution may be deemed to represent a fulfilment of the poet's humanistic undertaking in his quest for the thing signified.

At the end of the day – a long day indeed – the Franceschini trial has left the 'secret cause o' the crime' enveloped in mist; nevertheless, a final attempt to solve the enigma generated by the 'whydunit' may not come amiss.

To begin with, the description of the crime revolves around an event that has already taken place and therefore cannot be erased. Secondly, the narrative frame is supported by the characters' actions in sequences that have brought forth the issue of causality and made the logic behind the succession of events tightly interwoven with their chronological order. In this connection, the main character, a perpetrator of deadly violence, has nonetheless felt entitled to a payback; ergo he can be depicted as one link in the chain of distribution of socio-economic assets.

Thirdly, Guido tit for tat may well point up the cultural code of a patriarchal, male-dominated, class-conscious society, and a related topic has been that of a symbolic order based on moral and social prohibitions: take, for instance, the taboo of death which Guido has insouciantly violated.

In addition, the voices heard, formally monologic, have been substantially dialogic in virtue of the fact that 'every speech act' springs 'from previous utterances and is 'structured in expectation of a future response'[7]. Scenes have interrelated qua inherent in a symbolic order that has come on the scene as a realm created by language and bound to supersede the imaginary condition.[8]

Guido's language, for one, has significantly intimated the paranoid destructiveness and contextually the reparative anguish that often characterises a child's emerging sense of selfhood and is conducive to the reintegration of a split personality. Regrettably, the Count's schizoid desire has failed to have a *eureka* moment, attain a central position of power and be anchored in a 'symbolic order'; his unsteady self, alas, has become entangled in 'a field of 'play, that is to say, a field of infinite substitutions only because it is finite ... because ... there is something missing from it: a centre which arrests and ground the play of substitutions.'[10]

In the final analysis, Browning's verse novel has been spiced up by an enigmatic code inherent in its title, and the denouement has been deferred until the epilogue has revealed the search for truth as a primary theme of the work. On that score, it is highly significant that the author has asked at an early stage of the narrative, 'How heart moves brain, and how both move hand, what mortal ever in entirety saw?' and then, on approaching the end of his *tour de force*, he has concluded that 'Art remains the one possible way of speaking truth', with the caveat that it 'may tell a truth obliquely', – a conclusion that has anticipated the phenomenological tenet about an 'obligation of always approaching it [truth] sideways through the mediation of symbols, images, stories and ideologies.'[11] In this connection, it does help to take account of the view that 'art exists that one may recover the sensation of life; it exists to make one feel things, to make the stone *stony*.'[12]

On a New Year's Day, Browning has recounted, a young statue maker living at Asolo, in the Veneto Region, was led to the thought that by the sight of the silk-weaver Pippa passing by, 'One may do whate'er in Art: the only thing is, to make sure that one likes it – which takes pain to know.'[13] If that does happen, art, still endowed with the Renaissance hue that made it encompass every creation of the mind, justifiably 'makes no less a "claim to truth" than science' on the strength of being a clear glass reflecting truth, as it has been hermeneutically propounded.[14] In this connection, Utilitarians have preached from their pulpits about the dependence of social life on the respect of conventions such that of telling the truth.[15] For his part, the soldier poet Wilfred Owen told the world from the trenches: 'All a poet can do to-day is warn. That is why the true poets must be truthful.' Browning's related view has been: 'Truth remains true, the fault's in the prover[16], – an assertion consonant with the Victorian poet making Mr Gigadibs, Bishop Blougram's antagonist and a student of the Gospel, declare that 'truth is truth, and justifies itself by undreamed ways'[17]

When all is said and done, Guido Franceschini's multifaceted performance has made the issue of the search for truth a leitmotif in *The Ring and the Book*; consequently, it has provided a vital clue about the presentation of the Roman murder filling the pages of the *square old yellow book*: the blue-blooded culprit can be seen as a key function of the poet's use of an ironic metalanguage conducive to a poem that is 'rhythm, death, and future.'[18] Interistingly, Guido's attitude calls to mind the stance of the priest who says to Joseph K, the bank administrator equally undergoing trial, that 'it is not necessary to accept everything as true, one must only accept it as necessary.'[19]

Compliance with the law, it appears, is, as has always been, the name of the game. Consequently, is escape from its fetters beyond the bounds of possibility? Something of the kind has happened to the Count, for he has not ben able to state in tune with old Tiresias, 'I have escaped. The truth is what I cherish and that's my strength.[20] Indeed, he might have made utterances in harmony with the latter-day dictum that 'One is never happy making way for a new truth, for it always means making our way *into* it: the truth demands that we bestir ourselves. We cannot even manage to get used to the idea most of the time. We get used to reality. But the truth we repress.'[21]

At this concluding stage of *The Ring and the Book* it makes sense to wonder whether a 'univocal' reading of poem is fit for purpose and consequently no 'deconstructive' reading is required. In this respect, a straight answer with the help of the theory is that 'the obvious or univocal reading of a poem is not identical with the poem itself', for 'the relation in question is always a chain, that strange sort of chain without beginning or end in which no commanding element, – origin, goal, or underlying principle, – may be identified, but in which there is always something earlier or something later … which keeps the chain open, undecidable.'[22] In the light of the above assertion, it seems wise to maintain that a 'poem, like all texts, is *unreadable*, if by *readable* one means open to a single, definitive, univocal interpretation. In fact, neither the obvious reading nor the deconstructionist reading is univocal. Each contains, necessarily, its enemy within itself, is itself both host and parasite. The deconstructionist reading contains the obvious one and vice versa.'[23] The inevitable corollary may well be that Browning's contention that the *old yellow book* was utterly truthful and "fancy with fact is just one fact the more" highlights the issue of the reader's activity as a possessor of meaning and therefore interpretive 'not after the fact but of the fact … at once wholly present, – not waiting for meaning but constituting meaning, – and continually in the act of reconstituting itself.'[24] It seems befitting to end a birds-eye view of the poem with a realistic appreciation of the assumption that after describing Guido's murder 'in terms of black and white', the author has suggested that 'language can never present the absolute truth: pure truth is ever deferred and cannot be reached by any tragic vision. 'See it for yourself', the showman admonishes his audience and in so doing he leaves the listeners stranded in a verbal labyrinth. Once 'the rough ore' has been 'rounded to a ring', as hoped by the poet while rounding off his epic effort, it's worth remembering that 'a ring has at its centre only an empty space until it is fitted to the finger. Meaning is an abstraction until it is existentially appropriated.'[25] Reader, rest assured: a healthy deconstructive interpretation may well give a feeling of sanguinity about the possibility of solving the mystery of the *whydunit* which is at the core of *The Ring and the Book*.

1. Martin Heidegger, as quoted in *Literary Theory – An Introduction*, by Terry Eagleton, p. 64
2. Hans-Georg Gadamer, as cited in *Western Philosophy and Philosophers*, p. 117
3. P. F. Strawson, *Metaphysics* in *Op. Cit.* p. 203
4. As the Apostle Paul has put it in *Corinthians*, 13.12
5. Edmund Spenser, *The Faerie Queene*, Book I, Canto IX, 1
6. R. D. Laing, *The Divided Self*, Penguin Books, 1981, p. 205
7. Mikhail Bakhtin, *Ibid*, p. 124
8. Jacques Lacan's tenet, as propunded in *Ecrits*
9. See Jacques Derrida, *Structure, Sign and Play in the Discourse of the Human Sciences*, in *Modern Criticism and Theory*, pp. 118-119
10. Melanie Klein, in *Psychoanalytic Theory*, pp. 80-81
11. Paul Ricoeur, in *Western Philosophy and Philosophers*, p. 278
12. Victor Shklovsky, *Art as Technique* in *Modern Criticism and Theory*, p. 20
13. Robert Browning, *Pippa Passes, Noon*, ll. 306-310
14. Hans-Georg Gadamer, in *Western Philosophy and Philosophers*, p. 117
15. See *Utilitarianism*, in *Op. Cit.* pp. *318ff*
16. *Christmas Eve, l. 229*
17. *Robert Browning, Bishop Blougram's Apology, ll. 807-08*
18. *Julia Kristeva, The Ethics of Linguistics, in Modern Criticism and Theory, p. 233*
19. *Franz Kafka, The Trial, Penguin Books, p. 243*
20. *Sophocles, Oedipus the King, ll. 357-58*

21. *Jacques Lacan, The Insistence of the Letter in the Unconscious, in Modern Criticism and Theory*, pp. 99-100
22. J. H. Miller, *The Critic as a Host*, in *Op. Cit.* p. 282
23. J. H. Miller, *Op. Cit.* p. 285
24. Stanley Fish, *Interpreting the Variorum, Op. Cit.*, p. 319
25. See Clyde de L. Ryals, *The Life of Robert Browning: A Critical Introduction.*

www.ingramcontent.com/pod-product-compliance
Lightning Source LLC
Chambersburg PA
CBHW052009070526
44584CB00016B/1684